THE TWENTY-FIVE YEARS
OF PHILOSOPHY

THE TWENTY-FIVE YEARS
OF PHILOSOPHY

A SYSTEMATIC RECONSTRUCTION

Eckart Förster

Translated by Brady Bowman

HARVARD UNIVERSITY PRESS

Cambridge, Massachusetts

London, England

2012

This book was originally published in German as *Die 25 Jahre der Philosophie: Eine systematische Rekonstruktion*, copyright © Vittorio Klostermann GmbH Frankfurt am Main, 2011.

Library of Congress Cataloging-in-Publication Data

Förster, Eckart.
  [25 Jahre der Philosophie. English]
  The 25 years of philosophy : a systematic reconstruction / Eckart Förster ; translated by Brady Bowman.
      p.   cm.
  Includes bibliographical references (p.   ) and index.
  ISBN 978-0-674-05516-2 (alk. paper)
  1. Kant, Immanuel, 1724–1804.   2. Hegel, Georg Wilhelm Friedrich, 1770–1831.
3. Idealism, German.   I. Title.
  B2798.F6713 2012
  193—dc23   2011040581

For Gita

Contents

At the height of his career, in the preface to the *Metaphysical Foundations of the Doctrine of Right,* Kant declared that philosophy had not existed prior to the publication of his *Critique of Pure Reason* in 1781: "It sounds arrogant, self-seeking, and for those who have not yet relinquished their old system, belittling, to assert: that prior to the development of critical philosophy there had been no philosophy at all" (6:206)[1]. And yet he had no doubts about the truth of the statement he had committed to print and thus to posterity. As though that were not enough, Kant had concluded the *Critique of Pure Reason,* with which philosophy is supposed to have begun, by predicting that the completion of philosophy was now imminent and "it may be possible to achieve before the end of the century what many centuries have not been able to accomplish" (A856)—in less than nineteen years!

Things did not happen quite as Kant had predicted. Even so, it was a matter of fantastically few years before Hegel announced the end of the history of philosophy in a lecture held in Spring of 1806: "Herewith, this history of philosophy comes to an end" (TW 20:461).

If Kant and Hegel were right in what they assert, then the history of philosophy would be reduced to a span of *twenty-five years!* In light of the historical facts, which testify to a history one hundred times that long, one might be inclined to dismiss their assertions as expressions of unparalleled hubris and excess. Still, it is not easy to believe that Kant and Hegel would be liable to such egregious mistakes.

On the one hand, Kant of course knew as well as anyone else that philosophy had existed before him. Well known are the biographical

---

[1] For the method of citation, see the list of Abbreviations at the end of the book.

documents in which he acknowledges his debt to those who came before him: Hume is said to have 'awakened' him from his dogmatic slumber, Rousseau 'straightened him out,' and he asked that the *Critique* itself be understood as an 'apology for Leibniz'. His ethics are inconceivable without the example of the stoics. And the very passage in the *Metaphysical Foundations of the Doctrine of Right* from which the quotation above is taken leaves no doubt that Kant was far from diminishing the achievements of his predecessors.

On the other hand, neither did Hegel come to his view as a result of overweening hubris. It is true that in the lecture just mentioned he does assert that philosophy has come to an end, but not by dint of his own personal efforts. On the contrary. Immediately after announcing the end of philosophy he goes on to say, "The last philosophy thus contains the previous ones, includes all the stages, and is the product and result of all the ones that preceded it . . . [O]ne must rise above . . . one's own vanity, the notion that one has thought something special" (TW 20:461). And besides, Fichte, Schelling, and other great philosophers were at the height of their fame when Hegel spoke these words, and he can hardly have believed that the time had come for them to retire or look for a new profession.

How, then, are we to interpret these assertions by Kant and Hegel? That is the question I will pursue in the following. This book is an attempt to grasp and understand the *single* thought that philosophy begins in 1781 and ends in 1806. The wealth of intellectual phenomena that makes this period so rich also tends to obscure the *idea* that lies at the root of that thought. In order to make it visible, everything that does not strictly belong to it had to be isolated and put to one side. *The Twenty-Five Years of Philosophy* is therefore not intended as a contribution to the popular historical genre 'From Kant to Hegel'. My purpose is not to give an overview of the epoch. Many of the authors who would necessarily be included in such an overview are scarcely mentioned here or mentioned not at all; of those who are, the majority of their writings are left unconsidered.

Moreover, my chief aim has been to grasp the internal dynamic of that fundamental idea, to *reproduce* its immanent development; I have therefore also resolved to forgo discussion of the relevant secondary literature. This decision was the hardest to make since it is so easy to misconstrue. That being said, those who are familiar with the current state of debate in Kantian or Hegelian studies, for example, are also well aware of how controversial virtually every interpretation is—and how easily those controversies take on a life of their own. I resolved to avoid the opportunities for digression as far as possible, in order to focus all the attention on the internal dynamic of the idea that is at the center of my interest. Although I thereby run the occasional risk of appearing uninformed or dogmatic, that is the price I have to pay.

This decision naturally does nothing to change the fact that this book would have been impossible without the accomplishments of countless scholars of idealism, on whose work it builds and whose results, positive as well as negative, it gratefully presupposes. I have therefore listed the titles to which I am particularly indebted in the bibliography. I hope that I have not overlooked too many.

I would also like to thank the John Simon Guggenheim Memorial Foundation for a fellowship that freed me for a year from all academic duties. Of the many people without whose help this book could not have been written, I would like gratefully to acknowledge the following: Michael Williams, Robert B. Pippin, Charles L. Griswold, J. B. Schneewind, Adam Falk, Jürgen Stolzenberg, Katharina Mommsen, Nikola Wolther, and Yitzhak Melamed. Johannes Haag read every chapter and offered valuable comments. Over the course of many years, I have had the privilege of discussing the ideas of this book with Rolf-Peter Horstmann and of testing them out in seminars we taught together. For this I am especially grateful to him. Whatever mistakes and errors remain are, of course, my sole responsibility.

THE TWENTY-FIVE YEARS
OF PHILOSOPHY

Prologue: A Beginning of Philosophy

Why, according to Kant, was there no philosophy prior to the *Critique of Pure Reason*?

An initial, though tentative, answer to this question can be taken from one of Kant's letters to his former student Marcus Herz, written in 1772 and thus nine years before publication of the *Critique*. After briefly describing a book on which he has begun to work and which is to be entitled *The Limits of Sensibility and Reason,* Kant admits "that I still lacked something essential, something that in my long metaphysical studies I, as well as others, had failed to consider and which in fact constitutes the key to the whole secret of metaphysics, hitherto still hidden from itself. I asked myself this question: What is the ground of that in us which we call 'representation' to the object?" (10:130).

When we philosophize about a particular object, we generally assume that we are able to say something true about it. Yet what is the basis of this assumption? The relation between representation and object does not in principle pose any problem when the object is an object of sense perception or when it is the product of moral action. For in the first case, I am affected by the object and my representation of it is produced in me by the object in some as yet unspecified way. In the second case, I modify the present state of the world by way of moral action, and thus the object of my action is itself realized on the basis of my representation of what ought to happen. With the objects of classical metaphysics, however, the case is altogether different, for they are characterized precisely by being nonempirical and uncaused by us. Take, for example, the metaphysical claim that the soul is immortal. How can I know that? Neither is the soul the cause of my representation, nor is this representation the cause of my soul. But then how can my representation veridically refer to my soul at all? This question, of course, can easily be extended to all the objects of metaphysics:

1

What must be the case if our representations are to refer to non-sensible objects in such a way that it is possible for statements about those objects to be veridical? In other words, how is metaphysics possible at all, if it is to be more than the mere play of opinion? Kant addresses this question in the letter to Herz:

> In my dissertation [*De mundi sensibilis atque intelligibilis forma et principiis,* 1770] I was content to explain the nature of intellectual representations in a merely negative way, namely, to state that they were not modifications of the soul brought about by the object. However, I silently passed over the further question of how a representation that refers to an object without being in any way affected by it can be possible. I had said: The sensuous representations present things as they appear, the intellectual representations present them as they are. But by what means are these things given to us, if not by the way in which they affect us? And if such intellectual representations depend on our inner activity, whence comes the agreement that they are supposed to have with objects—objects that are nevertheless not possibly produced thereby (10:130–31).

Kant had indeed formulated the problem on whose solution the possibility of philosophical knowledge in the traditional sense depends, the problem namely of non-empirical, veridical reference. In a trivial, colloquial sense, of course, philosophy has existed for centuries, as a "natural disposition"[1] so to speak; a philosophy, however, which can make a genuine claim to truth and which is more than just a "random groping among mere concepts" (Bxv) must offer insight into the conditions of its own possibility and be able to articulate the criteria that distinguish genuine philosophical knowledge from mere opinion and the empty appearance of knowledge. Since that had never before been the case, Kant has good reasons for saying that hitherto there had never been any genuine (i.e., veridical and hence scientific) philosophy of non-sensible objects at all. Moreover, metaphysical questions will not be worth pursuing for as long as this problem remains unsolved. Is philosophy in the sense of metaphysics even possible? Can I, by sheer dint of thinking, come to know anything about the world that is not merely tautological but actually adds to my knowledge?

---

[1] "Metaphysics as a natural disposition of reason is real, but taken by itself it is . . . dialectical and deceptive" (4:365).

2

Though Kant's original question is easy to understand, his answer to it is anything but easy. Kant's announcement in the letter to Herz that "within three months" he would publish a "Critick" of pure reason that would solve the problem, proved to be all too optimistic: In the end it took him nine years. When the *Critique* was finally completed, Kant was aware that it demanded a revolution in thought that would pose significant obstacles to its reception. Consequently, even at this early stage he had conceived the plan for another work "according to which even *popularity* might be gained for this study" (10:269).

What is so difficult about Kant's answer? If the possibility of metaphysical knowledge is at stake, obviously the examination itself cannot be metaphysical in nature, for that would render the entire endeavor question-begging from the outset. The examination must not presuppose the very thing whose possibility it is intended to decide. Thus he is precluded from drawing on any resources from the tradition.[2]

This point is worth emphasizing. A casual reader of the *Critique of Pure Reason* might gain the contrary impression that Kant does after all place himself within the philosophical tradition. The traditional metaphysical disciplines were ontology, rational theology, rational cosmology, and rational psychology. Kant's predecessor Christian Wolff, for example, composed a classic metaphysical textbook entitled *Metaphysics or Rational Thoughts on God, the World and the Soul of Man, and on All Things Whatsoever.*[3] It might seem as though Kant's method for answering his original question consisted in successively examining each of these traditional metaphysical concepts in order to determine how it refers to objects. One might think that in the Analytic, Kant first examines how "rational thoughts" about "all things whatsoever" come to be formed, in order then to move to the Dialectic and the examination of how the concepts of "God" (the transcendental ideal), the "world" (the chapter on the antinomy), and the "human soul" (the paralogisms) refer to their objects. He would thus have done justice to the traditional areas of rational theology, rational cosmology, and rational psychology.

---

[2] "[A]nd the worst thing about it," Kant was later to write, "is that metaphysics, as much of it as might be present anywhere at all, could not give me even the slightest help with this" (4:260).

[3] *Metaphysik, oder vernünftige Gedanken von Gott, der Welt und der Seele des Menschen, auch allen Dingen überhaupt,* Halle 1720. By 1752 the work had gone into its twelfth edition.

If that were the case, the *Critique of Pure Reason* would not be the great work of philosophy that it is. Kant would have allowed metaphysics to dictate the plan upon which to examine the possibility of metaphysics. Fortunately, that is not what he does. In a lecture Kant gave immediately after publishing the *Critique* (the *Metaphysik Mrongovius*), he explains to his students that the examination of the possibility of metaphysics has called for a completely new kind of philosophy to which he has given the name "transcendental philosophy."

> Transcendental philosophy is the propaedeutic of metaphysics proper. Reason determines nothing here, but rather speaks always of only its own faculty . . . No one has had a true transcendental philosophy. The word has been used and understood as ontology, but (as it is easy to make out) this is not how we are using it. In ontology one speaks of things in general . . . one treated things in general directly—without investigating whether such cognitions of pure understanding or pure reason or pure science were even possible . . . *But I cannot speak this way in the Critique* . . . In transcendental philosophy we consider not objects, but reason itself . . . One could therefore also call transcendental philosophy transcendental logic. It is concerned with the sources, the extent, and the bounds of pure reason, and pays no regard to objects. Hence it is wrong to call it ontology. For there we do indeed consider things according to their universal properties. Transcendental logic abstracts from all that; it is a kind of self-knowledge (29:752, 756; emphasis added).

The investigation therefore had to be grounded in a completely new kind of philosophy, a 'transcendental philosophy'. This new philosophy is in fact free from metaphysical pretensions to a priori knowledge of objects, for it is not concerned with *objects* at all, not even with "all things whatsoever" in the sense in which they concerned traditional ontology, but rather with the possibility of non-empirical *reference* to such objects and hence with the *possibility* of metaphysics. Transcendental philosophy's topic is not a specific class of objects or their mode of being, but rather the possibility of a priori reference—precisely the question of the letter to Herz: "What is the ground of that in us which we call 'representation' to the object?"

If the relation of a priori reference is the real issue for transcendental philosophy, then we need a concept which can serve to designate the accusative of this relation (of thought), that to which a thinker believes himself to be referring, without already presupposing a specific object as actual or even as merely possible. What is required is the concept of a *place-holder* of which, in consequence, nothing can be predicated. Kant coins a term of art for this place-holder in order to distinguish it from "all things whatsoever," the possibility of which classical ontology merely presupposed: He calls it an *object in general (Gegenstand überhaupt)* and comments on it at some length both in the lecture just mentioned (29:811) and somewhat more briefly and cryptically in the *Critique of Pure Reason* itself, where he states, "The supreme concept with which it was customary to begin a transcendental philosophy [prior to Kant] is the division into the possible and the impossible. But since all division presupposes a concept to be divided, a still higher one is required, and this is the concept of an object in general, taken problematically, without its having been decided whether it is something or nothing" (A290).

The topic of transcendental investigation is defined accordingly: "I entitle *transcendental* all knowledge which is occupied not so much with objects [for then it would be metaphysical] as with our a priori concepts of *objects in general*" (A11–12; second emphasis added).

At this point, however, all we have is a more precise statement of the problem. How is the actual investigation to proceed? On what plan is it to be carried out? For obviously it must be based on some plan or idea of the whole. Just as a house cannot be built by piling up stones willy-nilly, neither can a scientific investigation be carried out by stringing together concepts without some guiding plan: "No one attempts to establish a science unless he has an idea upon which to base it" (A834).

Upon closer inspection, Kant's initial problem turns out to be three-fold: (a) The possibility of metaphysics is to be investigated; to this end, (b) a new philosophical discipline, a transcendental philosophy or critique of pure reason, has to be inaugurated, which (c) must be founded on a plan, an idea.

Our understanding of Kant's method is complicated by the fact that he himself does not mention this plan explicitly anywhere in the *Critique* since he was convinced that its suitability could only be judged on the basis of the completed whole and hence retrospectively.[4] Later, in the *Prolegomena*, he wrote that "although a mere plan that might precede the Critique

---

[4] In the *Critique* Kant merely states in the Introduction: "If we are to make a systematic division of the science which we are engaged in presenting, it must have first a doctrine of the elements, and secondly a doctrine of the method of pure

5

of Pure Reason would be unintelligible, undependable, and useless, it is by contrast all the more useful if it comes after. For one will thereby be put in the position to survey the whole, to test one by one the main points at issue in this science, and to arrange many things in the exposition better than could be done in the first execution of the work" (4:263).

In fact, however, the plan set out in the *Prolegomena* after the fact is different from the plan on which the *Critique* itself is based. It forms an *alternative* to the plan of the *Critique*—an alternative which Kant hoped would lend his results "popularity." Thus it cannot dispense us from reconstructing the plan on which the *Critique* itself is based.

Once again, the appropriate starting point for such a reconstruction is the basic question of how it is possible for a priori representations to refer veridically to their putative objects. In order to answer that question we must first determine whether we really even have such representations, and if so, how many and of what kind they are. Thus our first step must be to inquire whether our cognitive faculty contains a priori representations. Since according to Kant we possess three such faculties—namely, sensibility, understanding, and reason—a rough initial division of the investigation will result in three sections: the transcendental aesthetic (for sensibility), the transcendental analytic (for the understanding), and the transcendental dialectic (for reason). Each of these sections will have to contain an investigation revealing which "pure" or a priori representations are proper to each faculty. Let us call this investigation a "metaphysical deduction." As we know, Kant has concluded that sensibility contains two such representations (the representations of time and space), the understanding twelve (the categories), and reason three (the ideas).

In a second step, the investigation must also show that for each of these faculties we possess no further a priori representations and hence that the metaphysical deductions are complete. Since—in contrast to empirical investigations—here there can be no external input that might later force us to revise our results, we are in a position to pronounce a universally valid (conclusive) judgment on our cognitive abilities, albeit only on the condition that all of their elements have been investigated, properly derived, and mutually related to one another in such a way that it is possible both to recognize them as parts belonging to a common whole and at the same time to recognize that whole as such. Only then can we rule out

---

reason. Each of these chief divisions will have its subdivisions, *but the grounds of these we are not yet in a position to explain*" (A15; emphasis added).

that later on any new and previously unconsidered objections might be brought forth against the result of the investigation. The proof that its elements are complete thus also supplies a criterion for the correctness of the investigation: "That is why it can be said of such a critique, that it is never trustworthy unless it is *entirely complete* down to the least elements of pure reason, and that in the domain of this faculty one must determine and settle either *all* or *nothing*" (4:263, cp. A762). (We will later return to this point.)

The third step, which Kant calls a "transcendental deduction," will in each case consist in investigating whether and how these representations refer to the objects corresponding to them, and hence whether a priori knowledge of those objects is possible at all.

The broad outlines of the plan of investigation and the architectonic of the *Critique* thus derive from Kant's basic idea. Yet what, we may ask, entitles Kant to assume that we possess precisely *three* cognitive faculties, neither more nor less? That we possess understanding and reason, a faculty, that is, of forming concepts and a faculty of making inferences, may be accepted as unproblematic; not so the claim that sensibility is a separate cognitive faculty. After all, Kant himself repeatedly draws attention to the fact that Locke and Leibniz, for example, recognized only a difference of degree between concepts and perceptions (cp., e.g., A44, 270–71), and the claim that the faculty of sensibility differs in principle from conceptual abilities is Kant's own quite original position. What entitles him to that claim?

While Kant was still a student, his teacher Martin Knutzen introduced him to Newton's works, and in many respects he was to maintain a firmly Newtonian outlook for the rest of his life. Newton's conception of absolute space and absolute time, though, did not command his allegiance. Even in his first publication, Kant already subscribed to Leibniz' relational view of space and time, a fact which can probably be attributed to the influence of a book that made a deep impression on the young Kant: the correspondence between Leibniz and Clarke, in which Leibniz subjected various of Newton's assumptions to fundamental criticism.

Newton's very first Law of Motion, according to which "every body continues in its state of rest, or of uniform motion in a straight line, unless it is compelled to change that state by forces impressed thereon," already presupposes absolute space as a frame of reference. This space is infinite and exists necessarily, which is to say that it possesses attributes traditionally ascribed exclusively to the divinity. Newton plays down this fact by explaining that absolute space is a *sensorium dei,* a divine sense organ. In Query 28 of the *Opticks* (Appendix A), for instance, he states that "there is a being incorporeal, living, intelligent, omnipresent, who in infinite space, as it were in his sensory, sees the things themselves intimately, and thoroughly perceives them, and comprehends them wholly by their immediate presence to himself." For Leibniz, it was philosophically untenable to assume that God needs a "sense organ" in order to perceive his creation, or that space exists necessarily even when it is void of any objects whatsoever. In his fourth letter to Clarke he writes, "If space is an absolute reality; far from being a property or an accident opposed to substance, it will have a greater reality than substances themselves. God cannot destroy it, nor even change it in any respect. It will be not only immense in the whole, but also immutable and eternal in every part. There will be an infinite number of eternal things besides God."[5]

For Leibniz himself, space is nothing over and above the relations between things; thus if there were no things, space would not exist at all. Kant accepted this view until 1768, when he became convinced that he had devised a thought experiment that could demonstrate its falsity. In his essay "Concerning the Ultimate Ground of the Differentiation of Directions in Space," he discusses the problem in the context of incongruent counterparts, objects which in respect to size, proportions, and the disposition of their parts are perfectly equal and similar, but which nevertheless can have no boundaries in common and therefore do not coincide. The most familiar example for such incongruent counterparts are human hands: "The right hand is similar and equal to the left hand. And if one looks at one of them on its own, examining the proportion and the position of the parts to each other, and scrutinizing the magnitude of the whole, then a complete description of the one must apply in all respects to the other" (2:381).

Now let us imagine that the world had not yet been brought into existence and the first work of creation was a human hand. It must either be a right hand or a left hand. Contra Leibniz, whether it is the one or the other cannot be determined on the basis of its relations to other objects, for, *ex hypothesi,* that hand is as yet the only object in existence; the space it occupies would according to Leibniz necessarily be the only actual space there is. Nor will a complete description of the parts of the hand and their

---

[5] Leibniz/Clarke 1715/1716, 37.

relations help us any, for in this respect a right hand is indistinguishable from a left hand. And of course it is irrelevant whether we can *recognize* what sort of hand it is. The fact is that it must be either a right or a left hand; were a human torso the next thing to be created, then that hand would only fit on one of the arms and not on the other. The difference must therefore be based, as Kant says, on an "inner ground," and since at this point nothing else exists that ground can only be a space distinct from the hand. We must therefore accept the existence of such a space, even though—as he is prompt to admit—"there is no lack of difficulties regarding this concept when one wants to understand its reality (with the *intuition* of which inner sense is satisfied) by employing *ideas of reason*" (2:383, emphasis added).

Kant did not, however, long adhere to the assumption of an absolute space. For in his *reductio* of Leibniz' position, how absolute space was supposed to provide an inner ground for the hand's determinateness remained obscure. Very soon it became clear to him that the positions of Leibniz and Newton were not the only possible alternatives: Space (and time) could also be forms of human intuition. For present purposes we need not decide whether the example of incongruent counterparts was enough to lead Kant to this new position, or whether, as Klaus Reich has conjectured, an additional impulse came from Leonhard Euler's *Letters to a German Princess,* which appeared in German translation one year after the "Ultimate Ground" essay in 1769.[6] In letters 92 and 93, Euler points out that owing to the soul's effects on the body, its presence in the body can be thought, though it cannot be presented to the senses since the soul, as something immaterial, can have neither extension nor spatial coordinates. This view is clearly analogous to Kant's discovery: whereas the presence of the soul in the body can be thought, but not intuited, the difference of incongruent counterparts can be intuited, although it eludes description in conceptual terms. From this it follows that thought and intuition do not differ from each other merely by degrees, but must be understood as two fundamentally different sources of knowledge with their own peculiar structures and laws. In Kant's own words from the *Critique of Pure Reason:* "By way of introduction or anticipation we need only say

---

[6] Leonhard Euler 1769. Compare Klaus Reich's introduction to his edition of Kant's *De mundi sensibilis atque intelligibilis forma et principiis* (Hamburg: Meiner 1958), xiv. In sections 27 and 30 of that text, Kant himself refers explicitly to Euler. The problem of the presence of the soul in the body was already known to him; cp. 2:293.

that there are two stems of human knowledge, namely, *sensibility* and *understanding,* which perhaps spring from a common, but to us unknown, root. Through the former, objects are given to us; through the latter, they are thought. Now in so far as sensibility may be found to contain a priori representations constituting the condition under which objects are given to us, it will belong to transcendental philosophy" (A15).

The insight that sensibility is an independent source of knowledge does not by itself yield the consequence that space and time are its forms. In order to reach this conclusion an additional argument is required which Kant first developed in his inaugural dissertation of 1770, *De mundi sensibilis atque intelligibilis forma et principiis,* and whose result he carries over into the *Critique,* again without explicating it in any detail. The argument can be reconstructed as follows:

"*Sensibility* is the *receptivity* of a subject in virtue of which it is possible for the subject's own representational state to be affected in a definite way by the presence of some object" (2:392, §3). Not all of our representations are produced by us; we are in principle open to being sensuously affected by other things and thereby experiencing a change of state. The mechanism of this affection can remain undetermined for the time being; the important thing is that it allows us to undergo an effect resulting in a representation (perception) which must be understood as a subjective state: All representations are merely in us.

If all my representations are merely "in me," then how can I gain knowledge of any external objects at all? Obviously, this is only possible if I treat my representations not merely as modifications of my own state, but rather refer them to something distinct from myself (an *object*). Now, I have no other way of distinguishing something from myself other than representing it as being in a *different place.* Consequently, space cannot be an empirical representation, that is, one abstracted from external objects, for it is spatial representation which makes it possible for me to represent something as external to and distinct from myself in the first place: "The possibility, therefore, of outer perceptions as such *presupposes* the concept of space; it does not *create* it" (2:402, §15A). And, *mutatis mutandis,* the same is true of time. For neither can temporal representation have an empirical origin or result from abstracting from the succession of sensuous impressions. For the fact that one thing temporally succeeds another is something I recognize only by relating a present sensation to one which is no longer present. It is only in this way that the representation of something successive can arise. For in itself and without connection to anything else, every present impression is something singular and as it were primary, something whose being consists in its being perceived; it does not become something secondary and successive until I relate it back to something which was but is no more. "And thus the concept of time, regarded as if it had been acquired through experience, is very badly defined, if it is defined in terms of the series of actual things which exist one *after* the other. For I only understand the meaning of the little word *after* by means of the antecedent concept of time. For those things come *after* one another which exist at *different times,* just as those things are *simultaneous which exist at the same time*" (2:399, §14.1).

As Kant emphasizes in the Inaugural Dissertation, space and time can be neither substances nor determinations of substances (accidents), nor yet again objective relations. They cannot be anything real at all, but rather merely "something *subjective* and ideal; it issues from the nature of the mind [more precisely, from the nature of the human faculty of intuition] in accordance with an immutable law" (2:403, §15D)—namely the possible orderings of the material received by sensibility.[7] Such ordering is not achieved by sensibility as such, for as a purely receptive faculty sensibility is merely *passive,* pure *receptivity* for impressions.[8] The task of ordering falls to the imagination. Hence the fact that space and time are *forms* of intuition only means that any connection the imagination may forge within the material given in sensibility is limited and constrained by these forms: Every connection of appearances to something distinct from myself is inevitably spatio-temporal.

Thus did Kant arrive at the conception of space and time which he presupposes in the *Critique.* In the work of 1781 he maintains the arguments for the transcendental ideality of space and time as forms of human

---

[7] In the chapter on the antinomy, Kant refutes the obvious objection (first formulated by Trendelenberg, *Historische Beiträge zur Philosophie,* vol. 3 (Berlin 1867), 215–76) that it does not follow from the fact that space and time are subjective forms of intuition that they are not *also* real, mind-independent entities "in themselves." There he shows that such an assumption inevitably leads to contradictions (see A506–7).

[8] "The *intuition* namely of our mind is always *passive.* It is, accordingly, only possible in so far as it is possible for something to affect our sense. Divine intuition, however, since it is the ground and not the consequence of objects . . . is an original intuiting and for that reason perfectly intellectual" (2:396–97, §10).

intuition first presented in the Inaugural Dissertation of 1770 with only slight modifications.

We are now in a position to assess Kant's solution to the problem of the possibility of metaphysics. Before doing so, however, I must point out a general methodological problem which we will repeatedly encounter in what follows.

I started with Kant's claim in the *Metaphysical Foundations of the Doctrine of Right* that prior to the advent of his own critical philosophy there had been no philosophy at all, and I have attempted to determine the grounds for that claim. Although Kant's claim has in a way become more intelligible, there is also a sense in which it has actually become less intelligible. For what we have found so far would only entitle Kant to the claim that prior to the *Critique* there had been no *theoretical* philosophy, since we have not yet even touched on moral philosophy. On the contrary: in the letter to Herz with which we started, Kant introduces the problem of transcendental philosophy by specifically contrasting it with morality (and empirical perception). In moral contexts, representation makes its object possible by means of action, while in the case of perception the object causes the representation by way of sensible affection. The problem of how objective reference is possible only poses itself in the case of non-empirical theoretical knowledge. Here once again is how Kant characterizes the situation to Herz: He was "making plans for a work that might perhaps have the title, *The Limits of Sensibility and Reason.* I planned to have it consist of two parts, a theoretical and a practical . . . As I thought through *the theoretical part,* considering its whole scope and the reciprocal relations of all its parts, I noticed that I still lacked something essential, something that in my long metaphysical studies I, as well as others, had failed to consider and which in fact constitutes the key to the whole secret of metaphysics, hitherto still hidden from itself. I asked myself this question: What is the ground of that in us which we call 'representation' to the object?" (10:129–30, emphasis added)

The *Critique of Pure Reason* was intended to solve this problem only and thus to demonstrate the possibility of theoretical metaphysics. Accordingly, at the end of the preface to the 1781 edition Kant writes, "Such a system of pure (speculative) reason I hope myself to produce under the title Metaphysics of Nature" (Axxi). Here Kant does not view the possibility of a metaphysics of morals as in any way problematic (cp. A797ff.) and at this point in time Kant does not plan to write any further critique.

Since the problem of a priori reference simply does not arise in the case of morality, morality does not form part of transcendental philosophy: Kant explicitly states that practical questions are "not transcendental but moral" (A805), and that morality is therefore "foreign to transcendental philosophy" (A801).

Hence if we truly wish to understand Kant's remark in the *Metaphysical Foundations of the Doctrine of Right* (1797), we must pay special attention to the way he modified his original conception of transcendental philosophy in the intervening years to include morality. For soon after he published the first *Critique,* morality became an issue in a way he had not foreseen in 1781. In 1785 Kant published his *Groundwork of the Metaphysics of Morals,* upon which the *Critique of Practical Reason* followed three years later. Kant originally intended to integrate the latter work into the second edition of the *Critique of Pure Reason,* published in 1787 (cp. 3:556), and later we will need to clarify what finally made Kant drop that plan. It is therefore important to be aware of these changes in Kant's conception of his system, and to appreciate their true significance we must begin by concentrating on the first edition of the *Critique.* Our point of departure must therefore coincide with Kant's own historical starting point; we must begin by reading the first *Critique* as though there had never been a second edition nor any other critical works by Kant.

There are other reasons, too, for this way of proceeding. The *Critique* appeared in 1781 in an edition of one thousand copies and went out of print within just a few years. Early in 1786 Kant was already busy preparing the new edition requested by his publisher (cp. 10:441). We know that for this edition he completely rewrote key passages to take account of the new situation. We will have to examine this fact more closely later on. For now, however, it is important to remember that (with the exception of Jacobi) the later thinkers who followed upon Kant and with whom we will be dealing further on in this book were only familiar with either the second or even later editions of the *Critique.* The original edition did not again become available until 1838 when the first complete edition of Kant's works was published—seven years after Hegel's death! Today's practice of printing the first and second edition on facing pages or at least in the same volume was unknown in those days. Neither Fichte nor Schelling nor Hegel was familiar with the first edition of the *Critique,* and we must remain open to the possibility that this fact might have had consequences for the manner and extent to which they understood themselves to be engaged in a Kantian project.

PART I

"Kant has given the results . . ."

1

Kant's "Revolution of the Mode of Thought"

Let us turn, then, to Kant's solution to the problem of metaphysics. Here I can disregard the numerous problems of detail presented by the *Critique,* and concentrate on the three basic problems I referred to above as the 'metaphysical deduction', the 'completeness proof', and the 'transcendental deduction'. Kant must begin with the question of whether a priori representations are to be found in each of the three faculties sensibility, understanding, and reason, and if so, how many. To this end, each faculty must be considered in itself, excluding any influence from sources external to it. "In the transcendental aesthetic we shall, therefore, first *isolate* sensibility" (A22).

1. Transcendental Aesthetic

"What, then, are space and time? Are they real existences? Are they only determinations or relations of things, yet such as would belong to things even if they were not intuited?" (A23). Though Kant begins with this question, it quickly becomes clear that he has already ruled out these alternatives. Indeed we find only scattered and indirect references to the controversy between Leibniz and the Newtonian Clarke (e.g., at A39) discussed in the Prologue. Instead, Kant essentially repeats the arguments for the ideality of space and time he had given in the Inaugural Dissertation. To summarize for the case of space, Kant argues first that it is not a concept abstracted from outer experiences since it must be presupposed for me to distinguish anything from myself. Secondly, space is a necessary representation a priori since I can only represent something as outside of myself by representing it as spatial, while I can represent space itself as void of objects. Thirdly, space is a pure intuition, not a universal concept, for space contains spaces *within* it, whereas a concept's subordinate concepts fall *under* it.[1] Finally, we represent space as an infinite given magnitude since no limits are set to the progress of intuition.

Space is thus nothing other than the subjective condition of human sensibility, under which alone an intuition of something as distinct from myself is possible. This condition is what originally enables me as it were to separate representations (which as such are just subjective states of consciousness 'inside me', for instance, the occurrent color sensation 'red') from myself and refer them to a distinct object as its property ('a red object'). As soon as we depart from this subjective condition of intuition, we render talk of space incomprehensible according to Kant. Though we cannot on logical grounds alone rule out the possibility that beings with a constitution different from ours might relate to objects distinct from themselves in some non-spatial way, this possibility must remain empty for us since we cannot imagine anything determinate by it:[2] "It is, therefore, solely from the human standpoint that we can speak of space, of extended things, etc. . . . We know nothing but our mode of perceiving them—a mode which is peculiar to us, and not necessarily shared in by every being, though, certainly, by every human being" (A26, 42). The case of time is analogous.

That is the substance of what, in the second edition, Kant calls a metaphysical exposition and what I would like to call a metaphysical deduction: the demonstration that two a priori representations do in fact belong to sensibility, namely, space and time. And he also supplies an argument that these two representations complete the list and that there cannot be more than these: All further concepts belonging to sensibility (e.g., motion or change) already presuppose something empirical which moves or changes, and are therefore not a priori.

Now how does it stand with the transcendental deduction or the demonstration that these concepts veridically refer to objects? Obviously, the problem only arises for sensibility in a limited way: Since its forms refer only to what is given to it, object reference poses no special difficulty:[3]

---

[1] To clarify, while it is true that we have concepts of space and time, space and time are not themselves concepts, but rather pure intuitions.

[2] An interesting, though ultimately unsuccessful, attempt to illustrate a non-spatial mode of distinguishing objects from ourselves is undertaken in Strawson 1959, 59–86. Cp. Evans 1980, 76–116.

[3] Significantly, the term "transcendental deduction" does not even occur in the Aesthetic.

We have already been able with but little difficulty to explain how the concepts of space and time, although *a priori* modes of knowledge, must necessarily relate to objects, and how independently of all experience they make possible a synthetic knowledge of objects. For since only by means of such pure forms of sensibility can an object appear to us, and so be an object of empirical intuition, space and time are pure intuitions which contain a priori the condition of the possibility of objects as appearances, and the synthesis which takes place in them has objective validity (A89).[4]

This statement also supplies a clue as to why Kant believed that the *Critique*'s underlying plan could only become clear in retrospect and that it would only have confused the reader if it had been presented in advance. The real problem of transcendental philosophy, the question of how a priori representations can refer to *objects in general,* does not yet truly arise in the case of sensibility. Its pure representations refer only to objects of possible experience. The real problematic does not emerge until we get to the second cognitive faculty, the understanding. Hence Kant's remark:

In the case of the *pure concepts of the understanding,* it is quite otherwise; it is with them that the unavoidable demand for a transcendental deduction, not only of themselves, but also of the concept of space, first originates. For since they speak of objects through predicates not of intuition and sensibility but of pure *a priori* thought, they relate to objects universally, that is, apart from all conditions of sensibility. Also, not being grounded in experience, they cannot, in *a priori* intuition, exhibit any object such as might, prior to all experience, serve as ground for their synthesis. For these reasons, they arouse suspicion not only in regard to the objective validity and the limits of their own employment, but owing to their tendency to employ the *concept of space* beyond the conditions of sensible intuition, that concept also they render ambiguous; and this, indeed, is why we have found a transcendental deduction of it necessary (A88).

---

[4] This is the reason why, in the Transcendental Aesthetic, Kant only discusses this problem in the one case in which object reference might seem problematic, the case of geometry (cp. A46–47). If space and the objects in it were things in themselves, then there would according to Kant be no reason why geometric propositions are true of external objects with apodictic certainty; at the best, they would be inductive and hence empirical.

Since I can think of anything I like by way of the concepts of the under-standing (e.g. 'God') without having to take account of a possible intuition, I run the risk of ascribing spatial predicates to such a concept (e.g. 'omni-present') without considering the possibility of realizing them empirically. By thus extending the predicate beyond the limits of sensibility I render the concept of space "ambiguous." Hence the necessity of later revisiting the issue of intuition in connection with the understanding. However, be-cause the Transcendental Aesthetic is primarily concerned with isolating sensibility and investigating what it is in itself, in abstraction from con-ceptual determinations, this problem remains in the wings for the time being.

There is a further reason why the issue of intuition cannot be defini-tively settled in the Transcendental Aesthetic. For it is conceivable that if the understanding also has "*a priori* representations" (categories), then their objective validity could be proven in a way analogous to that of sensibility's a priori representations: the proof would show that just as nothing can appear to us in sensibility which is not subject to the conditions of space and time, so too nothing can be an object of experience for us which is not subject to the categories. And Kant did in fact proceed this way at first.[5] Very soon, however (in 1775, to be exact: cp. the so-called *Duisburg'schen Nachlass,* 17:643–73), he came to recognize the limits of this procedure. For the two stems of knowledge, sensibility and understanding, are disanal-ogous in that it is inconceivable that anything could appear to us that is not in space and time, whereas it is not inconceivable that something could appear in space and time which we are unable to bring under categories and which therefore could not become an object of experience. The re-sult of the deduction of the concepts of the understanding, assuming it to be valid at all, would then have only conditional or hypothetical validity— namely under the condition that we do in fact have objective experience. This strategy already assumes that there is experience and hence knowl-edge in the Kantian sense, and anyone who, like Hume, is skeptical about the a priori validity of, for instance, the causal principle need not share this assumption. As Kant himself puts it in the *Critique:*

> Let us take, for instance, the concept of cause, which signifies a spe-cial kind of synthesis, whereby upon something, A, there is posited something quite different, B, according to a rule. It is not manifest

---

[5] Cp. Wolfgang Carl 1989a. See also Carl 1989b.

a priori why appearances should contain anything of this kind (experiences cannot be cited in its proof, for what has to be established is the objective validity of a concept that is a priori); and it is therefore a priori doubtful whether such a concept be not perhaps altogether empty, and have no object anywhere among appearances . . . Appearances might very well be so constituted that the understanding should not find them to be in accordance with the conditions of its unity. Everything might be in such confusion that, for instance, in the series of appearances nothing presented itself which might yield a rule of synthesis and so answer to the concept of cause and effect (A90, cp. 100–1).

In order to defuse this doubt, then, Kant was forced to set a significantly more ambitious goal for the deduction of the concepts of the understanding. He would have to attempt to prove that nothing can even *appear* to us in sensibility which is not already subject to the categories and hence that the categories are not only valid for the objects of experience but rather for all possible appearances whatsoever. This argument, however, which takes apperception or the possibility of thought as its starting point, makes it necessary to revisit the issue of intuition once again.

The difficulties we face in gaining a clear understanding of Kant's deduction of the pure concepts of the understanding derive in part from the fact that he uses *both* arguments in the *Critique*—a fact to which he explicitly draws attention in the Preface. The Preface also gives his reasons for doing so. Hitherto, the history of philosophy has not been one of continuous progress, but rather a series of dogmatic assertions and skeptical refutations, in short an arena of endless disputes. This of course is the reason why the *Critique* is set up as a "tribunal" whose purpose is to determine the very possibility of metaphysics: "It will . . . decide as to the possibility or impossibility of metaphysics in general, and determine its sources, its extent, and its limits—all in accordance with principles" (Axii), thus vindicating its justified claims against the skeptics and dismissing its dogmatic pretensions once and for all. Kant first attacks the dogmatists: a primary aim of the *Critique* is to determine the limits of the metaphysics whose very possibility it seeks to establish. For this purpose, however, the weaker argument just discussed would be sufficient, according to which the categories have objective validity exclusively for objects of possible experience. Kant calls this the "chief purpose" of his book. However, in order to silence the skeptic, the stronger, and also significantly

21

more difficult, argument from the possibility of thought is required. Anticipating his readers' difficulties, Kant writes:

> I know no enquiries which are more important for exploring the faculty which we entitle understanding, and for determining the rules and limits of its employment, than those which I have instituted in the second chapter of the Transcendental Analytic under the title *Deduction of the Pure Concepts of the Understanding* . . . This enquiry, which is somewhat deeply grounded, has two sides. The one refers to the objects of pure understanding, and is intended to expound and render intelligible the objective validity of its a priori concepts. It is therefore essential to my purposes. The other seeks to investigate the pure understanding itself, its possibility and the cognitive faculties upon which it rests; and so deals with it in its subjective aspect. Although this latter exposition is of great importance for my chief purpose, it does not form an essential part of it. For the chief question is always simply this:—what and how much can the understanding and reason know apart from all experience? Not:—how is the *faculty of thought* itself possible? (Axvi–xvii)

We will, therefore, encounter both sides in the text itself. Before I can turn to the transcendental deduction, however, we must first consider the question of whether the understanding has any a priori representations at all, and if so, how many—the subject of the metaphysical deduction. To this end "we isolate the understanding—just as above, in the Transcendental Aesthetic, the sensibility—separating out from our knowledge that part of thought which has its origin solely in the understanding" (A62). As Kant himself emphasizes, the investigation must take its orientation from four points of reference: (1) The concepts are to be pure and not empirical. (2) They are not to belong to intuition and sensibility, but rather to thought and the understanding. (3) They are to be fundamental concepts, clearly distinguishable from those which are derived from or composed of them. (4) The table of such concepts is to be complete, covering the whole field of the pure understanding (cp. A64).

2. Transcendental Analytic

How does Kant proceed? He begins by distinguishing the understanding as the faculty of concepts from sensibility. Whereas intuition, being receptive, has its basis in affections, concepts have their basis in functions, by which Kant understands "the unity of the act of bringing various representations under one common representation" (A68). A concept is a rule for combining certain representations (and thus also a principle for excluding certain others). Thus the representations 'white', 'grainy', 'saline' are combined and ordered in the concept 'salt', while the representations 'colorless', 'liquid', 'tasteless' (say) are not. In this way a concept is a rule allowing me to unite certain representations and to bring them under a higher representation, i.e. the *concept.* Our thought is therefore discursive.[6]

"Now the only use which the understanding can make of these concepts," Kant continues, "is to judge by means of them" (A68). For a concept as such does not refer to anything at all distinct from myself and does not constitute knowledge. Only when I have combined it in judgment with further concepts (e.g. 'The ocean is salty'; 'all humans are mortal') does reference to an object and hence knowledge become possible. Thus since the understanding is the faculty of concepts, while concepts can only produce knowledge by way of being combined in a judgment, Kant can also say, "Now we can reduce all acts of the understanding to judgments, and the *understanding* may therefore be represented as a *faculty of judgment*" (A69).

Note, however, that Kant speaks of "reduction." Not all the acts of the understanding are themselves judgments, but they can be reduced to judgments: So for instance a question is a judgment with a question operator (Is it the case that) (s is p), a command is a judgment with a command operator (Make it happen that) (s is p), and so on. The basic form of judgment, to which the others can be reduced, is the subject-predicate form, and it is responsible for bringing about reference to objects.

Now Kant goes on to claim that since judgments are nothing but combinations of concepts (or representations), a complete enumeration of the functions of unity in judgments will yield all the elementary functions of the understanding (cp. A69). And he believes that such an enumeration has, in all essential points, already been accomplished by classical logic.[7]

---

[6] "With respect to the understanding, human cognition is discursive, i.e., it takes place by means of representations that take what is common to several things as the ground of cognition" (9:58).

[7] "Here lay before me now, already finished though not yet wholly free of defects, the work of the logicians, through which I was put in the position to present a complete table of pure functions of the understanding . . ." (4:323). Tonelli 1966 shows the extent to which this is in fact the case.

For if we abstract from the judgments' content and consider only their form, we discover according to Kant twelve fundamental forms (i.e. forms which are neither derivable from nor composed of others): With respect to their *quantity,* judgments are either universal, particular, or singular; with respect to their *quality* either affirmative, negative, or infinite; with respect to their *relation* categorical, hypothetical or disjunctive; and with respect to their *modality* either problematic, assertoric, or apodictic.

Since logic abstracts from any intuitive content in order to isolate the mere form of judgment, whereas transcendental philosophy must investigate how reference to objects can be possible at all, that is, how a possible intuition can be determinate with respect to one of the forms of judgment, the pure concepts of the understanding are precisely the rules which originally combine the manifold of an "intuition in general" (A79) (for we are isolating the understanding and abstracting from *our* sensibility) in such a way that a something can be thought which is determinable by means of one of the forms of judgment.[8] Since, however, the understanding itself does not produce a manifold of intuition, having instead to rely on the material for thought being supplied from some other source, the categories are accordingly conceptualizations of the pure syntheses which combine the manifold (regardless of how it is given) in such a way that it can be thought as an object, thus making it possible to formulate judgments about it. They are *concepts* and therefore combinations of representations; since they are *pure* concepts, they are pure syntheses in general, or in transcendental terms, they are the "concepts of *objects in general*" which "underlie all empirical knowledge as its *a priori* conditions" (A93).[9] Thus corresponding to the twelve forms of judgments there are twelve pure concepts of the understanding, or categories (cp. A80).

That, in rough outline, is the argument of the metaphysical deduction. It is striking that Kant offers no proof of the completeness of his table of the fundamental forms of judgment at this important point in the text. He merely promises that its completeness "will be shown" (A69) in the

---

[8] "The form of judgments (converted into a concept of the synthesis of intuitions) yielded categories which direct all employment of understanding in experience" (A321).

[9] Note the precision of Kant's use of language: taken merely as pure concepts of the understanding, the categories are "concepts of *objects in general*" [*Gegenstände überhaupt*]; however, if we take a possible intuition into account, they are concepts "of things in general [*Dinge überhaupt*], so far as the manifold of their intuition must be thought through one or other of these logical functions" (A245).

relevant section. Kant's contemporaries were the first to take exception to this fact (cp. 11:498), and the literature on the problem produced since that time is substantial. However, since we will be returning later to the question of whether the categories can be derived from the elementary acts of the understanding, I can pass over it here. At this point we must only take note of one fundamental criticism which, if accurate, would undermine Kant's whole approach—a criticism voiced by P. F. Strawson: "Current logic is usually presented in two parts: propositional logic, or the logic of truth-functions; and predicate logic, or the logic of quantification. At its basis there lie, correspondingly, two fundamental and underived ideas: first, the idea of truth-functional composition in general; second, the general idea of quantification . . . [A]s far as logical forms are concerned, the logician's choice of primitives *is* a choice."[10]

However, this objection is only valid from the point of view of a realism which holds that objects are somehow given *before* the logician makes his choice. But that is just what Kant disputes: Since he is concerned with explaining how, on the basis of representations, reference to something distinct from the subject is possible in the first place, he cannot take quantification over objects as primitive. Therefore an effective criticism of his treatment would have to be based on a deeper foundation than the conventions of contemporary logic, namely at the level of a theory of perception, the question of the given or the constitution of the given.

We now turn to the transcendental deduction of the categories. Here again, a brief summary will be sufficient for my purposes. We must however keep in mind that when Kant speaks of a 'deduction', he by no means intends a syllogistic proof; rather, he adopts the term from the legal practice of his day.[11] In addition to determining the relevant facts in a law suit, i.e. the question *quid facti,* a deduction in this sense also determines the claim's legitimacy, the question *quid iuris,* by demonstrating the origin of the claim (cp. A84–85). Thus to justify a claim to ownership, for example, in a court of law is to derive it from a valid contract of sale or inheritance; to justify a claim to an academic title is to demonstrate that the relevant examinations were taken and passed, and so on. If the deduction succeeds, then the lawsuit is concluded, the claim legitimated and irrefutable. Though a deduction is not a proof in the sense of formal logic, it nevertheless accomplishes

---

[10] Strawson 1966, 81, 80.
[11] This has been convincingly shown in Henrich 1989.

something analogous to proof by either establishing or refuting a claim in a way that is universally binding.

Now the "tribunal of reason" that is to decide the possibility of metaphysics—that is, the *Critique*—is in a comparable position. It is called on to decide a dispute as to the legitimacy of claims to knowledge. The dogmatist claims himself to be in possession of metaphysical knowledge, while the skeptic disputes the legitimacy of that claim. If the possibility of metaphysical knowledge is at stake, this dispute must be settled according to universally valid laws and a binding decision must be issued. What makes the present case particularly volatile, however, is that here reason is prosecutor, defendant, and judge all rolled into one.

The dogmatist's claim to be in possession of metaphysical knowledge and to be able to refer to supersensible objects by means of a priori concepts must, therefore, be subjected to scrutiny. The question *quid facti*: which a priori concepts does the understanding possess?, was already decided by the metaphysical deduction where it was ascertained that the understanding possesses twelve categories. The transcendental deduction must now determine the legitimate use of these concepts. In terms of the "chief purpose" Kant refers to in the Preface: what and how much can the understanding cognize with these concepts? It is now becoming clearer why he describes this question as "essential to my purposes" (Axviii), for by answering it, the legitimacy of the metaphysical claim to knowledge is decided and hence the possibility of metaphysics itself. For the reader who is in danger of getting lost in the details, he explains that, "on this matter, what has been said on pp. [A] 92–93 should in any case suffice by itself" (Axvii).

If we follow Kant's reference and turn to page 92 of the A-edition, what we find is the older, "objective" argument paralleling that of the Transcendental Aesthetic: All appearances necessarily conform to the formal conditions of sensibility because it is only on the basis of these conditions that they can be intuited at all: "The question now arises whether a priori concepts do not also serve as antecedent conditions under which alone anything can be, if not intuited, yet thought as *object in general*. In that case all empirical knowledge of objects would necessarily conform to such concepts, because only as thus presupposing them is anything possible as *object of experience*" (A93). Since sensibility itself furnishes only unconnected impressions, then, if an object is to arise from them, there must be an underlying concept by means of which the unity of the various predicates necessarily belonging to that object can be thought. If the categories are such concepts, then although they are concepts of *objects in general,* they are still only pure rules of synthesis. In other words, as long as they lack any material from intuition to combine, they are merely "the logical form of a concept" (A95), and cognize nothing. For this reason, the pure concepts of the understanding cannot produce knowledge until they are linked with intuition. Yet since they are concepts of *objects in general* and hence must underlie all determinate thought, the principle error of traditional metaphysics becomes readily apparent: "Certainly, *once I am in possession of pure concepts of the understanding,* I can think objects which may be impossible, or which, though perhaps in themselves possible, cannot be given in any experience. For in the connecting of these concepts something may be omitted which yet necessarily belongs to the condition of a possible experience (as in the concept of a spirit). Or, it may be, pure concepts are extended further than experience can follow (as with the concept of God)" (A96, emphasis added).

Thus Kant's reference to his "objective deduction." He does not tell the reader where to look for the "subjective deduction" and the explanation of how "the faculty of thought itself is possible," since his intention is precisely to steer the overwhelmed reader along the simplest possible path through the thicket of the deduction. Even so, the text of A97–98 hardly leaves a doubt that this is where the transition to the subjective deduction and hence also to the later of the two strategies takes place: Since there can be no object of knowledge without a relation of the understanding to intuition, we require an "explanation in regard to the possibility of such relation" and hence also of the "subjective sources" which "make possible the understanding itself—and consequently all experience as its empirical product" (ibid.).

Let's try to summarize Kant's argument.[12] As a faculty of receptivity, sensibility is passive. Thus the manifold contained by it is as such unconnected: every impression is "completely foreign to every other, standing apart in isolation" (A97). Whatever *we* are able to distinguish and separate in sensibility *is* separate and distinct in it.[13] The manifold must first

---

[12] The following interpretation is indebted to the groundbreaking research of Dieter Henrich 1976; see also 1988.

[13] Kant is thus by no means committed to the atomistic sensualism Henrich ascribes to him in Henrich 1976, 110, and which he is said to have "shared with the epistemology of his times" (17). If this were the case then Kant would be making a dogmatic and unverifiable assumption about what precedes consciousness and

be gone through or apprehended, that is, we must proceed from one impression to further impressions. However, lest every new impression count as the first and only one, the antecedent impression must not be lost: Secondly, therefore, the antecedent impression must be reproduced *as antecedent,* i.e. as an impression which was, but no longer is present. This is just as true of the representation of spatial extension and temporal duration ("the first parts of the line, the antecedent parts of the time period") as it is for the manifold contained in them, so that even though space and time as *forms* of intuition do not presuppose subjective activity of this kind, "the purest and most elementary *representations* of space and time" (A102, emphasis added; cp. A99–100) do.

In order for these conditions to give rise to consciousness *of something,* however, this is not yet sufficient. The impressions which have been run through and reproduced must not be connected with just anything given in consciousness, but with what belongs to it, i.e. with that which can be combined under a concept. This in turn requires that it be taken up in consciousness in order to be compared with other representations. A concept, as we have seen, is the representation of the unity of various related representations which at the same time excludes any and all representations not so related. So the sensibly given that I apprehend and combine under the concept 'dog' (say), does not include as one of its parts the blanket on which the dog is sleeping, though it does include past and possible future perceptions of a waking, barking, or feeding dog. This unity of consciousness in various representations is what Kant calls apperception, about which he writes:

> It is this apperception which must be added to pure imagination, in order to render its function intellectual. For since the synthesis of imagination connects the manifold *only as it appears in intuition* . . . it is, though exercised a priori, always in itself sensible. And while concepts, which belong to the understanding, are brought into play through relation of the manifold to the unity of apperception, it is only by means of the imagination that they can be brought into relation to sensible intuition (A124, emphasis added).

which for us can never be an object of experience. Kant makes no such assertion. Rather, for him the unconnectedness of the sensuous material follows *exclusively* from sensibility's passivity.

Hence the unity or rather identity of the consciousness in which the different representations are found is a necessary condition if we are to have consciousness of something at all. For if the representations were distributed across different subjects, it would be impossible to form a thought. Or, as William James once wrote (taking a cue from Brentano): "Take a sentence of a dozen words, and take twelve men and tell to each one word. Then stand the men in a row or jam them in a bunch, and let each think of his word as intently as he will; nowhere will there be a consciousness of the whole sentence" (James 1890, 1:160). In order for a series of words to come together to form a sentence, or for a series of representations to come together to form a thought, they have to occur in one and the same consciousness. And this is the case with any representations which can come to be present to me: "The identity of the consciousness of myself at different times is therefore only a formal condition of my thoughts and their coherence . . ." (A363).

Now what exactly is the identity of consciousness? Though Kant designates it by the term "I," he does not mean to refer to the empirical person that I am and which changes and develops over the course of my life, but rather to the invariable subject of thinking. Everything I have ever thought, am thinking, or will think, are thoughts by the same subject. I thus possess an a priori knowledge of my identity in all my states of consciousness, past as well as future: "We are conscious a priori of the complete identity of the self in respect of all representations which can ever belong to our knowledge, as being a necessary condition of the possibility of all representations. For in me they can represent something only in so far as they belong with all others to one consciousness, and therefore must be at least capable of being so connected" (A116). Yet how is such an a priori knowledge possible? In other words, how can I know now that in the future I will continue to be able to combine thoughts into a unity and make transitions from one thought to another? Obviously, that is only possible if the manner in which I make transitions from one thought to the next remains immutably the same, that is, if the forms of transition remain unchanged and independent of their content: "For this unity of consciousness would be impossible if the mind in knowledge of the manifold could not become conscious of the identity of function whereby it synthetically combines it in one knowledge" (A108).

Here we find an important difference between a priori knowledge and empirical knowledge. Thus I can for example know that, for as long as

I live, episode will follow episode in my biography, but I cannot know in advance in what those episodes will consist nor the order in which they will occur. I am forced to wait and see what life has in store for me. The facticity of every stage irrevocably eliminates all the previously open possibilities. In thought, by contrast, I can in principle move from any one thought to every other, initiating thoughts at will. This, however, means that I am utterly free from empirical conditions in these transitions, so that the totality of possible transitions continues to be available to me at every single moment. They must therefore always remain the same functions, for as Kant says, "the mind could never think its identity in the manifoldness of its representations, *and indeed think this identity a priori*, if it did not have before its eyes the identity of its act, whereby it subordinates all synthesis of apprehension (which is empirical) to a transcendental unity, thereby rendering possible their interconnection according to a priori rules" (A108, emphasis added).

But what are these immutable acts which effect the transitions from one representation to the next, thus making the unity and identity of consciousness possible? As we just saw, they are according to Kant the judgments to which we can reduce all the acts of understanding, such that the understanding can "be represented as a *faculty of judgment*" (A69). The unity of my thought which I designate by the word "I" is thus only possible because I form concepts and use them in judgment. The forms of judgment remain constant, or more precisely, that which remains constant in judgment and is independent of the content of representation is the function of referring concepts to something distinct from myself. The thought of something that is distinct from myself and in which different representations are unified is the thought of an object. The necessary unity of my consciousness is thus only possible by way of the thought of a necessary unity of representations. Therefore the understanding and my self-consciousness are possible only to the extent that I cognize objects.

Since, however, the unchanging relation to an object itself entails a three-fold synthesis (apprehension, reproduction, recognition), upon which the unity of space and time rest in turn, everything that can appear in space and time must be subject to the conditions under which alone the unity of self-consciousness is possible. "Now, since this identity must necessarily enter into the synthesis of all the manifold of appearances, so far as the synthesis is to yield empirical knowledge, the appearances are subject to *a priori* conditions, with which the synthesis of their apprehension must be in complete accordance" (A113).

With this, Kant has derived the objective reality of the categories in regard to all appearances whatsoever from the possibility of the understanding itself. He has not only shown (in an "objective deduction") that objects of experience are necessarily subject to the categories since we could not think any objects at all without them. He has shown in addition (in a "subjective deduction"), that the identity of self-consciousness of which we have a priori knowledge, would be wholly impossible without consciousness of objects. Consciousness of the I and consciousness of objects are thus two sides of the same coin.[14]

As he had done in the Transcendental Aesthetic, Kant again points out that he is arguing only from the human standpoint, i.e. the standpoint of a being who possesses sensibility in addition to understanding and to which therefore only appearances are given, which as such are not objects distinct from ourselves: "For since a mere modification of our sensibility can never be met with outside us, the objects, as appearances, constitute an object which is merely in us" (A129). If we possessed a productive intuition like the intellectual (divine) intuition discussed in the Inaugural Dissertation, which is conceived as the ground and not the consequence of objects (cp. 2:397, §10), then a transcendental deduction would be neither necessary nor possible. Since, however, our understanding is not the ground of its objects, having to rely on given material which to think and which it can only find in human sensibility, it must first connect it and thereby bring it to consciousness: "From this point of view, the only feasible one, our deduction of the categories has been developed" (A130).

3. Transcendental Dialectic

Let us now turn to the third cognitive faculty, reason. Kant proceeds here, too, in the way we have learned to expect: First he "isolates" reason in order to investigate whether it is "an independent source of concepts and judgments which spring from it alone, and by means of which it relates to objects" (A305). Here, too, he begins with what I am calling a metaphysical deduction. And he again takes formal logic as his point of departure: whereas the understanding is the faculty of concepts and judgments, reason is the faculty of drawing inferences. The *fundamental* inference of

---

[14] If I am already in possession of self-consciousness, I can of course ascribe 'merely' subjective states to myself. Kant's argument only shows that self-ascriptions of this kind are secondary in relation to successful reference to objects.

reason (*Vernunftschluss*) consists in a major premise, a minor premise which subsumes something under the major premise, and a conclusion in which reason uses the major premise to determine the thing that has been subsumed. To take an example, given the major premise "All x are p" and the minor premise "F is an x," the conclusion follows that "F is p." Thus reason seeks the condition of a judgment, an inference, by deriving it from a universal rule (the major premise) with the help of a minor premise.

In addition to the "logical" use of reason there is also a "real" or "transcendental" use (A299) which does not abstract from the content of cognition but rather refers to the concrete content supplied by the understanding in order to subsume it under principles and systematize it. For obviously we are not content to collect isolated insights rhapsodically; instead we constantly strive to combine them into larger wholes and to comprehend their connections with other insights. This would seem to indicate the presence of an undeniable need or, in contemporary terms, an interest of reason. Reason refers, then, immediately to that which is given by the understanding and by deriving it from principles seeks to integrate it into a greater whole. Now in principle reason can also further try to determine the content of the major premise by making it into the conclusion of a further inference, so that the condition in its turn comes to be regarded as subject to higher conditions which must again be sought out. And this continues until reason arrives at a unity which is underivable from higher principles. That this ultimate unity is *de facto* unattainable by us is not in itself an obstacle to reason's striving to approach ever nearer to it.

As Kant writes: "[T]his logical maxim can only become a principle of *pure reason* through our assuming that if the conditioned is given, the whole series of conditions, subordinated to one another—a series which is therefore itself unconditioned—is likewise given, that is, is contained in the object and its connection" (A307–8).

Now the result of the Analytic was that there are three forms of judgment by means of which the understanding thinks real relations: categorical, hypothetical, and disjunctive. If reason has concepts of its own with which to think that which is unconditioned in the results of the understanding, then they would have to be the following: first an unconditioned "of the *categorical* synthesis in a *subject*; secondly, of the *hypothetical* synthesis of the members of a *series*; thirdly, of the *disjunctive* synthesis of the parts in a *system*" (A323). For our representations may be related either to (1) the subject or to the object, and they may be related in turn to the object either as (2) appearance or as (3) an object of thought in general.

32

If reason's quest for unity is undertaken with regard to these three possibilities, then its goal is represented by the idea of an ultimate element in the series (the unconditioned for the given conditioned). Reason therefore also has a priori concepts or (since no empirically given object can be adequate to them) ideas, of which there are three: the absolute unity of the thinking subject, the absolute unity of the series of the conditions of appearance, and the absolute unity of the conditions of thought in general (A334): the soul, the world, and God. The first of these is the traditional object of rational psychology, the second that of rational cosmology, and the third that of rational theology. As we can see, Kant does not in this case adopt the basic themes of classical metaphysics merely as given by the tradition (as was the case in the Prologue in regard to Wolff); rather, he derives them from the nature of pure reason (cp. A334–35). These ideas do not therefore originate solely in reason itself; they are basically "categories extended to the unconditioned," which come about when reason *frees* "a concept of *understanding* from the unavoidable limitations of possible experience" and thus endeavors "to extend it beyond the limits of the empirical, though still, indeed, in terms of its relation to the empirical" (A409).

Kant's line of thought here is perhaps not fully convincing. Even if we concede that we are constantly striving to integrate our empirical results into an ever more inclusive nexus, does it really follow that reason must produce for itself a representation (or idea) of the ultimate element of such a series? Nor does Kant offer any further reason for the completeness of the ideas of reason; he apparently considers the matter to be self-evident since they are extended categories and since he believes there are only three categories of relation. However, it is not this metaphysical deduction of the ideas of reason which will concern me here, but the question of their transcendental deduction. For here we encounter a far greater obstacle in interpreting Kant's text. Let us first consider what he himself writes on the subject: "No *objective deduction,* such as we have been able to give of the categories, is, strictly speaking, possible in the case of these transcendental ideas. Just because they are only ideas they have, in fact, no relation to any object that could be given as coinciding with them. We can, however, undertake a subjective derivation of them [i.e. a metaphysical deduction] from the nature of our reason . . ." (A336). Later, however, he insists that a transcendental deduction is not only necessary, but that it is even the very culmination of the whole *Critique of Pure Reason:* "We cannot employ an a priori concept with any certainty without having first given a transcendental deduction of it. The ideas of pure reason do not, indeed, admit of the kind of deduction that is possible in the case of the categories. But if they are to have the least objective validity, no matter how indeterminate that validity may be, and are not to be mere empty thought-entities . . . a deduction of them must be possible . . . This will complete the critical work of pure reason, and is what we now propose to undertake" (A669–70).

This statement has confronted Kant's interpreters with considerable difficulties.[15] These difficulties are compounded by the fact that the three ideas of reason for which Kant attempts to provide a transcendental deduction are apparently not the ideas of the soul, the world, and God at all, but three altogether distinct ideas: homogeneity, variety, and affinity. In order to orient ourselves here, we must look back at Kant's development.

Historical Excursus

One of Kant's earliest philosophical experiences seems to have been his astonishment that the greatest minds of an age not only are incapable of reaching any agreement on the basic philosophical problems, but that their views on those problems are wholly disparate. I already mentioned the controversy between Leibniz and Newton's advocate Clarke which made a strong impression on the young Kant. Another seemingly irreconcilable disagreement in which Kant himself sought to mediate with his first publication was that between Leibniz and the Cartesians on the true nature of force and the proper method of expressing it mathematically. In the course of time, however, his astonishment gave way to a fundamental skepsis: Is the reason for this inability to reach agreement in philosophical questions perhaps that the questions are wrongly posed? Are they perhaps undecidable because the philosophical method of answering them is fundamentally misguided?[16] From this point on, Kant was increasingly concerned to determine the "proper method of metaphysics," and in the catalog of the Leipzig book fair of 1765 we already find a work by Kant advertised under this title (cp. 13:31). The work never

---

[15] Cp., e.g., the classic statement in Zocher 1966.

[16] We know from Herder's notes on Kant's lectures from the period that as early as 1762–64 Kant illustrated metaphysics' fundamental methodological mistake with the Leibniz-Clarke correspondence: "each believes himself to be wholly in the right, and takes the other to be merely an opponent, whereas he ought to explain the opponent's error" (cp. 28:157).

materialized, however, because in the meantime Kant had recognized that the root of the problems was deeper than he had at first assumed. In the following year he wrote to Moses Mendelssohn about "the value of metaphysics": "I cannot conceal my repugnance, and even a certain hatred, toward the inflated arrogance of whole volumes full of what are passed off nowadays as insights; for I am fully convinced that the path that has been selected is completely wrong, that the methods now in vogue must infinitely increase the amount of folly and error in the world, and that even the total extermination of all these chimerical insights would be less harmful than the dream science itself, with its confounded contagion . . . My feeling is not the result of frivolous inconstancy but of an extensive investigation. Admittedly, my suggested treatment will serve a merely negative purpose, the avoidance of stupidity (*stultitia caruisse*), but it will prepare the way for a positive one" (10:70–71).

It is not difficult to discern in this early passage the first traces of the path that will culminate years later in the *Critique of Pure Reason*. After his reflections on incongruent counterparts had led Kant to his insight into the fundamental difference between sensibility and thought in 1768, he again came to believe that he was close to a solution: In Section Five of the Inaugural Dissertation of 1770 he laid out the fundamental error of metaphysics, namely the confusion or conflation of the principles of sensibility with those of the understanding. For example the principle, "Everything that exists, is in some place," is based on such confusion (though its converse, "Everything that is in some place, exists," is not).[17] As Kant writes, "Every method employed by metaphysics, in dealing with what is sensitive and what belongs to the understanding, amounts, in particular, to this prescription: great care must be taken lest the principles which are native to sensitive cognition transgress their limits, and affect what belongs to the understanding" (2:411, §24). Kant therefore planned a "quite special, though purely negative science, general phenomenology (*phaenomenologia generalis*)" (10:98) which would precede metaphysics and prevent its being contaminated by principles of sensitive cognition: This science was to be the first section of the theoretical part of the work Kant mentions in his letter to Herz cited above, *The Limits of Sensibility and Reason* (cp. 10:129).

We have already seen why these plans failed to materialize. There is, however, a further problem on the way to the *Critique:* The error of metaphysics pointed out in the Inaugural Dissertation is not quite identical with the problem of the antinomy

---

[17] That everything that exists is in some place and at some time had been claimed for example by Crusius in *Entwurf der nothwendigen Vernunft-Wahrheiten, wiefern sie den zufälligen entgegen geseetztet werden.* Leipzig, 2nd ed. 1753, sect. 46–48.

in the *Critique,* namely the insight that reason is not only subject to contamination by the principles of sensibility, but that it must reckon with contradictions within its own legislations as soon as reason itself dares to overstep the boundaries of sensibility. In order for there to be an antinomy in the proper sense of the term, two statements or judgments, the validity of which has in each case been proven on the basis of principles of reason, must stand to each other in contradictory opposition. To Kant's own mind, what was revolutionary about his discovery of the antinomy problem was that it demonstrates that reason must contend with a *conflict of the laws of pure reason* (A407, cp. 28:620) whenever it leaves the realm of experience and attempts to determine something about things in themselves. For then, according to Kant, it is possible to derive contradictory propositions from principles of reason with equally valid arguments. In the interests of highlighting the systematic problem, Kant refrains in the *Critique* from any discussion of the historical positions represented by those statements; it is nonetheless obvious that he regards them as tenets that have in fact been held in the history of philosophy (cp. 4:379). Nor is it difficult to discover the corresponding positions.[18] From this vantage point it finally also becomes clear why there has been no agreement among the great thinkers: there *could not* be any since theoretical reason can equally well 'prove' either of two contradictory statements as soon as it abandons the ground of experience—and consequently cannot know anything at all.

It is in this context that the antinomy problem gains unique significance for the attempt to set limits to metaphysics. Looking back, Kant will later write that the antinomy of pure reason "is in fact the most beneficial error into which human reason could ever have fallen, inasmuch as it finally drives us to search for the key to escape from this labyrinth" (5:107). This key is nothing other than the doctrine of the ideality of space and time and the attendant distinction between appearances and things in themselves, so that the self-contradiction in reason can at the same time serve as an indirect proof of the doctrine's correctness. For the antinomy only, indeed inevitably, arises if space and time and the appearances in them are taken to be things in themselves.

In terms of its radicality, Kant's critique of metaphysics is not to be outdone. We need not feign a *genius malignus* with Descartes in order to contemplate the possibility of a fundamental delusion of reason. It lies in the very nature of reason to have deluded itself from the outset by taking appearances to be things in themselves, and the antinomy is simply the most conspicuous symptom of

---

[18] On the correspondence between Leibniz and Clarke, see Al-Azm 1972. More generally, see Heimsoeth 1970, 133–280. An excellent discussion is provided in Martin 1961, 51–54.

its fundamental error. Since however the distinction between appearances and things in themselves follows from the ideality of space and time and Kant was the first to prove this, the fundamental mistake of all pre-Kantian metaphysics is thus also manifest. Here we have a further reason why Kant was able to claim that prior to the *Critique of Pure Reason* (theoretical) philosophy had simply not existed. Any metaphysics which is not founded on the ideality of space and time has no choice but dogmatically to commit to one or the other antinomial propositions without being able even in principle to refute its contradictory opposite. Such a metaphysics cannot be veridical and hence it cannot become a *science*. Thus no real metaphysics existed prior to Kant.

Such being the case, it is hardly surprising that Kant would like to have begun the *Critique* with a presentation of the antinomy, "which could have been done in colorful essays and would have given the reader a desire to get at the sources of this controversy. But the school's rights must first be served; afterwards one can also see about appealing to the world" (10:270). In order to accomplish this, however, it would have been necessary not only to display the antinomy, but also to explain it. The basic nature of reason's relation to the understanding and the source of the illusions that arise from it must already be demonstrated before we can learn how to avoid them, if indeed metaphysics is to be established as a science. It must be shown that in the end the concepts of reason are categories which have been freed from the inevitable restriction to possible experience "by carrying the empirical synthesis as far as the unconditioned" (A409). Prior to that, however, it must be shown that as soon as the categories lack a possible intuition, they are no longer able to determine any object at all. Or as Kant explained it to his students, "the dialectic is the greatest end of transcendental philosophy. But the analytic must come before it" (29:805). To this end he had to introduce a fundamental distinction between understanding and reason in the *Critique* (terms which he had used interchangeably in the Inaugural Dissertation) and make clear how the latter is dependent on the former. Only then can the school's rights be served.

With these remarks, I return to the main topic of this chapter.

In the Transcendental Dialectic the antinomy is integrated into the general analysis of transcendental illusion, which arises when dogmatic reason fails to distinguish between appearances and things in themselves, thus transforming what is ultimately just a logical principle of the synthesis of appearances into an existential claim. As we pointed out, reason strives to integrate the conditioned which is given into ever larger unities, basing its striving on the idea of an unconditioned; therefore, when it fails to make the critical distinction, it assumes that the unconditioned is given along with the conditioned. In other words, reason hypostatizes the unconditioned, conceiving it in accord with the three ideas of the unconditioned as the absolute unity of the thinking subject (the soul), the absolute unity of the conditions of experience (the world), and the absolute unity of the condition of all objects of thought in general (God), which then become the objects of dogmatic metaphysics. A "semblance of objective assertions" (A61) thus arises which however cannot vouchsafe any knowledge of reality because in all three cases the subjective condition of thought has been confused with a cognition of the object.

I do not need to go into Kant's analysis of the fallacies of pure reason any further here; I will come back to them later as necessary. Here I will simply summarize Kant's results by saying that dogmatic reason, untouched by criticism, confuses in rational psychology the necessary unity of consciousness in all cognition with the cognition of a unified subject (paralogisms); in rational cosmology it confuses that which is set as a task, namely to seek the condition for any conditioned, with the unconditioned as something given (antinomy); and in rational theology, finally, it confuses the unconditional necessity of judgments with the absolute necessity of things (transcendental ideal).

Thus it is clear that there can be no transcendental deduction of these transcendental ideas of reason. In the absence of a corresponding intuition, the veridical reference to their objects cannot in principle be demonstrated. Nor of course is it possible to show that *nothing* real corresponds to these ideas. In regard to the absolute, the unconditioned, we must remain agnostic: "Indeed it is precisely in knowing one's own limits that philosophy consists" (A 727).[19]

Hence though reason is not suited to cognition of the unconditioned, it is on the other hand equally beyond doubt that it fulfills a positive function in the systematization of experience. Cognition does not consist merely in the collecting of phenomena; rather we strive to forge conceptual links between them and to grasp the laws of nature that are valid for specific classes of objects as cases of yet more general laws, whereby we are guided by the ideal of a unified explanation of nature. Such an explanation only makes sense, however, when we are justified in assuming that nature is in fact unified. And according to Kant, such an assumption is indeed justified.

---

[19] And not "in knowing *its* limits," as Kemp Smith and, more recently, Paul Guyer and Allen Wood have erroneously translated this passage.

For if there was such a great diversity among appearances that they could not be compared and combined into unities, we would be unable to form any concepts at all. On the other hand, concepts would be just as impossible if there were only an undifferentiated homogeneity among appearances, for in order to combine something into a unity, concepts must also distinguish and exclude what does not belong to that unity. And since there cannot be just one single concept (for these must necessarily form a systematic nexus), the appearances must also allow for such a continuity of all concepts among themselves.[20] Now since the understanding is the faculty of concepts, it would itself be impossible if nature did not supply in its appearances the necessary homogeneity, variety, and continuity or affinity. The transcendental unity of apperception, the highest point of all employment of the understanding, is therefore only possible because nature 'plays along' and allows for its activity. We thus arrive at a result which is decidedly beyond the scope of what was shown in the Aesthetic and the Analytic, and which highlights the positive function of reason: "Reason thus prepares the field for the understanding: (1) through a principle of the *homogeneity* of the manifold under higher genera; (2) through a principle of the *variety* of the homogeneous under lower species; and (3) in order to complete the systematic unity, a further law, that of the *affinity* of all concepts—a law which prescribes that we proceed from each species to every other by gradual increase of the diversity" (A657–58).

This transcendental deduction of the three principles of reason—homogeneity, variety, and affinity—would indeed "complete the critical work of pure reason" (A670). The principles' objective validity is demonstrated by the fact that their object is a condition of the possibility of concept formation, without which the understanding and any thought whatsoever would be impossible. In contrast to the categories, these principles of reason possess only an indeterminate objective validity, for the extent of the uniformity and diversity of natural appearances cannot be determined a priori, but only in the course of experience. The principles of reason thus have only a regulative employment, not a constitutive employment.

Kant does not stop here, though. For the line of thought just described really only succeeds in providing an a priori justification for the assumption of a thoroughgoing unity of nature. Nature must be conceived as cohering

---

[20] For as Kant writes in the B-edition, "the criterion of the possibility of a concept . . . is the definition of it" (B115). A definition in turn presupposes a genus (homogeneity) and specific difference (variety), and hence other concepts (affinity).

in such a way that it is amenable to conceptualization. In the actual systematization of experience, reason of course proceeds in such a way that it ascends to increasingly higher levels of universality, aiming at an ideal endpoint, a *focus imaginarius* "from which, since it lies quite outside the bounds of possible experience, the concepts of the understanding do not in reality proceed; nonetheless, it serves to give to these concepts the greatest [possible] unity combined with the greatest [possible] extension" (A644). These *foci imaginarii* are according to Kant nothing other than the ideas of the soul, the world, and God as the ultimate elements in the chain of conditions. It is *these* ideas in their regulative function for which he attempts to give a transcendental deduction by way of the principles of homogeneity, variety, and affinity.

Few commentators have found this last step convincing, nor do I. Whereas Kant's diagnosis of the illusions of traditional metaphysics are of undeniable philosophical significance, his success in securing a positive use for the ideas of reason in the systematization of experience is questionable. Since it will not play a role in the further course of my investigations, however, I can let the matter rest.

2

Critique and Morals

With the *Critique,* the "tribunal of pure reason" had passed a sentence on theoretical metaphysics that was universally valid and promised a lasting peace between the parties to the dispute: The pretensions of dogmatic reason have been dismissed once and for all since it has been shown that there cannot in principle be any theoretical cognition outside of possible experience. The fundamental objections of skeptical reason are also over-ruled, since it has been shown that, in relation to possible experience, a priori cognition is indeed real and demonstrable: "Reason, when employed apart from all experience, can know propositions entirely a priori, and as necessary, or it can know nothing at all. Its judgments, therefore, are never opinions; either it must abstain from all judgment, or must affirm with apodictic certainty" (A775).

However, if we go on to ask just what it is, according to this sentence, that can be known by theoretical reason with apodictic certainty, the an-swer is sobering to say the least:

1) All appearances are, in their intuition, extensive magnitudes (A162).
2) In all appearances, sensation and the real, which is its object, has intensive magnitude, that is, a degree (A166).
3) All appearances contain the permanent (substance) as the object itself and the transitory as its mere determination, that is, as a way in which the object exists (A182).
4) Everything that happens, that is, begins to be, presupposes some-thing upon which it follows according to a rule (A189).
5) All substances, so far as they coexist, stand in thoroughgoing community, that is, in mutual interaction (A211).
6) That which agrees with the formal conditions of experience, that is, with the conditions of intuition and of concepts, is *possible* (A218).

41

7) That which is bound up with the material conditions of experience, that is, with sensation, is *actual* (A218).
8) That which in its connection with the actual is determined in accordance with universal conditions of experience, is (that is, exists as) *necessary* (A218).

That is all that theoretical reason can know a priori. We cannot help but ask whether this answer is worth the effort that went into finding it. As Kant puts it, "It is humiliating to human reason that it achieves nothing in its pure [i.e. theoretical] employment, and indeed stands in need of a discipline to check its extravagancies, and to guard it against the deceptions which arise therefrom . . . The greatest and perhaps the sole use of all philosophy of pure reason is therefore only negative; since it serves not as an organon for the extension but as a discipline for the limitation of pure reason, and, instead of discovering truth, has only the modest merit of guarding against error" (A795).

For Kant, of course, there is more to the task of philosophy than just this, for besides its theoretical employment there is also a practical employment of reason: "Consequently, if there be any correct employment of pure reason, in which case there must also be a canon[1] of its employment, the canon will deal not with the speculative but with the practical employment of reason. This practical employment of reason we shall now proceed to investigate" (A797). The ultimate significance of the task of the *Critique* was that in restricting theoretical reason's claims to knowledge, it secured to morality a field exclusively its own: the *Critique* was to be followed not only by a metaphysics of nature, but also by a metaphysics of morals. For Kant was convinced that practical reason contains pure laws—the moral laws—which we can know a priori and which are not subject to a dialectic, thus allowing for a canon of the proper use of reason. The lesson of Rousseau, Kant believed, was that even the philosophically uneducated know what it is moral to do, so that the task of philosophy consists merely in explicating and bringing into view the underlying principle. In the *Critique's* Doctrine of Method, in the chapter on 'The Canon of Pure Reason', Kant writes that he is justified in assuming that there actually are such pure moral laws which command the will in a completely a priori manner, in that he can appeal "not only to the

---

[1]"I understand by a canon the sum-total of the a priori principles of the correct employment of certain faculties of knowledge" (A796).

proofs employed by the most enlightened moralists, but to the moral judgment of every man, in so far as he makes the effort to think such a law clearly" (A807).

Note, however, that Kant is not concerned here with the question, 'What ought I to do?', which as such is a purely practical question and hence "not transcendental but rather moral, and cannot, therefore, in and by itself, form a proper subject for treatment in this critique" (A805). The question that Kant treats is rather: 'If I do what I ought to do, what may I then hope?' As he emphasizes, this question is at once both practical and theoretical and therefore still part of the present subject. For it can serve to explain why reason, in spite of the dialectic and the theoretical agnosticism to which it leads, time and again ventures beyond the limits of experience and is compelled to confront three problems constituting the ultimate purpose of reason: the freedom of the will, the immortality of the soul, and the existence of God. The practical question, What ought I to do?, provides merely the "guiding thread" for answering the theoretical question. What is meant by this?

Since the answer to the first, practical, question is: 'Do that through which thou becomest worthy of being happy', the second question comes to mean: 'If I behave as I must in order to be worthy of happiness, may I hope *thereby* to obtain happiness?' In other words, Kant is asking whether the principles of pure reason, which prescribe the moral law a priori, also necessarily connect the hope of happiness with it. And, he claims, indeed it can: "I maintain that just as the moral principles are necessary according to reason in its *practical* employment, it is in the view of reason, in the field of its *theoretical* employment, no less necessary to assume that everyone has ground to hope for happiness in the measure in which he has rendered himself by his conduct worthy of it, and that the system of morality is therefore inseparably—though only in the idea of pure reason— bound up with that happiness" (A809). How does Kant arrive at this conclusion?

We can imagine a possible world in which all human action takes place in accord with the moral laws. In such a moral world, whose idea abstracts from all obstacles to morality, we ourselves would be the authors of both our own happiness and that of others, for the moral law prescribes that we further "what is best in the world, alike in ourselves and in others" (A819), i.e. each must make the happiness of others his duty. In such a world, the proportionality of virtue and happiness must therefore be "conceived as necessary" (A809). Moral happiness is the result of a reciprocal

exercise of virtue and is thus largely independent of nature.[2] In addition
to such moral happiness, Kant also acknowledges physical happiness,
which is dependent on nature and consists in the maximal satisfaction of
our sensuous desires (cp. A800, 806). Since my various desires are often
in conflict with each other, so that the fulfillment of one precludes the
fulfillment of another, the task of reason is to establish an order that allows for the greatest possible satisfaction overall. As a sensuous being
with needs and desires, I inevitably pursue such happiness, but it is ultimately empirically contingent and, without morality, it is not actually
true happiness.[3]

True happiness, which would reign in a moral world in exact proportion to virtue, thus presupposes that "*everyone* does what he ought"
(A810). In our actual world that is not, of course, the case. Hence the
moral happiness of individuals is *de facto* unachievable; physical happiness, on the other hand, is subject to empirical contingencies and stands
in a merely contingent relation to one's own morality. Additionally, in
our world we cannot abstract from the obstacles to morality. Not infre-
quently, moral demands starkly conflict with one's own desires, so that
moral action entails physical disadvantages for oneself. Nevertheless, the
obligatory force of this categorical 'thou shalt' remains unaffected by all
such concerns. Reason therefore finds itself compelled to assume a different connection between morality and happiness. For it is after all one and
the same reason which both posits the moral law and is responsible for
the equally paramount task—called "prudence" (A800, 806)—of promoting my empirical happiness. Were the two fundamental demands of
morality and prudence irreconcilable, reason would either despair or, at
the very least, be deterred from morality. Under such circumstances being
moral would be extremely imprudent, for it would be in no way to my
advantage. Though the moral law would allow us to conceive the idea of

[2] ". . . inasmuch as freedom, partly inspired and partly restricted by moral laws,
would itself be the cause of general happiness, since rational beings, under the
guidance of such principles, would themselves be the authors both of their own
enduring well-being and of that of others" (A809).
[3] In reflection 6907, written during the period in which Kant was at work on the
Critique, we read: "Happiness is twofold: either that which is an effect of the free
choice (*Willkühr*) of rational beings in themselves, or that which is only a contingent and external effect dependent on nature. By way of actions which are mutually
directed toward each other, rational beings can create True Happiness (*die Wahre
Glükseeligkeit*) which is independent of everything in nature and without it nature
cannot produce happiness in the proper sense" (19:202).

a perfect action, it could never provide any motivation to act. But such a state of affairs is irreconcilable with the categorical obligatory force of the law: "Since there are practical laws which are absolutely necessary, that is, the moral laws, it must follow that if these necessarily presuppose the existence of any being as the condition of the possibility of their *obligatory power,* this existence must be *postulated*" (A633–34, cp. 815). In order for the moral law actually to motivate actions, a proportion between virtue and happiness must at least be *possible,* even if experience does not appear to offer sufficient evidence of such a proportion. For Kant, however, the possibility of such a proportion is only given on the assumption of a just God and a life after death.

> Morality, by itself, constitutes a system. Happiness, however, does not do so, save in so far as it is distributed in exact proportion to morality. But this is possible only in the intelligible world, under a wise Author and Ruler. Such a Ruler, together with life in such a world, which we must regard as a future world, reason finds itself constrained to assume; otherwise it would have to regard the moral laws as empty figments of the brain, since without this postulate the necessary consequence which it itself connects with these laws could not follow. . . . It is *necessary* that the whole course of our life be subject to moral maxims; but it is *impossible* that this should happen unless reason connects with the moral law, which is a mere idea, an operative cause which determines for such conduct as is in accordance with the moral law an outcome, either in this or in another life, that is in exact conformity with our supreme ends. Thus without a God and without a world invisible to us now but hoped for, the glorious ideas of morality are indeed objects of approval and admiration, *but not springs of purpose and action.* For they do not fulfill in its completeness that end which is natural to every rational being and which is determined a priori *by that same* pure reason (A811–13, emphasis added).

Thus the theoretical and practical interests of reason are at last united in the idea of the highest good of a future world in which virtue and happiness correspond. We must be able to conceive of ourselves as belonging to such a world if reason is to accord with itself. "Thus God and a future life are two postulates which, according to the principles of pure reason, are inseparable from the obligation which that same reason imposes upon us" (A811).

With this I can conclude my present discussion of the *Critique of Pure Reason*. There is just one last point to which I would like to call attention. If the discovery of the main transcendental question and the problem of the antinomy had shown that prior to the *Critique* there could not have been any scientific philosophy based in pure reason, after the completion of this work Kant can now hold out the prospect of perfecting such a science "in a short time" (Axx), indeed "before the end of the present century" (A856). Since this science is "nothing but the *inventory* of all our possession through *pure* reason, systematically arranged," all that is required for its perfection is the enumeration of all the derivative concepts (for which Kant desires the "assistance of a fellow worker" [Axxi], as well as the systematic exposition of all possible cognition through pure concepts: "Such a system of pure (speculative) reason I hope myself to produce under the title *Metaphysics of Nature*. It will be not half as large, yet incomparably richer in content than this present critique, which has as its first task to discover the sources and conditions of the possibility of such a metaphysics" (Axxi).

Before Kant could begin working out the system in detail, however, he had planned a short book intended to facilitate understanding of the *Critique*. As mentioned above, Kant was aware of the extraordinary difficulties that such a completely new "mode of thought" and the comprehension of the underlying "plan" was bound to cause the unprepared reader. The *Critique* had only just left the press when he communicated to Marcus Herz that he knew he could not at first expect many readers who would carefully study his book, but that he was contemplating a plan for rendering the work more popular. That was not possible at the outset, "because the whole system of this sort of knowledge had to be exhibited in all its articulation" (10:269), but it could happen now that that had been accomplished. He presented this simpler plan two years later in the form of the *Prolegomena to Any Future Metaphysics That Will be Able to Come Forward as Science* (1783).

Whereas the *Critique* was forced to take the more difficult path of investigating reason itself and, "without relying on any fact whatever," to derive cognition from its original sources, the *Prolegomena* were to be a kind of preparatory exercise: "they ought more to indicate what needs to be done in order to bring a science into existence if possible than to present the science itself. They must therefore rely on something already known to be dependable" (4:274–75). So, in contrast to the *Critique*, they take an acknowledged "fact" as the starting point.

It is mathematics and pure natural science in which Kant finds such a starting point. For he sees both sciences as containing synthetic knowledge which is at once both apodictically certain and independent of experience, and thus a priori. Since the propositions of metaphysics (assuming its possibility) are also synthetic and a priori, it seems natural to ask whether the conditions of possibility of synthetic a priori judgments in mathematics and pure natural science are not also the conditions under which such judgments would be possible in metaphysics. "We have therefore some at least *uncontested* synthetic cognition a priori, and we do not need to ask whether it is possible (for it is actual), but only: *how is it possible,* in order to be able to derive, from the principle of the possibility of the given cognition, the possibility of all other synthetic cognition a priori" (4:275). Hence "the main transcendental question" on which the plan of the *Prolegomena* is based is not 'How can a priori representations veridically refer to objects in general?', as in the *Critique,* but rather: 'How are synthetic judgments *a priori* possible?' (cp. 4:280, 276).

The method of the *Prolegomena* has both advantages and disadvantages. The main advantage is that since the text begins with something familiar to the reader which is then analyzed step by step, the steps of the argument are easier to follow. The whole is thus capable of a certain popularity which the more strictly academic exposition of the *Critique* could not have hoped for. It is also far easier to recognize here than in the *Critique* what is crucial for the possibility of synthetic judgments a priori: namely the ideality of space and time. As Kant emphasizes, it is "the sole means for solving this problem" (4:377). The fundamental disadvantage is that the regressive-analytic method leads to a result which is valid only conditionally, valid, that is, only to the extent that the premise (the "fact") is correct. For though Kant is certain for his part that the propositions of mathematics and pure natural science are synthetic a priori, it is certainly possible to doubt that they are as Hume, for example, had done. The *Prolegomena,* therefore, can only supplement the *Critique* or follow upon it, not replace it. The method of the *Prolegomena* is useful against dogmatism because it makes clear the limits of possible knowledge from pure reason. It is less successful against skepticism, however, because it presupposes that there really are synthetic judgments a priori, instead of deriving them from the possibility of thought (apperception) as in the subjective deduction of the categories. And of course this method also excludes morality from transcendental philosophy; its possibility cannot be derived from that of pure mathematics and natural science.

Just as Kant was busy with the composition of the *Prolegomena*, the first review of the *Critique* was published in the *Göttingische Anzeigen von gelehrten Sachen*. The importance of this review for the further development of Kant's philosophy cannot be overestimated and hence I will deal with it here in somewhat greater detail.

Historical Excursus

In order properly to appraise the significance of the review, it is important to realize that in 1781, the same year as Kant's *Critique*, Berkeley's *Three Dialogues between Hylas and Philonous* were also published for the first time in German translation.[4] This work caused considerable puzzlement. One reviewer predicted that out of a hundred readers there would hardly be one who "will fail to view this idealistic system, so very appalling and confusing to the common understanding, as nonsense and as clear proof of the philosophers' aberrations, and throw away with indignation a book that contains such fantasies." For, as the reviewer goes on, in Berkeley's idealism "all matter is completely annihilated, its reality denied, and its existence reduced merely to the mind's representations of it."[5]

Although the tone of the Göttingen review of Kant's *Critique* is less disparaging, the association with Berkeley is present from the outset. For Kant's work, writes the reviewer, "is a system of higher, or, as the author calls it, transcendental idealism; an idealism that comprehends spirit and matter in the same way, transforms the world and our self into representations . . . All our cognitions arise from certain modifications of our self that we call sensations . . . Upon these concepts of sensations as mere modifications of our self (upon which Berkeley also mainly built his idealism), of space, and of time, rests the one foundation pillar of the Kantian system."[6]

This passage is sufficient to demonstrate that the reviewer has failed to understand the basic question posed by the *Critique*—and hence also the idea of transcendental philosophy. For the *Critique* is not at all concerned with objects

---

[4] The work was included in the volume *George Berkeleys, ehemaligen Bischofs zu Cloyne in Irland, philosophische Werke*. Part One. Leipzig: im Schwickertschen Verlag 1781.

[5] *Allgemeine Deutsche Bibliothek*, No. 52 (1782), 161–62.

[6] [Tr.: The Göttingen review is quoted from the appendix to Kant, *Prolegomena to Any Future Metaphysics*. Trans., ed. Gary Hatfield, Cambridge: Cambridge University Press 2004, 201–7, here 201–2.]

("matter"), but rather with our a priori concepts of *objects in general*.[7] Berkeley's idealism is metaphysical, Kant's is not. Kant is concerned instead with investigating the *possibility* of metaphysics. Indeed, it was for precisely this reason that he introduced the term '*object in general*' in order to cast into relief the difference from traditional metaphysics. The fact that the reviewer has utterly failed to notice this is also evidenced by his overall appraisal of the table of categories and the principles: "They are the commonly known principles of logic and ontology, expressed according to the idealistic restrictions of the author."[8]

Kant's reaction is documented by numerous handwritten remarks as well as by the three notes to section 13 and the appendix to the *Prolegomena*. In section 13 he again summarizes his theory of space as the form of outer appearances. Secondly, he points out that in contrast to all the other idealists he does not in the least deny the existence of external objects, but only claims that we do not know them as they are in themselves, but only by way of the representations they arouse in us. Thirdly, he rejects the criticism that his theory transforms the sensible world into "mere illusion"; on the contrary, his theory is the only way both to guarantee the certainty and exact applicability of mathematics to actual objects while at the same time guarding against the "transcendental illusion" by which metaphysics has always been deceived and which finds its starkest expression in the antinomy.

In the appendix, finally, Kant challenges the anonymous reviewer to step forward and enter into a public debate with him, and he invites him to choose any one of the antinomial propositions and to attack Kant's proof of the contradictory proposition. If Kant succeeds in defending the proof, "then by this means it is settled that there is an hereditary defect in metaphysics," since both the proposition and its contradiction are equally provable—an hereditary defect which cannot be explained, much less remedied, unless we examine pure reason itself: "and so my *Critique* must either be accepted or a better one put in its place, and therefore it must at least be studied; which is the only thing I ask for now" (4:379). At the same time, however, Kant also makes an important and highly consequential concession. Since the *Critique* as a whole is difficult to grasp, and

---

[7] "The word transcendental, however, which with me never signifies a relation of our cognition to things, but only to the *faculty of cognition*, was intended to prevent this misinterpretation" (4:293).

[8] Göttingen Review, ibid., 202. In his notes Kant writes that the reviewer "persists in the belief that I find myself together with him in the same field of metaphysics, whereas I have taken up a standpoint wholly outside of it from which I can judge the possibility of metaphysics itself; he however persists in judging me according to the codex of metaphysics, against whose validity I protest throughout the whole work" (23:57).

since a certain prolixity and obscurity cannot be denied, Kant makes the following "proposal": "I propose these *Prolegomena* as the plan and guide for the investigation, and not the work itself" (4:381). This means that the reader is not to start from the question how a priori representations can refer to an object in general, but rather from the question how synthetic propositions a priori are possible.

Not long after the publication of the *Prolegomena,* the author of the review did in fact contact Kant; he did so, however, not in order to carry on the discussion of the antinomy as Kant had suggested, but to explain how his review had come about. The well-known *Populärphilosoph* Christian Garve confesses that he took on the review of Kant's work without having read it. He soon came to see that he would not be able to do it justice, and his discussion of it grew to such length that the editor of the *Göttingische Anzeigen* shortened it by two-thirds and significantly rewrote important passages of the remainder. He could not recognize the printed version as his own.

Kant's answer was immediate. He praises Garve as the man of noble sentiments he had always known him to be. He goes on to write, "Furthermore, I must admit that I have not counted on an immediately favorable reception of my work . . . In time, a number of points will become clear (perhaps my *Prolegomena* will help this). These points will shed light on other passages, to which of course a clarifying essay from me may be requisite from time to time. And thus, finally, the whole work will be surveyed and understood, if one will only get started with the job, beginning with the main question on which everything depends (a question that I have stated clearly enough)" (10:338–39). The main question to which he refers is that of the *Prolegomena:* How are a priori synthetic propositions possible? Here again Kant suggests that one should take this question as the starting point.

On August 21, 1783, Garve sends his original version of the review to Kant. It is considerably more circumspect than the rewritten version that appeared in the *Göttingische Anzeigen.* Nor is the comparison with Berkeley to be found in Garve's own version. What lends Garve's original version its special importance, however, is something else. It is his judgment of the chapter on the canon of pure reason, which I mentioned above and in which God and a life after death are introduced as necessary postulates of reason in order to explain why moral actions are obligatory. On this point we read in the published review in the *Göttingische Anzeigen:* "We prefer to pass over without remark the way the author intends to use moral concepts to lend support to the common mode of thought after having robbed it of speculative concepts, for this is the part with which we find ourselves least able to agree. There is of course a manner of connecting the conceptions of truth and the most general laws of thought with the most general concepts and principles of right behavior which is grounded in our nature . . . But we do not recognize it in the guise in which the author dresses it . . . First and foremost, the right employment of the understanding must accord with the most general concept of right behavior, the basic law of our moral nature, that is, the promotion of happiness" (Malter 198–99).[9]

The notes Kant wrote while preparing the *Prolegomena* make it clear that he found this passage especially offensive: "Instruction by the reviewer in morality . . . I, too, learn—only not morality" (23:59). For the principle of happiness which is here promoted to the fundamental law of our moral nature can never lead to a pure morality, but only to a prudential doctrine oriented toward one's own advantage, in other words what today would be called instrumental reason oriented toward means and ends. The imperatives which have their source in instrumental reason are always conditioned and dependent on an assumed end, whereas moral imperatives command categorically and without regard to aims and interests. Thus there is either only instrumental reason or there is a completely different kind of practical reason as well, namely moral reason, which presupposes the possibility of an unconditionally commanding imperative. On this point Kant makes the following note: "Now the question is, how is a categorical imperative possible[;] whoever solves this problem has found the true principle of morality. The reviewer will probably not dare to undertake a solution to this problem as he has not dared to take on the important problem of transcendental philosophy which has a remarkable similarity to that of morality" (23:60).

Indeed, if instead of the question of the possibility of objective reference one starts from the main question of the *Prolegomena,* the similarity is striking. For the categorical imperative is also a synthetic a priori proposition. It connects my will with a deed, and it does so a priori and necessarily, without the connection being prescribed by a prior end willed by myself. What, then, is the third term that makes the synthetic connection a priori possible? Since it is not possible experience as in the case of theoretical propositions of this kind, what is it then?

Based on what Kant says in the "Canon of Pure Reason," we have to assume that it is the idea of a possible highest good, in which happiness is thought as proportional to virtue, that makes such a connection possible and is thus in a position to motivate action. But it is precisely this thought which Garve finds wholly unconvincing. He writes: "It is very true that it is only moral sentiment that makes the thought of God important to us; it is only the perfection of that sentiment which improves our theology. But that it is supposed to be possible to maintain this sentiment and the truths founded on it, after one has eliminated all the

---

[9] Garve's texts are reprinted in R. Malter's edition of Kant's *Prolegomena.* References are to this edition.

other sentiments that relate to the existence of things and the theory derived from them—that one is supposed to be able to live and abide in the kingdom of grace, after the kingdom of nature has disappeared before our eyes—this, I think, will find its way into the hearts and minds of very few people indeed" (Malter 237–38).

In the dialectic Kant had, on the one hand, shown that we cannot know anything about God and that theoretical cognition of supersensible objects must be ruled out as impossible in principle. On the other hand, he argues that certain propositions of practical reason cannot be true, or rather, cannot motivate action unless we can assume the existence of God and a future life. It is thus the validity and obligatory force of the moral law itself which re-introduces God into theoretical cognition, while at the same time it is the idea of God which serves to explain the bindingness and validity of the law. For "reason finds itself constrained to assume" the existence of God, Kant writes in the *Critique,* since "otherwise it would have to regard the moral laws as empty figments of the brain" (A811).

Kant is thus guilty of a *petitio principii* which only becomes clear to him through Garve's objection (for the published version of the review had passed over this point as incomprehensible). His explanation presupposes the very thing it is supposed to explain.

Hence it is equally clear that Kant still owes an explanation of how the categorical imperative is possible as a synthetic proposition a priori. What is the source of the obligation which connects the will with action in the absence of a determinate purpose? Whatever the case, a sufficient explanation cannot be derived from the *Critique's* Canon of Pure Reason.[10] And until such an explanation is given, the moral skeptic is just as entitled to claim that up to now there has been no metaphysics of morals, as Kant is in claiming that up to now there has been no metaphysics of nature.

The moral skeptic's counterpart is the moral dogmatist who insists that the moral laws can be derived from human nature and are thus subordinated to happiness. And this is the view shared by Garve and his editor in Göttingen. Garve, too, believes that morality can be determined on the basis of human nature, and he

---

[10] It is interesting to note that in the chapter on the Canon of Pure Reason (A 818–19) Kant himself had pointed out a possible case of circular reasoning. This circle is however not the one that Garve finds in the explanation of the obligatory force of the law, but one which would arise if we attempted to derive the moral laws from the will of God when it was the moral laws which led us to the idea of God in the first place. The moral law does not originate in a divine will ("we would have no conception of such a will"), but rather in reason itself, and we have a concept of God "which we now hold to be correct . . . because it completely harmonizes with the moral principles of reason" (A818).

explicitly questions whether "this worthiness counts as the final end of nature and for more than happiness itself" (Malter 240). And since he had just published his views on this matter with great success in a two-volume translation of Cicero's *De officiis,* commissioned by the King of Prussia himself and enlarged by Garve's commentary and annotations, Kant was forced to admit that the first principle of morality was not at all as clear and evident as he had assumed in the *Critique* under the influence of Rousseau. In place of the simple response to the Göttingen review he had initially planned, he now saw that he himself was still missing something. He could not possibly make a direct transition to metaphysics from the *Critique* and *Prolegomena.* Rather the first order of business would be to give a perfectly clear account of the supreme principle of morality and to demonstrate the possibility of a categorical imperative as a synthetic a priori proposition. In other words, he would have to write a *Groundwork of the Metaphysics of Morals.*

Before turning to that work, however, I would like briefly to address a further fundamental objection raised in the Göttingen review. Though Garve does not explicitly refer to Berkeley, he too questions whether Kant's principles provide a basis for explaining the difference between experience on the one hand and dream and fantasy on the other. For even in dreams we see what we imagine as though in space and time and as following causally upon what precedes it. Nevertheless, we later recognize it as unreal. Does Kant have a response to this objection?

Let us return, then, once more to the *Prolegomena.* After elucidating his doctrine of space and time as the a priori forms of all appearances, Kant writes: "From this it follows: that, since truth rests upon universal and necessary laws as its criteria, for *Berkeley* experience could have no criteria of truth, because its appearances (according to him) had nothing underlying them a priori; from which it then followed that experience is nothing but sheer illusion, whereas for us space and time (in conjunction with the pure concepts of the understanding) prescribe a priori their law to all possible experience, which law at the same time provides the sure criterion for distinguishing truth from illusion in experience" (4:375).

As it stands, this claim is hardly convincing. For in the third *Dialogue,* Berkeley had explained, "[I] place the reality of things in ideas, fleeting indeed, and changeable; however not changed at random, but according to the fixed order of nature. For herein consists that constancy and truth of things, which secures all the concerns of life, and distinguishes that which is *real* from the irregular visions of the fancy" (Berkeley 1713,

254). And Kant himself seems to share precisely this same view, which he had expressed for instance at A493 of the *Critique* and reaffirms in the *Prolegomena:* "The difference between truth and dream, however, is not decided through the quality of the representations that are referred to objects, for they are the same in both, but through their connection according to the rules that determine the connection of representations in the concept of an object, and how far they can or cannot stand together in one experience" (4:290). How, then, are we to interpret Kant's objection that Berkeley has no criterion of truth?

Let us suppose for a moment that Berkeley is right and space is not a priori but has an empirical origin in the abstraction from given appearances.[11] Initially, therefore, all we have are the appearances as representations in inner sense. They arise successively, in continuous flux, one after the other. In order for me now to form the representation of space, I require representations of something permanent or simultaneous. Two things are 'simultaneous', as Kant explains in the third analogy, when the perception of the one (A) can both follow and be followed by the perception of the other (B), that is, when apprehension (and not only thought) can proceed both from A to B as well as from B back to A. This, however, is not possible in inner sense, for there everything is successive and hence every new perception is later than the one which precedes it. Under these conditions, then, it is wholly impossible to represent a manifold as being simultaneous and thus to refer it to something distinct from myself. On the basis of inner sense alone, it is not possible to distinguish between representation and external object and hence neither is it possible to distinguish between illusion and reality. Or as Kant will later say, "No one can have inner sense alone, and indeed on behalf of cognition of his inner state, yet that is what idealism asserts" (18:616). Therefore, space cannot have an empirical origin as Berkeley supposed it to have. Experience is impossible—and hence self-consciousness, too, is impossible, as Kant has demonstrated in the transcendental deduction of the categories—if

---

[11] Berkeley assumes "that *distance* and *outness* is neither immediately of itself perceived by sight, nor yet apprehended or judged of by lines and angles, or anything that hath a necessary connexion with it; but that it is only suggested to our thoughts by certain visible ideas and sensations attending vision . . . by a connexion taught us by experience, they come to signify and suggest them to us" (Berkeley 1710, sect. 43).

space is not presupposed as an a priori form of intuition along with inner sense.[12]

This argument refutes Berkeley's theory of space, but it also has an important implication for Kant's own position. As we have seen, Kant demonstrated the objective validity of the categories by showing how they can refer to their object in an a priori manner. This, of course, could not take place a posteriori, but rather transcendental philosophy must, in a purely a priori fashion, "formulate by universal but sufficient marks the conditions under which objects can be given in harmony with these concepts. Otherwise the concepts would be void of all content, and therefore mere logical forms, not pure concepts of the understanding" (A136). At this point, however, it becomes obvious that Kant had not presented such "sufficient marks." Although he had shown in the schematism chapter how an object can be given *"in concreto"* (A138) as corresponding to the categories, he had done so only for the inner sense. For the schemata are "nothing but a priori determinations of time in accordance with rules" (A145). The reason for limiting schemata to inner sense seems to be that *all* appearances are to be met with in inner sense, whereas only some of them are present also in outer sense: "For the original apperception stands in relation to inner sense (the sum of all representations), and indeed a priori to its form" (A177, cp. 98–99). Thus Kant was able to believe that the schemata contain the necessary and hence "universal" conditions of the objective reality of the categories: "Thus an application of the category to appearances becomes possible by means of the transcendental determination of time" (A139).

In the course of his encounter with Berkeley, however, it becomes clear that there can be no temporal determination without space, since inner sense cannot contain the elements of permanence and simultaneity required for any temporal determination. Space itself, however, cannot be perceived. Rather, for us it must be represented by way of the simultaneity of the objects within it. Thus in addition to the schemata, there must also be

---

[12] When he was first distinguishing his position from that of Newton and Leibniz, Kant had concentrated all his attention on the point that space and time cannot be real quantities existing independently of the subject ("What, then, are space and time? Are they real existences?" A23), but only forms of intuition. The present context reveals a new aspect: it is only *together* that they make experience possible. No spatial determination without time; no temporal determination without space.

something like an 'a priori spatial determination in accord with rules' which can explain how we are able a priori to distinguish something, which is supposed to be an object of outer sense, from the space which it occupies. The following statement from the *Critique* cannot therefore be correct: "The schemata of the pure understanding are thus the true and *sole* conditions under which these concepts obtain relation to objects and so possess *significance*" (A145–46, first emphasis added). A *sufficient* demonstration of the objective validity of the categories still requires something along the lines of a schematism of space.

Thus it was the first review of the *Critique* which made Kant realize that not just one, but *two* books would be necessary before he would be able to turn to metaphysics: in addition to the *Groundwork for the Metaphysics of Morals,* which came out in 1785, another work as well, which, though completed in the same year, was not published until the year after: *Metaphysical Foundations of Natural Science.* In regard to this latter work, he wrote to Christian Gottfried Schütz on September 13, 1785: "Before I can compose the metaphysics of nature that I have promised to do, I had to write something that is in fact a mere application of it but that presupposes an empirical concept.[13] I refer to the metaphysical foundations of the doctrine of body . . . So I finished them this Summer under the title 'Metaphysical Foundations of Natural Science'" (10:406).

To these two works I now turn.

---

[13] For that space is not empty cannot be known a priori.

3

From A to B

Groundwork for the Metaphysics of Morals

In the preface Kant makes perfectly clear what it is he intends to accomplish with the work: "The present groundwork is . . . nothing more than the search for and establishment of the *supreme principle of morality*" (4:392). For that the principle of morality had remained largely misunderstood and that the possibility of a categorical imperative was yet to be demonstrated, had been revealed to Kant by Garve and the Göttingen review. Hence, as he goes on to say, "this [groundwork] must come first, and *without it there can be no moral philosophy at all*" (4:390; emphasis added). The metaphysics of morals must therefore be preceded by an investigation into the possibility of morality, just as the metaphysics of nature must be preceded by an investigation into the possibility of a priori cognition of objects. With this we have reached the standpoint from which it first becomes possible truly to understand Kant's later remark (which is also my starting point) that prior to critical philosophy there had been no philosophy at all. On the other hand, we are by the same token forced to ask how we are to conceive the relation of the two propaedeutics to one another. Is the *Groundwork* a science *in addition to* and fundamentally distinct from transcendental philosophy, yet having the same goal, namely the demonstration that a certain kind of metaphysics is possible? Or is it a *part* of transcendental philosophy even though it is not concerned with the possibility of a priori reference, but rather with the possibility of a categorical imperative? Kant postpones the answer:

> Indeed there is really no other foundation [for a metaphysics of morals] than the critique of a pure practical reason, just as that of metaphysics is the critique of pure speculative reason, already published. But . . . I require that the critique of pure practical reason, if

it is to be carried through completely, be able at the same time to present the unity of practical with speculative reason in a common principle, since there can, in the end, be only one and the same reason, which must be distinguished merely in its application. But I could not yet bring it to such completeness here without bringing it into considerations of a wholly different kind and confusing the reader (4:391).

Let us, too, postpone this question and turn directly to the *Groundwork* and hence to "the search for and establishment of the supreme principle of morality." Here the most suitable approach is the analytical method that Kant himself had just employed with success in the *Prolegomena* and which in addition to clarity in the steps of the argument also holds out the promise of popularity: It is not until the third chapter that (for reasons later to be discussed) Kant switches to the synthetic method. In this case, too, his point of departure is something for which he believes he can assume widespread assent, in order then to go on to investigate its condition of possibility: namely that there is something unconditionally good and not merely things good relatively such as suitable means to a given end. What is an unconditional good?

"It is impossible to think of anything at all in the world, or indeed even beyond it, that could be considered good without qualification except a *good will*" (4:393). Anything else that may appear good to us, be it happiness or ability, moderation of the passions, or fame, fortune and honor, ceases to be good when it serves dishonest ends. Even the mafia is said to have a code of honor, though we would not subscribe to it, and a crime committed with premeditation and cunning generally strikes us as more heinous than one which has arisen from the confusion of passion. Yet even when no criminal intent is present, but only an attitude that is closed to moral questions, we withhold our assent: as Kant says, "an impartial rational spectator can take no delight in seeing the uninterrupted prosperity of a being graced with no feature of a pure and good will, so that a good will seems to constitute the indispensable condition even of worthiness to be happy" (4:393).

Such a will must, of course, actually be a *will* and not a mere wish unconcerned to use all the means at its disposal. A good will must be accompanied as far as possible by the appropriate action. Even so, its value does not depend on its success. A good will does not cease to be good when circumstances beyond the agent's control prevent the action from achieving its goal. But what exactly is it then that makes a will good? If it is not the effect or the consequence of the action, its unconditioned quality can only consist in the action's form or conformity to law, which serves as the principle of the will: according to Kant a good will is one whose principle is never to act except in such a way that it could also will that its maxim should become a universal law (cp. 4:402). What exactly does this mean?

Our starting point was a being endowed with reason and a will determinable by reason. As a human being, however, I am not merely a rational being with a will, but also a sensuous being. As such, I suffer from various deficiencies and have needs and inclinations, the satisfaction of which is invariably particular and subjective: it is *my* hunger that is at issue, *my* desire, *my* pain. From the standpoint of reason, however, I consider things from a supra-subjective, universally valid point of view: theoretical reason is concerned here with truth, practical reason with that which is universally valid in practical regard, i.e. good. In formal terms, however, universal validity is nothing other than freedom from contradiction ("a universal, though merely negative, criterion of all truth" [A 151]), so that we could also say that what reason is concerned with is avoiding contradictions. "If we now attend to ourselves in any transgression of duty, we find that we do not really will that our maxim should become a universal law, since that is impossible for us, but that the opposite of our maxim should instead remain a universal law, only we take the liberty of making an *exception* to it for ourselves (or just for this once) to the advantage of our inclination. Consequently, if we weighed all cases from one and the same point of view, namely that of reason, we would find a contradiction in our own will, namely that a certain principle be objectively necessary as a universal law and yet subjectively not hold universally but allow exceptions" (4:424).

From the point of view of reason, an action which is only possible by my making an exception for myself stands in contradiction to the universal principles of rational action. The same is true of an action which is possible only if the intention or maxim behind it is concealed, as for example in the case of lying: if the person to whom the lie is addressed knows I am lying, I cannot deceive him. In order for an action to be good, its maxim has to be capable of being publicly declared without negating the action, or it must be capable of being adopted by everyone else in suitably similar circumstances, or, as Kant says, it must be suitable for universal legislation. Precisely this is what the categorical imperative prescribes. It is the supreme principle of morality and it can accordingly be analytically derived from a more explicit determination of the good will: a good will is a will which does not act on principles of self-love which have only subjective validity, but which instead can also will that its maxim become a universal law (4:402).

Still, the result is merely hypothetical: "Whoever holds morality to be something and not a chimerical idea without any truth must also admit the principle of morality brought forward" (4:445). But must one hold morality to be something true? "That morality is no phantom—and this follows if the categorical imperative, and with it the autonomy of the will, is true and absolutely necessary as an a priori principle—requires a possible *synthetic use of pure practical reason,* which use, however, we cannot venture upon without prefacing it by a *critique* of this rational faculty itself, the main features of which we have to present, sufficiently for our purpose, in the last section" (ibid.).

The analytic method of the first chapter must therefore be followed by a synthetic procedure in the third which demonstrates the real possibility of a categorical imperative. However, Kant interposes a further analytic chapter between these two entitled "Transition from popular moral philosophy to metaphysics of morals." This is surprising given that it is still the task of the *Groundwork* to prove the possibility of such a metaphysics and that this can only be achieved synthetically. Moreover, Kant goes on to offer numerous examples of various duties which presuppose empirical knowledge of human nature, even though he himself insists that the *Groundwork* must be completely pure and that one could not give worse advice to morality "than by wanting to derive it from examples. For every example of it presented to me must itself first be appraised in accordance with principles of morality, as to whether it is also worthy to serve as an original example, that is, as a model" (4:408). Why, then, does he do this?

Essentially, there are three reasons that can be offered in explanation of Kant's procedure. *First,* a capacity of judgment honed by experience is necessary in order to distinguish the cases in which the law is applicable (cp. 4:389). For this reason Kant had already introduced the concept of duty in the first chapter in order to "explicate" (*entwickeln*) under human conditions the concept of a good will which is really a "holy," i.e. pure rational will. A holy will knows neither duty nor imperative, but only the moral law or law of reason. Duties and imperatives result from humanity's dual nature of reason and sensibility. Since sensibility has its own legitimate demands, human reason is frequently confronted with obstacles which the imperative commands it to overcome when they stand in conflict with the demands of the moral law. Such cases of conflict therefore illustrate the good will under human conditions without however constituting the criterion of morality. The interpretation made popular by Friedrich Schiller, according to which my deed must be unpleasant to me in order for it to have moral value,[1] is a widespread caricature of the Kantian position arising from a misunderstanding of this point.

Second, Kant offers examples in order to provide the law, which as such is wholly abstract, "with access to the will of the human being and efficacy for his fulfillment of [it]," that is, "to bring an idea of reason closer to intuition . . . and thereby to feeling" (4:389, 436).

Thirdly, and in my opinion perhaps the most important reason, is a result of the context in which the *Groundwork* was written. Kant had initially planned to write an 'anti-critique' in response to Garve's review. When a copy of Garve's *Philosophical Annotations and Essays on Cicero's De Officii* [*Philosophische Anmerkungen und Abhandlungen zu Cicero's Büchern von den Pflichten*] fell into his hands and he saw how Garve followed Cicero in attempting to derive all the duties (as well as their obligatory force) from the four cardinal virtues of prudence, justice, courage, and moderation, which in turn are conceived as rooted in human nature,[2] he seems to have realized that "the search for and establishment of the supreme principle of morality" would have to take priority over a response to the review: The "anti-critique" turned into a *Groundwork for the Metaphysics of Morals.*[3] And although Garve is not explicitly named in the text, the debate with him is palpable in many passages. This is especially the case in chapter two, in which the "Transition from popular moral philosophy to the metaphysics of morals" is effected by demonstrating what a determination of the duties would have to look like if preceded by a genuine determination of the principle of morality. Here the duties are not

---

[1] Compare Friedrich Schiller's Xenion entitled "Qualms of Conscience" (*Werke,* vol. 1, 357): "I gladly serve my friends, yet I do so, alas, by inclination, / And thus it often rankles me that I am not virtuous." It is followed by "Decisum": "There's no other way about it: You must seek to revile your inclination / And then to do with loathing what duty bids you do."

[2] "Whoever examines the nature of that which is good," writes Garve, "examines the primary motivations of our desires, from which alone the foundations of morality can be derived" (Garve, *Werke,* vol. 10, 10).

[3] Compare Hamann, *Briefwechsel,* vol. 5, 129, 141.

arbitrarily derived from certain moral intuitions or from the vague concept of 'human nature', for example courage or moderation, where it remains unclear why there are supposed to be just four cardinal virtues and
not more or different ones. Instead, we are supplied with *examples* of how
one would have to proceed in order to develop a genuine metaphysics of
morals able to satisfy rigorous philosophical criteria. We are dealing here,
then, with an anticipation of the later metaphysics of morals. Even so, it is
still provisional upon the condition that the supreme principle of morality
is real and not a mere "figment of the brain."

The reality of the moral principle is not demonstrated until chapter
three, which in consequence proceeds synthetically. Here again, a brief
summary of Kant's line of reasoning will suffice. Assuming that we are free,
the human will is determined neither by inner nor by external causes. This
does not mean that free actions are arbitrary. Freedom does not signify
arbitrariness or lawlessness, but rather that its actions are determined
not externally (heteronomously), but through itself in a lawful manner. If
it is to be possible for freedom to remain free while at the same time being
subject to a law, then the law on which its actions are based is either chosen by itself (= practical freedom, freedom in the 'negative' sense) or originates in freedom itself (= transcendental freedom, freedom in the 'positive'
sense). So positive freedom is at the same time autonomy, and freedom in
this sense is the only kind that is relevant in the present context. Now this
freedom (to the extent that it exists) is limited by the freedom of other
rational beings, who consequently must also be conceived as autonomous.
The only law that freedom can give to itself and which at the same time
is valid for all is therefore the law of concordance with the freedom of all
other rational beings, and that is none other than the moral law that has
already been analytically derived. Thus it becomes clear how a categorical
imperative could be possible as a synthetic a priori proposition: namely,
on the assumption of freedom as autonomy. It would be the 'third term'
which would connect the will with the deed without having recourse to
something heteronomous as a source of motivation.

Yet how can we be justified in assuming freedom? After all, the *Critique* had shown that we cannot demonstrate the objective reality of a
non-sensible concept such as that of freedom. So is freedom anything more
than a figment of the brain? Here Kant introduces a new thought that
goes beyond the *Critique*. Although theoretical reason can neither prove
nor disprove the reality of freedom, it itself presupposes in all of its judg-

ments a freedom of judgment since otherwise it would be incapable of true judgments. Truth presupposes the possibility of error, and it is only given when, among distinct predicates each of which could be ascribed to a subject, I could also have chosen the false one. If the choice is causally conditioned, it is no longer a choice but an effect. Thus pure theoretical reason must regard itself as subject to no laws other than those it prescribes to itself (the laws of formal and transcendental logic), and hence also as free. Similarly, I must ascribe to myself freedom of action if my action is to count as one for which I can be held responsible. I must have caused it myself, for else it cannot be ascribed to me. "One cannot possibly think of a reason that would consciously receive direction from any other quarter with respect to its judgments, since the subject would then attribute the determination of its judgment not to his reason but to an impulse . . . Now I assert that to every rational being having a will we must necessarily lend the idea of freedom also, under which alone he acts. For in such a being we think of a reason that is practical, that is, has causality with respect to its objects" (4:448; cp. 8:14).

This means that we must presuppose freedom of the will in the case of agents (and thus hardly need do more than theoretical reason itself must do), but it does not also imply that freedom or its law does in fact determine the will, thus making the action moral. In other words, we are confronted by the same problem we encountered in the *Critique* where Kant presupposed moral laws and questioned the source of their motivational power. Even if I presuppose freedom along with its laws—what motivates me to accept it as binding upon me when to follow it will cause me physical disadvantage: "Why, then, ought I to subject myself to this principle?" (4:449).

At this point the debate with Garve is especially evident, even though his name is nowhere mentioned. Garve had raised three objections against Kant's chapter on the canon of pure reason, doubting (1) "that we recognize a certain behavior as absolutely worthy of happiness"; (2) "that this worthiness counts as the final end of nature and for more than happiness itself"; (3) that, "after one has eliminated all the other sentiments that relate to the existence of things and the theory derived from them . . . reason . . . still gives us certain a priori necessary rules for our behavior, which however are not true or at least cannot motivate our will if God and a future life" do not exist (Malter 240, 238).

Here is what Kant has to say:

It seems . . . that in the idea of freedom we have actually only pre-supposed the moral law, namely the principle of autonomy of the will itself, and could not prove by itself its reality and objective necessity[4] . . . for, if someone [= Garve] asked us why the universal validity of our maxim as a law must be the limiting condition of our actions, and on what we base the worth we assign to this way of acting—a worth so great that there can be no higher interest anywhere [= Garve's first objection]—and asked us how it happens that a human being believes that only through this does he feel his personal worth, in comparison with which that of an agreeable or disagreeable condition is to be held as nothing [= Garve's second objection], we could give him no satisfactory answer. We do indeed find . . . that mere worthiness to be happy, even without the motive of participating in this happiness, can interest us of itself; but this judgment is in fact only the result of the importance we have already supposed belongs to the moral law (when by the idea of freedom we detach ourselves from all empirical interest); but we cannot yet see, in this way, that we ought to detach ourselves from such interest . . . and how this is possible, and hence *on what grounds the moral law is binding* [= Garve's third objection]. It must be freely admitted that a kind of circle comes to light here from which, as it seems, there is no way to escape (4:449–50).

There is, however, a way out of the circle after all. The key to avoiding it is the same as that which allowed us to avoid the antinomy: the distinction between appearance and the thing in itself. It was the precise analysis of the process of perception which had made this distinction necessary. For among our representations we distinguish those which we produce ourselves through our own spontaneity from those which arise through affection without any activity on our part (perceptions). And in the case of the latter we were forced to assume non-sensible things with certain powers in order to be able to conceive perceptions as their effect on us, that is, "merely to have something corresponding to sensibility viewed as a receptivity" (A494). Now I myself am initially given to myself empiri-

---

[4] Garve had written in his review, "It is however evident that the author holds certain propositions to be higher and holier than his system, and that in the case of certain decision he paid more attention to the consequences, which he wanted to preserve, than to the principles which he had set down" (Malter 235).

cally as the object of inner and outer sense and thus as an object in the sensible world. Additionally, however, I must also assume "something else lying at their basis, namely the I as it may be constituted in itself" (4:451), and thus I view myself as belonging to the "sensible world" on the one hand and to the "intelligible world" on the other. And my use of reason does indeed distinguish me from all other things and from myself as a sensuously affected being, as we have just seen, and thus I myself lay the foundation for the distinction between two worlds. Now the crucial point for Kant is that these two worlds are not simply juxtaposed without further relation. Ontologically speaking, appearances are dependent on there being something which appears. Only the intelligible world exists independently; the sensible world is to be conceived as dependent on it, so that the laws of the intelligible world must also find expression in the sensible world: "But because *the intelligible world contains the ground of the sensible world and so too of its laws,* and is therefore immediately lawgiving with respect to my will (which belongs wholly to the intelligible world) and must accordingly also be thought as such, it follows that I shall cognize myself as intelligence, though on the other side as a being belonging to the sensible world, as nevertheless subject to the law of the intelligible world, that is, of reason, which contains in the idea of freedom the law of the intelligible world, and thus cognize myself as subject to the autonomy of the will; consequently the laws of the intelligible world must be regarded as imperatives for me, and actions in conformity with these as duties" (4:453–54).

Thus the obligatory force of the moral law is not to be explained by way of something distinct from myself operating as a motivating force. Rather what I *ought* to do as a sensuous being is nothing other than that which I must *will* as a free rational being: "The moral *'ought'* is then his own necessary *'will'* as a member of an intelligible world, and is thought by him as 'ought' only insofar as he regards himself at the same time as a member of the sensible world" (4:455). With this the real possibility of a categorical imperative has been shown for the first time. Only now can there be a genuine metaphysics of morals.

Kant had completed the *Groundwork* in September of 1784; it came out at Easter 1785. He seems then to have turned immediately to work on the *Metaphysical Foundations of Natural Science,* for as we know from a letter to Schütz (September 13, 1785) the *Metaphysical Foundations* were already finished by this time (even though the work did not come out till the following Easter).

Metaphysical Foundations of Natural Science

Intuitions are necessary in order to demonstrate the reality of our concepts. Since transcendental philosophy deals with concepts that are supposed to refer a priori to objects, it must also be able to demonstrate a priori the conditions for objects being given that agree with these concepts, if it is to guarantee their objective validity. Taken by themselves, the categories are "merely functions of the understanding for concepts; and represent no object" (A147). For this reason, the deduction of the pure concepts of the understanding was followed in the *Critique* by a 'schematism of the pure concepts of the understanding', which deals with the "sensible condition under which alone pure concepts of the understanding can be employed" (A136). It is thus only through the mediation of the schemata that the categories have "a relation to objects and so possess significance" (A146).

So what exactly is a schema? As Kant defines it here, it is the "representation of a universal procedure of imagination in providing an image for a concept" (A140). It is not the image or the intuition itself that is given by the schema, but an a priori rule that specifies how a sensible manifold is to be determined in accord with the form of inner sense so that it can "be connected a priori in one concept in conformity with the unity of apperception" (A142) and contain an objective time determination. "The schemata are therefore nothing but a priori determinations of time in accordance with rules" (A145).

If, however, as we have already seen, no temporal determination is possible without a spatial determination, then neither is the applicability of the categories possible solely on the basis of a transcendental determination of time as Kant had written in the *Critique* (cp. A139). The objective reality of the categories has, therefore, not yet really been demonstrated. Consequently, the schematism of inner sense must be supplemented by a schematism of outer sense, i.e. by the representation "of a universal procedure of imagination in providing an image for a concept," only now for the concept of "something that is to be an object of outer sense" (4:476). Since space itself is not perceptible, that which can sensibly represent it (objects intuited in space) must be capable of being exhibited a priori in intuition (i.e. constructed).

Kant made this explicit in the long preface to the *Metaphysical Foundations*, though only at the end. The general doctrine of bodies, he says

66

unmistakably, provides transcendental philosophy with an "indispens-able service" in realizing its "concepts and propositions, i.e. to give a mere form of thought sense and meaning." For "in order to provide meaning for its pure concepts of the understanding," space as a *form* of outer intuition does not suffice. Since space itself is not perceptible, the "form *and* principles of outer intuition"—space *and* the principles of a material filling up of space—are needed, and as long as these are "not exhibited completely" transcendental philosophy "gropes uncertainly and unsteadily among mere meaningless concepts" (4:478; emphasis added).

Initially, however, the preface seems to be about something alto-gether different: the exact specification of what science is. *First,* accord-ing to Kant science is not merely a rhapsodic collection of propositions, but a totality of knowledge ordered according to principles and hence systematic. Systematicity is only a necessary condition for science, how-ever, not a sufficient condition. For if those principles are merely em-pirical in nature, what we have is a systematic doctrine, but not a sci-ence in the proper sense. *Secondly,* therefore, the *principles* must be associated with a "consciousness of their necessity" (4:468). Hence they cannot be principles discovered on the basis of induction, mere generalizations from experience; they must be capable of being known a priori. "All *proper* natural science therefore requires a *pure* part, on which the apodictic certainty that reason seeks therein can be based" (4:469).

Now if something that actually exists is to be known a priori, we must have insight into its *real possibility.* The real possibility of a thing is not recognized merely by seeing that its concept is free from contradic-tions and hence logically possible; rather, it is necessary that "the *intu-ition* corresponding to the concept be given a priori, i.e. that the concept be constructed" (4:470). Science in the strict sense must therefore, accord-ing to Kant, be able to construct its basic concepts since that is the only way to generate a consciousness of the principles' necessity. This idea will occupy us again later in Part II. Here I would like to prevent a certain misunderstanding. When Kant goes on to write that, since "rational cog-nition is mathematical insofar as it constructs its concepts," no theory of nature can contain more science than it contains mathematics (4:470), he does not mean to say that every science must represent the world in math-ematical language—that is not Kant's point here, even though his manner of expressing himself occasionally seems to suggest so—but rather just that its basic concepts must be constructable.[5] As long as "no concept is found that is capable of being constructed," our theory of nature may be "a systematic art or experimental theory, but never a true science" (4:470–71).

Now we can also see the internal connection between the two trains of thought that make up the preface: The basic concept of a natural theory of the objects of outer sense is the concept of a body in general. This is also the basic concept of what I have called a schematism of space: the concept of "something that is to be an object of outer sense" (4:476). The a priori exhibition (construction) of this concept is thus the very thing that secures the objective reality of transcendental philosophy, on the one hand, and the genuinely scientific status of a theory of nature, on the other.

So what exactly are we to understand by 'construction'? "In its general meaning, all[6] *exposition* of a concept by (spontaneous) production of a corresponding intuition can be called construction" (8:192). "We *construct* concepts when we exhibit them in intuition a priori without experience" (9:23).

In any case of construction, then, we must distinguish the following: (a) the object brought about through a priori construction in intuition; (b) the elements from which that object is constructed; and (c) the constructive rule that places the elements in a specific relation to each other in such a way as to produce the object a priori.

(a) *The object of construction:* It has already become clear what the object of construction must be: namely whatever fills space to some degree, thus making it accessible to experience, or more generally: something that can be "an object of outer sense." It must therefore first be determined how this something can be distinguished from the space it fills. And here we already see an important difference from a purely mathematical construction. Space, as a form of outer intuition, lies within the subject and can be known a priori; but whether this form is empty or not can only be known on the basis of experience. The "metaphysical construction" (4:473) must therefore be based on *one* empirical datum, namely the fact that space is not empty, that is to say on the empirical concept of *matter in*

---

[5] Constructability is prior to the applicability of mathematics in natural science since it provides something, "that mathematics itself inevitably requires for its application to natural science" (4:479), so that "mathematics *can be* applied" (4:470, emphasis added).
[6] That is to say, not only mathematical exposition of concepts.

general (as distinct from the concept of a determinate empirical object).[7] Consequently, the schematism of space specifically consists, first of all, in the assumption of the empirical concept of matter. Then, secondly, in order to have any elements for the construction, this empirical concept of matter in general must be completely analyzed in such a way that "outside of what lies in this concept, no other empirical principle is used for its cognition" (4:470). And in the third place, finally, the "principles for the construction of the concepts that belong to the possibility of matter in general" (4:472) have to be specified.

(b) *The elements of the construction:* Matter in the intended sense is distinguished from the space it occupies by the fact that it can leave that space to occupy another one: Matter is that which is moveable in space (*quantity*). If we consider matter solely in respect to its movability (as a point) and to no other property, then the following phoronomic proposition is true of its construction or of the construction of its possible movement: "The composition of two motions of one and the same point can only be thought in such a way that one of them is represented in absolute space, and, instead of the other, a motion of the relative space with the same speed occurring in the opposite direction is represented as the same as the latter" (4:490).

If, on the other hand, we go on to consider matter with respect to its *quality* as well, then movability is joined by a further property, the ability to withstand the motion of other bodies that strive to penetrate into the same space, that is, the ability to fill a space. This property requires a force in order to be the cause of the decreased motion of the penetrating matter: "Thus matter fills its space through a moving force, and not through its mere existence" (4:497). Kant calls this repulsive force. We can now easily see, though, that this force by itself is not enough to construct the concept of matter. If there were only repulsion, matter would be infinitely dispersed and space would therefore be empty. The filling of space therefore requires a second fundamental force that acts in opposition to the first, limiting it to a specific extent: Kant calls it attractive force. But neither can there only be attraction as the fundamental force of matter, for then matter would contract to a point and once again space would be empty.

---

[7] What we have here is therefore a concept of matter "insofar as it is not yet empirically determined (the object of sensation in general)" (4:324), and "without assuming anything else empirical other than *that* . . . there is . . . something of this kind" (20:285). Cp. also 4:470, 481.

Thus neither can attractive force occur by itself; both forces must oper-
ate together in order for space to be filled. Hence the fact that bodies fill
space to a given degree and are thus of a specific density is only possible
on the basis of the action and reaction of these basic forces, or more precisely on the basis of the limitation of repulsion or expansion by means
of attraction.

For Kant, it is impossible to conceive more than these two moving
forces as *proper to matter* (cp. 4:498). In his opinion they are however
also sufficient for an a priori construction of how matter fills space and
thus also of the possibility of making space sensible. The differing densities of matter can arise if the relation between the two forces is variable.
And that is in fact the case. Repulsive force acts only at the surface of
contact, independently of how much matter is beneath this surface. It has
a specific degree beyond which greater or lesser degrees are always conceivable. Thus it can be originally different in different kinds of matter.
Attractive force, since it originally limits expansion and thus contains the
ground of a determinate filling of space, thus also contains the ground of
the possibility of physical contact. Hence it must precede every contact
and not depend on it as a condition. In other words, it must be an immediate effect of all matters on each other through empty space (cp. 4:512).
We of course know such an effect by the name of Newtonian gravitation,
with which Kant explicitly identifies his attractive force. It extends beyond
all determinate bounds to every other material object; it is a penetrating
force and thus always proportional to the quantity of matter (4:516). With
this the *analysis* of the empirical datum matter is complete: Repulsion and
attraction are the two elements from which the concept of matter is to be
constructed.

(c) *Constructive rule:* In order for the concept of matter actually to be
constructable, we need, in addition to the two elements, "a law of the relation of original attraction as well as of repulsion at varying distances between matter and its parts" (4:517). This law cannot be an empirical
discovery if the construction is supposed to be possible a priori; it must
itself be able to be known a priori. This means that it must be derivable
strictly on the basis of the two forces in their relation to space. Kant had
engaged in similar reflections as early as 1756 in the *Monadologia physica,*
and he can draw on them now. The repulsive force is supposed to radiate
from every point, filling the whole space in which it acts. Since it radiates
through the whole of the surrounding space, and since spherical spaces
are proportional to the cube of the distances, a force which is to fill the

70

entire spatial sphere of its action must decrease in inverse ratio to the spaces. The strength of the repulsive force must therefore vary in inverse ratio to the cubes of the distance.

The case of attractive force is different since it acts in the opposite direction. It can be represented by lines drawn from the points of an attracted spherical surface to the center of attraction. Thus it will decrease in inverse proportion to the spherical surfaces. Hence the strength of the attractive force must vary as the inverse square of the distances. And since the repulsive force decreases much faster, namely in proportion to the inverse cube, there will be some point along the diameter at which attraction and repulsion balance out—a point which thus determines the surface of the body and the degree to which it fills space (cp. 1:484). Kant appears to have these considerations in mind when he now writes in the *Metaphysical Foundations*: "Thus the original attraction of matter would act in inverse ratio to the squares of the distances at all distances, the original repulsion in inverse ratio to the cubes of the infinitely small distances, and, through such an action and reaction of the two fundamental forces, matter filling its space to a determinate degree would be possible. For since repulsion increases with the approach of the parts to a greater extent than attraction, the limit of approach, beyond which no greater is possible by the given attraction, is thereby determined, and so is that degree of compression which constitutes the measure of the intensive filling of space" (4:521).

This is what Kant needs for the construction of the concept of matter. The two following chapters of the *Foundations,* which correspond to the *dynamical* categories of relation and modality, round out the account by considering matter first as that which has moving force as a result of its own motion, i.e. mechanical force, which Kant associates with the category of *relation*. And finally it is considered as that which, insofar as it is moveable, can be an object of experience, so that criteria can be provided according to which possible, actual, and necessary motions can be distinguished (*modality*). These two chapters are necessary to show the applicability of the dynamical categories to the object of outer sense *in concreto;* for the construction of the concept of matter they presuppose, they add nothing new.

Historical Excursus

"I find it to be a very striking phenomenon that as often as your other writings have been used, explained, excerpted, elucidated, etc., it has been only a few up to now who have dealt with the *Metaph. Foundations of Natural Science*. I do not know whether the infinite value of this work has gone unrecognized or whether it has been found too difficult" (12:23). Kiesewetter wrote these words to Kant in June 1795—nearly a decade after publication of the book.

The importance that Kant himself attributed to the *Metaphysical Foundations* contrasts starkly indeed with the opinions voiced about the book immediately after its publication. However, since Kant's theory of matter will come to play an important role in the second half of the twenty-five years of philosophy, it is worthwhile to mention here a few of the reasons that initially hampered the reception of the *Metaphysical Foundations*.

1) At first, the significance of the work for the completion of transcendental philosophy went absolutely unnoticed. This was no doubt in part due to the fact that, at this point in time, transcendental philosophy as such was still a riddle to most of the public, as for example the review of the *Critique of Pure Reason* had shown. It was not until years later, in the context of the development of a *Naturphilosophie* that sought to follow Kant in raising the *constructability* of concepts to the criterion of scienticity, that this crucial point came to the fore. I will go into this in greater detail in Part II.

2) Kant himself did not help matters: He mentions the necessity for transcendental philosophy to have an a priori theory of matter exclusively in the preface, and even there only incidentally—as merely "another ground for commending this procedure" (4:473). The work was presented from the beginning as a metaphysical foundation for *natural science,* in which the realization of the categories was so to speak merely embedded. The few early attempts to come to terms with Kant's theory thus also took contemporary physics as their starting point. They completely ignored the constructability of matter and concentrated purely on the question whether repulsive force was really an essential property of matter. Kästner, for example, the Göttingen mathematician who himself advocated an atomistic conception of matter, wrote in his anonymous review of the *Metaphysical Foundations:* "Must one conceive of there being a moving force in the wall because the wall prevents one from going any further?"[8] And as late as 1793, the physicist Johann Tobias Meyer, one of Kästner's and Lichtenberg's most impor-

---

[8] *Göttingischen Anzeigen von gelehrten Sachen,* 191. Stück, December 2, 1786, 1914–18, 1916.

tant students, wrote that all the known proofs for the existence of original forces of repulsion had failed.[9] From the point of view of physics, Kant had not proven the impossibility of atomism and hence neither had he shown the necessity for a repulsive force to inhere in matter. We can accept this without having to abandon Kant's transcendental approach: the contemporary atomistic theory of matter, according to which matter consists of absolutely impenetrable atoms with empty spaces between them, can be reduced to the tautological 'explanation' that space is filled and therefore impenetrable, because matter in it (the atoms) is impenetrable. The cause of the impenetrability is thus—the impenetrability.

3) A further difficulty in understanding the text will also have arisen from the fact that Kant completely reduces matter to the two forces of attraction and repulsion, without assuming any underlying material substrate that *possesses* or *exerts* these forces—as he had still done in the earlier *Mondadologie physica* (1756). This set his theory apart from all other contemporary theories attributing attractive and repulsive forces to matter. R. C. Boscovich, for example, construed the two forces as *alternating* in the parts of matter, so that the one force can act only when the other does not, and vice versa. Herman Boerhaave, by contrast, advocated a theory according to which the two forces stand in conflict with each other, as they do on Kant's view, but yet are distributed among different types of matter: the regular parts of matter exert attraction while the parts of the caloric exert repulsive force. How both forces can stand in conflict with one another, as Kant thinks they do, yet without having any common substrate, is a point that is likely to have occasioned some doubt among his contemporaries.[10]

4) A further difficulty was first pointed out by J. S. Beck, who asked Kant in 1792 for a more detailed explanation of matter's differing densities. The explanation given by Kant in the *Metaphysical Foundations* is in fact untenable. Since he identifies attractive force with gravitation, and gravitational attraction is always proportional to mass (i.e. proportional to density, when the volume is taken into account), this implies, on the one hand, that the intensity of the attractive force must be the cause of the density, while on the other hand the density must in turn be the cause of attraction. Obviously, not both can be true. Kant frankly admitted this in his answer to Beck: "But this solution seems to lead to a kind of circularity

---

[9] Tobias Meyer, "Whether it is necessary to suppose a force of repulsion in nature" ["Ob es nöthig sey, eine zurückstossende Kraft in der Natur anzunehmen"], *Journal der Physik* 7 (1793), 208–37.

[10] For Kant, this is an unavoidable assumption because the possibility of filling space is supposed to be able to be known a priori and must therefore be constructable. Atoms, as substrates of forces, however, are not constructable.

from which I cannot see how to escape and I must give the matter more thought" (11:377).[11]

The resulting situation is astonishing, although its whole extent only gradually became apparent: an a priori theory of matter is, on the one hand, "indispensable" if the concepts and theorems of transcendental philosophy are to be *realized,* i.e. in order "to give a mere form of thought sense and meaning" (4:478). On the other hand, the theory as formulated by Kant in 1785 is circular and thus unable to provide its indispensable contribution. The conclusion drawn from this by the next generation will concern us in Part II.

Kant completed the *Metaphysical Foundations of Natural Science* in the Summer of 1785. By this time, all one thousand copies of the *Critique* had been sold and the publisher was pressing Kant for a new edition. In the same year, however, a book was also published by Friedrich Heinrich Jacobi who had previously been notable only as the author of two novels. This work was *Concerning the Doctrine of Spinoza in Letters to Herr Moses Mendelssohn* [*Über die Lehre des Spinoza, in Briefen an Herrn Moses Mendelssohn*], a book whose importance for the twenty-five years of philosophy can hardly be overestimated and which I therefore must discuss in greater detail before returning to Kant.

---

[11] Kant's own attempts to overcome these difficulties in his so-called *Opus postumum* need not concern us here. They remained unpublished for almost one hundred years and play no role in the period we are interested in here.

4

How to Become a Spinozist

While traveling in the Summer of 1780, one year prior to the publication of Kant's *Critique of Pure Reason,* Jacobi had met Lessing, the guiding star of the German Enlightenment, and learned to his surprise that Lessing was a professed Spinozist. At that time, Spinoza was a thinker seldom read, but much maligned as a purported atheist and spoken of by many in tones befitting of "a dead dog" (JWA 1,1:27/193). Many knew of him only through the defamatory article in Pierre Bayle's *Dictionnaire historique et critique* (1697)—an enormously influential work which went through five editions in the course of the eighteenth century and was published in German translation between 1741 and 1744.[1] Those with more philosophical pretensions also appealed to Christian Wolff's "refutation" of Spinoza in the second part of his *Theologia naturalis.* Jacobi, however, had devoted considerable time to a study of Spinoza's own works and hoped that Lessing would come to his aid against a philosophy whose intellectual rigor he admired, but which existential reasons compelled him to reject. From his youth, Jacobi had been filled with a powerful "yearning to attain certainty regarding the higher expectations of man"—a longing which came to be the "leading thread" (JWA 1,1:13/183) of all his endeavors. Someone with these sensibilities was bound to be repulsed by a God like Spinoza's, possessing neither will nor understanding and thus antithetical to the very notion of purposiveness. Yet in the course of studying Spinoza, Jacobi came to be convinced that this was the very position to which any attempt at a universal philosophical explanation or foundation must inevitably lead. For Jacobi, Spinoza's system with its exclusion of

---

[1] Cf. Bell 1984, 3.

a personal God of creation, its denial of human freedom and final causes, and its identification of the divine with nature as a realm of necessary law (*"deus sive natura"*) was the unavoidable result of a desire for a universal explanation and foundation which, in consequence, we must at all costs resist. Thus had he come to Lessing in hopes of receiving support in his own rejection of Spinozism. What Lessing had to say came utterly unexpectedly: "Become his friend all the way instead. *There is no other philosophy than the philosophy of Spinoza."* And: "The orthodox concepts of the Divinity are no longer for me; I cannot stomach them. *Hen kai pan!* I know nothing else" (JWA 1,1:18, 16/187; emphasis added).

Lessing died a few months later. When Jacobi learned that Lessing's friend Moses Mendelssohn intended to write a work on his character and writings, Jacobi asked him through the mediation of a common acquaintance whether he was aware that in his last days Lessing had been an avowed Spinozist. Mendelssohn, who could look back on a friendship with Lessing that had lasted decades and who was himself steeped in the philosophy of Leibniz and Wolff, naturally reacted with skepticism and requested further information. Thereupon Jacobi sent him a summary of his conversation with Lessing. The ensuing correspondence was for the most part mediated by third parties, a fact which provided wide margin for increasing personal suspicions and accusations, and after a great deal of to-and-fro Mendelssohn announced his intention to publish a work "against pantheism"[2] in which he would set down the "*statum controversiae.*" Hereupon Jacobi undertook the immediate publication of *Concerning the Doctrine of Spinoza in Letters to Herr Moses Mendelssohn* (1785), which came out almost simultaneously with Mendelssohn's book. In addition to an account of his conversations with Lessing and his letters to Mendelssohn, the book also included a letter to Hemsterhuis containing a fictional dialogue with Spinoza as well as a brief prospectus of Jacobi's own philosophical approach and two unpublished poems by Goethe.[3] And thus began the so-called "Spinoza Controversy," which saw the publication in rapid succession of Mendelssohn's reply, *To the Friends of Lessing* (1786), and Jacobi's riposte *Against Mendelssohn's Accusations*

---

[2] Moses Mendelssohn, *Morning Hours, or Lectures on the Existence of God* [*Morgenstunden oder Vorlesungen über das Daseyn Gottes*], Berlin 1785.
[3] Goethe's poem "Prometheus," which Jacobi had offered to Lessing to read, had been the original occasion for their conversation on Spinozism.

Relating to the Letters Concerning Spinoza's Doctrine (1786), only to be interrupted by Mendelssohn's sudden death early in 1786.[4]

The significance of the controversy for the philosophical climate of the time can hardly be overestimated. In order to bring home to his readers the full consequences of the Spinozist position, Jacobi had to present his opponent in his full strength, and for many this was the first real glimpse they had ever had of Spinoza's philosophical profile; indeed, the younger generation (including Fichte, Schelling, Hegel, and Hölderlin) was first introduced to Spinoza by Jacobi.[5] His main goal was to prove that every attempt at philosophical justification and explanation, consistently pursued, must necessarily issue in Spinozism, a position he identified with

---

[4] The background of the controversy is extraordinarily complex and cannot be presented here in any detail. The superb summary with which Kurt Christ prefaces his analysis of the controversy may suffice: "On the one side it is about the correct interpretation of Spinoza and about a trenchant and, in its ramifications, radical position laid claim to by a man who belongs to no particular philosophical school of thought, who, being of independent wealth, conceives of himself as an *homme de lettres,* who is for the most part an autodidact, a civil servant who publishes literary, philosophical and political essays but aspires to more because he owns an ambition knowingly fueled by his prominent friends and role models Wieland and Goethe, but to whom widespread acclaim and the final breakthrough have yet to come. On the other side we have the passionate champion of the trendsetting Berlin Enlightenment, Moses Mendelssohn, a man shaped by the traditional metaphysics of the Leibniz-Wolff school, highly respected and admired by Jacobi himself, who in the most roundabout ways tried repeatedly and unsuccessfully to establish a relationship with Mendelssohn. At a point in his life at which age and sickness are already taking their toll on his powers, this man receives a challenge to which he can hardly rise. Just as he is planning to crown his decade long friendship with Lessing with a so-called commemorative work in honor of the departed, Jacobi of all people, whom until then he had largely ignored and who was only briefly acquainted with Lessing, proclaims himself to be the sole heir of Lessing's most intimate and personal world view—a view, moreover, which Jacobi knows Lessing never to have revealed to Mendelssohn. Mendelssohn is quick to realize that in order to counter Jacobi's conviction that Lessing was a Spinozist, it will not suffice to mount a cramped defense of Lessing that merely contradicts Jacobi's statements. He finds himself forced to rescue Lessing *ex post* from being marginalized to the fringes of society. If he wants a water-tight argument, he will have to risk a "pass with the Spinozists"—and he even takes Jacobi to be a Spinozist in disguise—he will have to take them to court and refute them in order to rehabilitate Lessing indirectly and directly with the literary memorial which is to follow" (Christ 1988, 16–17).

[5] At this period Jacobi was not exaggerating when he said that "I think I know him as only very few can ever have known him" (cp. JWA 1,1:17–18).

fatalism and atheism and from which he thought we could only be rescued by a *"salto mortale"* of faith in an intelligent, personal cause of the world.[6] Although hardly anyone followed Jacobi in taking this final step, his claim that Spinoza's position was the only possible rational philosophy—a view which (according to Jacobi) Lessing, too, had held—was very much present in discussion and posed a fundamental challenge to Kant's *identical claim* for his own philosophy at a point in time when it was only just being formulated.

Apart from the debate with Mendelssohn, however, Jacobi was also involved in a second Spinoza controversy, one that has hardly been recognized in the philosophical literature, but which is by no means less significant: the Spinoza controversy with Goethe and Herder. Jacobi was friends with both and Herder had been privy to the developing quarrel with Mendelssohn from early on. Jacobi's wife and son had died in short succession at the beginning of 1784, and the two denizens of Weimar suggested that Jacobi come for an extended visit, an invitation which Jacobi accepted in September of the same year. Since he had already sent the text of the conversation with Lessing and the fictional dialogue with Spinoza to Weimar, Jacobi's Spinoza interpretation now became the topic of sympathetic yet pointed discussions. After his departure, Herder and Goethe immersed themselves in renewed study of Spinoza's *Ethics*.[7] When a short time later Goethe acquired the published version of Jacobi's book, he wrote to him, saying, "On this we agree and always have, that the idea you give of Spinoza's philosophy comes very much nearer to our own than what you said to us had led us to expect . . . I find it hard, however, to compare what you say of him with himself . . . You use a different order and different words to express his philosophy and I feel this is bound to break the real sequence of his most subtle ideas" (HABr 1:476).

Further on we will examine Goethe's and Herder's reactions more closely. Beforehand, though, I want to discuss Jacobi's interpretation of Spinoza in more detail since it formed the starting point for all these controversies.

---

[6] Jacobi: "I love Spinoza because he, more than any other philosopher, has led me to the perfect conviction that certain things admit of no explication . . . The whole thing comes down to this: from fatalism I immediately conclude against fatalism and everything connected with it" (JWA 1,1:28, 20/193, 189).

[7] "I'm training myself with Spinoza. I read him again and again," Goethe writes to Jacobi on January 12, 1785 (HABr 1:470).

1. Jacobi and Lessing

By Jacobi's account, Lessing asked him what he held to be the "spirit of Spinozism"—the spirit that "inspired Spinoza himself." Jacobi answered, "It is certainly nothing other than the ancient *a nihilo nihil fit* that Spinoza made an issue of, but with more abstract concepts than the philosophers of the cabbala or others before him.[8] In keeping with these more abstract concepts he established that with each and every coming-to-be in the infinite, no matter how one dresses it up in images, with each and every change in the infinite *something* is posited *out of nothing*. He therefore rejected any *transition* from the infinite to the finite. In general, he rejected all *causae transitoriae, secundariae* or *remotae,* and in place of an emanating *Ensoph* he only posited an *immanent* one, an indwelling cause of the universe eternally unalterable *within itself,* One and the same with all its consequences" (JWA 1,1:18/187–88).

This characterization of the "spirit of Spinozism" made history.[9] A decade later Schelling will attest, "I do not believe that the spirit of Spinozism could have been captured any better" (AA I,3:82; SW I:313). On closer examination, however, Jacobi's characterization exhibits several peculiarities. For one, we should note that Spinoza himself does not take the principle *a nihilo nihil fit* as his starting point, but rather begins with a definition of the concept of substance. As early as the *Treatise on the Emendation of the Intellect,* Spinoza already insists that in order to gain adequate knowledge of a thing, we must comprehend it either through its own essence or through its proximate cause. Thus if something exists in

---

[8] This "ancient" principle by which nothing comes from nothing is to be found as early as Melissus of Samos (see H. Diels, ed., *Die Fragmente der Vorsokratiker,* 53). Aristotle, *Physics* I, 4 ascribes it to Anaxagoras, as well. Empedocles (see *Die Fragmente der Vorsokratiker,* 185), Epicurus (see Diogenes Laertius, *Lives of Eminent Philosophers,* X, 38), and Lucretius (*De rerum natura* I, 149, 205 and II, 287) likewise appeal to the principle.

[9] Jacobi, who had first read Spinoza's *Ethics* in the German translation which Johann Lorenz Schmidt appended to his 1744 translation of Wolff's critique of Spinozism (cp. JW 2:188/282), seems to have based his conception of the "spirit of Spinozism" on Wolff's refutation. Wolff writes for example in the scholium to section 677, "Now since [Spinoza] considered that we can form no clear and distinct concept of creation in the proper sense of the term and which theologians refer to as the first creation, i.e. *creatio ex nihilo,* he rejected the concept of a creative force . . . *Hence Spinozism has its source in the impossibility of creation . . .*" (Wolff 1744, emphasis added).

and of itself or if it is its own cause, we must comprehend it by way of its own essence; if by contrast it requires an external cause for its existence, then it must be comprehended by way of its proximate cause (TIE sect. 92). Thus if knowledge is to take the form of a system, we will have to start with something whose concept does not presuppose the concept of anything else.

And this is precisely how Spinoza proceeds in the *Ethics*. According to Definition 3 of the *Ethics,* a substance is something which is in itself and can be conceived by itself and whose concept therefore does not presuppose the concept of any other thing (*cujus conceptus non indiget conceptu alterius rei*). Now if a substance could be produced by another substance, then knowledge of it (its concept) would depend on knowledge of its cause and, contrary to the original premise, it would not be a substance (E1p6). Thus for Spinoza it follows from the exact definition of substance that there can only be *one* substance which, in consequence, cannot be caused by or limited by another substance but is, on the contrary, eternal and infinite. That nothing comes from nothing would thus be at best a conclusion from this line of thought, and not its premise.[10]

Jacobi reverses this idea, as it were, and argues conversely. To explain something is to derive it from conditions. A consistent explanation of finite things from prior conditions leads, however, to an infinite regress, since these conditions in turn must be explained and derived from *their* conditions, so the explanation ends up explaining nothing. An original beginning and hence the origination of the finite out of nothingness is therefore also incomprehensible. Now since finite things which have arisen in time do in fact exist, they must be grounded in an eternal being. In other words, it is just as unthinkable that becoming can have had a beginning, as it is that being can have had one. Jacobi argues for this as follows:

> From all eternity . . . the impermanent has been with the permanent, the temporal with the eternal, the finite with the infinite, and whosoever assumes a beginning of the finite, also assumes a coming-to-be from nothingness . . . If it were produced by the subsisting

---

[10] The principle itself occurs almost nowhere in Spinoza's own works. In a letter to Simon de Vries (Letter 10) he mentions it as *one example among others* of an eternal truth of reason, and similarly at E4p20s. In his study of Descartes' *Principles of Philosophy* he also mentions that the principle occurs there in Part 1, sect. 49. And that's it.

thing from nothing, so too would the force or determination, in virtue of which it was produced by the infinite thing from nothingness, *have come* from nothingness; for in the infinite, eternal, permanent thing, everything is infinitely, permanently, and eternally actual. An action first initiated by the infinite being could not have begun otherwise than from all eternity, and its determination could not have derived from anywhere except from nothingness. Hence the finite is in the infinite, so that the sum of all finite things, equally containing within itself the whole of eternity at every moment, past and future, is one and the same as the infinite thing itself (JWA 1,1:94–95/217–18).

In a footnote, Jacobi further elucidates the point by referring to passages from Kant's transcendental aesthetic, "which are entirely in the spirit of Spinoza," but his real point of reference is Kant's pre-critical work *The One Possible Basis for a Demonstration of the Existence of God* (1763), which he had read years before with a feeling of "joy . . . that made my heart race" and which he had been forced to lay aside repeatedly "in order to restore myself to calm attention" (JW 2:191). This early text by Kant with its claim that being is not a property but rather an absolute positing and that the very possibility of anything at all absolutely presupposes a necessary being, forms the philosophical backdrop for Jacobi's appropriation of Spinoza. It is in the light of this text that Jacobi interprets Spinoza's substance as the "being in all beings" that cannot itself have had a beginning: "*Being* is not a *property;* it is not anything derived from some sort of power; it is what lies at the ground of every property, quality, and force—it is that which we designate with the word '*substance.*' Nothing can be presupposed by it, and it must be presupposed by everything" (JWA 1,1:59). Since we will be returning repeatedly to the Kantian idea at the heart of this passage, here is a sketch of the basic line of thought.

1. Possibility consists in the comparison of given concepts, i.e. something is said to be possible when the concepts combined in thought do not contradict each other.
2. The realities which the concepts express must be given, else there would be nothing to be compared and determined as possible.
3. If there were no realities, then there would be no possibility. The impossibility of possibility is however itself impossible, and hence all the realities thought in possible concepts necessarily exist.

4. These realities must make up a single, infinite being. For if the realities were distributed among different entities, the latter would be specifically limited and affected by privations. In contrast to realities, however, privations are not characterized by necessity. Accordingly, it is by unconditional necessity that the realities are wholly without privation and thus constitute a single infinite being.

5. Hence there is a being whose existence precedes its own possibility and the possibility of all finite things and which therefore must be recognized as existing with unconditional necessity (cp. 2:77–87).

Of course, Kant's critical insight that understanding and sensibility are separate yet interdependent sources of knowledge, and hence that the real possibility of a concept can only be explained with reference to a possible intuition, would later rob this argument of its force as a proof for God's existence. Even so, however, it was not to reduce it to utter insignificance. In the *Critique of Pure Reason,* the argument re-emerges in modified form in the chapter on the "Transcendental Ideal" as the principle of the complete determination of all things (A 571–83). There, however, what before was mistakenly conceived as an objective condition of the possibility of things in themselves is now argued to be a merely subjective condition of empirical thought: The unconditioned itself is never given to us together with what is conditioned; the case is rather that when the conditioned is given, the *task* of a regress in the series of its conditions is *imposed* on us. Yet as we will later see, even in the critical period Kant never abandoned the thought that human reason is forced to conceive a "transcendental substrate" or real ground: "In other words, I can never *complete* the regress to the conditions of existence save by assuming a necessary being, and yet am never in a position to *begin* with such a being" (A616).

At the time when he was working on the *Spinoza Letters,* Jacobi was not distinctly aware of this subtle but decisive shift in Kant's position. He seems rather to have seen in Kant's pre-critical argument precisely the kind of 'demonstration' that would make Spinoza's doctrine of the one substance necessary: "the *primal being,* the actuality that is unalterably present everywhere and cannot itself be a property, but in which, on the contrary, everything else is only a property it possesses—this unique and infinite being of all beings Spinoza calls 'God,' or *substance*" (JWA 1,1:98/219; cp. JWA 1,1:59).

According to Jacobi, being in this sense must be prior to any thought of determinate beings and their possibility, and therefore it cannot itself be anything merely possible, a mere thought. And since its becoming cannot have had a beginning, as he tries to show in the passage quoted above, a transition from the infinite to the finite by which finite things would attain separate existence is unthinkable. Therein lies Jacobi's reason for holding that the immanence of God in all finite things is not only a characteristic of Spinoza's position but the consequence of any rational metaphysics that seeks to establish the conditions of the conditioned and to provide a rational explanation of the finite on the basis of a first principle. In other words, Spinozism is *the only possible rational philosophy.*

Such a philosophy must, for the sake of consistency, deny the possibility of free action with an actual beginning. By the same token, it must also deny the existence of final causes since for the One Substance nothing can either be 'lacking' or be opposed to it such that Substance would have to achieve it or come into possession of it. On the contrary, all apparent becoming must rather be interpreted as an alternation internal to the One Substance itself and governed by necessary physical laws or, as Jacobi puts it, "Every avenue of demonstration ends up in fatalism" (JWA 1,1:123/234). As a consequence, such a philosophy cannot in principle be subject to *demonstrative* refutation (cp. JWA 1,1:21/189); and since Jacobi nevertheless finds it impossible to embrace this philosophy, he seeks to escape from it by way of a *"salto mortale."*

In 1785, Jacobi's own philosophical position is still somewhat vague and inchoate and it does not take on more distinct contours until 1789 with the second edition of his book. His basic point is that our quest for certainty itself presupposes a prior certainty. If this is true, then we must possess an immediate certainty that does not rest on reasons and demonstrations but is necessarily prior to them. "Grounds are only marks of similarity to a thing of which we are certain" (JWA 1,1:115/230). Our certainty that we have a body and that other bodies and thinking entities exist outside of us is one example. Jacobi refers to such 'groundless' certainty by calling it "faith" or "revelation." It is important to note that Jacobi does not mean faith of a kind that we come to have at some definite point in time and could abandon again if we chose; we have no choice but to believe: "We are all born in the faith, and we must remain in the faith" (JWA 1,1:115/230) Put differently, we are presented with a natural revelation, "that not only commands, but impels, each and every man *to believe,* and to accept eternal truths through faith" (JWA 1,1:116/231).

How does all this relate to Mendelssohn's position?

2. Jacobi and Mendelssohn

In his literary debut of 1755, *Philosophical Conversations* [*Philosophische Gespräche*], Mendelssohn had already painted a more positive picture of Spinoza than was common at the time, for he sought to prove that Leibniz (who by contrast was highly regarded) had derived his doctrine of pre-established harmony from Spinoza's *Ethics.* Although he found Spinoza's principles to be incoherent in places and also assumed the validity of Wolff's "refutation" of Spinoza in his *Theologia naturalis,* he carefully avoided polemics and concentrated instead on showing that most of Spinoza's propositions were "not so much false as merely incomplete" and that if only they were properly interpreted they were thoroughly "compatible with true philosophy and even with religion" (MGS 1:10, 11). "You are aware that the Leibniz' followers attribute as it were a twofold existence to the world. As they would put it, our world existed as one among many possible worlds in the divine understanding prior to God's decision. Because it was the best, God preferred it to all the other possible worlds and permitted it to become actual outside of himself. Now Spinoza halted at the former mode of existence. He believed that no world ever became actual outside of God and that everything we see before us was even now only to be encountered within the divine understanding. Thus Spinoza believed he could claim of the visible world what Leibniz' followers claimed of the plan of the world as it existed in the divine understanding (*antecedenter ad decretum*)" (MGS 1:17).

It was remarks such as this that made Mendelssohn a long-standing point of reference for Jacobi when it came to Spinoza. He had repeatedly sought Mendelssohn's acquaintance and was increasingly pained at the latter's unqualified rejection of his overtures. Mendelssohn's reaction to Jacobi's account of Lessing's Spinozism naturally also became a source of growing disappointment and embitterment. He must have realized that Mendelssohn had not returned to Spinoza since 1755 and even now, due to failing health, was unwilling to enter into a real examination of Jacobi's main points.

Moreover, Mendelssohn was obviously pursuing a strategy in his *Morning Hours* [*Morgenstunden*] that was very similar to the one he had followed in the early *Philosophical Conversation.* He sought to portray the quarrels among the various schools of philosophy as purely verbal disputes and to prove that a "clarified" or "reformed Spinozism" [*geläuterter Spinozismus*] was unproblematic since it could be made compatible with morality and religion. It was this Spinozism that Lessing must have meant. In contrast to Jacobi, Mendelssohn thought he was able to show that a rational refutation of Spinoza is indeed possible, and he undertook to provide such a refutation using the same arguments that Christian Wolff had used before him. He adopts Wolff's (false) argument according to which Spinoza conflated intensive with extensive infinity and conceived God to be composed of an infinitude of finite things (cp. MGS 3,2:106). If, however, God is to be truly self-subsistent and independent, then he must be infinite in respect to his power and not with respect to his extension.

Furthermore, Mendelssohn also follows Wolff in claiming that Spinoza's definition of the term "substance" is arbitrary. He does concede that there is a kind of substantiality proper only to a being whose existence is necessary and independent of any other thing. No finite being, but only God possesses substantiality or self-sufficiency in this sense. From self-sufficiency, however, he distinguishes what he calls "separate existence," which though dependent, can nevertheless be an entity separate from the self-sufficient being. If Spinoza refuses to call beings such as these substances, then according to Mendelssohn the dispute is merely verbal and far from constituting proof of their impossibility: "Instead of proving that all the things that exist separately are really only *one* thing, in the end all he shows is that there is only one self-sufficient being. Instead of demonstrating that the totality of the finite constitutes a single self-sufficient substance, he ends up maintaining that this totality must depend upon a single infinite substance. But all this can be conceded without settling the dispute. The real point of contention remains where it was at the start. His proofs are valid, but they fail to refute us" (MGS 3,2:107). By the same token, however, it might be pointed out that Mendelssohn himself has not proven (but here rather merely assumes) that there really are beings for themselves.

Finally, he offers a third argument to the effect that Spinoza's theory of substance with extension and thought as its attributes can only explain the material aspect of bodies and thoughts, but not their 'form': "Whence does the body receive its motion, an organic body its form, i.e. its purposive and regular movement, and every other body its figure? Where is its origin to be found?" (MGS 3,2:108). Motion cannot originate in the whole, for the whole is devoid of motion. Hence it must originate in the parts, which means that the parts must have "their own separate existence" and that the whole must be an aggregate of these parts. The same is supposed to be true of the attribute of thought. Since the whole of substance is incapable of desire, whence, Mendelssohn asks, do pleasure and pain and the expressions of desiring arise in the parts if these parts have no separate existence? The property of being able to think does not necessarily entail the property of being capable of assent; for this we must assume a source other than truth and falsity. "Thus we see that Spinoza's system is lacking in two respects. Both in regard to the corporeal world and in regard to thinking beings he has only taken care of the material side, and not of the formal side; yet how close must his system approach our own as soon as he takes on the formal side and attempts to explain the source either of motion on the one hand or of assent on the other" (MGS 3,2:109–10).

This criticism, too, misses its target, for it overlooks the fact that Spinoza interposes the infinite modi of motion and rest as well as will and understanding between the attributes and finite things (E1p23, 31). Jacobi rightly regarded Mendelssohn's attempts at a refutation, which hardly go beyond Christian Wolff, as insignificant. He was angered, though, by Mendelssohn's attempt to pass off Lessing's position as a "reformed" (and thus harmless) Spinozism. In the fourteenth lecture of the *Morning Hours,* Mendelssohn has Lessing take part in a fictional dialogue in which he advocates the position of a Spinozist. As it turns out, that position is identical with Mendelssohn's own in the *Philosophical Conversations,* the only difference being that now it is no longer Leibniz, but more generally a theist who represents the position opposed to Spinozist pantheism. While both start from the assumption that all reality is incessantly represented in God's understanding and thus has an "ideal existence," the theist differs from the pantheist in that he goes on to assert that God also gave the series of real things an objective existence outside of himself. That, however, has no consequences for our actions and is thus devoid of practical significance. Both the Spinozist and the theist will act on the premise that human happiness and misery depend upon the divine substance and upon how much we come to know it, how much we love it, and so on: "If my friend [Lessing], the advocate of a reformed Spinozism, admits all of that, as based upon his principle I am sure he would have, then morality and religion are secure. The Spinozist school differs furthermore from our own system merely as regards its subtlety in the fruitless question of whether

86

God allowed his thought of the best connection among contingent things to emanate or not, a question which can never gain practical significance" (MGS 3,2:123–24).

To Jacobi's mind, such a 'reformed' Spinozism presented no more than a trivialization of historical truth with which he did not wish to see Lessing burdened:[11] an "irresponsible" confusion of Spinoza's actual doctrine (as Jacobi had been able to reconstruct it from the primary sources) with a doctrine which Mendelssohn had arbitrarily thought up and attributed to Lessing and Spinoza "without the least proof" (cp. JWA 1,1:290).

In the fictional dialogue of the fourteenth lecture, Mendelssohn's fictionalized Lessing did in fact demand proof that we and the world about us have more than merely ideal existence in the mind of God and that we are therefore not just God's thoughts and modifications of his primal force (cp. MGS 3,2:116). And Mendelssohn himself was convinced that he could derive such a proof from the concept of a finite mind: "Indeed, it will suffice for me to show that I myself have a consciousness of my own and hence must be a substance existing for itself outside of God. From here it will not be hard to convince the pantheist of this conclusion" (MGS 3,2:119). Mendelssohn argues as follows.

(1) As a finite mind I am limited, i.e. I have no consciousness of realities which lie outside my consciousness. The infinite entity by contrast is aware not only of my limited consciousness, but of everything which lies beyond my limitations as well, for it is unbounded.

(2) No entity can imagine a reality greater than that which it possesses for itself. When we wish to imagine a more perfect entity, we simply imagine the limits that characterize ourselves to be indefinitely extended, without of course thereby gaining knowledge of realities which we do not ourselves possess.

(3) To the same extent, however, it is also true that no entity can ever divest itself of the least degree of its reality. When I imagine a blind person, I think of my own visual impressions as being darkened or I concentrate on my other senses; I can never manage to eliminate such impressions altogether. In the same

---

[11] "The reformed pantheism that is supposed to heal him [sc. Lessing] would make him into a half-wit [*Halbkopf*], and I will not have him posthumously trained to be that by Mendelssohn" (JWA 1,1:280).

way, God, who possesses all perfections, cannot imagine any entity utterly bereft of his own divinity.

(4) I myself, as a finite and thus actually limited mind, cannot therefore be a thought in God's mind, but must exist outside of God. Accordingly, the pantheistic 'One is All' must be false and something exists externally to God (cp. MGS 3,2:119–21).

Such is Mendelssohn's view. A reader of the *Morning Hours* familiar with Kant's critique of the paralogisms of pure reason will be quick to de-mask the fallacious inference from the unity of consciousness to a unified substance. In a letter to Christian Gottfried Schütz from November 1785, Kant himself described Mendelssohn's *Morning Hours* "in the main as a masterpiece of the self-deception of our reason" and as "the final legacy of a dogmatizing metaphysics," which however precisely because of its clarity offered "an enduring example for testing the principles" of the critique of pure reason and a touchstone for its success (10:428f.). Even so, however, Kant did not take sides with Jacobi. On the contrary: it was hardly com-prehensible, he wrote in a public statement on the controversy between Jacobi and Mendelssohn, how the former could believe that the *Critique of Pure Reason* encouraged Spinozism when in fact it contained the only certain antidote to such dogmatism (cp. 7:143). And a *salto mortale* into faith that was beyond all demonstration was something for which Kant could muster no sympathy.[12]

Although in light of Kant's recently published *Critique* the argumen-tative details of the controversy between Jacobi and Mendelssohn were bound to appear unsatisfactory or indeed as philosophically retro-grade, the fact remains that it forced the question of the true nature of Spinoza's philosophy into public awareness, and the significance of this event can hardly be overestimated. Lessing's authority (and Jacobi's elu-cidations) had secured Spinoza a hitherto unheard of importance and made him a factor to be reckoned with in the philosophical climate of the times.

---

[12] Thus in the second edition of the *Critique of Pure Reason* Kant characterized it as a "scandal to philosophy and to human reason in general" to maintain that the existence of things outside us "must be accepted merely on faith, and that if any-one thinks good to doubt their existence, we are unable to counter his doubts by any satisfactory proof" (Bxl, note).

3. Jacobi and Herder/Goethe

Goethe and Herder, though closer to Jacobi personally, also failed to embrace his position as he had hoped. Both these illustrious *Weimarer* shared a high opinion of Spinoza and thought that his philosophy deserved to be more widely known; Herder in particular urged Jacobi from early on to publish his conversations with Lessing. After having first read the Lessing conversation in 1784, Herder sent him a letter with the heading "Hen kai pan" in which he explicitly took sides with Lessing: "In all earnestness, dearest Jacobi, ever since I first cleared the ground in philosophy, time and again I have been struck by the truth of Lessing's dictum that the Spinozist philosophy is really the only one that is *completely at one with itself.*" He rejected Jacobi's own interpretation, as is particularly obvious when Herder reproaches him with insufficient conceptual rigor and recommends that he follow Lessing's example: "And thus, my dearest and best extramundane personalist, I humbly and sincerely beseech you: Take heed of some of the things that Lessing said and—armor your system with more reasons. If one has no need to do a *salto mortale,* then why should one?" (Herder, *Briefe,* 5:27–28).

Even after Jacobi's visit in Weimar, Herder sees no need to revise his judgment: "I fear, dear friend, that it is not I, but rather you who have mistaken Spinoza's intentions. After you left, I did not read all of him, but I did re-read various passages, and my first impression was again confirmed. . . . I wish you would read through the *Ethics* again from my point of view . . . for only [Spinoza's *Ethics*] unify all the various systems and ways of thinking. Since you've been away Goethe has read Spinoza and the fact that he understands him as I do is a touchstone for me. You have to come over to our side" (December 20, 1784, Herder, *Briefe,* 5:90–91).

Although it may seem at first that the standpoint that Goethe and Herder were urging against Jacobi was identical, in fact their positions differed considerably. Herder summarizes his interpretation and his criticism of Jacobi in a fictional dialogue on Spinoza's system entitled *God. Some Conversations* [*Gott. Einige Gespräche*] and published in 1787; it represented the fruit of some twenty years of study of Spinoza. His explicit aim in the book is to reveal Spinoza's true doctrine by freeing it from the constraints of the time in which it was written, chief among which are its dependence on Descartes and the insufficiently developed natural sciences of the period. "Spinoza's times were the childhood of natural history" (708), he has one of the participants of the dialogue to say, which is why scientists like Descartes identified matter with mere extension, thus distinguishing it sharply and absolutely from mind. They had yet to discover the powers inherent in matter itself, first recognized by Newton and extended by Herder without reservation to the realm of organic nature. A proper understanding of Spinoza only became possible with the concept of "substantial powers" and the reinterpretation of God's infinite attributes as such powers: God reveals himself through infinite powers in infinite ways (cp. 709 and Spinoza, E1p16). The supreme power must be conscious of itself, however, for else it would be a blind force liable to being overcome by the power to think. We must therefore ascribe understanding to God, although it in no way diminishes the necessity of his actions (cp. 743–44).[13] There is a basic difficulty with Herder's approach here which the fictive interlocutors Philolaus and Theophron unwittingly bring to the fore:

> *Philolaus.* I wish that Spinoza had been born a century later so that, unencumbered by Descartes' hypotheses, he could have philosophized in the freer, purer light of a truer natural history and the mathematical theory of nature; how different would have been the form even of his abstract philosophy!
>
> *Theophron.* And I hope that others will bravely continue along the road that Spinoza paved in the first dawn, and work out the laws of nature without worrying about God's particular intentions (737).

Herder's treatise is marked throughout by this basic tension: On the one hand he assumes that Spinoza's position can only be understood when it is reinterpreted in the light of late eighteenth century natural science;[14] on the other hand he claims that his interpretation expresses what Spinoza himself actually intended to say. I need not go into the details of Herder's interpretation here.[15] It is hardly surprising, though, that to Jacobi's mind it no more refuted his own interpretation than Mendelssohn's 'reformed Spinozism' had done. His concern was with what Spinoza had

---

[13] Of course, in order to ascribe this view to Spinoza, Herder is forced to claim "that Spinoza did not entirely understand himself in regard to these propositions" since he was still laboring under the influence of Cartesianism (see 724).
[14] To be precise, this is Herder's own position as he formulated it concurrently in his *Ideas for a Philosophy of the History of Humankind* (1784–91).
[15] Among others, Bell 1984 points out the weaknesses of Herder's approach.

actually written, not with what he should have written. Thus it was not hard for Jacobi to point out contradictions between Spinoza's text and Herder's interpretation (for instance in Supplements IV and V of the second, 1789 edition of the *Spinoza Letters*). In the end, Jacobi could rightly view himself as having carried away the victory not only against Mendelssohn, but against Herder as well.

To Goethe's objections alone Jacobi had no decisive rebuttal! To my mind they are the only objections to have come out of the Spinoza debate with Jacobi that were of genuine importance and consequence for the ensuing philosophical developments. Of course Goethe's own position only gradually took shape over the course of the debate, so we cannot find it spelled out in any any single text but have to infer it from numerous and scattered sources. This fact is presumably the chief reason why Goethe's contribution has been largely neglected by previous scholarship on German Idealism.

Goethe's engagement with Jacobi and Spinoza came at a period in which he was just embarking on an extensive study of the natural world. "Grand thoughts of a kind quite alien to younger men now fill my soul and occupy it with a new realm," he wrote to Lavater on November 2, 1779, to whom he had described his project one week before as "my appetite for the new *Systema Naturae*" (HABr. 1:281, 279). A German translation of Carl Linnaeus' magnum opus, *Systema naturae per regna tria naturae,* had been in print since 1768 and comprised three volumes (on animals, plants, and minerals, respectively). It represented a systematic classification of the phenomena of these three kingdoms that took the natural sciences to a new level. Its key was Linnaeus' method of binomial classification for products of nature in which the first term denotes the genus or general characteristic and the second denotes the species or *differentia specifica* (e.g. *canis lupus* for wolf, *canis familiaris* for the domestic dog, and so forth). To make this classification work, Linnaeus was forced to resort to superficial characteristics and properties which could serve to differentiate the various species from each other. Thus mammals are classified by their teeth, birds by their beaks, fish by their fins, while in the vegetable kingdom the classification is based on the number and disposition of the pistils and carpels, i.e. on the plants' sexual organs. Whether his system was 'true' and whether it represented the divine plan of creation was a question that Linnaeus himself repeatedly asked. He viewed his system of plants, in particular, as artificial and hoped for a system that would take the form of the plant as a whole into account.

Goethe, though he felt admiration for Linnaeus' achievement, nevertheless considered its classificatory principle to be wholly unsatisfactory.[16] His 'new *Systema Naturae*' was to replace the artificial, superficial system with one that was in accord with nature and which would display the wealth of natural forms on the basis of internal principles and nomological conditions drawn from the things themselves. As he was later to note, "For the time being, I confess that next to Shakespeare and Spinoza it was Linnaeus who had the greatest effect on me precisely because he provoked my disagreement. For as I tried to absorb his subtle and ingenious distinctions, his accurate, convenient, but often arbitrary laws, I felt a deepening conflict within myself: What he sought to separate by force, strove, by an inward need of my very being, toward unification" (HABr. 1:753).

Spinoza was destined to play a special role in Goethe's endeavor, and it is not hard to see which aspects of Jacobi's Spinoza interpretation were bound to disagree with him from the start.

In identifying Spinoza's 'spirit' with the principle *a nihilo nihil fit*, Jacobi commits him to a causal principle that cuts him off from the *scientia intuitiva* that Goethe saw as Spinoza's main concern and the source of his "most subtle ideas." In the appendix to the first part of the *Ethics*, Spinoza already mentions "another standard of truth" than the generally accepted one. It can be learned from mathematics, which is concerned with the "essences and the properties of figures" and which Spinoza contrasts with other ways of seeing the world "which are only modes of imagining, and do not indicate the nature of anything." This other standard of truth which comprehends things by their essences is referred to in the second part of the *Ethics* as "intuitive knowledge" (E2p40s2): it is the goal of *scientia intuitiva* and hence of the *Ethics* as a whole. Spinoza also calls it the third kind of knowledge and distinguishes it from two other, lower forms. The first kind of knowledge arises from hearsay

---

[16] "The task of denoting the genera and subordinating the species to them with any certainty seemed to me insoluble. I was of course aware of the method prescribed in his books, yet how could I hope to achieve a correct determination when even within Linnaeus' own lifetime a number of genera had been divided up anew and even whole classes declared invalid. The obvious conclusion seemed to be that even this man of utmost genius and acumen could subdue and master nature only in rough outline" (LA I,10:331; HA 13:161).

or indeterminate perceptions and manifests itself as opinion or mere imagination (e.g. the date of my birthday or the fact that I must someday die), while the second kind of knowledge results when we have "common notions" or adequate ideas of the *properties* of things and can make inferences on their basis (e.g. when I infer from the reflective properties of glass that a car in my rearview mirror is really closer than it appears). Spinoza calls this second kind of knowledge rational knowledge or reason [*atque hunc rationem, et secundi generis cognitationem vocabo*]. The third kind of knowledge is the highest and results when I recognize a thing's properties through knowledge of its essence or its proximate cause (e.g. when my knowledge of the nature or the essence of a plane triangle leads me to see that the sum of its angles is always equal to two right angles). As Spinoza writes, "The greatest striving of the Mind, and its greatest virtue is understanding things by the third kind of knowledge" (E5p25).

The substance of Goethe's critique of Jacobi should thus be obvious: Jacobi's view of Spinoza as the pinnacle of a rationalistic philosophy, i.e. a philosophy consisting of conceptual explications and derivations, limits Spinoza *de facto* to the second kind of knowledge and thus presents a fundamental misjudgment of the nature of his thought. For as long as we are concerned with the possibility or impossibility of a rational explanation of concepts or propositions on the basis of other concepts and propositions we remain at the level of that kind of knowledge. For Goethe, however, the decisive point is not whether every rational philosophy must inevitably lead to Spinozism, but rather the fact that, with his conception of a *scientia intuitiva*, Spinoza had put forward an ideal of knowledge that could claim superiority to any merely rationalistic explanation and which Jacobi failed even to notice (as did Herder, by the way).

Jacobi's reduction of Spinozism to a variety of "fatalism" and "atheism" could not therefore convince Goethe, for fatalism designates a blind, mechanical and hence external necessity (cp. JWA 1,1:75, 229), from which we must clearly distinguish the inner necessity that flows from the essence of a thing and which is the object of *scientia intuitiva*. Whereas Jacobi saw an atheist in Spinoza, Goethe was inclined "to praise him as Theissimum even Christianissimum," as he wrote to Jacobi shortly after the latter's departure from Weimar (HABr 1:475–76). Admittedly, it was above all in "*herbis et lapibus* [herbs and stones]" and in "*rebus singularibus* [singular things] . . . in whose profound and detailed study no one encourages us as much as Spinoza," that Goethe beheld the presence of the divine (HABr. 1:457–56). In regard to this claim he certainly had the authority of Spinoza on his side who states at E5p24, "The more we understand singular things, the more we understand God."

In a letter to Jacobi from May 5, 1786, Goethe is even more explicit: "I hold faith with the atheist's [i.e. Spinoza's] worship of God and leave to you what you have no choice but to call religion. If you say that one can only believe in God, then I reply that I place stock in *seeing*, and when Spinoza says of *scientia intuitiva: Hoc cognoscendi genus procedit ab adaequata idea essentiae formalis quorundam Dei attributorum ad adaequatam cognitionem essentiae rerum* [this kind of cognition proceeds from the adequate idea of the formal essence of certain attributes of God to the adequate knowledge of the essence of things; cp. E2p40s2], those few words give me the courage to devote my whole life to the contemplation of things . . . of whose *essentia formali* [formal essence] I can hope to conceive an adequate idea without in the least worrying about how far I'll get and how much is tailored to my mind" (HABr. 1:508–9).

And indeed, from this point onward Goethe devoted himself with unflagging vigor to the task of understanding individual things in Spinoza's sense. It was not long afterward that he departed for Italy where he continued the intensive botanical studies he had begun while still in Weimar. From there he sends word to Herder (with an unmistakable allusion to Jacobi) that "botany in particular has revealed a *hen kai pan*" (HA 11:395) that astonishes him in no small degree. The result of these studies is his *Essay on the Metamorphosis of Plants,* which was completed over the course of his Italian journey and published after his return to Weimar. In this work Goethe seeks to demonstrate how all the characteristics of an annual flowering plant can be derived from a single underlying "organ" or essence which manifests and metamorphoses itself in six successive stages of expansion and contraction. "We first noted an expansion from the seed to the fullest development of the stem leaf; then we saw the calyx appear through a contraction, the flower leaves through a contraction, and the reproductive parts through a contraction. We will soon observe the greatest expansion in the fruit, and the greatest concentration in the seed. In these six steps nature steadfastly does its eternal work of propagating vegetation by two genders" (*Metamorphosis of Plants,* sect. 73).

After Jacobi had received a copy of the work Goethe wrote to him, "I will continue my observations on every realm of nature in the way and along the lines you will have seen in my little botanical work . . . Time will tell what I shall achieve" (HABr 2:136). It is not however possible to tell either from Goethe's letter or from the *Metamorphosis of Plants* itself how the procedure could be extended to other parts of the natural world. The work contains no explicit reflection on method and merely describes the stages of the transformation undergone by a plant in the course of its annual life-cycle. What exactly is the method, we must ask, on which Goethe's investigation is based and which is supposed to be applicable to the other natural kingdoms? Is it an instance of Spinoza's third kind of knowledge at all?

Before I try to answer this question, it is necessary to get a clearer notion of how Spinoza understands the role of *scientia intuitiva* in the cognition of individual things.

Historical Excursus

We have already seen that, according to Spinoza, if we are to comprehend an individual thing in the third kind of knowledge, it must be comprehended and its properties derived from its proximate cause, namely the attributes of God. For this reason it is of the greatest importance to ensure that the concept or definition of the thing actually express its efficient cause. Spinoza customarily illustrates this point with examples from mathematics. If, for example, I define a circle as a figure in which all the lines drawn from the center to the circumference are equal to each other, I will not be able to derive all the properties of the circle from my definition. It expresses not the efficient cause of the figure's being a circle, but merely a specific property of circles. The case is different when we define the circle as a plane figure described by a line of which one end is fixed while the other is moveable. This definition is adequate and it expresses the efficient cause so that all the properties of the circle can be derived from it.

In his *Treatise on the Emendation of the Intellect* Spinoza emphasizes the importance of finding an adequate definition of a thing: "And though, as I have said, this does not matter much concerning figures and other beings of reason, it matters a great deal concerning Physical and real beings, because the properties of things are not understood so long as their essences are not known. If we neglect them, we shall necessarily overturn the connection of the intellect, which ought to reproduce the connection of Nature, and we shall completely miss our goal" (TIE sect. 95).

This point applies equally both to the non-created entity and to individual things, and it motivates Spinoza's decision not to begin the *Ethics* with the traditional idea of God as a perfect entity, but rather to define God as "a being absolutely infinite, i.e., a substance consisting of an infinity of attributes, of which each one expresses an eternal and infinite essence" (E1d6). From the necessity of God's infinite nature, therefore, infinitely many things flow in infinitely many ways (E1p16), from which it follows in turn that God is the efficient cause of all that can fall within the sphere of an infinite intellect (E1p16c1). In this case, too, Spinoza elucidates his thought with the aid of a mathematical example: Everything flows from God's infinite nature with necessity, he writes, in the same way that it flows from the nature of the triangle in all eternity that its three angles are equal to two right angles (cp. E1p17c2s).

However, any attempt to explicate the cognition of individual things on the basis of these propositions quickly leads to difficulties. To see how, it is best to begin with Spinoza's characterization of *scientia intuitiva* at E2p40s2 whose fundamental importance Goethe also points out in the letter to Jacobi quoted above: "And this kind of knowing proceeds from an adequate idea of the formal essence of certain attributes of God to the adequate knowledge of the essence of things."

Since the essence of a thing consists in that without which the thing can neither be nor be conceived, and since nothing can be or be conceived without God (E1p15), it follows (by p25), that "God is the efficient cause, not only of the existence of things, but also of their essence." "Each idea of each body, or of each singular thing which actually exists, necessarily involves an eternal and infinite essence of God" (E2p45).

God's essence is expressed by his infinite attributes (E1d3), although in the context of determinate individual things only the attribute of extension need interest us. Now whatever is finite and has a determinate existence cannot have been brought about directly by the unconditioned nature of one of the divine attributes, for whatever flows directly from the unconditioned nature of a divine attribute is (by E1p21) itself infinite and eternal. Therefore, the individuality and particularity of a thing can only flow from the formal essence of an attribute to the extent that the attribute has undergone some modification, which in turn must also be finite and have a determinate existence. The same of course goes for this latter modification as well. Accordingly, E1p28 states that "Every singular thing, or anything which is finite and has a determinate existence, can neither exist nor be determined to produce an effect unless it is determined to exist and produce an effect by another cause, which is also finite and has a determinate existence; and again, this cause also can neither exist nor be determined to produce an effect unless it is determined to exist and produce an effect by another, which is also finite and has a determinate existence, and so on, to infinity."

In the second part of the *Ethics* (E2p45s), Spinoza goes on to add, "By existence here I do not understand duration, i.e., existence insofar as it is conceived abstractly, and as a certain species of quantity . . . I am speaking, I say, of the very existence of singular things insofar as they are in God. For even if each one is determined by another singular thing to exist in a certain way, still the force by which each one perseveres in existing follows from the eternal necessity of God's nature."

Thus in addition to its determinateness and existence, every singular thing possesses an essence or a power, as well, which prevents it from changing its kind under the influence of external causes. E3p7 accords with this: "The striving [*conatus*] by which each thing strives to persevere in its being is nothing but the actual essence of the thing."

To sum up, then, the existence and particularity of every single individual thing flows from the universal order of corporeal nature (E1p11dem2), and its essence is the *conatus* or the striving to persevere in its being.

It is easy to see, though, that this is not sufficient for the intuitive knowledge of singular things, for the tendency to persevere in their being is common to all empirical things whatsoever, just as it is common to all geometrical figures to be forms of extension—a property from which it is impossible to derive more specific properties of, say, triangles, circles, ellipses, and so forth.

We must therefore conclude either that we cannot grasp individual things in the mode of *scientia intuitiva* because we do not really know their underlying idea, their efficient cause, or that we cannot grasp individual things in the mode of *scientia intuitiva* because we cannot derive their particularity, that is their *specific* properties, from the formal essence of the divine attributes, for otherwise all things, animate and inanimate, would have the same essence!

At this point it becomes obvious that it is no coincidence that Spinoza illustrates the third kind of knowledge exclusively with examples from mathematics. For only in the case of mathematical objects and in that of artifacts do we know the underlying idea and are thus able to derive all their properties from it, whereas we cannot do so in the case of the products of nature.

For this reason many students of Spinoza have denied that he held it possible to know particular things in the third mode of cognition. In my opinion, however, there are several points that tell against such a conclusion. In addition to the passage from the *Treatise on the Emendation of the Intellect* quoted above, not the least of them is the fact that at the beginning of the second part of the *Ethics* Spinoza explicitly states that in the following he will "limit" himself to the intuitive knowledge of the human soul and its supreme happiness—which can only mean that the limitation could also be removed and that other things *could in principle* be comprehended in the same mode.[17]

Goethe at any rate, as we saw above, did not doubt the possibility of a *scientia intuitiva* of particular things in Spinoza's sense of the term. Yet how could he be sure that the method he was employing was indeed Spinoza's? Indeed, how *could* it be the same method in view of the difficulties just sketched?

We must keep in mind that Goethe did not at first have any clear idea of the method he was employing in his investigation of nature. During his sojourn in Italy, what brought him to see the natural correlation that lay in the metamorphosis of plants was less the conscious application of a method than instinct, as it were, and 'intuition' in the more ordinary sense of the term. Goethe's own later account is highly revealing: "For the *Essay on the Metamorphosis of Plants* I had to develop a method that was in accord with nature; for to the extent that the vegetation presented its own procedure to me step for step I could not go astray, and if only I abstained from all interference I would be able to recognize the ways and means nature uses to bring the most enveloped state of being to perfection . . . *Yet the whole time over it was as though the light were only just beginning to dawn,* and nowhere could I discover the enlightenment I sought . . . But then the *Critique of the Power of Judgment* fell into my hands and I owe to it a most felicitous period of my life" (LA I,9:90–92; HA 13:26–27; emphasis added).

The *Essay on the Metamorphosis of Plants* was published in 1790; shortly thereafter Goethe became acquainted with Kant's *Critique of the Power of Judgment.* The work shed light on his problem in a manner which was utterly unexpected, and for Goethe it was as though he had stepped out of the darkness and into a well-lit room.[18] Hardly had the *Metamorphosis* essay come out, and he was already busy preparing a new version, the so-called *Second Essay on the Metamorphosis of Plants.* He got no further than the introduction, however, before interrupting his

---

[17] Later Spinoza will go on to say, "If it had been my intention to deal expressly with body, I ought to have explained and demonstrated these things more fully. But I have already said that I intended something else . . ." (E2lem7s).

[18] Related by Arthur Schopenhauer, *The World as Will and Representation,* vol. 2, book 1, ch. 15.

work on it. He devoted himself instead to the definitive formulation of his method and its application to the "other kingdoms of nature," just as he had announced to Jacobi, beginning with the origination of colors.

But that would be to anticipate much later developments. In order to understand the importance of the *Critique of the Power of Judgment* for Goethe's project, we must again take up the thread of our narrative where we left it in the last chapter—with Kant and the task of preparing a second edition of the *Critique of Pure Reason.*

5

From One Make Three

The task of preparing a new edition of the *Critique of Pure Reason* presented Kant with a whole series of problems. On the one side, there was the matter of answering the various objections which had been raised in reviews and of eliminating the obscurities of the first edition as far as possible. Especially affected were the transcendental aesthetic (in part), the deduction of the categories, and the paralogisms. Kant rewrote the corresponding chapters without changing their basic idea. At the same time, however, the *Groundwork for the Metaphysics of Morals* and the *Metaphysical Foundations of Natural Science* signaled the completion of a further phase in the development of the critical philosophy. How far were these changes to be incorporated into the second edition of the *Critique of Pure Reason*?

One of the main difficulties stems from the relation of transcendental philosophy to morality, as we have mentioned several times before. Originally (i.e. following the 1772 letter to Herz) the possibility of a priori reference to objects was the main question of transcendental philosophy, and morality therefore quite 'foreign' to it since its objective reference is not problematic. As Kant was later to confide to the students in his logic course, during the work on the *Critique* it was only "in the end [that] I found that everything could be captured in the question, Are synthetic propositions a priori possible?" (24:784). As we have seen, it was this question that he placed at the center of the *Prolegomena*. The Garve review, however, had also made him realize that when the problem of transcendental philosophy is understood in this way it has "a striking similarity with that of morality" (23:60).

Is morality a part of transcendental philosophy, then, after all, since in the categorical imperative it contains a synthetic proposition a priori, the possibility of which requires demonstration? Or is it *not* a part of transcendental philosophy, since it is unaffected by the problem of a priori reference to objects, even though moral philosophy, like transcendental philosophy, still must prove the possibility of an a priori synthetic judgment?

Since the subject of the 1781 *Critique* had been the possibility of metaphysics, and metaphysics consists in large part of synthetic a priori judgments, the first option is of course highly plausible. Indeed, Kant had insisted both in the *Prolegomena* and in the letter to Garve that the *Critique* is to be judged by its success in answering this question. This option has in fact only one disadvantage: If the question of the possibility of such judgments is promoted to the defining *criterion* of transcendental philosophy, then the structure of the *Critique,* its inner architectonic, and thus the basic idea of the work is rendered unintelligible. For its division into an aesthetic, analytic, and dialectic had been the result of the fact that, according to Kant, we have in sensibility, understanding, and reason three sources of knowledge which contain specific kinds of a priori representations whose objective reference is problematic and in need of investigation. If this is no longer the basic *idea,* because transcendental philosophy is no longer defined by the problem of a priori reference, but rather by the possibility of synthetic a priori propositions, then the architectonic of the *Critique* would have to be modified in the second edition to conform to the new conception.

Kant does in fact seem at first to have contemplated a revision of this kind: In May and September 1786 Kant informed Christian Gottfried Schütz, the editor of the *Jenaische Allgemeine Literaturzeitung,* of his work on the new edition. Shortly thereafter, on November 21, 1786, Schütz published the following announcement in the "brief notices" section of his journal: "Herr Kant in Königsberg is preparing a second edition of his *Critique of Pure Reason* due to come out next Easter . . . In addition to the *critique of pure speculative reason* contained in the first, a *critique of pure practical reason* will be added to the second edition, securing the principle of morality against objections which have been or may yet be made against it, and completing the whole of the critical inquiries which must precede the system of pure reason" (3:556).

So Kant had settled on the first option[1] and in the new edition was trying to combine the critique of theoretical reason with a critique of

---

[1] At this same time Kant writes to Johann Bering that the system of practical philosophy is "the sister of the [theoretical] system and requires a similar treatment, though the difficulties are fewer" (10:441).

practical reason. It is not hard to guess why he soon abandoned this plan. For once the organization center has shifted to the problem of synthetic a priori propositions, it becomes questionable whether "the whole of the critical inquiries" really is completed by a critique of pure speculative and pure practical reason as stated in the announcement. After all, in addition to the faculties of cognition and desire there is also a third faculty, namely taste or the feeling of pleasure and displeasure. If the principle of this faculty also turned out to be a synthetic a priori proposition, its possibility would also have to be demonstrated. Transcendental philosophy would have not two, but three parts! And a third critique—a critique of taste—would be too much to integrate into the new edition. Though the size of the resulting book alone would have been prohibitive, there is a deeper reason as well: Taste does not constitute a separate part of the metaphysical "system of pure reason" next to nature and morality, and therefore it has an exceptional status. But the prior question remains: does the faculty of pleasure and displeasure have a synthetic a priori principle of its own?

Kant's letter to Reinhold from December 1787 provides such eloquent testimony on this question that I quote in full:

> Without becoming guilty of self-conceit, I can assure you that the longer I continue on my path the less worried I become that any individual or even organized opposition (of the sort that is common nowadays) will ever significantly damage my system. My inner conviction grows, as I discover in working on different topics that not only does my system remain self-consistent but I find also, when sometimes I cannot see the right way to investigate a certain subject, that I need only look back at the general picture of the elements of knowledge, and of the mental powers pertaining to them, in order to discover elucidations I had not expected. I am now at work on the critique of taste, and I have discovered a new sort of a priori principles, different from those heretofore observed. For there are three faculties of the mind: the faculty of cognition, the faculty of feeling pleasure and displeasure, and the faculty of desire. In the Critique *of Pure* (theoretical) *Reason,* I found a priori principles for the first of these, and in the Critique *of Practical Reason,* a priori principles for the third. I tried to find them for the second as well, and though I thought it impossible to find such principles, the analysis of the previously mentioned faculties of the human mind

allowed me to discover a systematicity, giving me ample material at which to marvel and if possible to explore, material sufficient to last me for the rest of my life. This systematicity put me on the path of recognizing the three parts of philosophy, each of which has its a priori principles, which can be enumerated and for which one can delimit precisely the knowledge that may be based on them: theoretical philosophy, teleology,[2] and practical philosophy, of which the second is, to be sure, the least rich in a priori grounds of determination. I hope to have a manuscript on this completed by though not in print by Easter; it will be entitled "The Critique of Taste" (10:514–15).

With this development, the critical project had further expanded in an unanticipated direction. In the course of his work on the new edition of the First Critique, Kant realized that he would have to write two more critiques before he could finally turn his attentions to the metaphysics he had planned. Although the Third Critique was not published until 1790, its conception falls in the period during which Kant was revising the First Critique, the Winter of 1786/87 (cp. 3:557–58), and it is a direct result of the shift that has taken place in the point of departure or the definition of the problem.[3] We must therefore examine the effects this expansion had on Kant's project of a philosophy "that will be able to come forward as science."

1. *Critique of Pure Reason*, Second Edition

In the preface to the second edition, Kant explains the difference between the two editions: he says he used the opportunity to remedy the difficulties and obscurities as far as possible, without changing the form and completeness of the underlying plan (Bxxxvii). His enumeration of the "improvements" he has "attempted" in this new edition is not, however, complete. The reader does not, for instance, learn that the defining idea of transcendental philosophy has changed in comparison to the first edition. Kant also remains silent about the important changes in the introduction occasioned

---

[2] How teleology can be the principle of the feeling of pleasure and displeasure will become clear in the next chapter.

[3] Thus the footnote at A21 which denies an a priori principle of taste, is accordingly revised in the B-edition, opening the way for a 'Critique of Taste'.

by that shift (including the reformulation of the definition of transcendental cognition: cp. A11f./B25), and also about the changes in the chapter 'The Ground of the Distinction of all Objects in general into Phenomena and Noumena' (cp., e.g., A244f. with B288 and B291). While the changes which Kant himself mentions (bearing on the transcendental aesthetic, the deduction of the categories, the analogies of the understanding, and the paralogisms) were made in direct response to objections from readers and reviewers of the first edition, the changes he neglects to mention stem from Kant's efforts to adapt the second edition to the *Prolegomena* and to take account of the new definition of transcendental philosophy. I'll need to talk briefly about these changes since they had significant consequences for the reception of Kant's philosophy.

In 1781, Kant had already described the establishment of pure reason's boundaries and the limitation of theoretical knowledge to possible experience as the most important result of the Critique (cp. A795). The transcendental investigation leading to the establishment of these limits is not, of course, itself subject to them. Since it is concerned with our a priori concepts of objects in general, which in the further course of the investigation will be divided into "phenomena and noumena" (cp. A235)—the distinction that constitutes the boundary—the investigation is as it were at work in both domains, both on this and the other side of the boundary. Otherwise it would be impossible to recognize that the conditions of genuine cognition are only present in the domain of phenomena (appearances), but not in the domain of noumena (things in themselves).[4] Hence not only knowledge of how representations can refer to objects a priori is designated as 'transcendental', but knowledge of the corresponding errors of subreption in the employment of the understanding as well (cp. A583, 619). For there is also such a thing as "the transcendental employment or misemployment of the categories" (A296). Accordingly, a part of transcendental cognition, the "transcendental dialectic," deals with "transcendental illusion" (A293), for the trans*cendent* employment of the concepts of

---

[4] At A238 Kant justifies his procedure by pointing out, "that while the understanding, occupied merely with its empirical employment . . . may indeed get along quite satisfactorily, there is yet one task to which it is not equal, that, namely, of determining the limits of its employment, and of knowing what it is that may lie within and what it is that lies without its own proper sphere. This demands those deep enquiries which we have instituted."

reason constitutes a "trans*cendental* subreption" (cp. A583, 619). The task of the transcendental dialectic is to bring to light the transcendental illusion of transcendent judgments (cp. A297). Consequently the ideas of reason, which can never be given in experience and are also not conditions of possible experience, are also called "transcendental ideas"—a term which occurs no less than twenty-four times in the first edition.

The transcendental is therefore to be identified neither with that which is empirically immanent, nor with that which is transcendent. In the first edition, Kant formulates the distinctions between these three conceptual levels with the utmost clarity:

> We shall entitle the principles whose application is confined entirely within the limits of possible experience, *immanent;* and those, on the other hand, which profess to pass beyond these limits, *transcendent* . . . Thus *transcendental* and *transcendent* are not interchangeble terms. The principles of pure understanding, which we have set out above [i.e. the axioms of intuition, the anticipations of perception, the analogies of experience, and the postulates of empirical thinking], allow only of empirical and not of **transcendental employment, that is, employment extending beyond the limits of experience** [emphasis added]. A principle, on the other hand, which takes away these limits, or even commands us actually to transgress them, is called *transcendent.* If our criticism can succeed in disclosing the illusion in these alleged principles, then those principles which are of merely empirical employment may be called, in opposition to the others, *immanent* principles of pure understanding" (A295–96).

However, if transcendental knowledge ceases to be defined in terms of a relation to objects in general, and comes instead to be defined by the question of how synthetic judgments a priori are possible, this trichotomy is no longer valid. For although such judgments are only possible by way of "some third thing," this "third thing" is the possibility of experience itself, i.e. that which Kant identifies here with *immanent* or empirical employment. *Extending beyond* possible experience no longer makes any sense in transcendental terms, but must be considered as strictly *transcendent.* Kant first explicitly makes this correction in the *Prolegomena,* where he writes in regard to Garve's review: "The word transcendental—whose signification, which I indicated so many times, was not once caught by the reviewer (so hastily had he looked at everything)—**does not signify**

something that surpasses all experience, but something that indeed precedes experience (a priori), but that, all the same, is destined to nothing more than solely to make cognition from experience possible. If these concepts cross beyond experience, their use is then called transcendent, which is distinguished from the immanent use (i.e., use limited to experience)" (4:373–74, emphasis added).

The term 'transcendental' now coincides with 'immanent'. The result, however, is that talk of a 'transcendental dialectic', of 'transcendental ideas', not to mention a "transcendental object . . . [as] the intelligible cause of appearances" (A494/B522) is no longer appropriate, since they have no relation to the conditions of possible experience. However, Kant did not make the relevant changes in the new edition—regrettably, as we must concede, for by neglecting to do so he made the work considerably more difficult to understand.[5] Further below I will go into his reasons for refraining from such changes. First, however, we must consider how the shift in accent that takes place in the *Prolegomena* and the second edition of the *Critique* made an already difficult topic of Kantian philosophy, the so-called thing in itself, nearly incomprehensible.

In this connection it is important to recall that in 1781 Kant understands the *meaning [Bedeutung]* of a concept to be its "relation to the object" (A241, 240), while its *employment [Gebrauch]* consists in the determination, i.e. cognition[6] of an object. The categories have, therefore, an empirical employment, but no actual transcendental employment (A246). For if they are not related to any intuition, then their 'employment' consists merely in the unity of thinking a manifold in general (cp. A247), by way of which an object comes to be thought, but not determined. For this reason Kant says: "It may be advisable, therefore, to express the situation as follows. The pure categories, apart from formal conditions of sensibility, have only transcendental meaning; nevertheless, they may not be employed transcendentally, such employment being in itself impossible" (A248). However, as soon as 'transcendental' comes to be identified with 'immanent', the categories cease to have any transcendental meaning at all apart from sensibility. The *Prolegomena* in any case leave

---

[5] The equation of 'transcendental' with 'the conditions of possibility of experience', familiar today to every student of philosophy, is thus altogether false when applied to Kant's position in 1781; it is only valid from the *Prolegomena* on.

[6] To determine an object means to ascribe to it a predicate to the exclusion of its opposite (1:391, prop. iv; cp. A598).

no doubt about the matter: "Consequently, even the pure concepts of the understanding have no meaning at all if they depart from objects of experience and want to be referred to things in themselves (*noumena*)" (4:312; cp. 315, 316).

If Kant's terminology was not always consistent even in the first edition, the situation has now become wholly opaque. Jacobi, who hoped to penetrate Kant's *Critique* with the help of the *Prolegomena* and consulted the work as a commentary on the *Critique,* ran into insuperable difficulties in understanding the concept of the unknowable thing in itself. He formulated his criticism of this concept in a so-called appendix "On Transcendental Idealism" to his work *David Hume on Belief, or Idealism and Realism. A Conversation,*[7] which had appeared shortly before the publication of Kant's new edition of the *Critique.* Since the first edition was out of print and the *Prolegomena* and then the new edition of the *Critique* seemed to confirm Jacobi's interpretation, Jacobi's objection shaped the way the *Critique* would henceforth be read. The objection was almost universally accepted as valid and it has shaped our understanding of Kant up till the present. It is therefore worth quoting in full.

> However much it may be contrary to the spirit of Kantian philosophy to say of the objects that they make *impressions* on the senses and that in this way they bring about representations, still it is not possible to see how even the Kantian philosophy could find entry into itself without this presupposition and manage some statement of its hypothesis. For even the word "sensibility" is without any meaning, unless we understand by it a distinct real intermediary between one real thing and another, an actual means *from* something *to* something else; and it would be meaningless, too, if the concepts of "outside one another" and "being combined," of "action" and "passion," of "causality" and "dependence," were not already contained in the concept of it *as real and objective determinations.* In fact they are contained in such a way that the absolute universality and necessity of these concepts must equally be given as a prior presupposition. I must admit that I was held up not a little by this difficulty in my study of the Kantian philosophy, so much so that for

---

[7] *David Hume über den Glauben, oder Idealismus und Realismus. Ein Gespräch.* Breslau: Gottlieb Löwe 1787.

several years running I had to start from the beginning over and over again with the *Critique of Pure Reason,* because I was incessantly going astray on this point, viz. that *without* that presupposition I could not enter into the system, but *with* it I could not stay within it (JW 2:303–4/336).[8]

Jacobi's reasoning is clear: Since the objects of experience are, according to Kant, themselves constructs based on sensible representations, they cannot be the causes of these representations. We must however assume such causes, since otherwise "even the word 'sensibility' is without any meaning," for *qua* receptivity it must correspond to "what is real" as that from which it receives its impressions. Hence the categories of "'causality' and 'dependence' . . . *as real and objective determinations*" have in principle already been applied to this intermediary, which however can only be an illegitimate application of the categories outside the bounds of possible experience. Thus *without* this presupposition, Jacobi could not enter into the system, and *with* it he could not stay within it.

There can be no doubt that Kant's shifting terminology encouraged this interpretation, but to what extent is it really legitimate? Does Jacobi's objection apply? In my opinion, the key to answering this question lies in Kant's chapter on *phenomena* and *noumena,* more precisely in the distinction between the negative and positive senses of *noumena.* "The doctrine of sensibility is *likewise* the doctrine of the noumenon" (B307, emphasis added), Kant writes, and points out that the concept of the noumenon

---

[8] Twenty-eight years later, in the first complete edition of his works, Jacobi prefaced this 'appendix' with the following significant remark: "The following treatise makes constant reference to the *first* edition of the *Critique of Pure Reason,* the only one that was available at that time. A few months after this treatise was finished, the second edition of Kant's work was published . . . In the preface to this second edition (p. xxxvii ff.) Kant informs his readers of the improvements in *presentation* that he has attempted in the new edition, making no secret of the fact that this improvement also entails a certain loss for the reader since, in order to make room for a more easily graspable presentation, some things had to be left out or presented in an abridged form. —I think this loss very significant and hope that my opinion will encourage readers serious about philosophy and its history to compare the first edition of the *Critique of Pure Reason* with the improved second edition. The later editions are simply exact reprints of the second edition . . . Since the first edition has already become quite rare, at least public libraries and larger private collections should take care that the few copies still extant do not also disappear in the end" (JW 2:291).

is inextricably linked with the theory of sensibility.[9] The fact that our intuition is sensible (i.e. receptive) is the reason why we must think of noumena as corresponding to it if intuition is not to be empty. They are related to each other, then, as ground and consequence: just as the fact that a figure is a Euclidean triangle is the ground (though not the *cause*) of the fact that the sum of its angles are equal to two right angles, so too is the fact (if it is indeed a fact) that our intuition is receptive the ground for conceiving *noumena* as corresponding to it. For an intuition cannot be conceived as receptive if nothing corresponds to it from which it receives anything.[10] To this extent, then, Jacobi is right. And it is also true that if we conceive of such a *noumenon* corresponding to sensibility, we employ (non-schematized) categories in doing so. For "since I can think nothing without a category" (5:103), they are inevitably present in every intentional object, in every thought about something: "The categories accordingly extend further than sensible intuition, since they think objects in general, without regard to the special mode (the sensibility) in which they may be given" (A254).

Jacobi is mistaken, however, when he suspects a real *employment* of the categories of "causality and dependence" as well, which would indeed have to count as a "real and objective determination" of things in themselves. Kant himself has untiringly repeated that such a determination (i.e. the ascription of a predicate under exclusion of its opposite) is fundamentally impossible since no intuition can correspond to it. Yet neither is such a determination required in order to conceive a correspondence between sensibility and the thing in itself: "Two determinations *necessarily* combined in one concept must be connected as ground and consequent, and so connected that this *unity* is considered either as *analytic* (logical connection) or as *synthetic* (real connection), the former in accordance with the law of identity, the latter in accordance with the law of causality" (5:111). But as we have just seen, the connection of the concept of receptivity with that of the noumenon or thing in itself is analytic, not synthetic.

---

[9] Although this formulation is taken from the second edition, the thought behind it is to be found in both editions. According to A494, too, we have to assume a noumenal object, "merely in order to have something corresponding to sensibility viewed as receptivity."

[10] This is the reason why the concept of the thing in itself could be so effortlessly abandoned later on by Fichte (and by Kant himself in the *Opus postumum*)— namely as soon as sensibility ceases to be conceived as mere receptivity and its seeming passivity comes to be derived from unconscious acts of the self-positing I.

If reason sought to assert a noumenal causality, "it would have to try to show how the *logical connection of ground and consequence* could be *used synthetically with a kind of intuition different from the sensible,* that is, how a *causa noumenon* is possible; this it cannot do . . ." (5:49, emphasis added).[11]

The reference to 'a kind of intuition different from the sensible' sheds additional light on Jacobi's misunderstanding. Jacobi saw it as a crass inconsistency to assert the unknowability of things in themselves and at the same time to maintain that they exist; thus he concluded his criticism with the following challenge: "The transcendental idealist must have the courage, therefore, to assert the strongest idealism that was ever professed, and not be afraid of the objection of speculative egoism, for it is impossible for him to pretend to stay within his system if he tries to repel from himself even just this last objection" (JW 2:310/338).

The transcendental idealist would be ill-advised to submit to this challenge, however. For just as sensibility is determined as receptivity, as the faculty of receiving representations, so too are the understanding and imagination determined as spontaneity, as the faculty of producing representations on their own. Now if the concept of sensibility is inextricably linked with the concept of a noumenon, then the latter must not be an empty concept, an imaginary notion of something which a 'speculative egoist' could deny, for otherwise the distinction between receptivity and spontaneity would collapse—taking with it the distinction between two independent sources of cognition. This, however, as we saw at the outset of our reflections, is the fundamental presupposition of transcendental idealism. Consequently the thing in itself *must* be conceived in such a way that a being with a different, non-receptive intuition would in fact be able to perceive it and recognize it as actually existing.[12] This is the concept of

---

[11] For knowledge of a causal relation more is generally required than knowledge of a correlation between two events: one must also possess counterfactual knowledge to the effect that event A would not have happened if event B had not happened. Otherwise causal relations would be indistinguishable from wholly contingent, non-causal correlations. But where no experience is possible, neither can there be any such knowledge. Talk of a cause-effect relation would be empty in such a case.

[12] Hence Kant repeatedly emphasizes "that though we cannot *know* these same objects [of experience] also as things in themselves, we must yet be in a position at least to think them as things in themselves; otherwise we should be landed in the absurd conclusion that there can be appearances [i.e. objects of the passive faculty] without anything that appears" (Bxxvi).

the noumenon in the positive sense, of which Kant writes: "If we understand [by 'noumenon'] an *object* of a *non-sensible intuition,* we thereby suppose a special mode of intuition, namely, the intellectual, which is not that which we possess, and of which we cannot comprehend even the possibility" (B307). Kant explicitly claims that forming such a concept is "indispensable" in "setting limits" to our sensibility (A256) so as not to mistake it for the only possible form of intuition.

Before leaving the *Critique of Pure Reason,* I still need to address the question why Kant did not carry out all the necessary changes in the new edition. A partial answer already suggested itself at the beginning of this chapter: If transcendental philosophy is no longer defined by the problem of a priori reference, but rather by the possibility of synthetic a priori propositions, then the architectonic of the work would also have to be modified in accord with the new conception. But that is not feasible, as can easily be shown:

Kant introduces the problem of synthetic a priori propositions by way of the concept of judgment, more precisely by way of the distinction between analytic and synthetic judgments (cp. A6, 4:266, B10). Both presuppose a principle governing the connection of subject and predicate. Since analytic judgments are merely explicative, i.e. the predicate is part of the concept of the subject, the common principle of all analytic judgments is the law of non-contradiction. Synthetic judgments require a different principle. Since they are ampliative, it follows that "I must have besides the concept of the subject something else (X), upon which the understanding may rely, if it is to know that a predicate, not contained in this concept, nevertheless belongs to it" (A8). In the case of synthetic judgments a posteriori this 'X' is the perception of the object, "but in a priori synthetic judgments this help is entirely lacking" (A9). How then are such judgments possible? What is that 'something else (X)' in their case?

We are inclined to give the correct answer because we are already familiar with the *Critique,* but if this is the question from which everything starts, the question that defines the problem and with a view to which the work is to be carried out, of course we cannot already know the answer in advance.

There is however no way of arriving at a non-circular answer to this question if we start from the distinction between analytic and synthetic judgments as our premise. One could take putatively synthetic a priori propositions in mathematics and pure natural science as a starting point and investigate how *these* are possible, and then consider the general implications for all propositions of this kind. This is the path taken in the *Prolegomena,* and it determines the following "plan" of the work: "1) How is pure mathematics possible? 2) How is pure natural science possible? 3) How is metaphysics in general possible? 4) How is metaphysics as science possible?" (4:280). Apart from the fact that this plan is not the one on which the *Critique* is based, the validity of the result would of course depend on whether the propositions of mathematics and natural science are indeed the synthetic a priori propositions they were assumed to be. That is, to put it delicately, not apodictically certain; as Kant himself was well aware (cp. 4:272, 5:52), David Hume had famously believed that mathematical propositions are analytic. Thus Kant insists in the *Prolegomena* that it presupposes the *Critique of Pure Reason* and is only intended as a clarification "subsequent to the completed work" (4:263). Its method already presupposes the answer that the *Critique* sets out to discover, namely *whether* synthetic a priori propositions are possible at all. This question cannot therefore replace the initial question of the *Critique*.[13]

Since Kant wants to make the new edition conformable to the *Prolegomena,* he thought up a different strategy: in the Preface he recommends that the reader begin by tentatively assuming the correctness of his theory and treating it as a scientific "hypothesis." Taking the history of mathematics and natural science as cases in point, he first identifies the methodological "revolution" which placed initially erratic attempts at understanding on "the secure path of a science." He then goes on to ask whether in metaphysics, too, we should not imitate such a procedure "at least by way of experiment" (Bxvi). For the reader who accedes to Kant's proposal, he promises two means of verifying his hypothesis: first the "experiment" of the dialectic, the attempt to conceive of the unconditioned in non-contradictory terms (cp. Bxx), and secondly the possibility of morality. If the dialectic ends up showing that the unconditioned cannot even be thought without contradiction so long as one fails to distinguish between things in themselves and appearances, then "we are justified in concluding that what we at first assumed for the purposes of experiment is now definitely confirmed" (Bxx). On the other hand, the *Groundwork* had in the meantime demonstrated that if we can assume freedom of the will,

---

[13] Kant's original plan, mentioned above, to integrate a critique of practical reason into the new edition of the First Critique would have been tantamount to an entirely new conception of the work's architectonic.

morality is not a "chimerical idea" (4:445). This, however, is only possible, as Kant emphasizes, because the *Critique* teaches that "the object is to be taken *in a twofold sense*" (Bxxvii), so that human beings can conceive themselves as both free and (to the extent that they are appearances) subject to natural laws. It is only by way of the self-limitation of theoretical reason that it becomes possible for the doctrine of morality to "make good its position" (Bxxix).

However, in order for this position to be made good and for morality to be more than a mere possibility, it is necessary to prove the reality of freedom, and this is precisely the task of the *Critique of Practical Reason*. Is it surprising that Kant felt the need to turn his energies to this work instead of trying to eradicate the sources of any further misunderstanding of the First Critique? For in addition to the *Critique of Practical Reason* he was also planning to write a critique of taste, and after that the metaphysics of nature and the metaphysics of morality he had put off for so long. What should have priority: the completion of the system, of which as yet he had only finished the first part, or the thorough reworking of this first part of it in order to prevent possible misunderstandings?

The revisions do not extend beyond the paralogism chapter because, as Kant writes in the Preface to the new edition, "time was too short to allow of further changes; and besides, I have not found among competent and impartial critics any misapprehension in regard to the remaining sections" (Bxxxviii-xli). And a few pages later he adds, "In the course of these labors I have advanced somewhat far in years (this month I reach my sixty-fourth year), and I must be careful with my time if I am to succeed in my proposed scheme of providing a metaphysic of nature and of morals which will confirm the truth of my Critique in the two fields, of speculative and of practical reason" (Bxliii).

To this end, however, it was first necessary to work out the *Critique of Practical Reason,* and in its preface Kant gives us a further reason for his decision, likely the most important reason of all. The demonstration of the reality of freedom supplied by this work also contributes more to the understanding of the first *Critique* than a partial emendation of isolated passages ever could have: "Here, too, the enigma of the critical philosophy is first explained: how one can *deny* objective *reality* to the supersensible *employment* [!] *of the categories* in speculation and yet *grant* them this *reality* with respect to the objects of pure practical reason; for this must previously have seemed *inconsistent,* as long as such a practical use is known only by name" (5:5).

2. *Critique of Practical Reason*

The preceding remarks about Jacobi are not intended to suggest that Kant's position on the relation between the sensuous and the noumenal worlds had not continued to evolve since 1781. A comparison between the *Critique of Practical Reason* and the *Groundwork* shows indeed that it has. The *Groundwork* had been conceived as a foundation for the metaphysics of morality, and in its third, "synthetic" section it undertook to deduce the supreme principle of morality required by such a metaphysics. Hence the *Critique of Practical Reason,* also intended as a demonstration of the *possibility* of morality, does not replace the *Groundwork* but rather complements it. The second Critique "presupposes, indeed, the *Groundwork of the Metaphysics of Morals,*" as Kant explains, "but only insofar as this constitutes preliminary acquaintance with the principle of duty and provides and justifies a determinate formula of it; otherwise, it stands on its own" (5:8). As we recall, the task of the *Groundwork* had been to discover and establish the supreme principle of morality; now it is said to concern only the discovery of the principle and the justification of a "formula," but not the establishment of the principle. In other words, the third section's deduction of the moral law is not presupposed, and it is revealing to see why not.

In the *Groundwork,* Kant had aimed to deduce the concept of freedom from pure practical reason (4:447), in order then to show how the possibility of a categorical imperative becomes intelligible on the basis of the reference to the world of the understanding established in the course of the work. The fact that *theoretical* reason is already forced to distinguish between the sensuous world and the world of the understanding does not in itself tell us anything about the latter, leaving it undetermined. Even the resolution of the third antinomy could only prove that the laws of nature and causality through freedom do not necessarily contradict each other. This is why Kant's reference to the conditions of the act of judging in the third section of the *Groundwork* is so interesting: It shows that theoretical reason must already presuppose a freedom in regard to its judgments which it cannot itself justify.

There is admittedly no compelling reason to identify this freedom of judgment with moral freedom. For it is initially only freedom in the negative sense—freedom of choice in light of alternative predicates. It is true that theoretical reason is also free in the positive sense and hence

114

autonomous:[14] The laws which theoretical reason gives to itself—thus originally constituting itself as understanding and reason—are not moral laws, but rather the elementary laws of logic. Again, these laws belong not to the world of appearances, but to the world of the understanding only. As Kant had said in the first edition of the *Critique,* logic is a "pure doctrine of reason" containing "the absolutely necessary rules of thought," and to this extent it is analogous to "pure ethics which contains only the necessary moral laws of a free will in general" (A52–55).

From the point of view of theoretical reason, the laws of the world of the understanding are therefore none other than these "absolutely necessary rules of thought,"[15] and a further argument would be required to show that the moral law is also among them. As a subject that judges and combines representations in the unity of consciousness, I know of no other laws of the world of the understanding.

Thus in the third section of the *Groundwork* Kant speaks generally of beings which are rational *and have a will.* For it is only if I can ascribe *will* to myself that I must also ascribe to myself a form of freedom distinct from that of judgment, namely a *causality* which, independently of all external influences, can be determined to action by pure reason alone: "Freedom . . . holds only as a necessary presupposition of reason in a being that believes itself to be conscious of a will, that is, of a faculty distinct from a mere faculty of desire (namely, a faculty of determining itself to action as an intelligence and hence in accordance with laws of reason independently of natural instincts)" (4:459). Only on the assumption that I can ascribe to myself a will in this specific sense (and not merely an empirically conditioned faculty of desire), is it also possible for me to ascribe to myself freedom of action, thus placing myself in the world of the

---

[14] Reason must "regard itself as the author of its principles," is all that Kant writes here, "independent of foreign influence" (4:448). One year later, in "What Does it Mean to Orient Oneself in Thought?," he is more explicit: "Freedom of thought" means "not to subject reason to any other law than that which it gives to itself" (8:145).

[15] A passage in Kant's lectures on logic (9:52–53) indicates that what he has in mind here is 1) the laws of non-contradiction and of identity (logical possibility), 2) the principle of sufficient reason (logical actuality), and 3) the law of the excluded middle (logical necessity). The rules associated with the other categories are all part of what Kant ("contrary to the usual meaning of this title") calls "applied general logic" (A52–55).

understanding. This, however, is merely freedom in the negative sense, the independence from sensuous drives, and does not suffice as a deduction of the moral law. It only entails that reason can determine the will and is therefore practical. That the law to which freedom itself is subject is in fact the moral law is no more entailed by this reasoning than the laws of logic are entailed by the mere fact of the freedom of judgment.

How, then, do I know that I can ascribe to myself freedom in the positive sense of the term? This does not seem to follow from my mere consciousness that reason has determined the will to action, no matter how unusual and contrary to inclination the action might be. David Hume's basic objection will always apply to such actions: "We consider not, that the fantastical desire of shewing liberty is here the motive of our actions."[16] And finally, Kant himself emphasizes frequently enough that the morality of my own actions is just as concealed to me as the motives guiding other agents (A551; 4:407). The argument of the *Groundwork* fails, then, because it is impossible to deduce positive freedom (and hence the moral law) from any action at all other than the consciousness of negative freedom. On the contrary: we ascribe a will to ourselves and conceive of ourselves as free, not because of any determinate actions we perform, but rather because of those which *"ought to have been done* even though they *were not done"* (4:455, cp. A550).

Kant gives what is surely the most famous illustration of this theorem at the beginning of the *Critique of Practical Reason* with the example of a man in front of whose house a gallows has been erected and who is commanded by his prince, under threat of immediate execution, to give false testimony against an honest man whom the prince thus hopes to rid himself of.[17] Kant asks whether the man would believe it to be possible for him to refuse to give false testimony, even though doing so would probably mean the loss of his own life: "He would perhaps not venture to assert whether he would do it or not, but he must admit without hesitation that it would be possible to him. He judges, therefore, that he can do

---

[16] Hume 1777, 94.

[17] Kant's model for this example is presumably the report by Diogenes Laertius (IX, 5) according to which the tyrant Nearchus intended to force Zeno of Elea to betray those with whom he had plotted Nearchus' overthrow. Rather than speak, however, Zeno is said to have bitten off his own tongue and spat it out in the tyrant's face. Thereupon he was beaten to death. Boethius tells the same story in *The Consolation of Philosophy*, Book II, Ch. 6, without however mentioning the names.

something because he is aware that he ought to do it and cognizes freedom within him, which, without the moral law, would have remained unknown to him" (5:30).

If this line of thought is correct, then consciousness of the moral law is a fundamental fact that necessarily precedes the consciousness of positive freedom and cannot be deduced from it. Hence Kant refers to this consciousness in the second Critique as a "fact of reason because one cannot reason it out from antecedent data of reason, for example, from consciousness of freedom (since this is not antecedently given to us)" (5:31). Even without a deduction, this remark reveals the core of Kant's new foundation of morality: that even pure reason, taken in itself, is practical, in that it gives human beings a universal law of moral action which can determine the will. And it is through this law that we originally become conscious of our freedom: The moral law is the *ratio cognoscendi* of freedom, while freedom is the *ratio essendi* of the law. This law guarantees the actuality of freedom for beings "who cognize this law as binding upon them" (5:47)—and only for such beings.

Thus we come to see more clearly why it is that Kant believed the Second Critique was of fundamental importance for the First Critique as well, since it is only the Second Critique that allows us to see the connection between the intelligible and sensible world in a more distinct light: "Now the concept of freedom, insofar as its reality is proved by an apodictic law of practical reason, constitutes the keystone of the whole structure of a system of pure reason, even of speculative reason" (5:3–4). A keystone, of course, is the topmost stone in the apex of an arch. Until this stone has been inserted, the arch has to be supported by scaffolding or other reinforcements; thereafter the arch is self-supporting and the scaffolding can be taken down. The keystone is the last stone to be inserted, however; the construction cannot begin with it.

Kant was presumably deliberate in choosing just this metaphor. It casts a particularly distinct light on the relationship of the two Critiques to each other. It is evident that he could not begin with the concept of freedom before he had demonstrated that the laws of nature are valid only for appearances, and so that natural necessity and freedom do not stand in contradiction. The First Critique, however, could not even prove the real possibility of freedom, but only that it was free of contradiction. The real possibility of freedom is only proven in the *Critique of Practical Reason,* where the 'fact of reason' that rests on freedom as its presupposition proves both its actuality and hence also its possibility (for anyone who is conscious of the law), even though we are unable to comprehend the latter. For that would only be possible, as Kant re-emphasizes in this context (5:49, 99), for a faculty of intuition different from ours, namely for a non-sensible intuition of the same subject, which we, however, do not possess. Yet it is here that we reap the benefits of the distinction drawn above between the transcendent and immanent employment of a concept. From the perspective of the First Critique, any talk of human freedom is ungrounded and any employment of the concept transcendent. With the *experience* of the moral law, however, which *commands* us to perform certain actions, the employment becomes immanent: The moral law supplies the idea of freedom, the employment of which was previously extravagant, with an "objective, though only practical reality," since the consciousness of the obligatory force of the law "changes its *transcendent* employment into an *immanent* employment (in which reason is by means of ideas itself an efficient cause in the field of experience)" (5:48). In more precise terms, the relationship of the intelligible world to sensibility is as follows:

> This law is to furnish the sensible world, as a *sensible nature* (in what concerns rational beings), with the form of a world of the understanding, that is, of a *supersensible nature,* though without infringing upon the mechanism of the former. Now, nature in the most general sense is the existence of things under laws. The sensible nature of rational beings in general is their existence under empirically conditioned laws and is thus, for this reason, *heteronomy.* The supersensible nature of the same beings, on the other hand, is their existence in accordance with laws that are independent of any empirical condition and thus belong to the *autonomy* of pure reason . . . The law of this autonomy, however, is the moral law, which is therefore the fundamental law of a supersensible nature and of a pure world of the understanding, the counterpart of which is to exist in the sensible world but without infringing upon its laws. The former could be called the *archetypal world* (*natura archetypa*) which we cognize only in reason, whereas the latter could be called the *ectypal world* (*natura ectypa*) because it contains the possible effect of the idea of the former as the determining ground of the will. For the moral law transfers us, in idea, into a nature in which pure reason, if it were accompanied with suitable physical power, would produce the highest good, and it determines our will

to confer on the sensible world the form of a whole of rational beings (5:43).

If this is right, then it is understandable that Kant also believes it possible to make the reverse inference: "If, therefore, the highest good is impossible in accordance with practical rules, then the moral law, which commands us to promote it, must be fantastic and directed to empty imaginary ends and must therefore in itself be false" (5:114). For the moral law is not a merely negative law prohibiting certain actions, but rather a law according to which "the form of a world of the understanding" is to be imparted to the sensible world to the extent that it involves human beings. If the moral law could not be realized in this world, then it would be comparable to the plan of a house that could never be built—with the important difference that the law, but not the house plan, at the same time *requires* its "counterpart" in the sensible world. The law would be "in itself false," for a law that is in principle unrealizable is not a law. The transcendent employment of the concept of freedom could never be transformed into an immanent employment!

In the 'Dialectic' of the *Critique of Practical Reason* Kant therefore defines the "totality of the object of pure practical reason" as the highest good (5:108). At the same time, however, he also states that its realization presents a fundamental problem, indeed that it even plunges practical reason into an antinomy according to which the highest good on the one hand *ought* to be realized, while on the other hand it cannot be realized. Why so?

Here is a difficulty: The highest good ought to be realized *in the sensible world;* consequently, it must be compatible with the universal laws of nature. According to the First Critique, however, nature consists in a thoroughgoing causal determinism, i.e. everything that happens presupposes something upon which it follows according to the law of causality (second analogy). A purpose, by contrast, is something that does not arise on the basis of a preceding appearance, but rather on the basis of an idea of what ought to be. How something in the world can be both at the same time, how it could be possible to realize moral purposes in this world "though without infringing upon its laws," is a matter into which theoretical reason has as yet no insight.

This problem, which exists for all purposes, and not only ethical ones, is not solved by Kant until the Third Critique, where the concept of a purposiveness of nature is transcendentally justified. In the present case, however, not only the realizability of purposes in general needs to be secured; beyond that, the specific *object* which the law demands a priori must also be a real possibility in this world.

This gives rise to a second difficulty: for as we have just heard, pure reason would produce its object in the sensible world "if it were accompanied by an appropriate physical capacity." It does not possess a physical capacity, however, except to the extent that it is a human being. Only a human being can realize the moral law in the world of which it is also merely a part. As a human being, however, I have *two* supreme goals. The highest goal I set for myself as a natural being is the optimal satisfaction of my own needs, i.e. my own happiness. My highest goal as a rational being is the realization of the moral law. If the highest good is really possible, then happiness must be compatible with morality as embodied in my person, *although* the moral law so frequently demands the neglect and subordination of my own needs—namely whenever they conflict with it. But that is only possible if happiness can also belong to me *because* I act morally. For me as a human being, the highest, complete good is therefore only possible in the form of an *a priori possible correspondence* between the two: "Insofar as virtue and happiness together constitute the possession of the highest good by a person, while happiness distributed in exact proportion to morality (as a person's value and worthiness of being happy) constitutes the highest good of a *possible world:* both together constitute the whole, the complete good, where virtue as the condition always remains the highest good" (5:110–11).

It is the concept of the highest good *understood in this way* which according to Kant gives rise to an "antinomy of practical reason" that can be expressed as follows:[18]

Thesis: The highest good is possible.
Antithesis: The highest good is impossible.
Proof of the Thesis: The moral law demands its realization.
Proof of the Antithesis: The proportional connection of virtue and happiness is neither analytic nor synthetic a priori, nor given synthetically a posteriori.

Since this is obviously a different concept of antinomy than that of the First Critique, it is worthwhile to consider it here in greater detail.

---

[18] My formulation of the antinomy follows that by Lewis White Beck 1960, 248.

Historical Excursus

Like the concept of deduction, the concept of antinomy used by Kant in the *Critique of Pure Reason* was adopted from the legal practice of his day. In that context, 'antinomy' refers to a case in which "two laws are in conflict or indeed in contradiction with each other."[19] This is the way Kant too introduces the term: it is "a conflict of the laws (an antinomy) of pure reason" (A407/B434). For on the one hand reason establishes the law that everything that is conditioned must be derived from something unconditioned; on the other hand, though, its law is that every condition must in turn be considered as conditioned. This gives rise to contradictory propositions, each of which "meets with the conditions of its necessity in the nature of reason" (A421/B449).

On account of the contradiction in its own legislation, pure theoretical reason was forced to reflect on its own limits and to distinguish between appearances and things in themselves. For only when this distinction is assumed can the antinomy be avoided, so that Kant regards the antinomy as constituting an indirect proof for the truth of transcendental idealism.

Interestingly, none of this is true of the antinomy of practical reason. This antinomy is not a conflict between laws of reason, for the antithesis does not derive from a law of reason, but ultimately from experience. Nor is transcendental idealism the solution of this conflict; it is rather the case that the formulation of the antinomy already presupposes idealism. The most important difference, however, lies elsewhere (and this is the crucial point for Kant): whereas the antinomy of the First Critique forced theoretical reason to acknowledge its limits, the new antinomy forces reason to go beyond these limits in order to resolve the contradiction. In this way, Kant's new concept of antinomy continues a tradition that reaches back to Plato, although the latter did not refer to contradiction as an antinomy (since it was not a contradiction between νομόι), but as a "paraclete" (a 'helper', an 'advocate') that *provokes* us to ascend from what is transitory to true being, thereby striving for a higher level of knowledge. Thus Plato writes in Book VII of the *Republic* that a "turning of the soul" (521c) from the sensible to the supersensible becomes necessary when things occur in perception that are "summoners [παρακλητιό ʹ]￼ of thought . . . those that strike the relevant senses at the same time as their opposites" (524d). This provokes the mind, "summoning reason to consider whether each of the things announced to it is one or two" (524b). Since the contradictory sensory elements obtain at the same time without negating each other, reason

---

[19] See Zedler's *Großes vollständiges Universallexicon* (1732), 2:572.

feels summoned to investigate whether there is something higher, not itself present in perception, as whose *moments* the contradictory elements can be considered. Such a perception, that "goes off into opposite perceptions at the same time"
(523b-c), could be compared to the riddle of the Theban sphinx, which also presents us with something that seems self-contradictory—What goes on four legs in
the morning, on two at noon, and on three in the evening?—and which requires us
to find something that makes the contradiction disappear. "I'll point out, then, I
said, if you can grasp it that some sense perceptions don't summon the understanding to look into them, because the judgment of sense perception is itself adequate, while others encourage it in every way to look into them, because sense
perception seems to produce no sound result" (523a-b).

Traces of the Platonic tradition of the contradiction as a *paraclete* are also to
be found in Kant's time, although they are faint.[20] Whether or not Kant consciously belonged to that tradition is less relevant here than the actual similarities his position bears to it. For though Kant's starting point in the Second Critique is not a sensible perception, he does start with the *experience* of the moral
law as a fact of reason that is as certain as perception, and this distinguishes his
procedure here from that of the First Critique. In contrast to the third antinomy in
the First Critique, freedom is now a practical fact given in the experience of the
moral law and inseparably bound up with an object, namely the highest good as it
is to be realized in the sensible world. The realizability of this object (its real possibility), however, entails a contradiction in the subject who is to realize it—a contradiction that can be expressed as the antithesis of two propositions: "Thus either
the desire for happiness must be the efficient cause of virtue, or the maxim of
virtue must be the efficient cause of happiness" (5:113).

Both propositions are false and thus the highest good would seem to be impossible. Since, however, the highest good is "a necessary object a priori of our will
and inextricably bound up with the moral law" (5:114), reason finds itself *provoked*
to look beyond the sensible world and to seek the a priori possible correspondence between virtue and happiness in a source *beyond* the sensible world. This
antinomy thereby proves to be not a self-deception of reason, but its "most beneficial error," since it "finally drives us to seek for the key to escape from this labyrinth; and when this key is found it further discovers what we did not seek and yet
need, namely a view into a higher, immutable order of things in which we already

---

[20] For example in Goethe: "Since many of our experiences cannot be roundly formulated and directly communicated, I have for a long time now had recourse to
forms which, though opposed, seem to mirror each other, in order to reveal deeper
meanings [*den geheimeren Sinn*] to the attentive reader" (HABr. 4:250).

are and in which we can hence forth be directed, by determinate precepts, to carry on our existence in accordance with the highest vocation of reason" (5:107–8).

How does Kant go on to resolve the antinomy? It turns out not to be as serious as he initially led us to believe (for didactic reasons). The distinction between the sensible and intelligible worlds which theoretical reason had already drawn is sufficient to resolve it. For that distinction guarantees that it is not impossible that a kind of causality distinct from natural causality produces the connection required such that happiness can figure as the sensible effect of virtue: It is "not impossible," Kant writes, that "morality of disposition should have a connection, and indeed a necessary connection, as cause with happiness as effect in the sensible world, if not immediately, yet mediately (by means of an intelligent author of nature), a connection which, in a nature that is merely an object of the senses, can never occur except contingently and cannot suffice for the highest good" (5:115).

In this way the idea of such an intelligible author of nature is just as inseparably linked with the real possibility of a highest good as the idea of freedom is with the moral law. If freedom is the condition for the moral law, the idea of God is the condition for the real possibility of the *object* of a will determined by that law, and thus the conditions "of applying the morally determined will to its object given to it a priori (the highest good)" (5:4). According to Kant, of course, the possibility of the latter additionally requires the idea of immortality. For the supreme condition of the highest good is the complete accordance of disposition with the moral law. Its possibility is as crucial as that of the highest good itself, and according to Kant that possibility is only given on the assumption of the immortality of the soul. Thus in the *Critique of Practical Reason* God, freedom, and immortality become postulates of pure practical reason, by which Kant understands propositions which, though theoretical in nature, are not capable of theoretical demonstration, inasmuch as they are inseparably attached to an a priori unconditionally valid practical law (cp. 5:122).

In the First Critique's appendix to the dialectic of pure reason, Kant had already attempted to prove that the speculative ideas of reason are not ultimately without employment since they play a role in systemizing experience and thereby fulfill "their purpose, but in a manner which, though useful, is not in accordance with our expectation" (A804). Now he argues that metaphysical propositions concerning God, freedom, and immortality are indeed possible and rationally justifiable, only not as theoretical insights, but as postulates of pure practical reason.

This might seem to suggest that in the First Critique Kant had proven the impossibility of traditional metaphysics, and then, with the doctrine of the postulates, produced a practical transformation of metaphysics or rather limited it to a metaphysics of morals. That, however, would be a false assumption. For two years later, in the *Critique of the Power of Judgment,* Kant once more affirms that his next project will be a "metaphysics of nature and of morals" (5:170). How would it be possible for there to be a metaphysics of nature if this view were correct?

With this question, let us turn to the Third Critique.

6

The "Critical Enterprise": Complete?

No book by Immanuel Kant gained such immediate success as the Third Critique, which eventually came out in 1790. In contrast to the first two *Critiques*, which had initially met with incomprehension and rejection, this work was hailed with instant enthusiasm. Schelling for instance called it "Kant's deepest work, which, if he could have begun with it in the way he finished with it, would have probably given his whole philosophy another direction" (SW X:177). As I mentioned at the end of Chapter 4, Goethe too felt indebted to the book for a "most felicitous period" of his life, and the other great thinkers that will concern us in Part II were likewise deeply influenced by the work and paid tribute to it.

Yet the existence of the book is due solely to Kant's reorientation of transcendental philosophy, undertaken in response to the first review of the *Critique of Pure Reason*. For as the inquiry into the possibility of synthetic judgments a priori advanced to center stage to become the "main transcendental question" (4:280), the question inevitably arose whether the third "faculty of the mind," the feeling of pleasure and displeasure, was perhaps also grounded in such a principle. As late as 1781, Kant had still denied the existence of such a principle (A21). By 1787, however, he was already at work on a "critique of taste" which promised to reveal "a new sort of a priori principles, different from those heretofore observed" (10:514), as he wrote to Reinhold. Let us take a closer look at this critique of taste.

1. Critique of Taste

Like any good philosopher, Kant begins by *defining* taste, namely as "the faculty for the judging of the beautiful. But what is required for calling an object beautiful must be discovered by the analysis of judgments of taste" (5:203).[1] What is special about this kind of judgment?

A judgment of the form 'x is beautiful' is not a cognitive judgment for it fails to determine any object. Beautiful objects have no generic feature in common which makes them beautiful and to which one could point in order to end debate about whether or not they are beautiful. Differently from the judgment 'x is rectangular,' say, where the rule governing the use of the predicate 'rectangular' gives us a way to verify the statement, 'x is beautiful' offers no such possibility. To this extent, judgments of taste are subjective. Judgments of taste do not express any objective property of the object, but rather a subjective pleasure taken in the object.

On the other hand, though, judgments of taste clearly also differ from subjective judgments about merely agreeable things. For we expect, according to Kant, that other people perceiving the object we judge to be beautiful will agree with us, *as though* our judgment were objective. Such an expectation is not normally associated with expressions of the agreeable, in regard to which it is always possible to ask, 'Agreeable for whom?' Indeed, we are at liberty to judge something to be indifferent or even disagreeable which someone else experiences as agreeable. When it comes to beauty, though, we do not ask, 'Beautiful for whom?'—just as we would not ask, 'Rectangular for whom?', when someone informs us of the shape of a table. Though subjective, aesthetic judgments nonetheless lay claim to the same universal validity as an objective or cognitive judgment; and it is this property of aesthetic judgments which demands "no little effort" (5:213) on the part of the transcendental philosopher.

In his pre-critical period, Kant had been convinced that taste had no a priori principle of its own, even though he was perfectly aware that judgments of the form 'x is beautiful' demand consent and thus differ from judgments of what is agreeable. At the time, however, he was only able to explain the fact empirically by assuming the existence of a common sense, or *sensus communis:* "Taste is thus the power of judgment of the senses, through which is cognized what agrees with the sense of others; it is thus a pleasure and displeasure in community with others . . . Agreeable is that which agrees with the private sense; but beautiful is that which agrees with the communal sense" (28:251). To be more precise, when an object

---

[1] The sublime is therefore not part of the original project of a critique of taste. And it was only later that Kant worked it into the text after he had changed the original plan of the book.

agrees with the universal laws of sensibility and exhibits order, harmony, an idea of the whole and so forth, then it must afford universal pleasure. Rules of taste do, therefore, exist, only they are not a priori but empirical and based on what can only be recognized a posteriori.

The result is merely a *de facto* probability of our agreement, a prognostic expectation of others' consent. By 1790, though, Kant finds such mere probability insufficient: "When we call something beautiful, the pleasure that we feel is expected of everyone else in the judgment of taste as necessary, just as if it were to be regarded as a property of the object that is determined in it in accordance with concepts" (5:218). For Kant has now come to be convinced that the claim to universal consent is grounded in an a priori principle for which he can even supply a deduction. Therefore we have a "rightful claim" to everyone's agreement. When others judge differently, not only do we not grant them their opinion; we deny that they have any taste at all, at the same time demanding "that they ought to have it" (5:213). This is the only way to explain "how it is that the feeling in the judgment of taste is expected of everyone *as if it were a duty*" (5:296, emphasis added).

Between these two positions stands the *Critique of Pure Reason* with its new theory of the human faculties of knowledge and their interplay in the cognition of objects. It opened a new perspective on the problem of taste, which was henceforth to be formulated in terms of the general conditions of cognition. Let's have a closer look at the problem.

In the cognition of any object we find an interplay of the understanding and the imagination. The latter combines the manifold of intuition into a unity such that, in a judgment, it can be subsumed under a concept supplied by the understanding. Thus it is the power of judgment which determines the object. If however the object also happens to be beautiful, then the power of judgment senses that the act of subsumption does not exhaust the object or fully do it justice. Upon reflection, the power of judgment finds the understanding and imagination to be in a mutually invigorating and animating "free play" with one another. The subject experiences this state as agreeable and it is bound to be similarly experienced by anyone who possesses the same cognitive faculties: "The animation of both faculties (the imagination and the understanding) to an activity that is *indeterminate* but yet, through the stimulus of the given representation, *in agreement,* namely that which belongs to a cognition in general, is the sensation whose universal communicability is postulated by the judgment of taste"(5:219; emphasis added).

How can two activities be *indeterminate* and at the same time *in agreement*? To answer this question, let us start from the concept Kant uses to characterize the procedure of both the imagination and the understanding: the concept of *'exhibition'*. At 5:287 for instance we read that "taste, as a subjective power of judgment, contains a principle of subsumption, not of intuitions under *concepts,* but of the *faculty* of intuitions or exhibitions (i.e., of the imagination) under the *faculty* of concepts (i.e., the understanding)." And the First Introduction tells us of the understanding that, in the case of aesthetic judgment where no concept is available under which to subsume a given intuition, the power of judgment "holds the imagination (merely in the apprehension of the object) together with the understanding (in the exhibition of a concept in general) and perceives a relation of the two faculties of cognition" (20:223). Since Kant explicitly underscores that the faculty of exhibition "is one and the same as that of apprehension" (5:279) and also states that "the faculty of exhibition is the imagination" (5:232), it is clear that *exhibition* plays a key role for understanding the "free play" of the two cognitive faculties. But what exactly is exhibition?

In the First Critique, Kant had defined the phrase 'to exhibit an object' quite generally as meaning "to relate the representation through which the object is thought to actual or possible experience" (A156). In much the same vein he now explains that exhibition consists "in placing a corresponding intuition beside the concept" (5:192). These remarks clarify what Kant means when he speaks of the understanding as a faculty of exhibiting a concept in general: it is the faculty of applying concepts. Yet in what way can the imagination also be said to be a faculty of exhibition?

As Kant had worked out in the deduction of the categories, three syntheses must come together before cognition of a sensuous object takes place: First the manifold given in intuition must be run through successively before any unity of intuition can emerge (the synthesis of apprehension in intuition). Secondly, the content that has been run through in this way must be reproduced, for apprehension as such does not establish any connection between representations; the past representation must be reproduced alongside the newly apprehended one, for otherwise every new representation would (again) count as the first (synthesis of reproduction in imagination). It is in this context that Kant introduces the term 'imagination' (A101), which he defines more carefully in the second edition as the faculty of representing an object without its being present in intuition (B151). However, this reproduction in imagination must not be arbitrary, nor must it

128

combine the representations in the contingent order in which they occur in perception. Rather, those representations which belong together must be reproduced. The rule which governs the synthesis of reproduction is the *concept* of the relevant object (synthesis of recognition in a concept), for a concept, in Kant's terms, is "what combines the manifold, successively intuited, and thereupon also reproduced, into one representation" (A103).

Thus we see more clearly what it means to call the imagination a faculty of exhibition: It is the faculty of combining previous or possible perceptions of the *same* object with a given perception. When I see a sleeping dog lying on a mat, for instance, and recognize it *as* a dog, I do not merely trace its outlines in my mind in order to distinguish it from its background; rather, I also see it as a being which might jump to its feet at any moment and bark or run to its feeding bowl—even if I have never had any perception of this particular dog prior my present experience of it.[2]

Now that Kant's analysis of aesthetic judgment is coming into relief, we can appreciate how genuinely new it is even in comparison with his own pre-critical reflections. Such a judgment always presupposes a perceptual object to which it is applied. Intuition, imagination, and the understanding must already have worked together to constitute a sensuous object before we can make the judgment 'That is beautiful'. And on Kant's analysis, that judgment is nothing other than the expression of the feeling that the perceived object in its turn initiates a free, mutually animating 'play' between the imagination and the understanding: "The powers of cognition that are set into play by this representation are hereby in a free play, since no *determinate* concept restricts them to a particular rule of cognition" (5:217; emphasis added).

Now that was not the case in the perception of a dog. There the previous or possible perceptions which, as it were, are co-present in the occurrent perception, are previous or possible perceptions of this *dog*. Here the imagination is not free in its animating of the object with non-occurrent

---

[2] Cp. Strawson 1974, 53: "It seems, then, not too much to say that the actual occurrent perception of an enduring object as an object of a certain kind, or as a particular object of that kind, is, as it were, soaked with or animated by or infused with—the metaphors are *à choix*—the thought of past or possible perceptions of the same object."

perceptions, but rather bound to a determinate rule which is expressed in the concept 'dog' and dictated by the understanding.

If the activity of the imagination is truly free, then it must be able to present representations or non-occurrent perceptions without being restricted by any determinate concept dictated by the understanding. This, however, cannot mean that the imagination's activity is arbitrary or lacking any rule in such cases, for in Kant freedom is unthinkable without its own proper order or conformity with rules. The combining of representations by the imagination must not be "entirely groundless" (5:342), but rather of such a kind that the representations *could* belong together without losing their connection to the beautiful object. And if the free play is to be mutual, the representations of imagination must also be such that the understanding *could* apply concepts to them on the basis of the given perception—"indeterminate and *at the same time in agreement*." We are talking about a free play "where the imagination in its freedom arouses the understanding, and the latter, without concepts, sets the imagination into a regular play" (5:296). This last point requires further clarification.

The cognition of an object (of a dog, say) subjects the imagination to compulsion by the understanding; its possible varieties of presentation are restricted by the concept of the object supplied by the understanding. In the case of a beautiful object, however, the imagination is also "free to provide, beyond that concord with the concept, unsought extensive undeveloped material for the understanding, of which the latter took no regard in its concept" (5:317). Kant describes this extensive undeveloped material as "such a manifold of partial representations" or "supplementary representations" in the free employment of the imagination "that no expression designating a determinate concept can be found for it, which therefore allows the addition to a concept of much that is unnamable, the feeling of which animates the cognitive faculties" (5:316). The object judged to be beautiful induces the imagination to present a manifold of partial or supplementary representations of it which occasions much thinking, but can never be combined into a determinate concept. In this its free activity, the imagination demonstrates an "unsought and unintentional subjective purposiveness" (5:317) in regard to the presentation of concepts in general—and thus also its own agreement with the lawfulness of the understanding. For the imagination animates the understanding and expands its concept aesthetically by underlaying it with representations which, though they *could* be part of the presentation of that concept and

130

thus prove to be "related" to it, nevertheless "let one think more than one can express in a concept determined by words" (5:315).

We can now say more precisely what it is that Kant means by the 'free play' of the cognitive faculties. It denotes an essential inexhaustibility of the aesthetic object in the sense that it allows for an indeterminate number of interpretations, no single one of which is definitive or conclusive. The scope of possible interpretations is unlimited and varies over time; new concepts may stimulate the imagination to produce new and unforeseen representations, while the new and unforeseen representations of the imagination may in turn give rise to corresponding combinations of concepts that no one had thought of before. We experience this mutual stimulation of the cognitive faculties as arousing and invigorating, and we express this feeling by saying that the object is beautiful.

Such, then, is Kant's analysis of judgments of taste. Like analysis in general, it answers the question *quid facti,* but does not tell us *quid iuris.* It fails to explain why one "may at the same time demand that everyone should consent to it" (5:278) and why this consent "is expected of everyone as if it were a duty" (5:296). Up to this point the investigation is comparable to Kant's manner of proceeding in the *Prolegomena* or in the first two chapters of the *Groundwork of the Metaphysics of Morals* which also proceed analytically and are therefore in need of completion by a synthetic procedure for deducing the legitimacy of the underlying principle.[3]

That I may expect everyone's consent 'as if it were a duty' can, Kant believes, be explained on the assumption "that the mere universal communicability of his feeling must in itself already involve an interest for us" (5:296). Thus for example the pleasure we take in the good is always bound up with an interest, for it is an object of the pure will. And to will something and to take an interest in its existence are for Kant synonymous. It is for this reason that we as moral beings have an interest in the consequences of our deeds, for the ultimate purpose of our moral actions is precisely to bring the highest good into worldly existence. However, since we can only *postulate* the objective reality of the concept of

---

[3] "Thus the empirical exposition of aesthetic judgments may always make a start at furnishing the material for a higher investigation, yet a transcendental discussion of this faculty is still possible and essential for the critique of taste. For unless this has a priori principles, it could not possibly guide the judgments of others and make claims to approve or reject them with even a semblance of right" (5:278).

the highest good, that is, since we can do no more than *rule out the impossibility* of its being achievable within the world, we have an interest
that nature "should at least show some trace or give a sign" (5:300) that
its physical laws allow for the achievement of our moral purposes. Hence
"the mind cannot reflect on the beauty of *nature* without finding itself at
the same time to be interested in it" (ibid.). For beyond the mere regularity
of its products, nature's beauty shows a purposiveness in relation to our
cognitive faculties such that it sets them into free play. Such agreement of
nature's beautiful products with our faculties must therefore be of interest
to every human being with a sufficiently developed moral sensibility.

Though this would explain why we demand consent to our judgments
of natural beauty, the argument cannot be made to apply without modification to the fine arts. This is why Kant follows up his discussion of aesthetic judgment with an investigation into the nature of the work of art
itself.

What is art? First of all it is the work of an artist or, to use the language of the eighteenth century, the work of a genius. What, then, is a
genius? In addition to his great technical mastery, a genius is characterized by a creative originality which can neither be copied nor made the
object of instruction in accordance with a set of rules. Various abilities
must be learned and mastered before a work of art can emerge, but creative talent as such is a 'gift of nature' that cannot be imparted to students. "Since the talent, as an inborn productive faculty of the artist, itself
belongs to nature, this could also be expressed thus: *Genius* is the inborn
predisposition of the mind (*ingenium*) *through which* nature gives the
rule to art" (5:307).

Kant goes on to characterize this gift of nature as *spirit*, the animating
principle of the mind which, when applied to a given material, acts on the
powers of the mind as a purposive stimulus, setting them into free play.
"Now I maintain that this principle is nothing other than the faculty for
the presentation of *aesthetic ideas;* by an aesthetic idea, however, I mean
that representation of the imagination that occasions much thinking though
without it being possible for any determinate thought, i.e., *concept,* to be
adequate to it" (5:313–14). Aesthetic ideas, then, are the same representations of the aesthetic imagination we encountered before, and thus Kant
can also characterize genius as "the exemplary originality of the natural
endowment of a subject for the *free* use of his cognitive faculties" (5:318).
The artist presents aesthetic ideas by creating as it were "another nature"
(5:314) from the material which primary, actual nature supplies and in

which that second nature is realized. Presentation in the relevant sense is thus a transformation of the given stuff of physical nature in accordance with the paradigm of aesthetic ideas.

Having thus characterized artistic productivity, Kant begins with what he calls the 'dialectic of the aesthetic power of judgment'. Here as in the Second Critique, dialectic no longer consists in a "logic of illusion" (A61, 293); it constitutes instead the site at which the reader is compelled to resolve an antinomy by accepting a distinction between two worlds, namely the sensuously given world and the supersensible world underlying it. Thus for taste Kant again constructs an antinomy. *Thesis:* Judgments of taste are not grounded in concepts, for otherwise they would be verifiable. *Antithesis:* Judgments of taste are grounded in concepts, for otherwise they could lay no claim to others' consent (5:338–39).

Of all the Kantian antinomies this one is perhaps least likely to disturb the reader; basically it just repeats the two peculiarities of aesthetic judgments or their subjective universality. But then again, at this point it no longer takes much to persuade the reader of the plausibility of distinguishing two worlds, either. Even though the foregoing discussion does not make the fact explicit, it is already clear that the 'nature' which supplies art with a rule by endowing the genius with a special talent or 'gift' cannot be the physical nature of the First Critique, the one constituted by the transcendental principles of the understanding. The talent which enables the genius to use the material of the physical world to create a second world in accordance with the paradigm of aesthetic ideas is every bit as independent of the causal mechanism of the physical world as our cognitive powers are when they constitute sensuous objects.

At this point Kant only needs to make one last step in his argumentation to reach the goal of his deduction. Genius, as we said, creates as it were a second nature from the material of nature as it is initially given to it. It accomplishes this by using the material to present the representations characterized above as supplementary representations or aesthetic ideas of given concepts. In this way, the concepts are underlaid with a corresponding intuition, but not directly so, as would be the case with an empirical realization of the concept or with the schematization of a category, but rather indirectly by means of analogy. Here Kant introduces the term 'symbolic presentation', illustrating it with the following example. When a monarchic state is governed by the internal laws of the people, it is symbolized by a living body, but by a machine (e.g. a hand mill) when it is governed by a single absolute will. The hand mill which crushes its contents is used symbolically to indicate what the despot does to the citizens of his state. Although there is no similarity between a despotic state and a hand mill, there is a similarity in the way we reflect on their modes of action and the rules that guide our reflection. According to Kant, symbolic, analogical presentation is to be explained as a "transportation of the reflection on one object of intuition to another, quite different concept, to which perhaps no intuition can ever directly correspond" (5:352–53). At this point, then, Kant has gathered all the elements he needs to conclude his deduction and vindicate the claim to universal assent which we associate a priori with judgments of taste: "Now I say that the beautiful is the symbol of the morally good, and also that *only in this respect* . . . does it please with a claim to the assent of everyone else" (5:353, emphasis added). What is the substance of this thesis? In the first place we are dealing with two objects in the widest sense of the word: the beautiful on the one side, and the morally good, i.e. "the ultimate end of humanity" (5:298), on the other. If the first object, the beautiful, is a symbol of the other, the morally good, then there must be an analogy between the ways in which we reflect on both. In the case of the beautiful Kant says that "in regard to the objects of such a pure satisfaction" the power of judgment "gives the law to itself, just as reason does with regard to the faculty of desire" (5:353). We saw in the last chapter how it is that reason gives the law to itself with regard to the faculty of desire: "This law," Kant wrote in the *Critique of Practical Reason,* "is to furnish the sensible world, as a *sensible nature* (in what concerns rational beings), with the form of a world of the understanding, that is, of a *supersensible* nature, though without infringing upon the mechanism of the former" (5:43).

If we compare the mode of reflection in the two areas, we discover a previously unnoticed similarity. Moral reflection consists in the consciousness of a non-empirical law, the moral law with which we compare our maxims, and in the choice of a sequence of actions suited to realizing that which ought to be in the physical world. As moral agents, we change the state of the actual world in accordance with the idea of another world. We are "conscious through reason of a law to which all our maxims are subject, as if a natural order must at the same time arise from our will. This law must therefore be the idea of a nature not given empirically and yet possible through freedom, hence a supersensible nature to which we give objective reality at least in a practical respect, since we regard it as an object of our will as pure rational beings" (5:44). In a strictly analogous manner, the artist uses his creative talent (the gift of nature which supplies art with its rule) to create a second nature, as it were, from the material of the first by bringing about a presentation of aesthetic ideas. In each of these two cases, a new form is bestowed upon existing reality, a form which is to be regarded as the presentation of supersensible ideas, be they moral or aesthetic in character. To a certain extent, the beautiful symbolizes the act of a morally good human being, and it is for this reason (and only for this reason) that I have a right to expect that others will take pleasure in the beautiful just as they do in the good.

Kant's moral theory and his aesthetics are complementary and mutually reinforcing, and they could only take the form they did because of the groundwork Kant laid in the *Critique of Pure Reason*. The paradox of subjective universality that characterizes judgments of taste only becomes comprehensible against the background of Kant's ethics of autonomy whose fundamental concept, freedom, in turn presupposes the transcendental idealism of the First Critique. The enthusiasm with which Kant wrote to Reinhold of his discovery of the systematic nature of our cognitive powers is understandable. Yet there is more to it than this alone. For what does it mean for Kant to say that in regard to the beautiful the power of judgment "gives the law to itself," just as reason does in regard to the faculty of desire?

If Kant's analysis of judgments of taste is right and beauty consists in our awareness of the free play of imagination and understanding, we discover a further implication which could not have been foreseen from the outset. It follows, namely, that only beings with both these cognitive powers can be open and receptive to the beautiful. "Agreeableness is also valid for nonrational animals; beauty is valid only for human beings, i.e., animal but also rational beings, but not merely as the latter (e.g., spirits), rather as beings who are at the same time animal; the good, however, is valid for every rational being in general" (5:210).

Only human beings can experience beauty! Now beauty in nature is an empirical fact. Although the existence of beautiful natural forms is, of course, from the standpoint of the First Critique, pure coincidence, this is not the case when viewed from the standpoint of our reflective power of judgment. Just as it requires genius to make fine art out of the material of nature, so too does nature itself, in the very midst of its blindly mechanical causality, reveal within its beautiful forms something which defies mechanical explanation and "through which the object seems as it were to be predetermined for our power of judgment" (5:245). It is as though the object were predetermined to elicit in us that free play of our faculties and the mutual animation that goes with it—as though its beautiful forms were *intended* to draw us humans (and only us) beyond the sensuously given by creatively expanding our imagination and thus setting the faculty of intellectual ideas (reason) into motion and awakening the understanding, occasioning much thinking. Without the assumption of such an intention the experience would remain incomprehensible, though even with the assumption we are powerless to explain it since no such intention is actually known to us. Here the power of judgment is not determinative, but only reflective: it is aware of purposiveness only, without any (intentional) purpose.

Nonetheless: Since natural beauty is given *de facto*—"the reality of the beauties of nature is open to experience" (5:291)—and these beauties cannot be understood as exceptions to natural law (for then they would be miracles), the power of judgment finds itself compelled to base its reflection on the principle that nature, in its beautiful forms and their regularities, accommodates itself to the power of judgment. Or as Kant himself puts it, "The self-sufficient beauty of nature reveals to us a technique of nature, which makes it possible to represent it as a system in accordance with laws the principle of which we do not encounter anywhere in our entire faculty of understanding, namely that of a purposiveness with respect to the use of the power of judgment in regard to appearances, so that this must be judged as belonging not merely to nature in its purposeless mechanism but rather also to the analogy with art. Thus it actually expands not our cognition of natural objects, but our concept of nature, namely as mere mechanism, into the concept of nature as art: which invites profound investigations into the possibility of such a form" (5:246).

That invitation, however, must also extend to an investigation of the extent of the principle, for according to Kant the critique of a faculty invariably calls for determination of its sources, extent, and limits (Axii). Thus the critical project undergoes a further expansion, for teleological judgments prove to be just as much a part of the reflective power of judgment as aesthetic judgments are and to have the same principle as their basis, namely the formal purposiveness of nature. As Kant explains in the Introduction, written only after the whole of the work had been completed, it is obviously appropriate to regard natural beauty as the presentation of the concept of *subjective* purposiveness and natural organisms as presentations of an *objective* purposiveness, "the first of which we judge through taste (aesthetically, by means of the feeling of pleasure), the other

136

through understanding and reason (logically, in accordance with concepts)" (5:193; translation modified). Therefore a critique of teleological judgment must follow upon the critique of taste so that both together can comprise a *Critique of the Power of Judgment*.

Before I turn to teleology, one concluding remark on the overall systematic form and, indirectly, on the problem of the highest good that concerned us in the preceding chapter is in order. The principle of purposiveness, as established a priori by the power of judgment, makes it possible to reconcile both the legislation by theoretical reason and that by practical reason and also their realizability within the world, although this reconciliation takes place in the supersensible substratum. Purposiveness compels us "to look beyond the sensible and seek the unifying point of all our faculties a priori in the supersensible: because no other way remains to make reason self-consistent" (5:341). Therefore Kant is quite right when he states, in the Introduction, that a critique of pure reason would be incomplete if it did not include a critique of the power of judgment as a special part of itself (5:168). A self-sufficient systematic unity is impossible unless all three parts are taken together; in isolation, each of the works stands in need of the others.[4] Yet the ultimate condition of that unity lies in the supersensible realm—that is the result of Kant's critical philosophy. Our faculty of knowledge gazes inevitably into the intelligible, "and it sees itself, both on account of this inner possibility in the subject as well as on account of the outer possibility of a nature that corresponds to it, as related to something in the subject itself and outside of it, which is neither nature nor freedom, but which is connected with the ground of the latter, namely the supersensible, in which the theoretical faculty is combined with the practical, in a mutual and unknown way, to form a unity" (5:353).

---

[4] "Through the possibility of its a priori laws for nature the understanding gives a proof that nature is cognized by us only as appearance, and hence at the same time an indication of its supersensible substratum; but it leaves this entirely *undetermined*. The power of judgment, through its a priori principle for judging nature in accordance with possible particular laws for it, provides for its supersensible substratum (in us as well as outside us) *determinability through the intellectual faculty*. But reason provides *determination* for the same substratum through its practical law a priori; and thus the power of judgment makes possible the transition from the domain of the concept of nature to that of the concept of freedom" (5:196).

2. Critique of the Teleological Power of Judgment

We form the concept of natural purpose because experience shows that certain products (organisms), though subject to natural laws, are not susceptible to explanation by natural mechanisms: The form and function of such bodies would remain incomprehensible to us if we did not take recourse to a concept of purpose borrowed from the art of making artifacts. For whereas a mechanically produced entity can be explained as the sum of its parts, an organic product of nature seems to be characterized by mutual interdependence of part and whole. As Kant points out, we know of only one way in which the whole makes possible the parts (instead of being mechanically determined by and dependent on the parts) and that is the case of human determination of ends where the *idea* of the whole (e.g. of a house or a watch) precedes and determines the production and arrangement of the parts. The concept of human purpose, however, cannot be constitutive for organisms: organisms are products of *nature*, not artifacts, and cannot therefore be explained as purposes of a rational being external to them. This is why Kant speaks of '*natural* purposes'— here the parts and the whole are *by their own nature* reciprocally cause and effect of each other.[5] "Strictly speaking, the organization of nature is therefore not analogous with any causality that we know" (5:375).

Even so, the concept of purpose cannot simply be abandoned in our assessment of natural purposes because they cannot be made intelligible purely on the basis of the laws of motion (their "causality as a blind mechanism," 5:360). Purpose thus becomes a concept of the reflective power of judgment. Whereas in the case of natural beauty the power of judgment compared understanding and imagination, here its comparative reflection is directed toward the understanding and *reason*, for even empirical knowledge of the causes and effects of an organized being requires concepts of reason: "An organized being is thus not a mere machine, for that has only a *motive* power, while the organized being possesses in itself a *formative* power, and indeed one that it communicates to the matter, which it does not have (it organizes the latter): thus it has a self-propagating formative power, which cannot be explained through the capacity for movement alone (that is, mechanism)" (5:374).

---

[5] Hume, too, had characterized "all animals and vegetable" in *A Treatise of Human Nature* by "the reciprocal relation of cause and effect in all their actions and operations" (Book I, Part IV, Section VI).

Since the existence of organized beings is a fact of experience, the concept of a non-practical, *natural* purpose gains "objective reality" (5:376). Now, no organized, living thing can exist in isolation; it is part of a reproductive chain within its species and is in a constant process of exchange with its environment—with other living things that serve as food, for instance, but also with light, air, and water without which it could not exist. It is a quite general truth that, assuming the existence of purposes as the reason why certain things exist, means for achieving those purposes must also be assumed whose functions and laws are explicable in purely mechanical terms, but which are in themselves at the same time subordinate or secondary effects of the purposes. Thus one can conceive of a very extensive or even universal connection between mechanical and teleological laws in the products of nature, without however confusing or conflating the principles of their judgment:

> For this concept leads reason into an order of things entirely different from that of a mere mechanism of nature, which will here no longer satisfy us. An idea has to ground the possibility of the product of nature. However, since this is an absolute unity of the representation, while the matter is a multitude of things, which by itself can provide no determinate unity of composition, if that unity of the idea is even to serve as the unifying ground a priori of a natural law of the causality of such a form of the composite, then the end of nature must extend to *everything* that lies in its product. For once we have related such an effect in the *whole* to a supersensible determining ground beyond the blind mechanism of nature, we must also judge it entirely in accordance with this principle . . . [T]his concept necessarily leads to the idea of the whole of nature as a system in accordance with the rules of ends, to which idea all of the mechanism of nature in accordance with principles of reason must now be subordinated (at least in order to test natural appearance by this idea)" (5:377–79).

Of course this is not to imply that the purposiveness here assumed is *intentional*, but only that in reflecting about certain products of nature the power of judgment must employ the principle "that once we have discovered in nature a capacity for bringing forth products that can only be conceived by us in accordance with the concept of final causes, we may go further and also judge to belong to a system of ends even those things . . . which do not make it necessary to seek another principle of their possibility beyond the mechanism of blindly acting causes; because the former idea already, as far as its ground is concerned, leads us beyond the sensible world, and the unity of the supersensible principle must then be considered as valid in the same way not merely for certain species of natural beings but for the whole of nature as a system" (5:380–81).

Here, too, Kant points out an antinomy. For in mechanism and purposiveness (blindness and intention), two principles confront each other which, as far as our insight goes, cannot both be grounds for explaining one and the same object: what is only made possible by a purpose cannot be brought about by an efficient cause, and vice versa. Kant presents the antinomy as follows. "*Thesis:* All generation of material things is possible in accordance with merely mechanical laws. *Antithesis:* Some generation of such things is not possible in accordance with merely mechanical laws" (5:387). It might seem as though this antinomy were easy to resolve: For the power of judgment, mechanism and teleology are two maxims guiding our empirical description of nature, and they only begin to contradict each other when we employ them as *constitutive* principles for explaining the possibility of objects. In fact they are only rules for how the power of judgment (which does not have any constitutive principles of its own) ought to reflect upon *already given* objects of experience. Thus they only have any bearing on the appropriate use of our subjective faculties of cognition, not on the origin of the objects themselves.

If this were really enough, then we would not be dealing here with a genuine antinomy. It is constitutive for an antinomy that thesis and antithesis are *either* grounded in the legislation of the cognitive faculty itself (First Critique), and hence represent more than merely heuristic rules, *or* that they force us to overstep the bounds of experience in order to resolve the contradiction (Second Critique). One of these two alternatives must be the case here, as well, if what we are dealing with is in fact an antinomy of the teleological power of judgment.

In the context of "the resolution of the above antinomy," this last point occasions a "remark" (sect. 76) by Kant whose brevity and unimposing title are apt to disguise its extraordinary significance. It is a remark which according to Kant "would certainly deserve to be elaborated in detail in transcendental philosophy," but which "can come in here only as a digression, for elucidation (not for the proof of what has here been expounded)" (5:401). He could hardly have guessed what immense importance this episodic 'remark' was to have for the development of the philosophy that would follow him. I claim that its 'detailed elaboration' provides a key to understanding the movement of thought that culminates in Hegel and which we will consider at length in the second part of this book. Schelling remarked of this passage that "Never, perhaps, have so many deep thoughts been pressed together in so few pages as is the case in section 76 of the Critique of the Teleological Power of Judgment" (AA I,2:175; SW I:242). What, then, is the substance of this episodic 'elucidation'?

With the aid of three examples, Kant attempts to show generally and for all three human cognitive faculties that certain ideas of reason—such as that of natural purpose—possess incontrovertible validity for us humans, even though this does not license us to infer that the ground of their validity lies in the object. The nature of our cognitive faculties commits us to a certain view of the world without, however, entitling us to assume that there is anything in the objects corresponding to it.

Kant's first example pertains to the inevitable distinction between the possibility and actuality of things, crucial to the theoretical employment of reason. This distinction presupposes two heterogeneous, but interrelated cognitive components, namely the understanding and sensible intuition. Whatever is sensuously given is actual; whatever is not given, but can be conceived without contradiction, is possible. If the mere act of thinking sufficed to bring about the existence of the corresponding objects, everything would be actual for us. Our understanding is not intuitive, however, but discursive and thus dependent upon an intuition that is sensible, i.e. receptive, and in which the object of thought has to be given. We must not, however, be led to assume that every cognitive being is subject to such a condition. Thus Kant writes, "The propositions . . . that things can be possible without being actual, and thus that there can be no inference at all from mere possibility to actuality, quite rightly holds for the human understanding without that proving that this distinction lies in the things themselves" (5:402).

Kant's second example pertains to the faculty of desire. As a finite rational being endowed with a will, I have no choice but to attribute to myself causality through freedom and to assume a moral law entailing the necessity of certain actions. At the same time, however, since I am also a sensuous being and a part of nature, so that the prescribed actions are always contingent in regard to the causality of natural law and could just as well fail to occur, the moral law goes by the name of duty and appears as a commandment. For reason, in other words, the necessity that corresponds to the moral law takes the form of an '*ought*', and not that of being or of an event. For a faculty of reason whose employment was free from this subjective condition of sensibility, however, this distinction would collapse. The opposition between "what ought to be done and what is done, between a practical law concerning that which is possible through us and the theoretical law concerning that which is actual through us" (5:404; translation modified) is therefore only valid for a practical rational being which is also sensuous and whose causality does not coincide with that of the sensible world.

The third example, finally, is the one that is at the core of all these reflections and which Kant intends as the promised "elucidation" of the antinomy. Since in cognition our understanding, being discursive, always moves from the universal to the particular, it is incapable of making any cognitive judgment about the lawfulness of organized objects of nature until some universal law has been discovered under which it could subsume them and from which their specific features could be derived. Yet we know of no such law: from the standpoint of the transcendental lawfulness of nature, organisms are contingent. As products of nature, however, they are lawful. Since the "lawfulness of the contingent is called purposiveness" (5:404) and the concept of purpose is known to us only from the context of human action, "the concept of the purposiveness of nature in its products is a concept that is necessary for the human power of judgment in regard to nature but does not pertain to the determination of the objects themselves, thus a subjective principle of reason for the power of judgment which, as regulative (not constitutive), is just as necessarily valid for our *human power of judgment* as if it were an objective principle" (ibid.).

The possibility of a concept of natural purpose thus rests on a peculiarity of the human understanding, as section 77 goes on to elaborate. What makes it appear to be a constitutive principle is the fact that experience constantly supplies us with examples of such beings in which necessity and contingency seem to be simultaneously instantiated: "(the product itself) is given in nature, after all" (5:405; translation modified). Yet it is only due to the peculiarity of our discursive understanding that the simultaneity of blind necessity and intentionality appears to us as a contradiction. As Kant points out, though, we can only become aware of this peculiarity by contrasting it with "the idea of a possible understanding other than the human one (as in the *Critique of Pure Reason* we had to have in mind

142

another possible intuition if we were to hold our own to be a special kind, namely one that is valid of objects merely as appearances)" (ibid.).

In our discussion of Jacobi in the previous chapter we saw why it is that we have to take account of the possibility of a different kind of *intuition*. If the objects of intuition are appearances, then we must also assume there to be things in themselves which, although unknowable, must nevertheless be conceived as more than mere figments of the imagination, for otherwise we could not consistently conceive appearances as genuine representations of sensibility rather than of thought. This however implies that things in themselves must be conceived in such a way that a being with another, non-receptive intuition *could* in fact perceive them and know them to be actual.

But why does the resolution of the teleological antinomy now demand the assumption of another possible *understanding*? Though the transcendental concept of nature peculiar to our human understanding leaves the particulars undetermined, so that the diversity and multiplicity of particular products of nature is contingent, they must nevertheless accord with the lawfulness of nature and the unity of experience. "[I]n order for us to be able at least to conceive of the possibility of such an agreement of the things of nature with the power of judgment (which we represent as contingent, hence as possible only through an end aimed at it), we must at the same time conceive of another understanding, in relation to which, and indeed prior to any end attributed to it, we can represent that agreement of natural laws with our power of judgment, which for our understanding is conceivable only through ends as the means of connection, as *necessary*" (5:407).[6]

Kant is not claiming, then, that such a (divine) understanding exists, nor that the possibility of organisms actually presupposes the representation of

---

[6] Because of this, the principle of the reflective power of judgment "can be nothing other than this: that since universal laws of nature have their ground in our understanding, which prescribes them to nature (although only in accordance with the universal concept of it as nature), the particular empirical laws, in regard to that which is left undetermined in them by the former, must be considered in terms of the sort of unity they would have if an understanding (even if not ours) had likewise given them for the sake of our faculty of cognition, in order to make possible a system of experience in accordance with particular laws of nature. Not as if in this way such an understanding must really be assumed (for it is only the reflecting power of judgment for which this idea serves as a principle, for reflecting, not for determining); rather this faculty thereby gives a law only to itself, and not to nature" (5:180).

any end. His claim is only that the constitution of our discursive faculty of cognition forces upon us the concept of natural purpose and with it the idea of an understanding from which the distinctive features of natural purposes could be lawfully derived. Kant then goes on, however, to characterize this understanding as an intuitive faculty which "goes from the *synthetically universal* (of the intuition of a whole as such) to the particular, i.e., from the whole to the parts, in which, therefore, and in whose representation of the whole, there is no *contingency* in the combination of the parts, in order to make possible a determinate form of the whole" (ibid.). This characterization reveals that that other understanding which we must be able to conceive in order to resolve the antinomy of the power of judgment need not in fact be a divine or causative understanding. It suffices for it to be an intuitive understanding which goes from the whole to the parts; whether or not it is causally responsible for the whole need not be decided. For as Kant explicitly emphasizes, it is undeniably possible that "another (higher) understanding than the human one might be able to find the ground of the possibility of such products of nature even in the mechanism of nature, i.e., in a causal connection for which an understanding does not have to be exclusively assumed as a cause" (5:406). Note that Kant refers here to the *products* of nature and not necessarily to the whole of nature.

This is the real result of section 77. The antinomy of the power of judgment does indeed lead to the idea of a possible faculty of understanding different from ours. Yet in order to grasp that the concept of natural purpose is conditioned by the discursivity of our understanding, all we really need is the possibility of a non-discursive understanding, just as in the *Critique of Pure Reason* we needed merely to contemplate the possibility of a non-sensible faculty of intuition in order to be able to conceive sensible objects as appearances and thus resolve the antinomy of theoretical reason. In contrast to his rather sporadic remarks about a different possible faculty of intuition in the First Critique, however, Kant here works out his ideas systematically and in a way that applies to all three faculties of the mind, the faculties of cognition and desire, and the power of judgment: *Because* understanding and intuition are two independent stems of knowledge, we are forced to distinguish between possibility and actuality (which would not be the case for an intellectual intuition); *because* we are both sensuous and rational beings, the moral law appears to us as an ought, not as a being or willing (which would not be the case for a holy will); *because* our understanding is discursive, we inevitably judge organisms as natural ends (which would not be the case for an intuitive understanding).

Now what I find most significant is the fact that Kant's considerations here bring not one, but *two* alternative faculties of cognition into play, neither of which can be reduced to the other. First we have a non-sensible, i.e. *intellectual intuition* for which possibility (thinking) and actuality (being) coincide. And secondly an *intuitive understanding* which goes from the intuition of the whole to its parts and thus perceives no contingency in the way the parts are assembled into a whole. Previous Kant scholarship has failed to recognize that these are in fact two distinct faculties. Astonishingly, the literature persists in identifying the two despite the fact that they are not the same—for in the first case the faculty is characterized by the opposition between receptivity and spontaneity, and in the second case by that of discursivity and intuition. Just as little as discursive understanding and sensible intuition are identical, neither are their alternatives: intuitive understanding and intellectual intuition. In order to gain more clarity about how Kant intended the distinction it will be helpful to consider the origin of this pair of concepts.

Historical Excursus

In 1753 the Prussian Academy of Sciences announced a prize competition to be judged in 1755. The task it set was to compare the 'system' of Alexander Pope, expressed in the proposition: "Everything is good," with Leibniz' system of optimism or divine choice of the best, expressed in his theodicy with its doctrine of the actual world as the best of all possible worlds. Beyond mere comparison, the Academy also demanded an account of "the most important reasons either for upholding this system or for destroying it."[7] The competition stirred considerable controversy with its barely disguised attack on Leibniz; the intention was obviously to reduce Pope's 'optimism' to absurdity and do away with Leibniz' at the same stroke. Protest was widespread. Lessing and Mendelssohn for example co-authored a text which, though they did not submit it, they published anonymously in the same year as the presentation of the prize with the title, "Pope—a Metaphysician!" In it they argued that it was illegitimate to criticize a poet like Pope as

---

[7] On the prize competition, its background, and the offense it caused, see Adolf Harnack 1901, 310–14. Pope's "system" refers to Alexander Pope's treatise in verse, entitled *Essay on Man* (1734); Mineola, NY: Dover 1994 which contains the dictum, "Whatever is, is right" (I, line 295).

though he were a philosopher, and sought to defend Leibniz against the indirect attack that had been launched against him.

Kant, too, who at the time was just twenty-nine years of age, seems to have seriously considered entering the competition whose challenge, astonishingly, he took literally: We find, for example, at the top of the third surviving page of his manuscript the title, "Comparison of Pope's System with Optimism; Superiority of the Former" (17:233). So he not only views Pope as a metaphysician, but even considers him (in this point) to be superior to Leibniz! To understand why, it is best to begin with the summary of the doctrine of the origin of evil that Leibniz himself gives in section 335 of the *Theodicy*. The ancients took matter, which they believed to be uncreated and independent of God, to be the cause of all evil in the world. Such a view is no longer possible today, Leibniz writes:

> Matter in itself is indifferent to all forms, and God made it. Evil springs rather from the *Forms* themselves in their detached state, that is, from the ideas that God has not produced by an act of his will, any more than he thus produced numbers and figures, and all possible essences which one must regard as eternal and necessary; for they are in the ideal region of the possibles, that is, in the divine understanding. *God is therefore not the author of essences in so far as they are only possibilities. But there is nothing actual to which he has not decreed and given existence;* and he has permitted evil because it is involved in the best plan existing in the region of possibles, a plan which supreme wisdom could not fail to choose. This notion satisfies at once the wisdom, the power and the goodness of God, and yet leaves a way open for the entrance of evil. God gives perfection to creatures in so far as it is possible in the universe.[8]

Kant finds two fundamental flaws in this theory. God contemplates the eternal essences in his understanding, sees that their partial incompatibility allows for various combinations, and then decides to actualize the best possible one, which happens also to contain evils. Or as Leibniz puts it, God wills "*antecedently* the good and *consequently* the best" (sect. 23). He does not, however, explain why it is that the essences are incompatible in the first place so that such a conflict within God is even possible, and that means for Kant that he does not really explain the origin of evil, but simply shifts it to another level: The whole mistake is rooted in the fact that "Leibniz identifies the scheme of the best world on the one

---

[8] [Tr.: Leibniz, *Theodicy*, ed. Austin Farrer, trans. E. M. Huggard (London: Routledge and Kegan Paul, 1951), sect. 335, emphasis added.]

hand with a kind of independence, and on the other hand with dependence on the will of God" (17:237).

The second flaw Kant finds is no less serious. Leibniz' explanation only justifies the evils and absurdities we perceive in the world if we are already convinced that God exists and that he wills the best, whereas on the contrary the "universal agreement of the arrangements of the world, if they can be acknowledged to exist in and for themselves, itself furnishes the most beautiful proof of the existence of God and of the universal dependency of all things on Him" (17:238). The 'most beautiful proof' refers here to the physico-theological proof which recognizes God by the "excellent arrangements which the world everywhere displays," and this proof is "invalidated by Leibniz' theoretical scheme" (ibid.). If the essential possibilities are independent of God's will and antecedent to his decision, then divine wisdom cannot be recognized by the ordering of things within the world: "The being of the world is not as it is simply because God wishes to have it so, but because it was not possible in any other way" (17:238).

Surprisingly, Kant finds the outline for a solution to the problem in Pope who, according to him, has chosen a path which "is the best suited of all possible paths. This path—and it is precisely this which constitutes the perfection of his system— even subjects every possibility to the dominion of an all-sufficient original Being; under this Being things can have no other properties, not even those which are called essentially necessary" (17:233–34).

We need not decide here whether Kant is entirely faithful to Pope's intentions in this matter. What is important is, first of all, that Pope (as Kant understands him) subjects the eternal essences themselves and thus all possibility whatsoever to the will of God, and that he is able to do this, secondly, precisely because he searches out creation for whatever seems to lack harmony and then shows that even the things we might wish were absent from the course of the world ultimately serve the advantage of all else, *and that they do so according to the law of nature:* "The essential and necessary determination of things, the universal laws which are not placed in relation to each other by any forced union into a harmonious scheme, will adapt themselves as if spontaneously to the attainment of purposes which are perfect" (17:234).

Kant did not take part in the Academy's competition; instead, he took up the points he had interpreted as Pope's strengths relative to Leibniz and gave them book-length treatment in two works that both appeared in 1755, the same year in which the Academy awarded its prize—the *Universal Natural History and Theory of the Heavens* (each of the three parts of which bore an epigraph taken from Pope's *Essay on Man*) and the *Nova Dilucidatio*.

147

In the *Universal Natural History,* which is also intended as a physico-theology, Kant starts from the assumption that matter was originally dissolved in a primordial chaos, and then attempts to demonstrate how the interplay of Newton's two basic forces of attraction and repulsion suffice to generate from that chaos the harmonious interconnections we know as our solar system and the system of the fixed stars. "When her forces are left to themselves nature is fruitful in splendid developments even in chaos, and the formation subsequent to it brings along such magnificent relations and harmonies for the common benefit of creation that even in the eternal and unchanging laws of their essential properties they reveal to us with unmistakable certainty that great Being in which by means of their common dependence they unite to a total harmony" (1:293).

In the *Nova Dilucidatio* Kant develops the idea that the possibilities or eternal essences cannot in any way be conceived as independent of God. It is the same idea we encountered in Chapter 4 when we observed how Jacobi employed it in his interpretation of Spinoza.[9] It is the idea, namely, that possibilities require realities to serve as the material for possible concepts, and that these realities must be united in a single being. Kant expresses this idea in the *Nova Dilucidatio* when he writes, "There is a Being, the existence of which is prior to the very possibility both of Itself and of all things. This Being is, therefore, said to exist absolutely necessarily. This Being is called God."[10]

The point of discussing the Academy's prize competition on optimism has been to illuminate the physico-theological background against which the distinction between an intuitive understanding and intellectual intuition reveals its contours. The former concept primarily refers to the way in which the divine understanding, which contains the sum of all possibilities, intuits itself, while the latter denotes its faculty of actualizing the combinations chosen from among those possibilities. For the basic concept of physico-theology (as Kant had presented it for example in the latter part of the 1770s in the so-called *Metaphysik Pölitz*) is that of a primordial being as the cause of nature. Because that being is the substratum of the possibility of all things, the possibility of all order and perfection must also be contained within it. Since a non-contingent order is inconceivable in the absence of an understanding, we must also attribute understanding to the primordial being. Since objects can only exist through the understanding of the primordial being, it possesses knowledge of all

---

[9] Jacobi adopted the idea from Kant's *One Possible Basis* where it appeared again in 1763 in a slightly modified form.

[10] "Datur ens, cuius exsistentia praevertit ipsam et ipsius et omnium rerum possibilitatem, quod ideo absolute necessario existere dicitur. Vocatur Deus" (1:395, prop. vii).

possible objects just insofar as it possesses knowledge of itself. To see how this is so, we must start with the assumption "that He knows the parts through the whole, and not the whole through the parts, for he knows everything and determines all things *limitando*" (28:328). Since there is nothing outside of God and God is essentially one, determinations must be conceived as limitations of God's essence (in a way analogous to geometry where figures arise as limitations of space). Divine knowledge is therefore non-conceptual, for concepts according to Kant are representations, formed by abstraction, of general marks or features of particular things. Conceptual knowledge moves by way of abstraction from the particular to the universal, whereas divine knowledge moves by way of limitation from the universal to the particular. "The primordial understanding is therefore intuitive" (28:329)—that is, it is an intuitive understanding.[11]

If God knows of all possibilities of things insofar as he knows himself, then how does God know things *in their actuality*? Not in the way that we do: He knows things not by way of affections, that is by the effect objects have on him, for the divine understanding is independent of things; rather, he knows them by being conscious of having created them: "God knows all possible things insofar as he is aware of Himself; He knows all actual things insofar as He is conscious of His decision to create them" (28:331). What Kant is referring to in this lecture when he speaks of God's consciousness of his decision to create the things of actuality is the same as what he normally calls intellectual intuition: "Divine intuition, however, which is the ground of objects, and not the consequence of objects, is, since it is independent, an original intuition and for that reason perfectly intellectual."[12]

The lecture on metaphysics belongs to Kant's pre-critical period, but we would be wrong to reproach him here with dogmatism. He explicitly states that no human can grasp what the divine understanding is. Our knowledge is merely symbolic. We have nothing to go on but our own discursive understanding and all we can be certain of is that the divine understanding must be intuitive rather than discursive. "Yet we cannot comprehend the manner in which this understanding intuits, for we have no other intuition than the sensible" (28:330). From the standpoint of the critical philosophy, however, neither do we need to comprehend the

---

[11] This is also the reason why there are no concepts to be found in the divine understanding, but only ideas: "An idea is a cognition *which is itself the ground of possibility for its object.* Divine cognitions contain the ground of possibility for all things. The divine *intuitus* contains the ideas according to which we ourselves are possible; *cognitio divina est cognitio archetypa*, and his ideas are the archetypes of things" (28:329).

[12] "Divinus autem intuitus, qui obiectorum est principium, non principiatum, cum sit independens, est archetypus et propterea perfecte intellectualis" (2:397).

way this understanding does its intuiting since it now serves only as a limiting concept, as a possible alternative to keep in mind lest we are tempted to believe that our cognitive faculty is the only possible kind. And so it happened that with Kant's critique of rational theology and his insight into the impossibility of a physico-theological proof, this pair of concepts soon blurred into a *mere*—and seemingly singular—limiting concept unworthy of sustained attention. As the critical philosophy developed further, however, and continued to gain in complexity, so too the question became increasingly acute what exactly these concepts were intended to delimit.

Let us return one last time to the *Critique of the Teleological Power of Judgment.* As we have seen, Kant distinguishes between purposiveness in particular products of nature and a purposiveness of nature as a whole. We have also seen that he characterizes the intuitive understanding in two different ways. On the one hand he gives a merely negative characterization of it as non-discursive, as an understanding "which does not go from the universal to the particular and thus to the individual (through concepts)" (5:406). In the case of *particular* products of nature such an understanding is able to "represent the possibility of the parts (as far as both their constitution and their combination is concerned) as depending upon the whole" and thus to determine the particular on the basis of the "synthetically universal" (5:407). On the other hand, however, the intuitive understanding is also characterized as an understanding which has nature as a whole, "indeed the whole of nature as a system" (5:409) as its object and would thus have to be conceived by us "as cause of the world" (5:410).

But let us also take a closer look at intellectual intuition. Kant says that when reading the *Critique of Pure Reason,* the idea of intellectual intuition is just as essential to our conception of intuition as sensibility, as the idea of an intuitive understanding is in the Third Critique if we are to conceive of organisms as natural purposes. Kant's remark refers on the one hand to the revised version of the deduction in the second edition, in the course of which he insists no less than six times (B135, 138f., 145, 149, 153, 159) that the deduction is only valid for an understanding that does not create its own objects and whose function it is exclusively to produce a priori connections within the manifold of a given intuition and to bring it under the unity of apperception. If our intuition were not sensible but productive, a deduction of the categories would be impossible, but also superfluous: "an understanding . . .

through whose representation the objects of the representation should at the same time exist—would not require, for the unity of consciousness, a special act of synthesis of the manifold. For the human understanding, however, which thinks only, and does not intuit, that act is necessary" (B139).

Now in section 77 of the Teleological Power of Judgment, Kant also refers to intellectual intuition as a logically possible intuition of the non-sensible substratum of appearances, i.e. of the thing in itself, thus continuing a line of thought from the chapters on phaenomena and noumena from the First Critique. There too he had explicitly pointed out that our way of intuiting things is to be distinguished from the way those things are in themselves and that our sensibility must not be taken to be the only kind that is possible. If we understand by 'noumenon', he writes there, "an object of a non-sensible intuition, we thereby presuppose a special mode of intuition, namely, the intellectual, which is not that which we possess, and of which we cannot comprehend even the possibility" (B307). Intellectual intuition in the sense relevant to this passage is not, however, identical with the *productive* intuition discussed in the deduction. In this passage what is at issue is not the creation of things in themselves, but only awareness of them by means of a non-sensible intuition.[13]

---

[13] In classical antiquity the belief was widespread that we possess such a faculty of intuition. In those times an emission theory of perception was dominant, according to which a ray is emitted from the eye in order to scan the object. On this theory, then, sight makes the entities themselves directly available to us and not mere appearances. Plato for example says in *Theaetetus*, 188e, "A man who is seeing any one thing is seeing something which is." A similar statement is to be found in the third postulate of Euclid's *Optics:* "Let it be assumed . . . that those things upon which the rays of vision fall are seen, and that those things upon which the rays of vision do not fall are not seen." An opposition between appearances and things in themselves would have made as little sense in this context as skepticism about the external world would have. The things I see are touched by me and it is thus that I know them; therefore they must be there, for otherwise I could not touch them. This emission theory was extremely widespread: in addition to Plato and Euclid, who based his optics on it, we also find it in the optics of Ptolemy, in Hipparchus and in Galen, and also in the poets such as Pindar and Sophocles to name only a few of its most weighty proponents. That today we no longer subscribe to the theory is the result of fundamental changes in the science of optics wrought in the course of its Arabic reception and culminating in a new theory of sight in the work of Alhacen (965–1039): compare Alhacen, *De aspectibus*, and also Lindberg 1976.

Thus we find in sections 76 and 77 of the teleological power of judgment *two distinct* faculties of cognition that Kant takes to be conceivable, but humanly unrealizable, each of which in turn is susceptible to two distinct interpretations. In each case, the one interpretation harkens back the pre-critical context of physico-theology and the characterization of God, while the other originates in the critical characterization of human understanding and sensibility to which it forms a contrast. Consequently we must make the following distinctions:

First of all, the intuitive understanding as (a) an original, self-intuiting understanding (the origin of all possibilities) is to be distinguished from intuitive understanding as (b) a synthetically universal understanding.

And secondly, intellectual intuition as (a) the productive unity of possibility (thought) and actuality (being) is to be distinguished from intellectual intuition as (b) the non-sensible intuition of things in themselves.

Although Kant viewed these merely as limiting concepts, by continuously differentiating them and making them more precise he created a conceptual arsenal that allows us to achieve greater clarity about that *in relation to which* they function as limiting concepts, namely our human faculty of cognition, about which we will learn more in the next chapter.

7

The "Critical Enterprise": Incomplete

"Thus with this I bring my entire critical enterprise to an end," Kant writes in the preface to the *Critique of the Power of Judgment.* "I shall proceed without hindrance to the doctrinal part, in order, if possible, to win yet from my increasing age some time still favorable to that" (5:170).

In the space of just a few years, the original question of the possibility of metaphysics—more precisely, of a metaphysics of nature with a defensible claim to being scientific—had given rise to something which at first was quite unforeseeable, namely a system of transcendental philosophy which now had come to a provisional conclusion with the *Critique of the Power of Judgment.* In the beginning, only the possibility of veridical, non-empirical reference to objects had been at stake, but very soon the original concern was widened to include the question of the possibility of synthetic a priori truths in general. The question of the possibility of a categorical imperative arose in turn, entailing the further question of whether it is possible to realize the moral law in this world. Finally, the investigation of the power of judgment in its reflective activity showed that it, too, is grounded in an a priori principle and that we can thus conceive respective legislation of theoretical and practical reason as united in a supersensible substrate. Inevitably, Kant's promised system of metaphysics was put off time and again.[1]

---

[1] It was not until early in 1797 that Kant published the *Metaphysical Foundations of the Doctrine of Right,* upon which the *Metaphysical Foundations of the Doctrine of Virtue* followed six months later. The two volumes were then bound together and published under the title, *The Metaphysics of Morals in Two Parts.* Whether the addition of two 'Metaphysical Foundations' equals a metaphysics of morals in the proper sense is a question which I need not go into here. Kant never published a metaphysics of nature.

Initially, then, it was the system of transcendental philosophy that attracted all the philosophical attention and provoked the most varied reactions. Since my concern here is to present not an historical survey, but the development of a thought, in what follows I will only deal with those receptions of Kant which agree with him in demanding that philosophy become a science, while objecting that this goal has not yet been achieved by Kant himself. From this point of view, the task of philosophy is to complete the project begun by Kant. "Philosophy is not yet at an end. Kant has given results; the premises are still missing. And who can understand results without premises?"[2] Such was Schelling's expression of this mood in a letter to Hegel on January 6, 1795.

Karl Leonhard Reinhold was the first to be seized by this thought. He had initially gained public recognition with his *Letters on Kantian Philosophy* which contained a popular account of Kant's moral philosophy and appeared serially in the journal *Teutscher Merkur* between 1786 and 1787. Thus he became the first popularizer of the critical doctrine. Soon after, Kant publically expressed his gratitude to Reinhold and declared him to be the foremost interpreter of his thought (cp. 8:183). In addition, Reinhold's *Letters* brought him the position of *professor extraordinarius* at the University of Jena, which under his aegis proceeded to become the center of Kantianism in Germany.

In Jena, Reinhold developed his so-called *Elementarphilosophie,* which he first presented to the public in 1789 and thus prior to Kant's publication of the Third Critique. This "Elementary Philosophy" is based on the assumption that the apex of a philosophy must consist in a proposition from which all its other propositions can be derived. At first glance this might appear as a relapse into a pre-critical rationalism guided by the methodical ideal of a *mos geometricus* in the style of Christian Wolff or Spinoza. In reality, however, Reinhold is seeking to solve a fundamental problem by which he sees Kant's philosophy encumbered.

As I pointed out in the Prologue, to the extent that philosophy is an a priori discipline, this fact implies for Kant that philosophy's scientific status depends on its elements being derivable from a common principle: Philosophy cannot be scientific unless it is systematic; and it cannot be systematic unless its various theorems can be produced from a fundamental principle. Consequently, a scientific whole must be 'articulated' in the same

---

[2] *Briefe von und an Hegel,* 1:14.

way an animal body is, and not merely form a 'heap'. Or as Kant also writes, "that which we call science . . . is not formed in technical fashion . . . but in architectonic fashion, in view of the affinity of its parts and of their derivation from a single supreme and inner end, through which the whole is first made possible" (A833). Until we have examined all the elements, derived them from a single principle, and determined their mutual relations, thus ensuring the recognizability of the whole *as such* along with that of its parts, we cannot rule out the possibility that later on new and hitherto unconsidered objections might be raised against the investigation's results.[3]

As Reinhold saw it, Kant had failed to supply a satisfactory proof of this kind. For Kant had made neither the inner link between practical and theoretical reason nor the distinction between sensibility and understanding sufficiently clear. The derivation of the categories from the forms of judgment was equally unsatisfactory: "The completeness of these forms must itself be proven; it must be shown both that only the four enumerated moments (quantity, quality, relation, and modality) and only the three forms of judgment in each, neither more nor less, are possible" (Reinhold 1790: I, 315). So it is not Kant's results Reinhold is criticizing, but their derivation, and this criticism is paired with his insistence that philosophy cannot become scientific until a convincing derivation from a first principle has been supplied.

In this matter, Reinhold could appeal to Kant's own authority. Otherwise it would be baffling that Johann Gottlieb Fichte could write to Reinhold, saying, "Like Kant, you have introduced something to humanity that will remain with it eternally. He taught us that we must begin by investigating the subject, and you have taught us that the investigation must be conducted on the basis of a single principle. The truth you have spoken is eternal" (GA III,2:282).

---

[3] Thus Kant writes in the *Prolegomena,* "Nothing can be more desirable to a philosopher than to be able to derive a priori from one principle the multiplicity of concepts or basic principles that previously had exhibited themselves to him piecemeal, in the use he had made of them *in concreto,* and in this way to be able to unite them all in one cognition. Previously, he believed simply that what was left to him after a certain abstraction, and that appeared, through mutual comparison, to form a distinct kind of cognitions, had been completely assembled: but this was only an *aggregate;* now he knows that only precisely so many, not more, not fewer, can constitute this kind of cognition, and he has understood the necessity of his division: this is a comprehending, and only now does he have a *system*" (4:322).

Though Fichte was mistaken in this latter opinion, it can hardly be denied that Reinhold had indeed cut to the quick of Kantian philosophy. The search for a first principle that could finally transform philosophy into a science was soon to produce the most curious effects. Today, those effects hold only historical interest, and Reinhold's own principle must be reckoned among them; his importance lies in what he initiated. Admittedly, he had the advantage of having followed Kant's own example as faithfully as possible.

In the *Critique of Pure Reason*, Kant himself refers to the principle of the synthetic unity of apperception as the "supreme principle of all employment of the understanding," the "highest point, to which we must ascribe all employment of the understanding, even the whole of logic, and conformably therewith, transcendental philosophy" (B136, 134). Since Reinhold takes statements like these to mean that Kant's *Critique* is itself a philosophy with a fundamental principle, his perception that its putatively fundamental principle does not guarantee the derivability of its parts motivates him to develop a principle which in his view is even more general than the principle of the synthetic unity of apperception.

If such a principle exists (and according to Reinhold it must exist if philosophy is capable of becoming science), it must fulfill at least four criteria. *First,* it must be immediately justified in and of itself, for if its validity depends on any other propositions it is not a principle. *Second,* its truth must be immediately evident; insight into it must not be the result of inference. *Third,* the concepts involved in the principle must be comprehensible solely on the basis of the principle itself. *Fourth,* the concepts involved must be the most general of all, and the state of affairs expressed by the principle must be the most general fact, for otherwise the concepts would be subordinate to yet higher concepts (as species concepts to the concept of a genus) and the principle could not be comprehensible in and of itself.

Now Reinhold is convinced that the fact of consciousness is the fundamental fact and that the concept of representation constitutes the most comprehensive genus, so that the sought-after principle is to be found in the following 'Principle of Consciousness': "In consciousness, the subject distinguishes the representation from the subject and the object and relates the representation to both" (Reinhold 1790: I, 167).

Why is the concept of representation supposed to be the most fundamental? For one thing, according to Reinhold it is the fundamental concept in the *Critique of Pure Reason,* as well, although it is insufficiently clarified by Kant. For example, on page 320 of the A-edition Kant sets out a serial arrangement of all possible kinds of representation that is extraordinary to say the least:

> The genus is representation in general (*repraesentatio*). Subordinate to it stands representation with consciousness (*perceptio*). A *perception* which relates solely to the subject as a modification of its state is *sensation* (*sensatio*), an objective perception is *knowledge* (*cognitio*). This is either *intuition* or *concept* (*intuitus vel conceptus*). The former relates immediately to the object and is single, the latter refers to it mediately by means of a feature which several things may have in common. The concept is either an *empirical* or a *pure concept*. The pure concept, in so far as it has its origin in the understanding alone (not in the pure image of sensibility), is called a *notion*. A concept formed from notions and transcending the possibility of experience is an *idea* or concept of reason.[4]

The concept which forms the apex of this conceptual pyramid, however, the genus-concept of representation as such (which includes unconscious representations as well) is nowhere explained by Kant, and Reinhold is certainly right to insist that it is in need of explanation. However, Reinhold may well have had a further reason for wanting to base his principle on the concept of representation. As we have just seen, Kant speaks of the synthetic unity of apperception as the highest point or the supreme principle of our employment of the understanding. He also says of this representation that it is the representation 'I think', which must be able to accompany all other representations. This representation, he goes on to say, is an act of spontaneity and cannot be conceived of as belonging to sensibility. It consists in that self-consciousness "which, while generating the representation '*I think*' (a representation which must be capable of accompanying all other representations, and which in all consciousness is one and the same), cannot itself be accompanied by any further representation" (B132).

To Reinhold's mind, then, Kant's formula of 'the representation: I think' supplied not only the fundamental principle of all employment of the understanding, but also implied a connection between subject, representation, and object which would enable him to render the concept of representation

---

[4] Cp. also 9:64–65: "The *first* degree of cognition is: to *represent* something; the second: to represent something with consciousness, or to *perceive* (*percipere*); the *third* . . ."

itself more distinct than Kant had done. Reinhold's principle is probably best interpreted as a more explicit formulation of Kant's 'representation: I think'.[5] However, rather than focusing on this representation that must be able to accompany all my other representations, i.e. on the activity of combining representations in consciousness, Reinhold intends to give an even more elementary exposition of *representing as such,* an exposition of 'I represent'.

Here I can pass over Reinhold's attempts to derive the various components of Kant's theory from this concept of representation, and turn instead to the reception of his principle itself among his contemporaries. The most important critique was published anonymously in 1792 in a book entitled *Aenesidemus or Concerning the Foundations of the Elementary Philosophy Issued by Professor Reinhold in Jena Together with a Defense of Skepticism against the Pretensions of the Critique of Reason.* The unnamed author—Gottlob Ernst Schulze—agrees with Reinhold that any philosophy claiming scientific status must be grounded in a principle and that this principle must consist in an explication of the most fundamental of all concepts. Although he concedes that the concept of representation meets this criterion, he nevertheless denies that the Principle of Consciousness is the hoped for principle of all philosophy. Schulze's objections essentially boil down to the following three.

(1) The Principle of Consciousness cannot be the first principle, since it is subject in turn to the highest rule of judgment, the principle of non-contradiction.
(2) The concepts contained in the principle cannot be understood on their own and independently of any other concepts. The concept of 'relating' is unclear, i.e. it is not clear whether the relevant relation is one of cause and effect, substance and accidence, part and whole, sign and signified, or of matter and form. The concept of distinguishing is similarly unclear.
(3) The Principle of Consciousness is not a priori at all, but is taken from experience.

The first point of interest is that Schulze, too, shares the view that philosophy must be grounded in a *single* principle if it is to be scientific. That is indeed something that Reinhold "introduced to humanity," as Fichte

---

[5] Here I am following Bernecker's (1997) interpretation.

put it. The demand that philosophy must be scientific has, of course, often been voiced, but notions of what that entails have changed with time. The notion that philosophy must be systematic in order to be scientific can, it seems, be traced back to Descartes,[6] who took his orientation from Euclid's *Elements*. Of course, Euclid does not start with a single principle but rather with twenty-three definitions, five postulates, and five axioms, from which he derives a total of 465 propositions. Descartes, too, initially assumed several principles, and in June 1646 he writes to Clerselier, "One must not make it a condition of a First Principle that it be so constituted that all the other propositions can be derived from it or proved by it. It is enough if it is such that, taking it as a starting point, other things can be discovered and that no other principle occurs on which it depends or that could be discovered prior to it. *For it might be the case that there is no principle in the whole world from which alone everything else can be derived*" (emphasis added).[7]

Kant represents the next stage in this development in that he insisted that the derivation from a single principle is superior to any derivation requiring several principles. Thus he had tacitly set the theme of the ensuing years: Find the first principle! Admittedly, he himself does not seem at first to have contemplated the possibility that *all* of philosophy could be derived from a single principle. In order to avoid confusion, it is important here not to lose sight of the distinction between transcendental philosophy and metaphysics. Kant does not initially assume a first principle for transcendental philosophy, while he does assume such a principle in the case of metaphysics.[8] In the introduction to the *Critique of Pure Reason* Kant says that the work is intended to outline the entire plan for a transcendental philosophy "architectonically, i.e. from principles" (A13; translation modified), in plural, and Kant does in fact discover different principles for each of the various faculties of sensibility, understanding, and reason. Yet since reason itself comprises the entire higher faculty of knowledge, or more precisely "the faculty of principles" (A299), it is conceivable

---

[6] See for example Descartes' letter to Picot which was later to be used as the preface to the French edition of Descartes' *Principles of Philosophy*.

[7] Quoted in Lauth 1998, 8.

[8] Metaphysics, Kant writes, "is nothing but the *inventory* of all our possessions through pure reason, systematically arranged. What reason produces entirely out of itself cannot be concealed . . . *as soon as the common principle has been discovered*" (Axx; emphasis added).

that reason and understanding have a common root. In the case of understanding and sensibility, on the other hand, Kant is more cautious, saying only that they "*perhaps* spring from a common, but to us unknown root" (A15, emphasis added). As long as we are concerned merely with the possibility of a priori reference to objects, however, there is no need to inquire into this root. At the end of the *Critique*, though, Kant anticipates the character of a still to be constructed metaphysics: "The legislation of human reason (philosophy) has two objects, nature and freedom, and therefore contains not only the law of nature, but also the moral law, presenting them *at first in two distinct systems, but ultimately in one single philosophical system. . . .* In accordance with reason's legislative prescriptions, our diverse modes of knowledge must not be permitted to be a mere rhapsody, but must form *a single* system" (A840, 832; translation modified, emphasis added).

This pronouncement applies to transcendental philosophy, as well, however, as soon as it comes to include morality. For then the systematic connection between theoretical and practical reason must already be accounted for at the critical level since it is of course only "one and the same reason" which in the one case, as theoretical reason, determines *what is,* and in the other, as practical reason, determines *what ought to be.* Giving such an account proved more difficult than Kant had originally anticipated. Thus he was forced to admit in 1785 that he could only present the *Groundwork of the Metaphysics of Morals,* and not a critique of practical reason because the latter, "if it is to be carried through completely, [would] be able at the same time to present the unity of practical with speculative reason in a common principle, since there can, in the end, be only one and the same reason, which must be distinguished merely in its application. But I could not yet bring it to such completeness here" (4:391). He was still unable to do so three years later, though, when the *Critique of Practical Reason* was published. He could only hope "of perhaps being able some day to attain insight into the unity of the whole pure rational faculty (theoretical as well as practical) and to derive everything *from one principle*—the undeniable need of human reason, which finds satisfaction only in a complete systematic unity of its cognitions" (5:91, emphasis added).

I will not try to judge Kant's success in ever achieving such an insight.[9] In any case, Reinhold persuaded his contemporaries that the Kantian

---

[9] If Kant ever did in fact succeed in such an endeavor, he did not do so until a decade later in his *Opus postumum.* Since this work was never published during his life, however, I can leave it out of the present consideration.

system was still lacking a foundation. And Schulze's *Aenesidemus* persuaded those same contemporaries that Reinhold had not supplied the missing foundation. It was in this sense that the thirty-one-year-old Fichte, who had agreed to review *Aenesidemus* for the *Jenaer Allgemeine Literaturzeitung,* wrote to the Tübingen professor J. F. Flatt at the end of 1793, "*Aenesidemus,* which I reckon among the notable products of our decade, has persuaded me of what I had previously suspected, namely that even after Kant's and Reinhold's labors philosophy has not yet attained the status of a science; it has rocked the foundations of my own system and forced me, since one cannot very well live without a roof over one's head, to rebuild from scratch" (GA III,2:18).

Preparatory to his review of *Aenesidemus,* Fichte subjected Reinhold's 'Elementary Philosophy' to a painstaking line-by-line study which he documented in writing and which has fortunately been preserved. The manuscript reveals how Fichte went about 'rebuilding from scratch'.[10] It starts with a problem—and a Cartesian echo: "Is it possible, as Reinhold set out to do, to demonstrate the categories and the forms of sensibility, time and space:—sensibility, understanding, reason, the cognitive faculty and the faculty of desire—to demonstrate the necessity of all these things—or more precisely, can the whole of philosophy be built upon a single fact, *or must one resort to more than one?*" (GA II,3:26, emphasis added).

By mid-December, after six weeks of work, he can report to his friend Heinrich Stephani, "I have discovered a new foundation from which it is very easy to develop the whole of philosophy. —Taken altogether, Kant has the right philosophy, but only in the results, not according to the reasons. I marvel increasingly at this singular thinker; I believe he has a genius who reveals the truth to him without showing him the reasons for it!" And in regard to the review he is working on, Fichte adds, "From the standpoint I have recently attained . . . it strikes one as droll to see Reinhold make representation into the genus of what goes on in the human soul" (GA III,2:28).

What does he mean by this? Let us recall for a moment Reinhold's principle: "In consciousness, the subject distinguishes the representation from the subject and the object and relates the representation to both."

The subject. Reinhold's principle obviously presupposes a knowledge which the subject must have of itself in order to be able to ascribe the

---

[10] See Reinhard Lauth's pioneering work, "Die Entstehung von Fichtes 'Grundlage der gesammten Wissenschaftslehre' nach den 'Eignen Meditationen über Elementarphilosophie'," in Lauth 1989, 155–79.

representation either to itself or to the object. It must already have a knowledge of itself which *cannot* be the result of a prior self-ascription of representations, for otherwise it could not know that it was ascribing the representations to *itself* and not to the object.[11] Consequently, this 'original' knowledge of myself, as Fichte calls it, cannot have the intentional or propositional structure described by Reinhold's principle. Indeed, it cannot be knowledge on the basis of representations at all, and hence the concept of representation cannot be the most fundamental. In his review of *Aenesidemus,* Fichte puts it this way: "The subject and object do indeed have to be thought of as preceding representation, but not in consciousness qua an empirical mental state, which is all that Reinhold is speaking of. The absolute subject, the I, is not given by empirical intuition; it is, instead, posited by intellectual intuition. And the absolute object, the non-I, is that which is posited in opposition to the I. Neither of these occurs in empirical consciousness except when a representation is related to them" (GA I,2:48; W 1:10).

The second sentence of this passage contains Fichte's discovery in a nutshell: All the empirical objects and facts that are present in consciousness have a being that does not originate in the subject; in order to cognize them, something must be given to me in empirical intuition. However, the I only has being to the extent that its being is brought about by its own activity. Something is expressed in the thought 'I am' that cannot come to me as it were from outside. No one else can cause this thought to occur in me or say 'I' for me:[12] no 'I' is present until one's own activity has apprehended itself. In the cognition of all other things, I am receptive; in the case of the 'I', I am productive, the creator of the I. This is the reason why Fichte states in the sentence quoted above that the I is not given in empirical intuition, but posited by intellectual intuition: The I is not *only* something that is thought, it is actual at the same time. On the other hand, it is actual *only* when it thinks itself.[13] The 'I' cannot be intuited unless one intuits

---

[11] This is the thought that Dieter Henrich (1967) has dubbed as "Fichte's original insight."

[12] "Even God himself cannot do this" (GA I,3:254; W 2:443). The implicit allusion to Descartes is hardly a coincidence. Just as little as an omnipotent being can deceive me about the fact that I am thinking while I am thinking, neither can an omnipotent being bring about in me the thought "I" if I do not do it myself.

[13] This is the reason why Fichte also says that 'to posit oneself' and 'to be at once both subject and object' mean the same thing. "I is that which cannot be a subject without, in the same undivided act, being an object, and which cannot be an object with-

oneself as the creator of this I. As an intuition, it is not receptive, but productive, or in Kant's terminology: it is an intellectual intuition. In self-consciousness, thinking is not only identical with what is thought; it also presents what is thought to intuition.

If this is correct, then the I is not only a "representation of apperception" which arises when representations are to be combined in the unity of consciousness and which for this reason must be able to accompany all other representations, as Kant thought (4:334). Kant conceives the I on the model of objective unity as a representation of the unity of spontaneity: "I think myself only as I do any object in general from whose mode of intuition I abstract" (B429). According to Fichte, the I must remain incomprehensible as long as we continue to interpret it as an abstraction on the basis of given representations.

At this point we encounter a fundamental difficulty. Fichte's claim cannot be proven in a descriptive manner; rather, it can only be borne out in one's own deed (*Tat*) of thinking oneself. Hence in order to understand what is crucial for Fichte, it is not enough merely to read his texts; since the I is only accessible in the perspective of the first person singular, the reader must perform an interior action (*Handlung*). Now Fichte believes that not everyone is able to do this; many people can imagine even the I only from an external perspective: "It would be easier to make most people imagine themselves to be a piece of lava on the moon than an I . . . Whoever has not yet come to an agreement with himself on this point cannot understand a thoroughgoing philosophy, nor is he in need of one. Nature, whose machine he is, will guide him in all the affairs he is to perform without the least effort on his part. To philosophize requires independence, and this can be granted to one only by oneself" (GA I,2:326; W 1:175).

Fichte's discovery is unprecedented in the history of philosophy: it is the insight that the proposition 'I am' expresses an utterly different kind of being than any existential proposition about a thing or state of affairs:[14] "The initial incorrect presupposition, and the one which caused the Principle of Consciousness to be proposed as the first principle of all philosophy, was precisely the presupposition that one must begin with a fact. We

---

out, in the same undivided act, being a subject. And vice versa, whatever is thus, is an I: both expressions mean absolutely the same thing" (GA I,3:253; W 2:442).

[14] Ernst Tugendhat (1979, 36) attributes this discovery to Martin Heidegger. In this matter, however, Heidegger's merits are merely those of an 'innovator' who has neglected to name his sources.

certainly do require a first principle which is material and not merely formal. But such a principle does not need to express a *deed* [Tat*sache*], it can also express an action [Tat*handlung*], if it is permissible to wager a proposition which can neither be explained nor proven here" (GA I,2:46; W 1:8).

I will examine the substance of this statement in more detail in the next chapter. His criticism of Reinhold, however, can be summed up as follows. In itself, Reinhold's principle is correct, but it is not a fundamental principle. It expresses nothing more than the empirical unity of consciousness and hence presupposes both subject and object. Over against this, empirical consciousness *of something*—intentional consciousness—is only possible on the basis of something which itself cannot be described either as intentional consciousness or as a deed (*Tatsache*), but only as a presuppositionless activity which is moreover accessible to experience only by way of an intellectual intuition.

On several occasions Fichte described to friends how he had arrived at this result. Henrik Steffens records one such story in his memoires:

I recall how once in a small and intimate circle Fichte told us how his philosophy originated and how its seminal thought suddenly surprised and took hold of him. He had long surmised that truth consisted in the unity of thought with the object; he had recognized that this unity could never be discovered within sensibility, and where it emerged, for example in mathematics, it produced only a rigid, lifeless formalism completely alienated from life, from deed [*Tat*]. And then suddenly he was seized by the thought that the action [*Tat*] by which self-consciousness grasps and takes hold of itself is manifestly a kind of cognition. *The I recognizes itself as produced by itself;* the thinking I and the thought I, cognition and the object of cognition are one, and all cognition begins with this point of unity, not with a scattered reflection that has time and space and the categories given passively to it. Now, he asked himself, what if you *isolated this first act of self-consciousness purely for itself* that is presupposed by all of human thinking and acting and lies concealed in all the fragmented opinions and actions, *and followed out everything it strictly entails,* wouldn't you be able to discover and present the same certitude we possess in mathematics within that vitally active and generative act? —This thought took hold of him with such clarity, force, and confidence that he felt as if com-

164

pelled by the spirit that had come to hold sway within him not to rest in his attempt to establish the I as the principle of philosophy. Thus did the idea for a *Wissenschafts-Lehre* and then this doctrine itself come about (Steffens 1840–44, 4:161–62, emphasis added).

"The I recognizes itself as produced by itself": Just as a mathematical figure is produced and presented to intuition by way of constructing it, so too is the I produced by the act of thinking itself—with the important difference that in the former case product and producer are separate from each other, whereas—crucially—in the case of the I they are not. Now this initial act of self-knowing, the pure action by which the I produces itself, is clearly not arbitrary, but takes place in a regular manner. Thus if this action were to be "isolated purely for itself" and everything it entails followed out in its consequences—might we not then discover that the original *Tathandlung* contains all the theorems which according to Reinhold Kant had failed to deduce? That, anyway, was Fichte's conjecture in December 1793. After finishing the *Aenesidemus* review, he planned to work out this conjecture in peace and quiet over the next few years and thus to provide the foundation that Kantian philosophy had lacked hitherto.

We have now arrived at the half-way point of these twenty-five years of philosophy. If we pause for a moment to look back over the path we have traveled, we make a surprising and remarkable discovery: Twelve and a half years after Kant's epoch-making endeavor to raise philosophy from a mere natural disposition to the status of science, Kantian philosophers stand divided over two quite disparate conceptions of what 'science' means.

One conception, the one that arose from transcendental philosophy's own dynamic, culminates in Fichte. It rests on the assumption shared by Kant and Reinhold that philosophy must be systematic and therefore must be derived from a first principle. According to Fichte, however, such a principle is accessible to cognition only in the intellectual intuition of one's own I.

The *other* conception, one which we have already encountered in Chapter 4 arose in the context of Goethe's Spinoza reception. It is inspired by Spinoza's view that scientific knowledge consists in the ability to derive an object's essential properties from its proximate cause or definition. Spinoza had only been able to give mathematical examples to illustrate the procedure of a *scientia intuitiva*. Goethe's theory of metamorphosis had led him to a similar result in botany, but he had lacked an explicit methodological consciousness. He had, however, recognized his procedure in the passages of the *Critique of the Power of Judgment* where Kant characterizes the intuitive understanding as an understanding which moves from the whole to the parts to grasp their reciprocal causation. This conception seemed to promise a methodological foundation for the idea of a *scientia intuitiva*.

Thus both positions follow Kant, yet both do so by vindicating notions which Kant had introduced as mere abstract possibilities and solely with the purpose of describing the limits of human cognition: intellectual intuition and intuitive understanding. While Kant viewed both modes of cognition as unrealizable for human beings, Fichte insisted that intellectual intuition is realized in each and every self-intuition of an I, and Goethe insisted that he had in fact based his *Metamorphosis of Plants* on a method of intuitive understanding and thereby proven the reality of such a faculty in practice.

As I mentioned above, the *Critique of the Power of Judgment* had such an effect on Goethe that once he had read it he immediately began working on an expanded edition of his *Essay on the Metamorphosis of Plants,* despite the fact that the first version had only just been published.[15] The introduction to this *Metamorphosis of Plants: Second Attempt,* as he called it, has been preserved among Goethe's posthumous works. Although it comprises only a handful of pages, they suffice to show that Goethe intended to provide a theoretical foundation for the first *Essay.*[16] After sketching the various inadequate conceptions which have previously hampered the study of organic creatures and which "would have to be got rid of in the best interest of science," Goethe writes in section 7: "Here, too, the student of nature can rest his fears and continue unimpeded on his way

---

[15] Both the *Critique of the Power of Judgment* and Goethe's *Metamorphosis* essay came out in 1790 at the Easter book fair. On July 9, 1790, Goethe writes to Knebel: "If I ever manage to find long hours, I will write the second piece on the metamorphosis of plants, and the essay on the forms of animals: I would like to publish both next Easter" (HABr. 2:128).

[16] Dorothea Kuhn, who produced the Leopoldina edition of the fragment, rightly remarks that "although Goethe got no further than the beginning of an introduction, his reflections take us beyond the *Essay on the Metamorphosis of Plants*. It seems that the earlier work was to be supplemented by something theoretical" (LA II, 9A:551).

since the recent school of philosophy, following the directions of its teacher (see Kant's *Critique of the Teleological Power of Judgment*, sect. . . .), will certainly make it its duty to introduce this manner of thought more widely, and here the student of nature must not miss the opportunity to join in the discussion" (LA I,10:66–67).

Goethe does not specify a particular section as he obviously did not have the book in front of him and did not recall the exact numbering. However, since the preceding sections of the introduction are devoted to arguing that science must 'get rid' of the assumption that living beings and their parts possess a relative purposiveness defined in relation to externally imposed ends, and that the concept of inner purposiveness alone is suited as the "key concept . . . from which one must not stray" (ibid., sect. 6), we can safely guess which sections Goethe had in mind. Kant introduces the distinction in section 63 of the *Critique of Teleological Power of Judgment* and goes on in sections 76 and 77 to give the philosophical justification for the view that Goethe so admired. Furthermore, Goethe also addresses this topic in the essay "The Intuitive Power of Judgment" [*Anschauende Urteilskraft*] and directly quotes a "highly significant" passage from section 77 of the Third Critique. Hence we can assume that he is referring to the same section here as well. The passage cited is this: "We can also conceive of an understanding which, since it is not discursive like ours but is intuitive, goes from the *synthetically universal* (of the intuition of a whole as such) to the particular, i.e., from the whole to the parts. — And it is not at all necessary here to prove that such an *intellectus archetypus* is possible, but only that in the contrast of it with our discursive, image-dependent understanding (*intellectus ectypus*) and the contingency of such a constitution we are led to the idea of an *intellectus archetypus,* and that this does not contain any contradiction" (LA I,9:95; HA 13:30, quoting [inaccurately] Kant 5:407–8).

Goethe continues, "Though the author seems to be referring to a divine intellect, yet just as we are able to elevate ourselves to a higher region in the ethical sphere through our belief in God, virtue, and immortality, the case might be the same in the intellectual sphere, so that by intuiting a continuously creative nature we make ourselves worthy of intellectual participation in its productions. My restless pursuit of the archetypical [*das Urbildliche, Typische*] had at first arisen unconsciously and from an inward drive, and then I had even succeeded in developing a mode of presentation in conformity with nature [i.e., the *Essay on the Metamorphosis of Plants*], so now surely nothing could keep me from courageously plunging myself into the *adventure of reason,* as the sage of Königsberg himself has called it" (LA I,9:95–96; HA 13:30–31).

Goethe did not, however, carry out his *Second Attempt,* but decided instead to see whether the Kantian idea of an intuitive understanding could be made to bear fruit for his Spinozist project of a *scientia intuitive* in another field, the lawfulness of colors. Here a few prefatory remarks are in order.

Historical Excursus

Even before his Italian journey, Goethe, who was an enthusiastic painter, had been struck by the fact that although he could distinctly perceive the beauty of colors and the differences between them, he was unable to put them into words or explain the laws that govern them. In Italy, therefore, he sought out the company of painters in order to have them explain these regularities. Soon, however, he was forced to acknowledge that they too practiced on the basis of instinct or feeling, but not in any case on the basis of an explicit theory of color. Goethe thus resolved upon his return to Weimar to get to the bottom of the matter in its physical aspects. As a student in Leipzig, he had attended lectures on Newton's optics and was convinced of its truth: "Like the rest of the world, I was convinced that all the colors were contained in light; no one had ever told me any differently, and never had I found the least cause to doubt it since I had taken no further interest in the matter" (LA I,6:417; HA 14:256). Now he was interested. Since the lectures in Leipzig had not included experimental demonstrations, he initially planned to catch up on them himself. An elongated room in his new house was able to serve as a large, walk-in *camera obscura,* and he borrowed the necessary prisms from Court Counselor Christian Wilhelm Büttner. Other business and obligations repeatedly prevented him from carrying out his plan, however. Finally, in February 1790, Büttner, who had in vain requested the return of his instruments, sent a servant to fetch them personally. Goethe gave them back, but not without at least taking a quick look through one of the prisms. They were standing in a completely white room, and Goethe expected to see the light that was reflected from the white wall "to be split up into a certain number of colored lights": "But how astonished I was when the white wall, viewed through the prism, remained white, showing a more or less discernible color only in the places where it bordered on something dark, so that in the end it was the window frame that had the most intense color, whereas not a trace of coloration was to be seen in the light grey sky. It did not require much reflection to realize that an edge is necessary to produce colors, and I said so aloud, as though by instinct, that the Newtonian theory was wrong. Returning the prisms was now out of the question. With all kinds of cajolery and promises of favors, I tried to calm their owner, in which I succeeded. I now began to simplify the contingent phenomena I encountered through the prism inside and out, and raised them to the level of easy experiments by using black and white panels" (LA I,6:420).

Whether Goethe is right to assume that Newton's theory is incapable of explaining the phenomenon he observed is less interesting to me in the present context than the fact that he concludes that an edge is needed for colors to emerge—an opposition of light and dark. Goethe was immediately convinced that this must be the essence of color, from which a *scientia intuitiva* would be able to derive all the properties of color. Recall Spinoza's admonition in the *Treatise:* "To be called perfect, a definition will have to explain the inmost essence of the thing, and to take care not to use certain *propria* in its place" (TIE sect. 95). From this point on, Goethe will charge Newton with having made exactly this mistake of explaining what is original from what is merely derived when he assumed that the spectral colors must already be contained in white light.[17]

Goethe's subsequent attempts to bring to bear Kant's characterization of an intuitive understanding are interesting. It must have been immediately clear to him that a single experiment, an *experimentum crucis* in the Newtonian sense, would not reveal the essence of the phenomenon in question (no more than a part could reveal the nature of the whole). Nor does his own glance through the prism, taken in itself, prove anything either. A single experiment cannot prove the truth of a theory. Rather, all the experiments that are directly connected with the phenomenon must be performed before the whole *as a whole*—and hence too the relation of whole and part, essence and property—can come into view. Until then, it is impossible to make any scientific statement at all in the sense of *scientia intuitiva*.[18] For since it is only in the case of mathematical objects (and artifacts) that we know the underlying idea, and not in the case of the

---

[17] "He [Newton] makes the mistake of basing his hypothesis on a single, and moreover artificial, phenomenon and wanting to explain from it the most various and limitless appearances" (LA I,11:301–2; HA 13:50). Compare *Theory of Colors: Didactic Part,* §176 and §718: "The worst thing that can happen to physics as well as many another science is when the derivative is mistaken for the original, and since the original cannot be derived from the derivative, the attempt is made to explain the original on the basis of the derivative."

[18] Here is not the place to go into Goethe's controversy with Newton. I will merely say that it cannot be decided on the basis of current physics since what is at stake is *scientia intuitiva* precisely as a *methodological alternative* to current physics.

products of nature, in this latter case our first step has to be to discover all the properties belonging to a thing or living being, in order then to consider these parts (properties) in light of the whole and to see how they depend on the whole as their efficient cause. The reason why section 77 of the *Critique of the Power of Judgment* met with Goethe's enthusiasm is obviously that this section seemed to him to illuminate the path that led beyond Spinoza to an application of *scientia intuitiva* in the kingdoms of nature: The direction of the method had to be reversed. Instead of moving directly from the efficient cause to the properties, in the case of products of nature the intuitive understanding must move from the totality of the properties to their efficient cause. In other words, we must first (additively or discursively) constitute a whole, in order to make it possible to intuit if the whole causes the parts.

This characterization is still somewhat vague. In the ensuing years, Goethe would make energetic attempts to render it precise. After reading the *Critique of the Power of Judgment* in 1790, however, his conception of the method must already have been sufficiently distinct for him to interrupt work on the *Second Attempt* at a theory of metamorphosis in order to devote himself to the laws of color. He published his results in installments he called *Contributions to Optics*. Goethe's method is worth examining in detail.

In the first of his *Contributions to Optics,* Goethe begins by describing how we normally encounter colors and then specifies a first experiment that can stabilize the phenomenon and make it reproducible: the view through the prism. He describes how colors are visible at the edges. The second experiment is devoted to the opposite situation: we look through a prism at a surface which is not bounded by edges or borders—the blue sky. No other colors are visible; perceived through a prism, the sky still only appears blue. Is this due to the blueness of the sky? In order to decide the question, we direct our view through the prism toward further monotone (edgeless) surfaces of black and white. Again, no other colors are visible through the prism except the color of the surface.

However, other colors do become visible as soon as clouds appear in the sky and we view them through the prism. Similarly, colors become visible when the surface is uneven (e.g. fibers in white paper, protrusions along the white wall, etc.). In order to eliminate such deviations, Goethe included plates in the treatise which enable us to observe the phenomena under ideal conditions. That it is not the irregularities which produce colors, but the contrast between light and dark is shown by a third experiment involving a white surface with black, wormlike lines: If one "puts plate no. 1 in front of the prism, one will see how the colors cling to the worm-shaped lines" (LA I,3:19).

The fourth experiment investigates whether regular alternations of light and dark also produce regular colors through the prism. To this end, a plate is furnished on which small black and white squares alternate with each other. "One will be pleased to see one square colored as the next." If, however, the plate is rotated in relation to the prism, the play of colors changes, too. This phenomenon is further considered in the next experiment, the fifth: A black background with white stripes parallel to the axis of the prism. The colors of the rainbow appear on a black background. The sixth experiment, involving black stripes on a white background, reveals a contrary phenomenon: Here the view through the prism shows the colors in an order inverse to that of the rainbow; yellow is at the bottom, above it is red, then violet, then blue. Seventh experiment: "We have seen in the previous experiments that the orderings of the colors are reversed; we must further investigate this law. Therefore we place plate no. 8 in front of the prism . . ." (LA I,3:19–21).

This sample of Goethe's method may suffice without adducing further experiments. I hope that it has become clear that the last experiment must again be followed by a contrary experiment, and that the common feature which is thus revealed to the viewer must in turn be diversified in further experiments. In this way, a chain of experiments is produced in which no gaps remain, and in which one experiment gives way to its polar opposite until all the appearances that make up the phenomenon have been exhausted and reveal themselves as a totality. In the first part of the *Contributions,* of course, such a degree of completeness is still a long way off; nevertheless, Goethe is already willing to conclude that "the edges show colors because they are where light and shadow share a boundary" (LA I,3:30). In the second part of the *Contributions* Goethe is even more explicit: "All these experiments are derived *from a single experience,* namely, that we must view two opposed edges whenever we want to see all the prismatic colors at once, and that we must move these bands closer to one another if we want the separate and opposed appearances to combine and form a continuous series of colors joined by gradual transitions" (LA I,3:50, emphasis added).

Goethe published the first two parts of his *Contributions to Optics* in 1791 and 1792. The *Contributions* were to comprise four parts altogether and were intended as a *chef d'oeuvre* that would implement his method in exemplary fashion. He promised parts three and four for the following year, but they never appeared. The *Contributions to Optics* were never finished, and it was years until they were replaced by another work, the *Theory of Colors*. Goethe's reason for abandoning work on the *Contributions* can be gleaned from an autobiographical sketch he wrote around 1800, entitled "An Account of the Author's Work in this Discipline": ". . . colored shadows. Early interest in this. Manifold experiments. Appearance attributed to stronger and weaker light. Realistically objective mode of explanation a long-term hindrance . . . So-called accidental colors. Insight into the physiological part. Foundation sought in the organ. The colored shadows are brought under this heading. Great benefit" (LA I,3:363).

How are we to interpret this sketch? In August 1793 Goethe had sent the third, as yet unpublished part of the *Contributions to Optics* to Georg Christoph Lichtenberg and asked for his opinion. This installment included Goethe's explanation of colored shadows—a phenomenon that had already puzzled Leonardo da Vinci and which had first captured Goethe's attention in 1777 during his descent from the snow-covered summit of the Brocken. In the third installment Goethe gives a "realistically objective" explanation that harmonized with his core experience of color: Since colors are produced at the boundary between light and dark, the fact that the shadows are colored is the result of the relation between "stronger and weaker light." That is, if there is only one source of light, the shadow it casts on a white surface will be black; if however the shadow is also illuminated by another light source of different intensity, then the shadow appears to be blue when the second source is weaker than the first, and yellow when it is stronger (LA I, 3:70–71, 78).

In a long reply dated October 7, 1793, Lichtenberg voices skepticism about Goethe's explanation. At the end of his letter he also points out a phenomenon which is similar to that of colored shadows and which we refer to today as successive contrast or colored afterimages. Lichtenberg writes, "It is, for example, certain that if one looks for long through a red glass and then suddenly removes it from before one's eyes, objects will briefly take on a green cast; if, on the contrary, one looks through a green glass, they will then at first have a red cast. This is connected to Buffon's *couleurs accidentelles,* which we notice in our eyes" (LA I,3:85).

Goethe's response to this is extraordinarily interesting. He wholeheartedly concedes the affinity between colored shadows and the "so-called *couleurs accidentelles,*" but objects to calling them *accidental* colors since they can be methodically produced in repeated experiments just as colored shadows can be. More importantly, though, Goethe admits that he can offer no explanation for the similarity between the two groups of phenomena. "Your Excellency have not failed to notice how nearly these experiments are related to the so-called *couleurs accidentelles*. In their case, too, it is possible to conduct a beautiful series of experiments matching the others in every respect; here there is nothing accidental, but there is an agreement of different experiences, the diversity of which we recognize through the senses, but whose agreement we cannot grasp with the intellect, much less express in words. As too often, alas, our mind finds itself in the predicament of having either to let the phenomena stand in isolated juxtaposition or to invent a hypothetical unity that tangles them more than it ties them together. How much is still left for us, how much is left for our descendents to do" (LA I,3:88).

Successive contrasts cannot be understood on the basis of Goethe's 'realistically objective' explanation of colored shadows, i.e. on the basis of 'stronger and weaker light'. Rather, they appear to point to a "foundation in the organ [of sight]," as Goethe emphasizes in the autobiographical sketch and as Lichtenberg also suggested. In other words, the two phenomena, despite their seeming affinity, cannot be integrated in a complete series of properties such that their common efficient cause or their underlying essence could be determined with any certainty. It is unclear how both kinds of phenomena could be explained on a unified basis. Moreover, Goethe, who had reproached Newton for confusing a mere property of light with its essence, was now confronted with a case which forced him to admit that he himself had no insight into what was the essence and what was the property, what was original and what derivative. Further publication of the *Contributions* was out of the question. He had still not achieved clarity on the right method for *scientia intuitiva*.

At this point in time, Goethe must have been painfully aware that his repeated efforts to cooperate with philosophers on methodological questions had failed to bear fruit. After returning from Italy he had devoted himself first to a study of the *Critique of Pure Reason* that cost him no little effort. He had hoped to be able to meet with Reinhold in Jena and hold a "long conference" on the subject, but this plan, too, came to nothing.[19] Then, after having read Kant's *Critique of the Power of Judgment*

---

[19] In a letter to Reinhold dated February 18, 1789, Wieland has this to report of Weimar: "For some time now Goethe has been studying Kant's *Critique of Pure*

and been "passionately inspired" by it,[20] he had again been forced to admit that he had "met with little approval among the Kantians." He was unable, as he later wrote, "to bring myself into line with the Kantians: they heard what I had to say, but were unable to respond or to benefit me in any way" (LA I,9:92; HA 13:28). And so when it came to philosophy, Goethe had only himself to rely on.

In the summer of 1793, Reinhold was offered a chair in Kiel and threatened to leave Jena. Regarding possible successors, Goethe's colleague C. G. Voigt, who shared responsibility with him for professorial appointments at the University of Jena, wrote to him (on July 17, 1793) that among others "the author of the *Critique of all Revelation* (which at first had been attributed to Kant himself), Fichte, who is presently travelling in Switzerland," was most likely available. Goethe's reply: "Keep your eye on Fichte" (GVB I,104, 108).

Reinhold accepted the appointment in Kiel, and Fichte was offered a professorship in Jena. On December 26, 1793, he received an official appointment letter. Fichte, who had announced his "discovery" to Heinrich Stephani only two weeks before and was hoping for "unoccupied leisure" in the coming months in order to work out the details of the plan implicit in his discovery ("building anew"), asked to be allowed to defer for a year: "A teacher of philosophy must have a system which is, at least for himself, wholly tenable. At the present, I have none that wholly satisfies me. I would be unable to meet the gracious expectations to which I owe this honorable proposal" (GA III,2:43).

This was not to be. For one thing, those in Weimar did not want to leave the chair in Jena vacant for a whole year; for another, Fichte made

---

Reason etc. with great diligence, and has set himself the goal of holding a long conference with you about it in Jena" (cited in Steiger 1982–96, III:13). Why nothing came of this plan can be gleaned from a letter Goethe wrote to Jacobi six years later: "Reinhold . . . was never able to go out of himself, and to be anything at all he needed to remain within a narrow circle. It was impossible to have a conversation with him, and I have never been able to learn anything through him or from him" (HABr 2:194).

[20] While Goethe was visiting Dresden for eight days at the end of September 1790, Schiller received a letter from his Dresden friend Körner saying, "I was soon able to get to know him better and he was more communicative than I had expected. You will hardly guess where we found the most in common. Where else but—Kant? In the critique of the teleological power of judgment *he has found nourishment for his philosophy* (Schiller, *Werke*, 43,1:32, emphasis added).

such progress over the course of the next few weeks that by February 4 he could already write "that I can at least see the glimmering of the conclusion, and thus even now could ascend to the philosophical lectern with confidence" (GA III,2:55). Thus it was agreed that the customary disputation in Latin could be postponed until later and Fichte would instead submit a "programmatic introduction in German as an invitation to students" (ibid.). Since he had no textbook upon which to base his lectures, it was also decided that he could publish the lecture course in single installments as he went along "as a handbook for my audience" (GA III,2:71).

In Jena, Goethe himself took care of finding a suitable publisher for the two projects. In this connection Fichte, who was still in Zürich, learned from his Weimar confident Böttinger that "Bertuch would take on the publication of your programmatic introduction with pleasure . . . Bertuch will also be happy to publish the textbook you will be bringing out serially and only for your students . . . Your whole idea enjoys Goethe's approval especially, who was present throughout the deliberations and has long since proved to be your affectionate friend" (GA III,2:84).

Late in the evening of May 18, 1794, Fichte arrived in Jena. On the morning of that day he had stopped in Weimar to introduce himself to Goethe and he presented him a copy of his programmatic introduction *Concerning the Concept of the Wissenschaftslehre [Über den Begriff der Wissenschaftslehre oder der sogenannten Philosophie]*. This copy is preserved today in the Goethe National Museum in Weimar. The numerous underlinings and marginal notes attest to Goethe's intensive study of the text.[21] What he read there must have been more than welcome to him. For Fichte characterized his philosophy, which he now referred to as *Wissenschaftslehre,* as the discipline which philosophically grounds the possibility of every other science. Since every science must have a systematic form, and since such form can only be derived from a first principle, the *Wissenschaftslehre* must at the same time establish principles for every other science. Those principles must, if they are truly to be principles, be incapable of further proof: "All those propositions which serve as first principles of the various particular sciences are, at the same time, propositions indigenous to the *Wissenschaftslehre.* Thus one and the same proposition has to be considered from two points of view" (GA I,2:128; W 1:56)—as a proposition contained within the *Wissenschaftslehre* and also as a first

---

[21] The late Professor Dr. Géza von Molnár graciously supplied me with a photocopy of this text.

principle standing at the pinnacle of some particular science. For Goethe, this formulation must have augured well for future cooperation.

Goethe also perused the first printed installment of the lecture on the *Foundation of the Entire Wissenschaftslehre* as soon as he received it in July, and then wrote to Fichte:

> I thank you kindly for the first installment of the *Wissenschafts-lehre,* in which I already see the hopes fulfilled which the introduction [i.e. *Concerning the Concept of the Wissenschaftslehre*] inspired in me; it contains nothing which I do not understand or at least take myself to understand, nothing which does not willingly conform to my habitual way of thinking . . . As for myself, I will owe you the deepest gratitude if you reconcile me with the philosophers whom I could never do without and whom I could never join. I await the further continuation of your work with yearning, *in order that it correct and consolidate something of my own,* and as soon as you are less occupied with urgent work I hope to be able to speak to you about various matters whose treatment I am postponing until I see more distinctly *how that which I am confident of achieving may conform with that which we expect from you* (HABr. 2:177–78, emphasis added).

". . . the premises are still missing"

8

Fichte's "*Complete* Revolution of the Mode of Thought"

Kant's renewal of philosophy, his attempt to raise philosophy to the level of a science, had originally begun with the question of how non-empirical, veridical reference to objects is possible, and it ultimately had led to a system of transcendental philosophy that comprised three Critiques. Initially, the first two critiques comprised two freestanding works with no integral connection to each other. For while on the one hand freedom is defined in explicit opposition to the laws of nature, it is supposed on the other hand to be capable of realization in the natural world. It is only the *Critique of the Power of Judgment* which makes possible the inner unity of the theoretical and practical faculties by teaching us "to look beyond the sensible and to seek the unifying point of all our faculties a priori in the supersensible: because no other way remains to make reason self-consistent" (5:341). The unity of Kant's transcendental philosophy is thus made possible through reference to the supersensible, though of course Kant denies any possibility of *cognitively* linking this supersensible point of unity with the sensuous realm.

Not so Fichte. He once characterized the essence of the *Wissenschaftslehre* he began teaching in Jena in May 1794 as consisting "precisely in the exploration of what for Kant was unexplorable, namely the common root linking the sensible and supersensible worlds, and in the real and comprehensible derivation of the two worlds from a single principle" (GA II,8:32; W10:104).[1] Just as Kant had been led to this common root

---

[1] In a letter to Reinhold from July 2, 1795, Fichte had already stated that the essence of the *Wissenschaftslehre* consists in such a derivation. He says that he is "firmly convinced that if you [Reinhold] had constructed your system after the appearance of all three *Critiques* (as I did) you would have discovered the *Wissenschaftslehre*. You would have discovered the unity underlying all three *Critiques*,

by way of reflection on the play of the subjective powers of cognition in the experience of beauty, Fichte too takes the subject's cognitive acts as the starting point for his exploration and determination of that root.

He does not, however, start with the cognitive acts of the *empirical* I. For the *Wissenschaftslehre* itself had originated in his critique of Reinhold and the attendant insight that the Principle of Consciousness expresses only the empirical unity of consciousness, whereas that unity itself is in turn made possible by an activity that is not present to empirical consciousness. Thus, in order to investigate this activity, it is necessary to free oneself from sensible intuition and rise to a non-sensible, *intellectual* intuition. As Fichte writes in the *Aenesidemus* review, "The absolute subject, the I, is not given by empirical intuition; it is, instead, posited by intellectual intuition" (GA I, 2: 48; W 1: 10). Now common sense is by nature realistic. It knows nothing of the I's non-sensible actions as revealed by philosophy. Hence it also forms a notion of self-consciousness as something intuitively given. It distinguishes self-consciousness from other forms of consciousness by saying that in the case of self-consciousness the I has itself as its object rather than something else. Such a description, however, is external to the phenomenon, given from a third-person perspective as though self-consciousness could disclose itself to observation in the same way that other modes of being do. Common sense thus fails actually to *carry out* the thought of the I; instead it merely describes what it takes to be that thought. It inevitably takes its own I to be something that exists independently of its activity and which is already there prior to the self-apprehension of that activity. However: "The I is nothing outside of the I, but it is itself the I" (GA I,2:326; W 1:176).

I mentioned above that Fichte reproached his contemporaries for their inability to rise above sensible intuition and that he saw this as the reason why they failed to understand the *Wissenschaftslehre*.[2] For every-

---

just as surely as you correctly discovered the (just as unobvious) unity of the critique of speculative reason. (I acknowledge that your Principle of Consciousness is, at any rate, an announcement of the unity of speculative reason, concerning which we do not at all disagree.)" (GA III,2:346).

[2] The very first review of Fichte's prospectus for the students in Jena, *Concerning the Concept of the Wissenschaftslehre,* shows how right he was. The reviewer (F. A. Weißhuhn) concludes his discussion with the statement, "that I do not enjoy the view from the standpoint to which Professor Fichte has led us, for the reason that my natural eyes are shown things they cannot grasp, and of which, in its activity [*Tun*], the natural understanding understands nothing." In *Philosophisches*

thing depends on precisely this ability. Just as Plato refused to admit anyone into his Academy who was untrained in mathematics, i.e. who was incapable of rising up to a mode of thought liberated from sensibility, so too according to Fichte no one will gain access to the inner core of philosophy—and philosophy henceforth refers to *Kantian* philosophy—who is not in a position to raise himself up to the intellectual intuition of the I.[3]

What, then, must Fichte show? Let us suppose for a moment that he is right to believe that the I is not given by empirical intuition, but rather posited exclusively in intellectual intuition. Then two things must be true:

(1) The I is what it is only *through itself*—the self-positing of the I. And since an I which is not conscious of itself would not be an I,[4] it must also be true that

(2) The I is what it is *for itself*—the self-consciousness of the I.

Fichte must therefore show, *first,* how the I posits itself and, *second,* how it comes to be conscious of this act. Obviously the first step must precede the second, despite the fact that they remain inseparable from one another. And we can already anticipate the form which this first step will have to take: If the I originally posits *itself,* then it does not posit just anything, but something determinate or determinable (an I). Since determinability always presupposes an opposite (*omnis determinatio est negatio*), the I must therefore equiprimordially posit something in opposition to itself that is not the I—i.e., something which is not posited by the I. Since it must posit this in opposition *to itself,* it must occur in the same

---

Journal für Moralität, Religion und Menschenwohl (ed. C. Chr. E. Schmid), 4,1 (Jena 1794): 139–158, 157, cited in Fuchs 1995, 1:252.

[3] In *sensible* intuition, something given is intuited; in *intellectual* intuition it is one's own activity which is intuited: "Intellectual intuition is the immediate consciousness that I act and of what I do when I act. It is because of this that it is possible for me to know something because I do it. That we possess such a power of intellectual intuition is not something that can be demonstrated by means of concepts, nor can an understanding of what intellectual intuition is be produced from concepts. This is something everyone has to discover immediately within himself; otherwise he will never become acquainted with it at all" (GA I,4:217; W 1:463).

[4] Meister Eckhart's dictum: "For were I a king, but knew it not myself, then I were no king" (1963; Nr. 36), is equally valid for the I: "What does not exist for itself, is not an I . . . The I exists only to the extent that it is conscious of itself" (GA I,2:260; W 1:97).

consciousness. Fichte must therefore show how something which is posited *as not posited* can occur in consciousness. In short, he must show how the I can be at once both determinant and determined.

I.

Fichte's initial manner of introducing the *Wissenschaftslehre* was shaped by the special situation in Jena, for there it was inevitable that his new foundation for transcendental philosophy on the basis of the I would be compared with Reinhold's system. Fichte is responding to Reinhold's recent modification of his position, published shortly before he left Jena. Its details need not interest us here;[5] it is, however, the reason why Fichte takes common sense as the starting point from which to work out his own position. Accordingly, he has to discover a transition to the intuition of the I's activity from concepts that would be familiar to common sense. He does so by assuming a proposition which "everyone will grant us without objection" (GA I,2:256; W 1:92), in order then to spell out the presuppositions of that proposition. Later he was to opt for other, more direct paths leading to the experience of one's own *Tathandlung*.

The proposition with which he begins in his 1794 lectures is the proposition $A = A$, recognized by 'common sense' as absolutely certain. Yet what is the nature of this undisputed certainty? It obviously does not concern the *existence* of A: The existence of A is here neither asserted nor in question. On the contrary, the proposition wholly abstracts from existence, for even if A stood for a self-contradictory state of affairs, the existence of which would thus be impossible, the certainty of $A = A$ would remain. The certainty thus lies not in A itself, but in the act of thinking: *If* A *is thought*, then it is true that $A = A$. What is decisive is the necessary connection between the two sides.

What is the origin of this connection? Evidently, it is only present when the first A occurs in the same consciousness as the second one. The certainty which everyone associates with the proposition $A = A$ is therefore rooted in the identity of the thinking subject: $I = I$, so that this proposition is equally as certain as $A = A$.

With this step Fichte has brought the members of his audience to what is for him the crucial point mentioned in the previous chapter: "The

---

[5] On this, cp. Stolzenberg 1994.

proposition 'I am I' has, however, a meaning wholly different from that of 'A is A' (GA I,2:258; W 1:94). In the case of the proposition A = A, whether something actual corresponds to the predicate A depends on conditions which are not given with the act of judgment itself; that is the reason why we were able to abstract from A's existence. In the case of the proposition I = I, by contrast, it is impossible for us to abstract from existence: "In it the I is posited, not conditionally, but absolutely, with the predicate of self-identity; hence it really *is* posited, and the proposition can also be expressed as *I am* . . . Hence it is a ground of explanation of all the facts of empirical consciousness, that prior to all positing in the self, the self itself is posited" (GA I,2:258; W 1:95).

Put differently, to express the identity of A with itself is a judgment, a mental act. At the basis of this act lies, as we have just seen, the identity of consciousness, I = I. This identity is in turn also the result of an act—an act, however, which is identical to the product of the act: Activity and that which is produced by the activity, deed and action, are one and the same. Accordingly, Fichte avoids talk of a fact or *Tatsache* that could be distinguished from the action, and prefers to speak of a *Tathandlung* (a 'deed-action') whose expression is found in the proposition 'I am'.

Hence all other acts and facts of consciousness distinct from this one presuppose the self-positing of the I in the form 'I am'. Thus the principle of the *Wissenschaftslehre* has been discovered: "The I originally and absolutely posits its own existence" (GA I, 2:261; W 1:98).

This principle not only precedes all empirical consciousness; as Fichte expressly emphasizes, it is also prior to logic. Let us recall: Aenesidemus' objection to Reinhold had been that the Principle of Consciousness could not qualify as a principle since it was itself subject to the principle of non-contradiction. Thus it is that Fichte insists in section 6 of his prospectus *Concerning the Concept of the Wissenschaftslehre* that every logical principle must be proven on the basis of the *Wissenschaftslehre*. If in the case of the proposition 'I = I' we abstract from the determinate content, namely the I, and consider only the form of being posited, then the principle takes on the form of the classical logical principle of identity, A = A. If, on the other hand, we abstract from all determinate acts (judgments) of the mind and direct our attention only to the *kind* of action expressed by the first principle, then we obtain according to Fichte "the *category of reality*." For the I posits itself and posits in the I that something be: A or A = A, respectively. If the *Tathandlung* described by Fichte is the condition of all empirical consciousness, then it is also the condition of all reality.[6] Thus the fact that reality can be predicated of anything at all presupposes the *Tathandlung* described by Fichte: "Everything to which the proposition 'A = A' is applicable, has reality, *insofar as that proposition is applicable to it.* Whatever is posited in virtue of the simple positing of some thing (an item posited in the I) is the reality, or essence, of that thing" (GA I,2:261; W 1:99).

The meaning of these statements will become clearer as we proceed.

Now one of Fichte's fundamental insights is that empirical consciousness cannot be explained on the basis of a single action. The fact that the I posits itself absolutely is not sufficient for the possibility of empirical consciousness. Determinate consciousness entails not only identity but difference as well, not only reality but negation, too. In order to show that this too rests on an original act of the I, Fichte once more begins with a propositions which 'everyone' holds to be certain: –A not = A.

Here again the certainty does not arise from the content of A, which we continue to disregard. The certainty relates exclusively to the form of the proposition: *If* anything at all is posited in opposition to an A, then it is not identical to A. This proposition cannot, however, be derived from the first principle, for position as such contains no negation. The form of opposition is not contained in the form of positing as such. Hence it must be an act of the I that is just as primitive and underivable as the act of positing expressed by the first principle. Fichte puts it this way: "As certainly, therefore, as the proposition '–A not = A' occurs among the facts of empirical consciousness, there is thus an opposition included among the acts of the I; and this opposition is, as to its mere *form,* an absolutely possible and unconditional act based on no higher ground" (GA I,2:265; W 1:102).

Now of course nothing can be posited in opposition to A unless A itself is already posited, and hence the act is on the other hand also conditioned. More precisely, it is unconditioned in respect to its *form,* and conditioned in respect to its *content.* Additionally, A must be posited in the same consciousness in which its opposite is to be posited, since other-

---

[6] Reality must not therefore be confused with existence; it expresses 'whatness' (*'Sachheit'*) as it were, not existence. As a category, reality is a category of quality, not of relation; it belongs to the mathematical categories, not the dynamical ones. Thus it is that Kant, too, defines the real as that, "which corresponds to sensations in general, as opposed to negation = 0" (A175/B217). For Fichte, in the context of the self-positing of the I, reality is identical to activity.

wise the latter positing would not be a positing *in opposition* but rather itself a positing. Since, however, originally nothing is posited but the I, the original opposition can only be an opposition to the I. The I therefore posits its own opposite, i.e. something whose being does *not* consist in positing. Since at this point no other predicates apply to this opposite besides its being the negation of the I, Fichte's designation of it as a *non-I* is perfectly justified. "As surely as the absolute certainty of the proposition '–A not = A' is unconditionally admitted among the facts of empirical consciousness, just as surely is a non-I opposed absolutely to the I" (GA I,2:266; W 1:104). This proposition may thus be taken as the second principle of all human knowledge.[7]

If we now go on to abstract from the determinate content of this second principle (i.e., the I and non-I), and consider only the form of being posited, we again obtain a principle of classical logic, namely the principle of non-contradiction: –A not = A, which Fichte provisionally refers to as the "principle of opposition." It is however also possible to abstract from the determinate act of judging and direct our attention merely to the form of the inference, which moves from the fact of being opposed to the non-being of that which was previously posited. In a word, this is the *category of negation*. And thus the second of Kant's categories of quality has also been derived from the I's original *Tathandlung*.

Yet this, too, is still insufficient. A third principle is necessary before the possibility of consciousness can be established. If only the first two principles held, then the I would posit itself as contradiction. For the non-I can only be posited in the I, since all opposition presupposes the identity of the I (the unity of consciousness). It is however posited as the opposite of the I, in consequence of which the I is negated and annulled: "Thus the I is not posited in the I, insofar as the non-I is posited therein" (GA I,2:268; W 1:106). Of course a negation is only possible in relation to a reality; therefore, the non-I cannot be posited unless the I is posited. That

---

[7] The expression 'non-I' has given rise to misunderstandings. Many readers have interpreted Fichte's non-I as a thing in itself, as something that could exist independently of the subject, although Fichte himself points out the "shallowness of this explanation" (GA I,2:266; W 1:104). For the non-I has no reality whatsoever independently of the I: No non-I without the I. On top of that, at this stage of Fichte's argument there cannot be any talk of things anyway—indeed, not even talk of representations: "For at this point the non-I is nothing; it has no reality" (GA I,2:285; W 1:125). What is at stake is rather the very possibility of the I's positing something in opposition to itself and distinguishing itself from it.

is, the I simultaneously posits in the I both the I and the non-I. The two principles which arise from the I's original *Tathandlung* result in a contradiction, and this contradiction must not persist: For if the derivation of these two principles is correct so far, then "the identity of consciousness, the sole absolute foundation of our knowledge, is itself eliminated. And hereby our task is now determined" (GA I,2:269; W 1:107).

What precisely is the task that Fichte has in mind? Since the unity of consciousness would not be possible on the basis of the two principles described so far, though it is in itself actual and indubitable, a further act must be ascribed to the I which guarantees the compatibility of the two principles without infringing on their validity. The possibility of such an act does not follow from the principles themselves; thus the relevant act must again be original and underivable. In Fichte's terms, it is unconditioned in respect to its content, while being conditioned by the other two principles in respect to its form: "Hence . . . we must make an experiment and ask: How can A and –A, being and nonbeing, reality and negation, be thought together without mutual elimination and destruction?" (ibid.; W 1:108).

The answer to this question is easy: They can only be thought together if they do not cancel each other out completely but only partially, that is, if they mutually *limit* each other. Applied to our present case, what this means is that both the I and the non-I are posited as capable of limitations (i.e. as "divisible"). "Only now, in virtue of the concept [of divisibility] thus established, can it be said of both that they are *something*. The absolute I of the first principle is not *something* (it has, and can have, no predicate); it is simply *what* it is, and this can be explained no further. But now, by means of this concept, consciousness contains the *whole* of reality; and to the non-I is allotted that part of it which does not attach to the I, and *vice versa* . . . [C]onsciousness is one: but in this consciousness the absolute I is posited as indivisible; whereas the I to which the non-I is opposed is posited as divisible. Hence, insofar as there is a non-I opposed to it, the I is itself in opposition to the absolute I" (GA I,2:271; W 1:109–10).

Accordingly, Fichte's formulation of the third principle reads: "In the I, I oppose a divisible non-I to the divisible I" (GA I,2:272; W 1:110).

That the category of limitation results when we abstract from the form of this action is obvious. According to Fichte, when we abstract from its content we obtain a logical principle "hitherto known as the principle of grounding" or the principle of sufficient reason: Every opposite is like its opponent in one respect (for else they could not be related to each other); and every like is opposed to its like in one respect (for else they would be one). Such a 'respect' is called a ground: in the former case a ground of relation, and in the latter case a ground of distinction.

As we can see, the three acts that Fichte has discovered so far cannot be independent of each other. Consequently they must not be conceived as temporally successive but rather as one and the same *Tathandlung*: It is only in our reflection that their three components come to be distinguished. Let's begin by trying to spell out the implications of this thought. The three principles contain three necessary acts by the I, acts which belong together and at this stage are still inseparable: Positing (*Setzen*), positing in opposition (*Entgegensetzen*), and unification of the opposites. Or thesis, antithesis, synthesis. A synthesis is only possible where two opposites are present; opposition is only possible where something has been posited. Something determinate can only be posited when something is opposed to it. Something can only be posited in opposition to something to which it is related. The third principle thus expresses the first and fundamental synthesis (Synthesis A). If further synthetic a priori propositions are to be possible, then they must already be implicitly contained in the first synthesis.[8] Since all synthesis involves the unification of opposites, the oppositions, that is, the contradictions of thesis and antithesis resolved in those subsequent syntheses must also be contained in the first synthesis. The remaining course of the *Foundation* is thus determined: It must systematically seek out the contradictions which are contained in the I's original synthesis—and which are always already synthetically resolved in every actual consciousness since otherwise the unity of consciousness would be impossible.

> In every proposition, therefore, we must begin by pointing out opposites which are to be reconciled. —All syntheses established must be rooted in the highest synthesis which we have just effected, and

---

[8] "The celebrated question which Kant placed at the head of the *Critique of Pure Reason:* How are synthetic judgments a priori possible? —is now answered in the most universal and satisfactory manner. In the third principle we have established a synthesis between the two opposites I and non-I, by positing the divisibility of each; there can be no further question as to the possibility of this, nor can any ground for it be given; it is absolutely possible, and we are entitled to it without further grounds of any kind. All other syntheses, if they are to be valid, must be rooted in this one, and must have been established in and along with it" (GA I,2:275; W 1:114).

187

be derivable therefrom. In the I and the non-I thus united, and to the extent that they are united thereby, we have therefore to seek out opposing characteristics that remain, and to unite them through a new ground of relation, which again must be contained in the highest ground of relation of all. And in the opposites united by this first synthesis, we again have to find new opposites, and to combine them by a new ground of relation, contained in that already derived. And this we must continue so far as we can (GA I,2:275; W 1:114–15).

The search for contradictions is thus set in motion by *our* reflection, by an activity of the philosophical observer. Yet what is revealed in its course is a structure of the 'object' of observation, the self-positing I. In order properly to understand the method of the *Wissenschaftslehre,* we must therefore take care to distinguish these two levels or series. At the same time, however, it also turns out that the further we carry out the investigation, the more the two series converge: "The I under investigation will itself arrive eventually at the point where the observer now stands; there they will both unite, and by this union the circuit in question will be closed" (GA I,2:420; W 1:291).

Of course we are still far from that point here. So far the third principle is all we have to work from: *I posit in the I a divisible non-I in opposition to the divisible I.* With this, the I and non-I are posited as *capable* of mutual limitation. If we now reflect on this principle, we find that it is open to two mutually exclusive interpretations:

A1) The I posits the non-I as limited by the I.
A2) The I posits itself as limited by the non-I.

Since a limitation is also a determination of that which is thus limited, the following holds:

A_p) The I posits the non-I as determined by the I; that is, the
          I determines the non-I—it acts or is *practical.*
A_t) The I posits itself as determined by the non-I; that is, the
          I posits itself as affected, it perceives or is *theoretical.*

The practical part of the *Foundation* is based on the first principle, the theoretical part on the second. Theoretical and practical philosophy are consequently not two disciplines seemingly independent of each other

188

whose connection is still waiting to be discovered; for Fichte, they are both equally rooted in the third principle. If this could be confirmed, the result would be an astonishingly direct solution to the problem of unifying theoretical and practical reason which was raised by Kant and further urged by Reinhold.

At this early juncture, of course, it is impossible to unify the two principles synthetically, since up to this point the non-I still has no reality (so far it is still only the negation of the I). Thus it remains puzzling how the I could alter it and negate reality in it. Therefore the practical part of the *Foundation* cannot be tackled until the determination of the theoretical principle has been completed. Let us therefore begin by turning our attention to this principle.

II.

A$_t$) The I posits itself as determined by the non-I.

Reflecting upon this proposition we discover that it again contains two further propositions related to each other as thesis and antithesis:

B1) The I *is determined by* the non-I, i.e. it is passive.
B2) The I *posits itself as determined,* or it determines itself, i.e. it is active.

The one proposition negates what the other asserts. The first (theoretical) corollary thus harbors a contradiction which, if it were to remain unresolved, would nullify this corollary. By implication, the fundamental synthesis formulated in the third principle (Synthesis A) would also be impossible, thus destroying the unity of consciousness. Since that is clearly not the case, a unification of the two propositions (Synthesis B) must already have been carried out in consciousness, and so our next step will be to uncover that unification: "All contradictions are resolved by more accurate determination of the propositions at variance" (GA I,2:392; W 1:255).

Synthesis B: If two contradictory propositions do not mutually negate each other, then they must contradict or negate each other only partially. That holds true in the present case as well. "The I thereby *determines itself in part,* and *is in part determined*" (GA I,2:288; W 1:129). That means that the I is active *to the extent* that the non-I is not active, and passive *to the extent* that the non-I is active.[9] Each thus limits the other and hence they reciprocally determine each other. With this the original Synthesis A that was formulated in the third principle reaches a further stage of determination, for if the I and non-I were initially posited merely as *divisible,* it now becomes clear that their division must be the result of a reciprocal limitation or determination which Fichte accordingly refers to as "reciprocal determination" (and which corresponds to the third Kantian category of relation). The question remains, however, *how* this is accomplished. For upon closer inspection we find that each of the propositions B1 and B2 contains a further contradiction.

Let's begin with B1. In order for the non-I to be able to determine the I, it must itself possess reality. Up to this point however, the non-I is determined solely as the negation of the I and as such it possesses no reality. How, then, can it determine the I? Thus in B1 we again have two contradictory propositions which, if the unity of consciousness is not to be destroyed, must be compatible with each other:

C1) The non-I has reality in itself (for otherwise it could not determine the I).
C2) The non-I is mere negation and consequently has no reality in itself.

If these are to be compatible with each other, it must again be shown that both propositions only partially hold.

Synthesis C: If the non-I has any reality at all, then, according to the principle of reciprocal determination just derived, it can only gain it as a result of the reality in the I being negated and transferred from the I to the non-I. Now this of course does not decrease what was originally posited in the I: The total sum of reality (activity) is conserved, though it is differently distributed. Since the opposite of activity is *passivity*,[10] it holds that decreased activity must correspond to an equal degree of passivity. "In

---

[9] Note that at this point nothing else is given besides the I and the non-I, activity and its negation.

[10] "*Passivity* is the mere negation of the concept of activity just established, and it is the quantitative negation, since the concept of activity is itself quantitative; for the mere negation of activity, when we abstract from the quantity of activity $=0$ would be rest. Everything in the I that is not immediately contained in the proposition *I am*, everything that is not posited by the positing of the I itself, is passivity (affection in general) for the I" (GA I,2:293; W 1:135).

light of the above, if the absolute totality of the real is to be conserved when the I is in a state of passivity, then, in virtue of the law of reciprocal determination, a similar degree of activity must necessarily be carried over into the non-I" (GA I,2:293–94; W 1:135).

Hence passivity can be ascribed to the I only in proportion as an equal degree of activity (reality) is assigned to the non-I. An 'activity' of the non-I, in respect to which the I is passive, is referred to in philosophical terminology as 'affection', and this is also how Fichte uses the term: "At least as far as we can see at present, the non-I has reality for the I only to the extent that the self is affected, and in the absence of such affection it has none whatever" (ibid.).

When we first introduced the concept of reciprocal determination, we left the question open as to which of the terms was doing the determining and which was undergoing determination, which of the two possessed reality and which was mere negation. This question has now been decided, however: Activity is posited in the non-I *in proportion to* the passivity of the I. Proportional correspondence between activity and passivity, however, is what we call causality, that is, the non-I is conceived as the cause of the passivity (the affection) of the I. Hence Fichte refers to this Synthesis C as the synthesis of *efficacy*. The category on which it is based is that of causality, the second Kantian category of relation.

What this synthesis fails to explain, however, is *how* the I, which is supposed to be nothing but activity, is able to negate activity in itself and thereby posit passivity in itself. Let us therefore turn to the second proposition B2, which evidently revolves around just this problem: *The I posits itself as determined, that is, it determines itself.* In this proposition we again find two further contradictory propositions:

D1) The I *determines* itself; it is active in determining.
D2) The I determines *itself*; it is passive in being determined.

This contradiction too can only be resolved if both propositions hold just partially, that is, if the I can be both active and passive in one and the same state.

Synthesis D: How can a state of passivity be posited in the I? Since the I is originally nothing but activity and since nothing outside of itself is there for it, the passivity of the I can also be nothing but a decrease in the activity of the I that it has brought about by itself. This means that it excludes something from the sphere of its activity. The I limits itself by positing itself as limited, affected, in short as a finite I. To be more exact, we must say that the *absolute* I posits itself as a *finite* (theoretical) I *by way of* partially transferring its activity to the non-I. It is only as a finite I that the I can be simultaneously active and passive, simultaneously determinant and determined. For purposes of clarification, Fichte again takes recourse to established philosophical terminology: The essence of the (absolute) I consists in its positing itself as being (first principle). That which exists of itself, requiring no other support or substrate in order to exist, is traditionally called 'substance'. The finite (theoretical) I by contrast exists only as a determination or limitation of this substance—what is traditionally referred to as 'accident'. As the sum of realities, the I is substance; the changing, limited realities are its accidents. "There is originally only *one* substance, the I; within this one substance, all possible accidents, and so all possible realities, are posited" (GA I,2:300; W 1:142).

The contradiction in B2 is thus resolved: the I can be simultaneously active and passive to the extent that we consider it by turns first as an absolute I and then as a finite I—as a quasi Spinozan substance (*causa sui*) and then as the limitation of that substance.[11] Hence the categorial determination at the basis of Synthesis D is the first Kantian category of relation. "Insofar as the I is regarded as embracing the whole absolutely determined realm of all realities, it is *substance*. So far as it is posited within a not absolutely determined sphere of this realm . . . to that extent it is *accidental* or *has an accident within it*" (GA I,2:299; W 1:142). Thus, in addition to the three categories of quality, Kant's three categories of relation have now also been derived from the I's original act.

To sum up, 'The I posits itself as determined by the non-I' (A_t) means that in self-consciousness the subjective activity is unified with the opposed objective activity. This unification is only possible on the basis of a reciprocal determination of I and non-I (Synthesis B). In turn, this reciprocal determination presupposes the causality of the non-I (Synthesis C) and the substantiality of the I (Synthesis D). More explicitly, we understand what it means (on Fichtean assumptions) that the I is determined

---

[11] The I "is *determinant,* insofar as it posits itself, through absolute spontaneity, in a determinate sphere among all those contained in the absolute totality of its realities; and insofar as we think merely of this absolute positing without regard for the limits of the sphere. It is *determinate,* insofar as it is regarded as posited in this particular sphere, without regard for the spontaneity of the positing as such" (GA I,2:298; W 1:141).

by the non-I when we consider the relation of the non-I to the I in terms of the category of causality; and we understand what it means that the I posits itself as determinate when we conceive of the I in terms of the relation of substance and accidence. Even so, however, we have not come a single step closer to understanding the first main proposition (A_t): The I posits *itself* as determined by the non-I.

So far we have determined only the two contradictory propositions B1 und B2, but they have not yet been synthetically unified. On the contrary: it now appears as though they cannot be unified. For if we consider them from the point of view of causality (Synthesis C), the passivity in the I is the effect of the non-I and determined by it; if on the other hand we take the point of view of substantiality (Synthesis D), the passivity in the I is a self-limitation of the I and thus determined by it. Fichte formulates the contradiction this way: "if the I posits itself as determined, it is not determined by the non-I; if it is determined by the non-I, it does not posit itself as determined" (GA I,2:304; W 1:148).

That is the result of a careful consideration of reciprocal determination. Reciprocal determination had proven to be the condition of possibility of the *ur*-synthesis contained in the third principle. Considered thus, reciprocal determination also implies a contradiction, and consequently it, too, can only partially hold if this contradiction is to be resolved.

Synthesis E: Up till now the principle of reciprocal determination required that an activity must correspond to every state of passivity, and a state of passivity to every activity in the opposite pole. The present contradiction can only be resolved however on the condition that this principle, too, holds only partially: In other words, there must be a certain measure of activity both in the I and in the non-I, to which no passivity corresponds at the other pole—an activity which is thus partially independent of the reciprocal determination: "[A]n activity is posited in the I, which is not opposed to any passivity in the non-I, and an activity in the non-I, which is not opposed to any passivity in the I. Activity of this sort we shall term for the moment *independent* activity" (GA I,2:305; W 1:149).

This activity must, firstly, be independent, and secondly, since it is supposed to resolve the contradiction, it must be related to and determined by the alternation of activity and passivity in the I and non-I—partially independent, partially conditioned.

To begin with the first point, the activity is partially independent of the alternation because it is what makes this alternation possible in the

193

first place. For that which is supposed to alternate—the two terms—mutually exclude each other as opposites; the existence of the one is wholly incompatible with that of the other. In themselves they are wholly isolated and singular. Thus in order for there to be *two* terms at all which can alternate with each other, they must somehow be *brought together*. Consequently, this must be the result of an activity in the I which is independent of the terms themselves. "The positing I, through the most wondrous of its powers . . . holds fast the perishing accident long enough to compare it with that which supplants it. This power it is—almost always misunderstood—which from inveterate opposites knits together a unity; which intervenes between elements that would mutually abolish each other, and thereby preserves them both; it is that which alone makes possible life and consciousness, and consciousness, especially, as a progressive sequence in time; and all this it does simply by carrying forward, in and by itself, accidents which have no *common* bearer, and *could* have none, since they would mutually destroy each other" (GA I,2:350; W 1:204).

It is thus an activity without which there could be no combination and consequently no unity of consciousness. It takes two elements which are isolated in themselves and *forms* (*bilden*) something common which as such can become an object of consciousness. Fichte therefore calls this independent activity "imagination" (*Einbildungskraft*). It proves to be the fundamental faculty of the self-positing I, without which no realities could become conscious at all: "Our doctrine here is therefore that all reality—*for us* being understood, as it cannot be otherwise understood in a system of transcendental philosophy—is brought forth solely by the imagination" (GA I,2:368; W 1:227). To this extent, imagination is an activity independent of alternation.

This activity is, however, in the *second* place, also necessarily related to and conditioned by something. Without terms to be connected, no independent activity would arise, just as little as there would be *alternating* terms without this activity. Now, the activity is supposed to determine the alternation by bringing together, comparing, and juxtaposing both terms. Imagination "oscillates," as Fichte says, between the terms and holds them together, comparing them in respect to their determinability. For this to take place, both elements, activity and passivity, the subjective and objective, must be present in the I. "Only in the I, and by virtue of this act of the I, do they become alternating components; only in the I, and by virtue of this its act, do they come together" (GA I,2:353; W 1:208).

It is *only* possible for the two opposed terms to come together in the I, however, if they have something in common, a common 'boundary' which as the ground of their relation allows for their combination. Herein lies a final difficulty: "Something in general must be present, wherein the active I traces out a boundary for the subjective, and consigns the remainder to the objective" (GA I,2:351–52; W 1:206).

What this difficulty comes down to is that the common 'boundary', without which there could be no alternation, is not conditioned by the imagination; rather, it is already presupposed by the activity of the imagination. Yet neither can it be conditioned by one of the terms themselves. For if the boundary lay in the I, the I's activity would be limited by itself and not by the passivity of the non-I. If the boundary lay in the non-I, however, its passivity would in turn be conditioned by itself and not by the activity of the I.

Consequently, reciprocal determination *both* presupposes a common boundary between its terms *and* rules out that this boundary could have its ground in the terms themselves. How, then, can something be in the I which makes possible an alternation between the subjective and objective without depending on these poles themselves and without having been produced by the imagination?

The objective to be excluded has no need at all to be present; all that is required—if I may so put it—is the presence of a check [*Anstoß*] on the self, that is, for some reason that lies merely outside the self's activity, the subjective must be extensible no further. Such an impossibility of further extension would then delimit—the mere interplay we have described, or the mere incursion; it would not set bounds to the activity of the self; but would give it the task of setting bounds to itself. But all delimitation occurs through an opposite; hence the self, simply to do justice to this task, would have to posit something objective in opposition to the subjective that calls for limitation, and then synthetically unite them both, as has just been shown; and thus the entire presentation could then be derived. It will at once be apparent that this mode of explanation is a realistic one; only it rests upon a realism far more abstract than any put forward before; for it presupposes neither a non-I present apart

195

from the I, nor even a determination present within the I, but merely the requirement for a determination to be undertaken within it by the I as such, or the *mere determinability* of the I (GA I,2:354–55; W 1:210).

To summarize, reciprocal determination requires an independent activity which determines the terms of the alternation. A determination, however, can only take place if the terms have a common boundary. Therefore, prior to all determination, there must be something in the I which provides what Fichte calls the *Anstoß* for the reciprocal determination of the I and non-I. Hence any determinability of the I presupposes an *Anstoß*. Of course we must not imagine that at this point a thing in itself has unexpectedly found its way into Fichte's philosophy. Though the *Anstoß* is not posited by the finite I, it only emerges when the I posits itself. The *Anstoß* is a check and impetus to the activity of the I and to that extent it is not something that exists outside the activity of the I: "no activity of the I, no *Anstoß*" (GA I,2:356; W 1:212).

The *Anstoß* is thus, on the one hand, not something that exists independently of the I's activity; on the other hand, though, it is independent of the I which posits itself as determined by the non-I, the finite I or "intelligence." Fichte's choice of the ambiguous term "*Anstoß*," which can mean both a check and an impetus or summons, was most likely motivated by this dual aspect. What exactly the *Anstoß* is cannot fully become clear until we examine the practical part of the *Wissenschaftslehre*. Here, where we are concerned only with the question of how the determinability of the theoretical I becomes possible, Fichte anticipates later developments by characterizing the *Anstoß* as 'feeling'. And just as a feeling is something that we find in ourselves without consciously having produced it, but which also has no existence external to the I, so it is with the *Anstoß*, too.[12]

Figure 8.1 provides an overview of Fichte's line of reasoning so far.

---

[12] The theoretical part of the *Wissenschaftslehre* demonstrates only "that the consciousness of finite creatures is utterly inexplicable, save on the presumption of a force existing independently of them, and wholly opposed to them, on which they are dependent in respect of their empirical existence. Nor does it assert anything beyond this opposing force, which the finite being feels, merely, but does not cognize" (GA I,2:411; W 1:280).

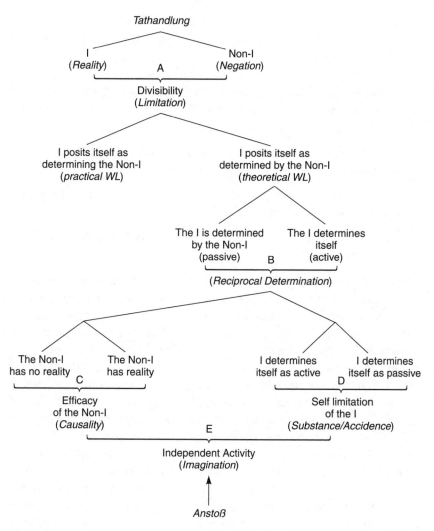

Figure 8.1

III.

The whole of the investigation so far has been carried out on the assumption that two absolutely opposed terms (I and non-I) are indeed capable of being unified in consciousness; the question was merely *how* they can be thus unified. The answer we have given is that the original activity of the I experiences an *Anstoß* and the imagination mediates between the two. Imagination thus proves to be an original power of the I, while the *Anstoß* is established as "a primordial fact occurring in our mind" (GA I,2: 362; W 1: 219).

If the deduction was correct, then the investigation's initial point of departure must be derivable from this original power and primordial fact. That is to say, the possibility of self-consciousness has to be explainable on their basis. We had said at the beginning:

(1) The I is what it is only through itself; and
(2) The I is what it is for itself.

At this point, however, it is also becoming clear that, taken together, these two propositions imply a third:

(3) The I cannot *simultaneously* be through itself and for itself, but only *successively*.

Why do they imply (3)? Anything at all which the I posits must be posited *for it*, that is, it must present it to consciousness. However, it cannot accomplish this in one and the same act, but only by means of a further act. For initially the I *is* the act. Recall that "the I's own positing of itself is thus its own pure activity . . . It is at once the agent and the product of action; the active, and what the activity brings about" (GA I,2:259; W 1:96). In the case of sight, for instance, we begin by seeing *something*; it is not originally the act of seeing itself that we see. Similarly, the act of positing has to be interrupted in order that not only the product but also the activity as such may become conscious. This happens when the product is reflected and thereby determined. Yet now it is the activity of reflection which is the unconscious element, and it must in a further step be made the object of a new reflection in order to become conscious to the I. "When the I reflects, it does not reflect on this act of reflecting itself. It cannot simultaneously act upon an object and upon its own acting. Thus it is not conscious of the activity in question; instead, it forgets itself entirely and loses itself in the object of the activity" (GA I,3:171; W 1:364).

Precisely because the self-conscious I is both activity *and* consciousness of its activity, it has a genesis or history behind it; and it is the reconstruction of this genesis that Fichte characterizes by the notion of a "pragmatic historiography of the mind." The task of the *Wissenschaftslehre* is now to reconstruct this genesis of consciousness in order to see whether it leads back to the starting point of the investigation so that the circle closes upon itself. "Hence in the future series of reflections, the object of reflection will not first be *brought forth* by that same reflection, but simply elevated *into consciousness* . . . The *Wissenschaftslehre* is to be a pragmatic history of the human mind" (GA I,2: 364–65; W 1:222).

The rest of this chapter will be devoted to the reconstruction of this pragmatic history. We begin with the fact of the *Anstoß*: "Upon the occasion of the check [*Anstoß*] on the original activity of the I (which remains completely inexplicable and incomprehensible at this point), the imagination, which is suspended between the original direction of the I's activity and the [opposed] direction which arises from reflection, produces something which is composed of both directions. Since nothing can be found in the I which the I has not posited within itself, the I must posit the fact in question within itself. That is, it must originally explain this fact to itself; it must completely determine it and establish its foundation" (GA I,3:143; W 1:331). How are we to think of this process?

(F′) Originally the I is nothing but activity. However, it cannot become conscious of this fact unless the activity meets with something which checks it and thus prevents it from trailing off into infinity. Without an *Anstoß* the I could never posit itself *as* I; it could never become finite and conscious of itself. How, then, does it come to be conscious of itself?

It is the *Anstoß* which impedes the activity proceeding from the I and throws it back upon itself. In the realm of the physical it obtains that two equal forces acting in opposite directions cancel out; the result is immobility, rest. This cannot be the case in the I which is by definition activity, for otherwise the I itself would be canceled out, annihilated. Clearly, however, the I is not cancelled out in this way; instead, it is to be limited without ceasing to be an I. Thus it acts upon the reflected activity: qua imagination, it is suspended or oscillates between both directions and produces something common from them: a feeling of impeded activity, a feeling of incapacity. We as observers can say: 'The I has sensation'. The self-positing I itself, however, which we are observing, must be said *to be* sensation at this stage. *For it* activity and product are indistinguishable for it cannot simultaneously intuit itself while in the midst of production. Thus it is only conscious of the product of its activity: the I is mere sensation (limitation).

(E′) At the next stage the I is to become conscious of the activity through reflection on it (i.e. it is supposed to become conscious of itself *as* sensing). For this to happen, it must determine the product of the activity, for all reflection presupposes determination of that which is to be reflected upon. Therefore the I reflects upon the sensation and determines the feeling of being checked or impeded. In order to determine it, reflection posits something in opposition to feeling that is not feeling: an impeding factor. By its very act of determining, reflection thus necessarily goes beyond the limitation (*Schranke*) and transforms it into a boundary (*Grenze*). With this the *ground* is laid for a distinction between 'inside' and 'outside', between subject and object. The I can now become conscious of its activity since it can posit something in opposition to it. The activity of the I now appears as bounded by *something which is doing the bounding* and which is thus 'outside' the I. Hence the product of reflection upon sensation is something that imposes boundaries, a non-I. And since it is conscious not of its reflection but only of the result, it completely coincides with and is absorbed by this result: it is 'intuition' (of *something*, and no longer mere sensation).

(D′) At the ensuing stage the I again becomes conscious of its activity, which at this point is the act of positing the intuited non-I. "Furthermore, the I is supposed to posit its product (the opposed and bounding non-I) *as* its product . . . The distinguishing feature of such a product is that it could also be different than it is and could be posited as such" (GA I,3:178–79; W 1:374). To the extent that the product is recognized *as* product, the I must unify within itself the elements of both its own and the other's activity: in this way intuition is simultaneously limited and free, that is, it is an image or representation of the non-I.

(C′) That is the one point. The other is this: An image (*Bild*) is not only something made, something formed (*gebildet*). An image in the proper sense of the term is an image *of* something that is not itself an image but rather that *of which* the image is an image. This fact however also implies a standard or measure: It is an image of *this* and not of something else; it is this to which the image must conform. "Insofar as the I posits this image as a product of its own activity, it necessarily opposes to it something which is not a product of this activity, that is, to something which is no longer determinable but is instead completely determined by itself . . . This is the *actual thing* to which the creative I conforms in designing its image, and of which it must necessarily have a vague notion as it forms this image" (GA I,3:179; W 1:375).

It might seem as though nothing could be there for the I besides the image, but that would be misleading. For the image only comes about as the product of repeated reflection; the thing itself is nothing other than the product of the previous action which has now been interrupted: the limiting factor that was intuited as such. It is only because the I cannot simultaneously produce and be conscious of its production in reflection—because, that is, reflection always lags behind production—that the difference arises between the reflected image and the originally posited thing: "The entire distinction between ideality and reality, between representation and thing, arises from the impossibility of any consciousness of a free action" (GA I,3:176; W 1:371).

The imagination thus differentiates itself into a productive and a reproductive imagination, whereby the thing is conceived as a limiting factor which is determinate in itself (i.e. independent of the activity of the I). The image or representation is intuition conceived as the free activity of the I.

(B') At this stage[13] the image-forming, representational activity (imagination) is supposed to become conscious. This is an activity which duplicates (*nachbilden*) intuitions, oscillating between opposites, and, like intuition itself, it continues on indefinitely. Thus, in order to become determinate, it must be brought to rest, captured, and fixated. This of course does not mean that the activity is to cease; it does however need to pause to an extent sufficient for its activity to become *determinate* and distinguishable from others. This is brought about by combining it in a concept, thus bringing it to a halt. If that is possible, then there must also be a corresponding faculty, and this faculty Fichte calls understanding.[14] The name of course is not really important, and even the etymological affinity between 'stand' and 'understand' (present also in German and to which Fichte alludes) is ultimately irrelevant. It does however seem right

---

[13] In the 1795 *Outline of the Distinctive Character of the Wissenschaftslehre*, in which Fichte offers a detailed presentation of the first steps of his pragmatic history of the human mind, the deduction of space and time follows at this point. In the *Foundation*, he merely alludes to such a deduction: "Kant demonstrates the ideality of objects from the presupposed ideality of space and time: we, on the contrary, shall prove the ideality of space and time from the demonstrated ideality of objects. He required ideal objects to fill up space and time; we require space and time in order to locate the ideal objects" (GA I,2:335; W 1:186). I am leaving out the deduction here so as not to further complicate a line of thought which is complicated enough as it is. It should be noted, however, that in strict terms such a deduction is indeed required at this point in order to explain how it is possible for the image and the thing to correspond or agree with each other.

[14] Cp. Kant: "The *unity* of apperception in relation to the synthesis of imagination is the *understanding*" (A119, emphasis added).

that imagination, if it is to become conscious, must be capable of becoming fixated.

If the unconscious activity of fixation involved here (i.e. concept formation) is to become conscious, then the I must reflect on the fixated product. The I therefore determines itself to conceptually determine the concept (of the object). It is precisely here, though, that the spontaneity of reflection comes to light, for positive determination involves the exclusion of everything else from which one has abstracted for purposes of determination. The product of this new reflection is the consciousness of a freedom to reflect on something and thus to abstract from other things, to combine specific features while separating others out. Fichte calls this the *power of judgment*: "The power of judgment is the faculty, free till now, of reflecting upon objects already posited in understanding, or of abstracting from them, and, on the strength of this reflection or abstraction, of positing these objects more determinately in understanding" (GA I,2:381; W 1:242).

Here we see that understanding and the power of judgment reciprocally condition and determine each other. For without the objects contained in the understanding (concepts), the power of judgment could not reflect on them or abstract from them; on the other side, it is the activity of the power of judgment which determines the object as an object for the understanding. Kant of course was the first to have drawn attention to this point: On the one hand the understanding can "make no other use" of concepts "other than using them to judge" (A68), while on the other hand concept formation itself presupposes judgment, since "the criterion of the possibility of a concept . . . is the definition of it" (B115), that is, judgment with reference to *genus* and *differentia specifica*.

(A_t) The power of judgment is thus the act by which an object in general is determined. It too must finally be raised to consciousness if the I is to become conscious of everything which is posited within it. If this is to be possible, the power of judgment must be determined by reflection and hence differentiated within itself: "The activity determinant of an object in general is determined by one which has no object at all, an intrinsically nonobjective activity, opposed to the objective activity" (GA I,2:382; W 1:243).

The possibility of abstracting from a *determinate* object comes to be conscious on the background of an ability to abstract from *all* objects whatsoever. This faculty of absolute abstraction is what Fichte calls reason. The faculty of abstracting from everything objective, though, is the

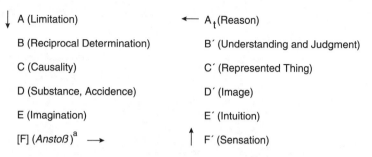

A (Limitation)	← A$_t$(Reason)
B (Reciprocal Determination)	B´ (Understanding and Judgment)
C (Causality)	C´ (Represented Thing)
D (Substance, Accidence)	D´ (Image)
E (Imagination)	E´ (Intuition)
[F] (*Anstoß*)[a] →	↑ F´ (Sensation)

[a] I include the *Anstoß* here as item [F] merely in order to provide a more useful overview; it should be noted, however, that it does not represent a proper synthesis.

Figure 8.2

faculty of self-consciousness, in which the I distinguishes itself from everything not itself: "Everything that I abstract from, everything I can think away . . . is not my I, and I posit it in opposition to my I merely by regarding it as something I can think away. The more a determinate individual can think away from himself, the closer does his empirical self-consciousness approximate to a pure self-consciousness" (GA I,2:383; W 1:244).

Fichte's "pragmatic history of the mind" thus culminates in the consciousness of the ability to abstract absolutely from all objects whatsoever. Consciousness of freedom consists in the consciousness that one need be determined by nothing but oneself. If the I is determined by an object, then it determines itself to be so determined. But this is just what is expressed by the fundamental proposition of the theoretical *Wissenschaftslehre* (A$_t$), to which we have now returned: *The I posits itself as determined by the non-I.* The circle is complete.

The course of the *Foundation* as just sketched can be put in the diagrammatic form shown in Figure 8.2.

The pragmatic history of consciousness, in turn, is shown in Figure 8.3.

Though in the end the circle of the theoretical *Wissenschaftslehre* has been completed, at the same time a new, "main antithesis" arises, namely that between the I as representational and limited, and the I as actively positing and unlimited. The I is on the one hand dependent on the non-I, but on the other hand it is also independent. Both, however, are supposed to be one and the same I. Fichte characterized the contradiction by saying, "the absolute I and the intelligent I (if we may put it as though they

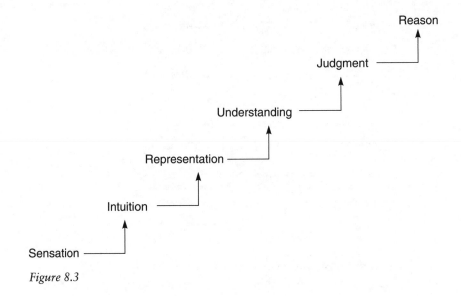

Figure 8.3

consisted of two I's, though they can only constitute one) are not one and the same, but are opposed to each other; which contradicts the absolute identity of the I. This contradiction must be removed" (GA I,2:387; W 1:249).

The removal of this contradiction requires a transition to practical philosophy. It can no longer be resolved within theoretical philosophy. It was in the following semester that Fichte's lectures turned to this part of his philosophy, which we will take up in the next chapter.

9

Morals and Critique

I.

At the beginning of the last chapter we derived two corollaries from Fichte's determination of the third principle of the *Wissenschaftslehre:*

A_p) The I posits the non-I as determined by the I; that is, the I determines the non-I—it acts or is *practical*.

A_t) The I posits itself as determined by the non-I; that is, the I posits itself as affected—it perceives or is *theoretical*.

So far we have only dealt with the second proposition, the basis of the theoretical part of the *Foundation*. This part culminated in an "main antithesis" between the I as a representational, limited, finite I ("the I as intelligence"), and the I as an actively positing, unlimited, absolute I: Qua intelligence, the I is dependent on the non-I, while the I as a being which posits absolutely is independent of the non-I. Both, however, are supposed to be one and the same I. How is this contradiction to be resolved?[1]

---

[1] The practical part of the *Foundation* is even more obviously marked by the haste with which Fichte was forced to work than is the theoretical part. More especially, however, this part also exhibits all the uncertainties of a first attempt. For while the theoretical part could take at least some orientation from the Kantian precedent, such as the (albeit underived) table of categories, Fichte's foundation of the practical has no historical forerunners. In the present case too, then, we find to be true what Kant said of the "common fortunes of the understanding in its investigations," namely that "the shortest way is commonly not the first way that it becomes aware of" (4:476). In my opinion, Fichte's division of the text into consecutively numbered paragraphs and "theorems" does not really mirror the content and it occasionally causes confusion. For example, the fact that this part of the *Foundation* is also composed of an analytic and of a pragmatic history of the human mind, is nowhere made explicit. The account I give here will therefore be situated at a certain distance

Here again, the unification of contradictory propositions is possible only if it can be shown that each of them holds only partially. This would be the case if the I was partially dependent on the non-I and partially independent of it. In other words, if the absolute I was (in some as yet unspecified way) the cause of the non-I, then it would also indirectly be the cause of the I qua intelligence. The I would ultimately be dependent on and determined by itself alone. The contradiction that is to be resolved could then be formulated this way:

H₁) The I is to have causality in relation to the non-I: it posits the non-I;

H₂) the I cannot have causality in relation to the non-I because the latter would then not be a non-I, but a product of the I.

Fichte begins by treating this as a hypothesis and asks which conditions must be fulfilled if the hypothesis is to be true. In order to be the cause of the non-I (and thus also of the limitation of the I by the non-I), the I would itself have to be the unity of two opposed activities: one of positing (*Setzen*) and one of positing in opposition (*Entgegensetzen*). Both would have to be the same activity, that is, it would have to be simultaneously limited and unlimited. This, however, is only possible if the activity, insofar as it is limited, persistently goes beyond the limit, and instead of being negated by it, renews itself as it were at the limit. And there is in fact such an activity: it is what we call striving. For striving is present whenever there is a check or hindrance which is resisted, such that the activity, rather than being negated, aspires to overcome it. The concept of striving is the concept of a cause which is not a cause—that is, one which does not bring about an effect outside itself but is only accessible to inner experience. The original activity of the I must be a striving in just this sense if it is to mediate between H₁ and H₂.[2] If it were *more* than a striving and thus had causality (i.e. realized itself), such that the I came to occupy an infinite extent, then it would not be *limited* and hence no

---

from Fichte's own text, which as we must not forget was conceived as a "handbook for his audience" and intended to be elucidated and supplemented by his lectures.

[2] "The striving . . . aspires to be a cause. If it does not become one, it fails in consequence to attain its goal, and becomes *limited* . . . The striving is not limited by *itself*, for it is implied in the concept of striving that it aspires to causality. If it limited itself, it would not be a striving" (GA I,2:417; W 1:286f.).

I could be posited. If the activity was *less* than a striving and failed to go beyond the limit, then it would be unable to posit anything in opposition to itself and hence it could not posit itself as something *determinate*: it would again fail to be an I. "Thus the I itself would have to posit in itself both the inhibition of its activity and the restoration thereof, as surely as it is to be the activity of an I that is inhibited and restored. But *this activity can be posited as restored only insofar as it is posited as inhibited; and as inhibited, insofar as it is posited as restored* . . . Hence, the states to be united are already in and for themselves in a synthetic unity; they cannot be posited at all, except as united. But *that* they are posited at all is inherent in the mere concept of the I, and is postulated along with the latter. And thus the curbed activity, which has indeed to be posited and thence restored, would simply require positing in and through the I" (GA I,2:401; W 1:266).

In other words, *if* the essence of the absolute I consisted in striving, this would also imply the *Anstoß* (even if it is not yet understood), since all striving entails an obstacle that is to be overcome. The question, then, is whether the essence of the I does in fact consist in such a striving? To answer this question, we must first decide how the I can experience any limitation at all. For the self-positing I can only experience an obstacle to the extent that it goes out beyond itself. But why should the I go out of itself? Indeed, in its first positing of itself it is wholly self-identical and self-contained. Why then should it go out of itself? If there is a reason, it must somehow be distinct from the I's self-positing as such. "It must be possible to provide a ground for this excursion of the I out of itself, whereby an object first becomes possible. This outgoing process, which precedes all resistant activity and is the foundation of its possibility in regard to the I, must be founded exclusively in the I" (GA I,2:404–5; W 1:271). What, then, requires explanation, is how it is possible *in principle* for an alien influence to be present in the I prior to any *Anstoß*. Why, then, does the I's activity come to be directed outward?

The answer lies in what we already know: The I posits itself, i.e., it is what it is *through itself*. And to this extent, nothing different from itself can be present in it. However, self-consciousness is equally essential: The I is what it is *for itself*. Thus it is essentially both—positing and reflection. To reflect on itself, it must make itself into an object for itself. This requires that it begin by distancing itself from itself; in order to reflect, it must go out of itself, and to this extent its direction must become "centrifugal" (as Fichte says for lack of a better word), outwardly directed.

207

However, it must also return into itself, and to this extent the direction of its activity is "centripetal." "Thus the centripetal and centrifugal directions of activity are both grounded alike in the nature of the I; both are one and the same, and are distinguished merely inasmuch as there is reflection upon them as distinct" (GA I,2:407; W 1:274).

In order not to lose sight of the whole, let us again summarize the development so far:

1. The I is *Tathandlung*—activity directled purely at itself (it posits itself).
2. The I is what it is for itself (it must be conscious of itself).
3. To be conscious of itself, it must reflect on itself.
4. To reflect on itself, it must
   (a) distinguish itself from itself; it must distance itself from itself—proceed beyond itself—its activity must be "centrifugal."
   (b) become an object for itself; its activity must at the same time take on the opposite direction, it must be "centripetal."[3]

At this point, however, some clarifications are in order which up to now I have been postponing. Through reflection, the I is supposed to become *for itself* what it is *in itself*. Now, the I is *Tathandlung*; i.e. originally it is purely active and absolute, unlimited and not passive. To this extent it contains all reality within itself: "the I is everything and nothing, since it is nothing *for itself*, and can distinguish no positing or posited within itself" (GA I,2:399; W 1:264). In order to become conscious of itself, it must go out beyond itself: "It is equally implicit in the concept of the I, that it must reflect about itself, *whether it really includes all reality within itself*. It bases this reflection on the foregoing idea, and thus carries the latter out to infinity, and is to that extent *practical*: not absolute, since it actually goes out of itself, through the tendency to reflection; and yet not theoretical either, since its reflection rests on nothing save this idea deriving from the I itself, and wholly abstracts from the possibility of an *Anstoß*, so

---

[3] This is an important result to which I shall later return: The self-conscious I is essentially constituted by opposed activities, centrifugal and centripetal activity. It thus has a structure analogous to that discovered by Kant in objects of outer intuition: Such objects also consist, as we saw, in the interplay of opposed, i.e. outwardly and inwardly directed forces, namely the forces of repulsion and attraction. We shall revisit this fact a little later in connection with Schelling.

that no actual reflection is present" (GA I,2:409; W 1:277; emphasis added).

In order to determine itself (i.e. reflect on itself), as necessitated by its essence, the I must therefore become practical, it must go out beyond itself with the idea of its absoluteness, *and* it must make itself into the object of its reflection, thus limiting and distinguishing itself from what is other. Again, let us summarize:

5. The I (according to its idea) is all reality.
6. In order for it to be *for itself* what it is *in itself,* it must be for itself all reality.
7. In order to be for itself, it must reflect on itself.
8. In order to reflect on itself, it must be limited and thus finite, i.e. it cannot be all reality.
9. It cannot be both, but it *ought* to be since it is one and the same I.
10. The identity of the I is not given (*gegeben*), but assigned as a task (*aufgegeben*): it *strives* for self-identity.

The necessity that the I is both the positing and the reflection of itself is grounded in its essence, and from this it follows that the fundamental activity of the I is striving. Once again, however, this line of thought also contains a moment still in need of clarification. The activity of the I required for reflection is simultaneously centrifugal and centripetal—it initially comprises both in one movement. The two directions must however also be distinguishable if the I is to become conscious of them. We can distinguish the two directions, but is the self-positing I able to as well?

Up to now, it is not. For in order for two things to be distinguishable, they must be related to a third thing, in relation to which they are distinct. So far, though, we have nothing but two directions, both of which are equally rooted in the I. *As such* both directions coincide—they are indiscernible and hence one and the same. Strictly speaking, we cannot yet even speak of directions. Without a boundary there can be no outside in opposition to an inside (which in turn is an inside only in opposition to an outside). Consequently, it is only by way of a boundary that an outwardly directed activity can be distinguished from one which is inwardly directed. Only when the activity of the I runs up against a point C which checks it and reflects it back onto itself do these directions become recognizable as distinct: one activity that strives beyond C, and another completely opposite activity which is reflected back into the I by the *Anstoß* in C. "Through limitation, whereby only the *outward* direction is eliminated, but not the direction *inward,* this original force is as it were divided . . . *That* this occurs, as a fact, is absolutely incapable of derivation from the I, as has frequently been pointed out; but we can show, at all events, that it must occur, *if* an actual consciousness is to be possible" (GA I,2:423, 408; W 1:294, 275).

At this point a resolution of the "main antithesis" between the I as intelligence and the absolute I is beginning to emerge: Because the I is practical, it goes out of itself. Because it goes out of itself, it opens itself to the experience of an *Anstoß* independent of itself. Because it experiences an *Anstoß,* it can reflect on itself. By way of this reflection on itself, a consciousness (feeling) of its limitation originates. The reflection on its limitation necessarily posits something opposed to it as a limiting factor (the non-I). And so on.

The non-I and the *Anstoß* must therefore be distinguished. The I opens itself to the *Anstoß* by going out beyond itself; otherwise it could not experience an *Anstoß* to its activity. To this extent, the *Anstoß* is conditioned by the I itself. Yet without an *Anstoß* from outside itself, the I would not reflect and hence not become conscious of its activity. To this extent, the I is conditioned by the *Anstoß.* Since the *Anstoß* must be homogeneous with the I in order to have this effect, we can at this point already see that the *Anstoß* must in no way impinge on the I's freedom and must therefore primarily originate in free beings, i.e. in other Is through which the self-positing I is "summoned" (as Fichte says), to determine itself. In his *Foundations of Natural Right, according to the Principles of the Wissenschaftslehre,* which appeared soon after in 1796, Fichte was to make this meaning of the *Anstoß* explicit.[4] Whether this interpretation of the *Anstoß* is already at work in the *Foundation* of 1794 is the subject of some controversy in the literature.[5] Considering the fact that

---

[4] If it is "to find itself as the *object* (of its reflection)," the subject "cannot find itself as *determining itself* to spontaneous activity . . . but [only] as determined to such activity by an external *Anstoß* which, however, must still allow it entirely to retain its freedom of self-determination. For otherwise the first point is lost, and the subject cannot find itself as an I . . . But this is not, and cannot be, otherwise conceived than as a mere summons to the subject that it should act . . . if there are to be humans at all, there must be more than one . . . The summons to free spontaneous activity is that which we call education [*Erziehung*]" (GA I,3:343, 342, 347; W 3:33, 39).

[5] A representative advocate of the view that intersubjectivity as a condition of self-consciousness is already present (at least implicitly) in the *Foundation* of 1794 is

Fichte argues solely on the basis of transcendental philosophy in the *Foundation* and is therefore *forced* to abstract from all *determinate* things independent of the I, the debate seems pointless to me. All that can be said from the standpoint of the *Foundation* is that the *Anstoß* is something alien and opposed to the I which determines it to self-determination. Since however the *Anstoß* must be experienced *in the I*, it must also be in some way homogeneous with the I.[6] Fichte himself summarized this line of thought as follows:

> The I posits itself absolutely, and is thereby complete in itself and closed to any impression from without. But if it is to be an I, it must also posit itself as self-posited; and by this new positing, relative to an original positing, it opens itself, if I may so put it, to external influence; simply by this reiteration of positing, it concedes the possibility that there might also be something within it that is not actually posited by itself. Both types of positing are conditions for the influence of a non-I; without the first, there would be no activity of the self to undergo limitation; without the second, this activity would not be limited for the I, and the latter would be unable to posit itself as limited. Thus the I, as such, is originally in a state of reciprocal action with itself, and only so does an external influence on it become possible (GA I,2:409; W 1:276).

II.

The "main antithesis" at the end of the theoretical part of the *Foundation* has issued in a conceptual possibility for how the I can be simultaneously dependent and independent of the non-I: If the contradiction between the finite and the infinite I, between dependence and independence from the non-I is to be resolvable, then the original activity of the I must

---

R. Lauth ("Das Problem der Interpersonalität bei Fichte," in Lauth 1989). The opposing view, according to which the theory of the *Anstoß* "underwent a dramatic development between 1794 and 1796," is argued in Breazeale 1995, 96. The latter text contains further references.

[6] It does indeed seem improbable that Fichte would have been unaware of this aspect of the *Anstoß* in 1794, especially given his statement at the very beginning of the 1794 Winter semester (i.e. in September) that "human beings must necessarily undergo development by their own kind" (GA II,4:37). R. Lauth points to a passage in the *Foundation* (GA I,2:337; W 1:189): "No you, no I; no I, no you."

be a striving. If the derivation was correct, then the actuality of practical self-consciousness must in turn be derivable from this activity together with the experience of resistance, which Fichte characterizes as a fact that is primitive in the sense that it is an original and underivable feature of the mind. It is necessary to demonstrate how the I in fact strives to restore its self-identity (which is simultaneously impinged upon and so-licited by reflection) in the products of reflection—sensation, intuition, imagination, understanding, the power of judgment, reason—and how the multiplicity of practical modes of behavior emerge from this striving as the I becomes increasingly conscious of it.

The remaining task is therefore set. Just as in the theoretical part of the *Foundation* the argumentation was divided into an analytic part and a "pragmatic history of the mind" reconstructing the I's emerging consciousness of its theoretical activity, an analogous course must be fol-lowed in the practical part, even though Fichte does not explicitly draw attention to the fact. What is now thematic is the I's activity of striving. Since it is aimed at unifying the opposed moments in the I itself (rather than the I and non-I), the genesis of consciousness now comes to be pre-sented as a deduction of feeling,[7] analogous to the deduction of repre-sentation in the theoretical part of the work. "In the theoretical part of the *Wissenschaftslehre* we have had to do solely with *cognition;* here we are concerned with that which is *cognized.* There, the question was, *how* is a thing posited, intuited, thought, etc.; here it is, *what* is posited? . . . Hence arises the series of those things that *ought* to be, and are given through the I alone; in short, the series of the *ideal*" (GA I,2:416, 409; W 1:285, 277).

III.

We turn, then, to the genesis of practical self-consciousness and its cor-respondence to the stages of theoretical reflection.

(F″) Striving, we had said, is causality that does not produce an object (for else it would no longer be a striving), but which is also not annihi-lated by resistance (for else it would again no longer be a striving). Hence it can only produce and continually renew itself: "But a self-productive striving that is fixed, determinate, and definite in character is known as a

---

[7] Feeling is that *in the I* which is experienced as given because its production re-mains unconscious.

drive" (GA I,2:418; W 1:287). In this way, striving, resistance, and their equilibrium are continuously unified in the drive. In order for a drive as such to become conscious, it must be reflected.

Now on the one side the drive is rendered unsatisfied by its obstruction, for it cannot become efficacious; on the other side, however, it nevertheless gains a certain satisfaction, for the I is supposed to become conscious of itself and consciousness is only possible on the basis of limitation. Hence any drive is necessarily also a drive toward limitation, toward an object. The condition of reflection is fulfilled by the limitation and the activity is thrown back onto itself. In this way, the limitation becomes conscious, that is, something felt comes into being—a feeling of compulsion, of restricted striving. The I is driven and feels this force in the obstacle as a feeling of incapacity (*Nicht-Können*). At this stage, then, it is merely a "feeling of force." It feels, yet without the activity that produces that feeling (reflection) emerging into consciousness: "There is something present *for which* a thing might be, though it is not as yet present *for itself*. But there is necessarily present for it an inner driving force, though since there can be no consciousness of the I, or of any relation thereto, this force is merely *felt*" (GA I,2:424; W 1:295).

(E″) There is something there, *for which* something can be there. That is, we, as observers, can already recognize the presence of the I as soon as feeling is there, for the I is always at once both that which feels and that which is felt, the active and the passive. The observed I, by contrast, is unable to recognize this. It is still wholly and exclusively the feeling of incapacity: "Its activity is eliminated *for itself*." Since however the I must also come to be *for itself* what it is *in itself*, it cannot remain at this stage: "As surely as it is an I, therefore, it must restore this activity, and restore it *for itself*, that is, it must at least put itself in the position of being able, if only in some future course of reflection, to posit itself as free and unlimited" (GA I,2:426; W 1:297f.). The new action thus arises spontaneously, and only because the I has to become conscious of itself. It depends only on the I and is determined by the I alone, and therefore it can only relate to something already present in the I: the feeling posited in the first reflection. The new action is thus a reflection on reflection; its object is something of the same kind as itself and it can only find itself therein. Since the I is simultaneously both that which does the determining and that which is determined, in the new reflection it transfers this essence (unconsciously, since it does not reflect on this action) to that which is to be determined and posits it as I—i.e., in this case as that which is simultaneously that which feels and that which is felt (in reciprocal action with itself). Fichte calls the resulting feeling *Selbstgefühl,* "self-feeling."

Let us take a closer look at this "self-feeling." In the earlier case of the feeling of force, the feeling subject and that which was felt were not yet separate and distinct. If that feeling is to be posited as an I, both that which feels and that which is felt must be posited as an I: the fact that it is simultaneously active and passive must therefore appear twice. And this is indeed the case—*for us:* (a) That which feels is as such active; but as something *driven* to reflection it is at the same time passive. (b) That which is felt is active as the act of driving to reflection, yet also passive as the object of reflection. *For the I,* however, things appear rather differently than they do for us:

As regards (a), that which is active in the first reflection knows nothing of the origin of its activity; for it, its felt passivity must consequently have a different ground. Since (qua reflection) it must necessarily be directed toward an object which it determines, it therefore *must* set a limit and hence posit something that is doing the limiting (a non-I), all without reflecting on its own activity: "Hence the felt compulsion to posit something as actually present" (GA I,2:428; W 1:300). At this stage the I is not conscious of the fact that it is itself the agent which has posited a limiting factor in opposition to itself.

As regards (b), that which is felt in the first reflection also fails to become conscious that it is itself the active source of the drive and thus the cause of its own suffering or passivity (limitation by reflection). For it, its suffering or passivity must therefore have its ground in the fact that it is limited by a non-I. Now, that which feels and that which is felt are one and the same I. In other words, the I ineluctably places the cause of its suffering or passivity in the non-I which it has itself (unconsciously) produced through reflection. Although the cause of suffering lies in the I, it is inevitably transferred to the non-I as that which limits the I.

With this, the feeling of compulsion is determined. Thanks to the second reflection, the I is now also *for itself* something for which something else exists. It has posited itself *as* a feeling subject. This "self-feeling" is inseparably bound up with the feeling of something distinct from itself, by which it is delimited—a reality independent of the I: "The productive I was itself posited as *passive,* as was that which is felt in reflection. *For itself,* therefore, the I is always *passive* in relation to the non-I, is quite unaware of its own activity, and does not reflect thereon. Hence the reality of the thing appears to be felt, whereas it is only the I which is felt. (Here lies the ground of all reality. Only through that relation of feeling to the I, which has now been demonstrated, is the reality either of the I, or of the non-I, possible for the I" (GA I,1:429; W 1:301).

If the feeling of force was still a purely subjective feeling of incapacity, the self-delimitation present in self-feeling makes it possible for the first time to distinguish between inside and outside.

(D″) From the previous reflection it is apparent that although the I has posited itself as feeling subject, it is, for itself, now limited by a non-I. The drive itself has remained unconscious and hence must be made into an object at the next stage of emerging consciousness. Up to now, the drive was described as an urge to go out beyond itself and produce a reality external to itself, which, however, it is not capable of doing: it is a restricted drive toward production. In the present reflection, this outwardly directed drive is supposed to become conscious. Thus the I comes to appear as "driven *out of itself—within itself*." Since—"as always"—the I does not reflect on the reflection itself, as a consequence what it reflects upon appears to it as given in the I, i.e. as feeling. What sort of a feeling is this? "It is an activity *that has no object* whatever, but is nonetheless *irresistibly driven out towards one,* and is merely *felt.* But such a determination in the self is called a *longing;* a drive towards something totally unknown, which reveals itself only through a *need,* a *discomfort,* a *void,* which seeks satisfaction, but does not say from whence. The I feels a longing in itself; it feels itself in want" (GA I,2:431; W 1:302f.).

Thus in addition to the limitation, the will to go beyond it, the outwardly directed drive, is now also posited for the I. If what was posited in self-feeling was a relatively indeterminate non-I limiting the I, longing now posits something indeterminate which the I, determined by the drive, would make actual if it possessed causality, "and which we may provisionally call the *ideal*" (GA I,2:432; W 1:304).

Just as the self-limitation that occurs in self-feeling is the prerequisite for distinguishing between inside and outside, so too in the feeling of neediness does an external world become manifest for the first time within the I which longingly relates to it—it feels a *void* that seeks repletion. Why ought the void to be filled?

(C″) Since everything implicit in the I must become conscious to it, it must also reflect upon that which remained unconscious at the previous stage: that which is active in the feeling of longing. Since we are in the

215

practical part of the *Foundation* and nothing in the I is without a drive, this means that the drive at the basis of longing must become determinate. Now a drive must effect as much as it can. It can only have effect, however, on the reflective activity of the I. For the drive can neither produce nor eliminate the real which is posited in the feeling of limitation; hence it can only direct itself toward that which determines it in an attempt to move or impel it: "The outgoing drive . . . becomes therefore in this respect a drive to the *determination* or *modification* of something external to the I, namely the reality already given by feeling in general. The I was at once the determinate and the determinant. That it is impelled outwards by the drive, is to say that it must be the determinant" (GA I,2:434; W 1:307).

The drive is thus the drive toward determination. Since it has no causality and the limiting non-I is posited as something determinate in itself, the drive can only manifest itself as an urge toward the duplication (*Nachbildung*) of the reality given in the feeling of limitation: "The requirement is simply to bring forth in the I a determination, as it exists in the non-I" (GA I,2:436; W 1:310).

This implies, first, that it is the *I* which is to do the determining, and second, that the determining can only be a duplication (*Nachbilden*) of the thing. Now we noted above, in the context of the genesis of theoretical self-consciousness, that an image (*Bild*), if it is to be an image *of something,* requires a criterion. Here the criterion of determination is supposed to lie in the reflecting I itself. Its criterion, though, consists in the necessity for the I to posit itself in its action as both the determinant and the determinate. Now that it is driven to reproduction, it transfers its criterion into the thing. The longed-for object is thus an object reproduced in accord with the real non-I and it carries the stamp (the criterion) of the I, or an actuality appropriate to the I; the drive toward determination is not satisfied until an opposed feeling arises in which the I can posit itself as simultaneously determinate and determinant.

(B″) If the I is to become conscious of this, it must be capable of becoming conscious of the longed-for object. So far, however, the object of longing has been entirely indeterminate: it was merely "*something other, posited in opposition to* that which is present." If longing is to become determinate, "the *other which is longed for* must be demonstrated" as posited in opposition (GA I,2:444, 447f.; W 1:320, 324). That in opposition to which the longed-for object is posited, is the present feeling of limitation, and since this feeling has till now remained indeterminate, so

216

has the longed-for feeling.[8] But a determinate, opposed feeling must now arise. Thus, if the I is to posit itself in this feeling as determinant, it must first determine the feeling of limitation itself.

Now, determining as such is delimitation and distinction: "Without opposition, the entire non-I is something, but not a determinate or particular something" (GA I,2:444; W 1:319). Something *else* must therefore also be posited; the drive toward determination is necessarily a "drive towards alteration in general," and since what is real manifests itself in the feeling of limitation, the drive finds expression in the desire for other such feelings, for the alteration of feelings of limitation that can mutually determine each other. Thus together with the drive toward reciprocal determination of feelings, striving (the alternation of obstruction and restoration) is also posited in the I.

Of course, up to now this is the case only for us, the observers. For it is as yet unclear how this can as such also become conscious for the I. For in order to be able to become conscious of the alternation of feelings, the alternating terms must be capable of being united in the I. However, the I cannot feel opposed terms at the same time, for a feeling arises just when the I is being limited: "it cannot be *limited at* C and at the same time *unlimited at* C" (GA I,2:445; W 1:321). That which is opposed cannot, *as such,* be felt at all.[9] On the other hand, the first feeling is determinate only in relation to the second; without a real opposition the present limitation cannot be felt as determinate: Thus if this condition is not fulfilled, "the I feels nothing *determinate,* and hence feels *nothing at all*; it is not alive, therefore, and is not an I, which contradicts the presupposition of the *Wissenschaftslehre*" (ibid.).

(A$_p$) Opposition must therefore come about, and the question is, how can the I itself become aware that its state of feeling has changed? Obviously, that depends on there being a common boundary between the alternating feelings, so that it is impossible to reflect on *one* of the feelings without reflecting on *both*. But this is only the case when two feelings

---

[8] Though the non-I was posited in self-feeling as the limiting factor and hence as something determinate *in itself,* the *feeling of limitation* itself has remained entirely indeterminate since it has not as yet been distinguished from anything else.

[9] The problem corresponds to the one we previously encountered in the theoretical part (*Synthesis E*), where the two opposed terms activity and passivity were only able to occur simultaneously in consciousness because they had been brought together by the imagination.

intrinsically refer to each other as longing and satisfaction do. For "[t]he feeling of longing cannot be posited without some satisfaction toward which it is directed; nor can the satisfaction be posited without presupposing a longing that is to be satisfied. At the point where longing ceases, and satisfaction begins, the boundary lies" (GA I,2:448; W 1:324). The feeling of limitation, then, can only come to be determinate for the I if satisfaction is possible.

Let us sum up: As the I determined itself in the second reflection, a feeling of limitation (reality) arose along with self-feeling. Now the I is driven to determine itself to alter the feelings of limitation (reproduction of the present reality). In order to do so, it brings its own criterion along with it, according to which it is supposed to be at once both determinate and determinant. When the I has altered its feeling of limitation in accord with its criterion, the drive to determine is satisfied and must now find expression in a new feeling: "*Drive* and *action* are now one and the same; the determination demanded by the former is possible, and occurs. The I reflects *upon this feeling,* and *on itself* therein, as at once the determinant and the determinate, as wholly at one with itself; and such a determination of feeling we may speak of as *approval.* The feeling is accompanied by approval" (GA I,2:448; W 1:325).

But this means that *when* the feeling of approval comes about, it must necessarily relate back to the original feeling, no matter how it may be otherwise determined, and hence that feeling too comes to be determinate for the I. Now, this is not merely possible: *insofar* as the I is conscious of itself as something determinate, the action demanded by the drive to determine has already become actual. But the presupposition of the entire chain of reasoning up till now has been that the I *is* conscious of itself as something determinate and posits itself as such. In other words, in the feeling of approval, the I not only posits itself as determined by the non-I, but also as determining it. This, however, is the principle A_p on which the practical part of the *Foundation* was based. The genetic description of practical self-consciousness has thus returned to the point at which this part began.

(G1) It has not yet, however, reached its end. For it started with the assumption that the I strives to realize its self-identity. Though the harmony of drive and action has now been posited in the I—it is at once both determinant and determinate—the drive to determine has still not determined itself. Up till now, it has realized itself only in the determination of things, so that the harmony it has achieved remains dependent upon such things. The final drive is therefore a drive toward absolute unity and completion of the I in itself. In order for the I to be conscious of itself as unrestrictedly self-determining, drive and action must reciprocally determine each other.

This is the case when the drive leads to an action which is done for the sake of the drive or when the action satisfying the drive is the drive itself. Such a drive toward actions for the sake of the drive is the moral drive, i.e. the will insofar as it is determined only by itself. The I experiences its harmony with itself (albeit only briefly) in moral action. "The harmony exists, and a feeling of *approval* ensues, which in this case is a feeling of *contentment,* of repletion, of utter completeness" (GA I,2:450; W 1:328).

Hence the final step is no longer the self-determination of the I by way of the non-I, but rather unconditional self-determination, the immediate unity of deed (*Tat*) and action (*Handlung*): the I posits itself absolutely. With this the argumentation has returned to the first principle of the *Foundation* and thus to its beginning: the circuit has been closed. Confirmation of what Fichte had already announced in his prospectus *Concerning the Concept of the Wissenschaftslehre* has been achieved: "A first principle has been exhausted when a complete system has been erected upon it, that is, when the principle in question necessarily leads to *all* of the propositions which are asserted and when *all* of these propositions necessarily lead us back to the first principle . . . In some future exposition of the *Wissenschaftslehre* it will be shown that this theory really does complete this circuit, that it leaves the inquirer at precisely the point where he started" (GA I,2:130f.; W1:58f.)

Even so, the *Foundation* does not conclude with the first principle as such. Why doesn't Fichte bring the work to a close with a renewed formulation of the principle? The answer lies in the two distinct standpoints constitutive for the *Foundation*.[10] In the beginning is the *Tathandlung*, the intellectual intuition of the I as the principle of a philosophy which is able to come forward as science, together with the analysis of its necessary implications. In order to confirm the correctness of the procedure, however, it was necessary to show that self-consciousness does in fact arise from the elements thus derived. And to this end, the reader had to posit arbitrarily "another I" upon which to perform the "experiment" of observing the genesis of self-consciousness. Fichte explains in advance that

---

[10] Wolfgang Schrader 1979, 343–344 has rightly pointed out this fact.

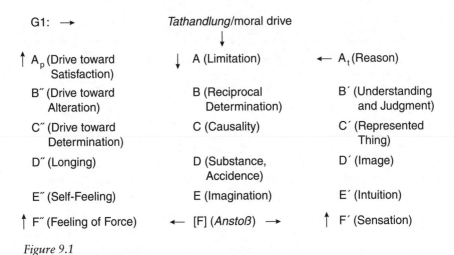

G1: → Tathandlung/moral drive
            ↓

↑ A_p (Drive toward   ↓ A (Limitation)   ← A_t (Reason)
    Satisfaction)

B″ (Drive toward   B (Reciprocal   B′ (Understanding
    Alteration)   Determination)   and Judgment)

C″ (Drive toward   C (Causality)   C′ (Represented
    Determination)   Thing)

D″ (Longing)   D (Substance,   D′ (Image)
                                Accidence)

E″ (Self-Feeling)   E (Imagination)   E′ (Intuition)

↑ F″ (Feeling of Force)   ← [F] (*Anstoß*) →   ↑ F′ (Sensation)

Figure 9.1

"the I under investigation will itself arrive eventually at the point where the observer now stands; there they will both unite, and by this union the circuit will be closed and the task completed" (GA I,2:420; W 1:290f.). That has now in fact happened. By way of the experience that the I under observation has undergone, the starting point has acquired a determinacy which it did not have at the outset: at the end the I has become the idea of the natural, rational human being: "The I exists in this [initial] form only *for the philosopher;* and insofar as one grasps it in the form, one thereby raises oneself to the level of philosophy. But the I is present as an Idea *for the I* itself, i.e. for the I the philosopher is observing. The philosopher does not portray this as his own I, but rather as the Idea of the natural, albeit completely cultivated [*ausgebildet*] human being" (GA I,4:266; W 1:515).[11] Although in the end the *Foundation* returns to its beginning, the "feeling of contentment . . . of repletion, of utter completeness" characterizes only the goal that has been attained, not the starting point of the investigation.

The schema shown in Figure 9.1 is intended to facilitate an overview of the course of the *Foundation* in its entirety.

---

[11] It is the "I as intellectual intuition, from which the *Wissenschaftslehre* commences, and the I as an Idea, with which it concludes" (GA I,4:265; W 1:515).

IV.

Historical Excursus

"After Reinhold's departure, which was rightly perceived as a great loss for the academy, Fichte, who in his writings had professed grand but perhaps not altogether appropriate opinions on the most important questions of morality and the state, was daringly, nay audaciously, called to take his place.[12] He was one of the most capable figures ever to have been seen, and his views were, in a higher sense, irreproachable; but how could he ever have been expected to keep in step with a world that he considered to have been created as his possession?" (HA 10:440–41).

Thus was Goethe's view of things in retrospect, many years later. Fichte's extraordinary success as a teacher was indeed plagued from the outset by recurring cases of slander, intrigue, and contention. In his very first semester, Fichte was forced to defend himself against the charge that he was a Jacobin who predicted in his lecture course 'Morality for Scholars' that in ten to twenty years there would be neither kings nor princes. By publishing the lectures he had held up to that point in the book *The Vocation of the Scholar,* Fichte was initially able to rebut the charge. The following semester, when he responded to the excessively high numbers of enrollment by rescheduling his lectures for Sunday morning, he was accused at court of seeking to replace the Sunday sermon with a cult of reason: this time the duke suspended the lectures until the authorities had had time to investigate the charges. The semester after that, Fichte even had to leave the university for several months and retire to the country in order to escape physical assault.

At this time a controversy occurred that found little public resonance, but which is all the more important in the present context: the so-called *Horenstreit* with

---

[12] In 1793, Fichte had published two texts on the current political situation: *Reclamation of the Freedom of Thought from the Princes of Europe, Who Have Oppressed It Until Now,* and *Contribution to the Rectification of the Public's Judgment of the French Revolution.* In the latter text, he had described "Europe's princes" as follows: "They who for the most part have been brought up in lassitude and ignorance, or who, when they do learn something, learn only a truth that has been fashioned expressly for them; they who cease, as all know, to further their education once they begin to rule, who read not a single new book unless it be watered-down sophistry, and who lag behind their own age by at least as many years as they have been in power" (GA I,1:207f.; W 6:45). Following the advice of Goethe and Voigt, one such prince, Karl August von Sachsen-Weimar-Eisenach, had appointed Fichte as Reinhold's successor in Jena.

Schiller. Schiller, who had initially also been among Fichte's audience, had begun publishing a literary journal called *Die Horen,* in which his *Letters on the Aesthetic Education of Man* also appeared in several installments. Fichte was persuaded to act as the journal's joint editor, and Schiller invited him to contribute articles as well. When, after several requests, he submitted "Concerning the Difference between the Spirit and the Letter within Philosophy. A Series of Letters," Schiller was forced to acknowledge that this placed Fichte in competition with his own *Letters on Aesthetic Education.* Indeed, Fichte went so far as to declare that Schiller's approach was circular since aesthetic education already presupposes the freedom it seeks to develop.[13]

Schiller responded by refusing to print the article. However, before returning it to Fichte he made a copy in order to discuss it with Goethe in hopes of finding support for his decision. Fichte, who felt certain of his case, demanded that Goethe act as referee. Schiller prevented this, thus interposing himself between Goethe and Fichte. The aggrieved Fichte withdrew, and Goethe must by this time have sensed that his hopes of scientific cooperation with Fichte were unlikely to be fulfilled.

When in 1798 an opportunity arose to bring the young Schelling to the University of Jena, Goethe (after some hesitation) decided to support the initiative. He had not originally been impressed by Schelling's *Ideas for a Philosophy of Nature.* The author did not seem to him to be entirely sincere, and the book itself failed to address organic nature. "Schelling's book has given me occasion to notice once again that we cannot expect much help from contemporary philosophers" (HABr. 2:325), he wrote to Schiller on January 13, 1798, one of Schelling's supporters in Jena. Yet when, at the end of May, he became personally acquainted with Schelling at Schiller's house and even found opportunities on the following days to perform experiments with him on the theory of color, Goethe gained a far more favorable impression: "he is visiting at the moment and I have very much enjoyed his conversation," Goethe promptly communicated to Voigt: "I am convinced that he will make us proud and be a boon for the academy" (GVB 2:74). After reading Schelling's *World Soul,* which had come out that same month and dealt with the organic sphere

---

[13] "Hence the epochs and regions of servitude are also those of tastelessness; and if it is inadvisable, on the one hand, to set people free before their aesthetic sense has been cultivated, it is impossible, on the other, to cultivate that sense before they are free; and the idea of aesthetic education as a means of raising up mankind to the worthiness of freedom and thence to freedom itself, leads us around in a circle as long as we have not already found a means of awakening the courage in individuals from among the great mass of people to be the lord of none and the servant of none" (W 8:286–287).

that had been omitted from the *Ideas*,[14] Goethe became a strong supporter of Schelling's appointment: "Schelling's brief visit made me very happy; I hope for his and for our sake that he is brought here . . . he would be of great benefit to me in my work" (GVB 2:79).

And so it happened that Schelling, hardly twenty-three years old, came to Jena in 1798 as an extraordinary professor. When Fichte became embroiled in the so-called "Atheism Controversy" in the following year, threatening to leave Jena should he be publicly rebuked, the Weimar court took Fichte to be giving notice. After just five years, his professorship in Jena had reached its end.

V.

Schelling

We can begin to understand Schelling's basic approach to philosophy by unpacking a remark I cited in the first part of the book. It is found in his early text *On the I as the Principle of Philosophy* [*Vom Ich als Princip der Philosophie*], which Schelling wrote while he was still a student at the protestant seminary in Tübingen, the Tübinger Stift. He says, "Never, perhaps, have so many deep thoughts been pressed together in so few pages as is the case in section 76 of the Critique of the Teleological Power of Judgment" (AA I,2:175; SW I:242). Why is this section 76 so extraordinarily important to Schelling?

If it is true, as Kant argues there, that the contradiction between mechanism and teleology is rooted only in our discursive mode of thought, and not in objects themselves, then this also says something about the objects' being in themselves. To understand this, we must make somewhat finer distinctions than we did in Chapter 6. There we saw that an organism is a product of nature in which part and whole are reciprocally conditioned by one another: the parts make the whole possible, and the whole makes the parts possible. This is the reason why, according to Kant, organisms are inexplicable to us, since for a discursive understanding these two relations are distinct and incompatible. They are *distinct* because, if the

---

[14] The complete title of the text, which was published in May of 1798, is *On the World Soul, a Hypothesis of Higher Physics for Explaining the Universal Organism* [*Von der Weltseele, eine Hypothese der höhern Physik zur Erklärung des allgemeinen Organismus*]. Goethe wrote of it to Voigt: "[I]t contains very beautiful views and stimulates that much more vigorously my wish that its author become more and more acquainted with the details of experience" (GVB 2:79–80).

parts make the whole possible, we are dealing with a mechanical relation; whereas, if the whole makes the parts possible, we are dealing with a relation of intention or purpose. They are *incompatible* because efficient causes and final causes cannot *both* be principles of the possibility of one and the same sensuous object.

If however the concept of a natural purpose cannot be adequate to its object, are we then justified at all in basing our inquiries into nature upon it? According to Kant, we are, and he offers two reasons why. First of all, because it is only on the basis of this concept that we can make organisms comprehensible to ourselves at all. And second, because organisms, too, are only appearances, and hence a non-sensible substrate underlies them. We need not think of this substrate as containing within itself a contradiction between mechanism and purposiveness, for the contradiction arises only from the subjective conditions of our cognition. This was the crucial point for Kant: Since mechanism and intention cannot both simultaneously be principles of the possibility of one and the same thing, they can only hold simultaneously for our inquiries into natural objects if no such opposition is to be met with in the objects supersensible ground. The distinction between the sensible and supersensible worlds thus secures "at least the possibility that both [mechanism and teleology] may be objectively unifiable in one principle (since they concern appearances that presuppose a supersensible ground)" (5:413).[15]

Such is Kant's resolution of the antinomy of the teleological power of judgment: the contradiction between the thesis and antithesis arises from the "particular [subjective] constitution of our understanding"; in objective terms, however, both may well be capable of unification in a single principle. Here a comparison with the First Critique is illuminating: just as, for example, the forms of intuition space and time are subjective principles that lead to an antinomy when applied to things in themselves, so too the subjective principles of mechanism and teleology lead to an antinomy when we refer them to the substrate that underlies natural ends. In the latter case, however, we would not be dealing with a mathematical,

---

[15] In section 70 Kant had already considered the possibility that "in the inner ground of nature itself, which is unknown to us, physical-mechanical connection and connection to ends may cohere in the same things, in a single principle: only our reason is not in a position to unify them in such a principle" (5:388). In his copy of the Third Critique, Goethe put three exclamation marks next to this passage! See Molnár 1994, 332.

but rather with a dynamical antinomy, i.e. one in which thesis and antithesis can both be true. Indeed, in the present case we *must* in fact assume that both are true. For organisms are "still given in nature" (5:405), and since they are products of nature and not of art, in this case it is nature itself which organizes its matter. In contrast to artifacts, the purpose is not in the present case ("technically") imposed on matter from without; and so matter must, in its supersensible ground, already be so inseparably bound up with what we call purposiveness that both are strictly indistinguishable. In this case, purposiveness is immanent in the product and inseparable from its mechanism, so that both must have the same unified ground. This however means that a fundamental opposition between matter and intention, nature and spirit can no more have any basis in the object, i.e. in the supersensible substrate, than the opposition between mechanism and purposiveness can.

VI.

Schelling realized this while he was still a student. As someone who had intensively studied not only Kant but also and especially Jacobi's book on Spinoza, he recognized that, taken to their logical conclusion, the ideas of section 76 bring Kant into an astonishing proximity to Spinoza: In Kant's supersensible substrate, spirit and nature are just as inseparably one as they are in the one substance of Spinoza (*deus sive natura*).[16]

Yet with one important difference: For Kant, the unifiability of spirit and nature in their supersensible substrate is only an object of the reflective power of judgment, and though philosophy is compelled to conceive a connection between the supersensible and the sensible worlds, it is in principle incapable of cognizing such a connection. For precisely this reason Schelling could not become a Kantian, despite his enthusiasm for section 76 of the Third Critique. For he had just received from Fichte the first sheets of the *Foundation of the Entire Wissenschaftslehre*,[17] in which Fichte (as we saw in the last chapter) transforms the connection between

---

[16] Thus Schelling again writes in his *Ideas for a Philosophy of Nature:* "The *first* to have viewed spirit and matter as one, thought and extension as mere modification of the same principle, was *Spinoza.*" (AA I,5:76; SW II:20). Cp. Spinoza, E2p7s.

[17] These sheets are what inspired Schelling to write *On the I as the Principle of Philosophy,* from which the statement on the unique significance of section 76, cited above, is taken.

the supersensible worlds from a *merely thinkable* relation (as it is according to Kant) into a *knowable* relation: the *Wissenschaftslehre* consists "precisely in the exploration of what for Kant was unexplorable, namely the common root linking the sensible and supersensible worlds, and in the real and comprehensible derivation of the two worlds from a single principle" (GA II,8:32; W10:104).

Yet neither could Schelling become a Fichtean. For Fichte had shown how the two worlds cohere *only in the case of the I*. If however the result of section 76 of the *Critique of the Power of Judgment* is right, then a corresponding demonstration must also be possible for knowledge of the natural world, assuming that both are indeed merely humanly conditioned manifestations of a single essentially indivisible reality.[18] And so it is that on February 4, 1795, Schelling, hard at work on the text *Vom Ich,* writes to his former classmate Hegel: "In the meantime I have become a Spinozist! Don't be astonished. You will soon hear how."[19]

In 1795 Schelling has become neither a Fichtean nor a Kantian, but a Spinozist instead, the reason being that, after Kant and Fichte, the exposition of the *unity* of nature and spirit and their derivation from a common root was philosophy's only remaining *desideratum*. If Kant is right and we follow section 76 to its logical conclusion, then (according to Schelling) there *must* be a philosophy of nature which can be placed next to transcendental philosophy as its complement and in which the Schellingian *Naturphilosoph* approaches nature just as the transcendental philosopher approaches the I, namely by constructing a systematic presentation of

---

[18] In the present context it is irrelevant that Fichte himself rejected this appraisal of his achievements; cp., e.g., GA II,8:16; W 10:96f. It is however true that his *Foundation* does not contain a philosophy of nature, and nor did he provide one later: "There is an a priori philosophy of nature. It will be worked out. However, I do not find myself able to do so." ("Platner- Vorlesung 1798/99", GA II,4:267). Lauth 1984 has a different views on this matter, however.

[19] *Briefe von und an Hegel,* 1:22. One month earlier he had already written to Hegel, saying, "I am now receiving the beginning of the detailed exposition by Fichte himself, the *Foundation of the Entire Wissenschaftslehre* . . . Now I am working on an ethics à la Spinoza. It is designed to establish the highest principles of all philosophy, in which theoretical and practical reason are united. If I have the courage and the time, it will be finished by the next book-fair or by next summer at the latest. I'll be happy enough if I can be one of the first to greet Fichte, the new hero, in the land of truth!" Cp. *Briefe von und an Hegel,* 1:15.

their origination from a common root (cp. SW III:12).[20] Thus at the beginning of his career, Schelling's chief efforts are devoted to a philosophy of nature that he later came to describe as a "Spinozism of physics."

VII.

In 1795, of course, all that is still only a project. Schelling has just turned twenty, and a philosophy of nature requires thorough knowledge of the various natural sciences, which of course the young seminarian had yet to acquire.[21] So he began with an attempt to clarify the notion of a supersensible substrate or the ultimate ground of reality (the unconditioned, the absolute) as the unity of the subjective and objective. Kant and Spinoza are therefore the two main addressees of the text *On the I* (Fichte is not mentioned by name). The basic Spinozist concept of a single substance is to be brought into line with Kant's results: the ultimate ground of appearances cannot be determinable as an unconditioned object. In its blind mechanism it must also be purposive, i.e. *rational* and hence I-like in nature. Thus Schelling provisionally defines this *dynamical* ground of appearances as the I—as an absolute I, however, not as an individual and not as a conscious I.[22] "For now," he writes, it is "defined as that *which can absolutely never become an object*. For the time being it is not to be further determined" (AA I,2: 90; SW I:167).

Schelling's main objection to Spinoza, then, is that he defined the absolute as an absolute *object* or substance and thus failed to give a genuine derivation of the phenomenal world on the basis of his principle: "Just as practical reason is constrained to resolve the conflict between the laws of freedom and those of nature in a higher principle, in which freedom is itself nature and nature is freedom, so too must theoretical reason in its teleological employment arrive at a higher principle, in which mechanism

---

[20] At the beginning of his Jena lectures Schelling insists that we must dare to view nature, too, "from the standpoint of the unity of reason." Cp. Steffens, *Was ich erlebte,* 4:76.

[21] On Schelling's education in the natural sciences at the Tübinger Stift, see Durner 1991; concerning his studies at the University of Leipzig, see Durner 1990.

[22] Fourteen years later, on the occasion of the re-printing of his text *On the I* in the first volume of his philosophical works, Schelling characterizes the work: It "shows idealism in its freshest form, and perhaps in a sense that it was later to lose. At least the I is here still understood throughout as absolute, as the identity of the subject and object, and not as something subjective" (AA I,2:81; SW I:159).

and teleology coincide, but which for precisely that reason cannot by any means be determinable as an object" (AA I,2:175; SW I:241f.).

On the other hand, if Kant is mistaken in thinking that the supersensible is in principle only thinkable, but not knowable, then the decisive question comes to be *how* it can be known. This question will be at the heart of the coming chapters. For the time being, though, I am only concerned to provide as accurate an account as I can of the origin of Schelling's plan for a *Naturphilosophie,* since the question has yet to be settled in the scholarship on Schelling.

Schelling later gave the following retrospective account of his beginnings as a *Naturphilosoph:* "The fundamental concept of Spinozism, spiritualized [*vergeistigt*][23] by the principle of idealism (and modified in one essential point), gained a living basis in the higher view of nature and the acknowledged unity of the dynamical with what is spiritual, and from that basis sprang the *Naturphilosophie,*[24] which as mere physics would have been complete in itself, but which in relation to the whole of philosophy must always be considered as merely its real part [*reeller Teil*], which can only be integrated into the proper system of reason when it is complemented by the ideal part [*ideeller Teil*], in which freedom reigns" (SW VII:350).

The ideal part of philosophy (= transcendental philosophy), in which freedom reigns and the outlines of which had been given in Fichte's *Foundation,* is also modified by Schelling 'in one essential point.' Since he understands transcendental philosophy as just one of the two fundamental sciences, the other being *Naturphilosophie,* the supreme or absolute unity of the two must be the identity of spirit and nature, not the unity of an absolute I lying behind or before self-consciousness, as it was for Fichte. Thus for Schelling transcendental philosophy must begin with self-consciousness, i.e. with the act by which the I becomes an object for itself, while the *Naturphilosophie* begins in turn with the act by which active nature (*natura naturans*) becomes an object for itself. From this a number of important consequences flow:

First, the I becomes an object *for itself,* i.e. it does not become an object for something other than itself, and it *becomes* an object for itself

---

[23] Namely, Spinoza's being has been dynamicized and transformed into activity.

[24] If this is right, then recent attempts in Schelling scholarship to locate the origin of his *Naturphilosophie* in his early studies of the *Timaeus* must appear dubious. See for example Krings 1994, Jantzen 1998, and Baum 2000.

because originally it is not an object. Originally it is activity and as such unlimited. If the I makes itself into an *object,* thus limiting itself, then it has not made *itself* into an object, for the I itself can never become an object. Without limiting itself, however, it can also never attain consciousness (cannot, therefore, be "for itself"), and thus it cannot be an I. Hence it is by its own *essence* a "conflict" between finite and infinite activities, a duplicity which is irreducible to a prior positing and opposing such as we find in Fichte: "It consists wholly in this conflict, or rather it is itself this conflict of opposite directions" (AA I,9,1:83; SW III:392).

A *second* consequence is the parallelism, so important for Schelling, with the concept of matter as analyzed by Kant: Matter too, according to Kant, is the product of an essential conflict between two opposed forces, repulsive and attractive, which can neither be derived from nor reduced to a substantial unity prior to and outside of themselves.

Third, it emerges that the *Anstoß* integral to Fichte's explanation of self-consciousness is part of the very essence of the I itself. This is the most important modification in relation to the *Wissenschaftslehre.* Years later, in a lecture on the history of modern philosophy, Schelling will recall, "The limit which Fichte supposed to fall outside the I, now fell within the I itself, and the process was transformed into a wholly immanent one in which the I was occupied solely with itself, with the contradiction posited within its own self of being at once both subject and object, finite and infinite" (SW X:97).

Fourth and finally, the immanence of this process determines Schelling's philosophical method. The movement of the I's self-objectivation, once begun, must necessarily proceed, for it is the nature of the I never to be simply an object, but rather "to re-emerge victorious from every finitude, as subject" (SW X:99)—only to objectify itself again once more and to become conscious of what it is. The philosopher must reconstruct this process, and in doing so the methodical procedure can be no other than to demonstrate "that that which was posited only subjectively in the preceding stage becomes objective in the next one" (SW X:108). Since self-consciousness and nature are to be understood as two sides of the same activity, Schelling insists that his method must be just as applicable to *Naturphilosophie* as it is to transcendental philosophy.

How this procedure works in practice is the subject of the next chapter.

10

Spiritus sive natura?

I.

When Schelling arrived in Jena as a newly appointed professor in October 1798, he was twenty-three years old. His reputation, established by his numerous publications, preceded him, and the students were filled with anticipation. They were not disappointed: "Indeed, there was something marvelous, something magical about the man, the way he stood at the lectern in the auditorium, which though not especially large was crammed full . . . two candles before him that left the rest of the room almost dark, and the whole audience at the very height of anticipation. How I felt when, speaking of the ascending series of creatures, he recited the monologue from *Faust* that begins 'Erhabner Geist, du gabst mir Alles' " (Abeken 1904, 42).

The reference is to the "Forest and Cavern" monologue, from Goethe's 1790 *Faust. Ein Fragment,* which in Coleridge's translation reads: "Oh, thou great Spirit, thou hast given to me / All, all that I desired. Thou hast not turned/Thy beaming countenance in vain upon me./Thou gav'st me glorious Nature for a kingdom, / The faculty to feel and to enjoy her./Thou didst not merely grant a cold short glimpse, /But laid her deepest mysteries open to me,/As a friend's bosom."[1]

Schelling certainly did not lack self-confidence! He was indeed deeply convinced that he would be able to work out both *Naturphilosophie* and transcendental philosophy as complementary sciences and to derive them from their common root. He immediately began to lecture on both,[2] and

---

[1][Tr: Frederick Burwick and James C. McKusick, eds., *Faustus. From the German of Goethe,* translated by Samuel Taylor Coleridge. (Oxford University Press 2007), 52.]
[2] In the Winter of 1798/99, on *Naturphilosophie* and the introduction to transcendental idealism; in Summer of 1799, on the whole of transcendental idealism and

the most important texts of this period originated in these lectures: the *First Outline of a System of the Philosophy of Nature* [*Erster Entwurf eines Systems der Naturphilosophie*] and its separately published *Introduction* (both from 1799), as well as the "Universal Deduction of the Dynamic Process [*Allgemeine Deduktion des dynamischen Prozesses*]" (1800); and the *System of Transcendental Idealism* (1800).

II.

In the foreword to his *System of Transcendental Idealism* Schelling emphasizes that this work is a necessary counterpart to his texts on *Naturphilosophie*. "For in this work it will become apparent, that the same powers of intuition which reside in the I can also be exhibited in nature ... The author's chief motive for devoting particular care to the depiction of this coherence, which is really an *ascending series* [*Stuffenfolge*] of intuitions, whereby the I raises itself to the highest power of consciousness, was the parallelism of nature with intelligence; to this he has long since been led, and to depict it completely, neither transcendental philosophy nor the philosophy of nature is adequate by itself; *both sciences* together are alone able to do it, though on that very account the two must forever be opposed to one another, and can never merge into one" (AA I,9,1:25; SW III:331).

The *System of Transcendental Idealism* is intended to complete one of these two tasks by deriving the "whole system of knowledge" from the principle of the *Wissenschaftslehre*, "I am." As his starting point, Schelling takes the original contradiction within the essence of the I, namely that it can never become an object for itself without ceasing to be a subject, but that it must become an object for itself so as to become conscious of itself. Schelling's model for his reconstruction of the resulting stages through which consciousness arises is Fichte's pragmatic history of self-consciousness. "Philosophy therefore has only to enumerate those acts that mark new epochs, so to speak, in the history of self-consciousness, and to exhibit their connections with each other" (AA I,9,1: 91; SW III:398).

The "first epoch" goes from original sensation to productive intuition (representation) and shows how the I comes to recognize itself as having

---

Naturphilosophie; in the Winter of 1799/1800, on organic physics according to the principles of *Naturphilosophie* and on the basic principles of the philosophy of art; in the Winter of 1800/1801 on the philosophy of art, *Naturphilosophie,* and transcendental idealism.

boundaries. The "second epoch" goes from productive intuition to reflection and shows how the I comes to recognize itself as productive. The "third epoch" leads from reflection to the absolute act of willing and hence to the transition to practical philosophy, in which further "potentiations of self-intuition" then follow.

With regard to the "parallelism of nature with intelligence," the first epoch with its three acts of self-objectivation—sensation, intuition, productive intuition (representation)—is especially important. For according to Schelling, these acts are to be rediscovered in the three forces of matter and in the three moments of its construction: "It is manifest that up to this point, nature is in step with the I . . . and passes through the same potentiations" (AA I,9,1:332–33; SW III:632–33), and so the history of freedom begins only after this point.

To understand this, we therefore have to turn to the philosophy of nature, though only in order to develop its basic idea and without entering into the details.

III.

Just as transcendental philosophy depicts the epochs of spirit's self-constitution, so too *Naturphilosophie* depicts the epochs in the development of nature. Both spirit and nature are thus viewed in a state of becoming: "We must observe that which is [now] an *object* in its *first origin* . . . To philosophize about nature means to *create* nature"—thus Schelling's own description of his project in the *First Outline of a System of the Philosophy of Nature* (AA I,7:78; SW III:13). Nature, then, is conceived first and foremost as *natura naturans,* as an unlimited and hence infinite productivity whose end is to become an object, *natura naturata.* Since its creative work is as it were frozen or rigidified in its products, while the ground of this retardation can only lie in productive nature itself, there must be something within nature that arrests its activity, an equally unlimited force of retardation which acts against nature's activity and without which a finite product could never arise. The original productivity must therefore be conceived as dual, as "duplicity in identity."

As long as there is nothing besides these two activities, however, they remain indistinguishable. In order for them to become distinguishable and to appear as *two,* there has to be a boundary or a point at which they can emerge as opposed, for this is the only way that directions can be distinguished ('toward the point', 'away from the point'). This point now allows the original activity to emerge as an alternation of expansion and retardation or contraction. "In this alternation of expansion and contraction, there necessarily arises something common to both, but which only exists *in the alternation.* If it is to exist *outside* the alternation, as well, the *alternation itself* must be fixated" (AA I,8:62; SW III:308).

For this to happen, the alternating factors must balance out and form a product. Since all further explanation of natural processes starts here, we must first of all clarify how a boundary is set to the original activity and how a fixation of the alternation of expansion and contraction becomes possible. Schelling rightly considered this to be the most important step in the explanation; everything that comes later depends on it. (I will return to this point a little further on.) With the fixation of alternation, however, "the series is concluded, and a new *series of stages* of processes begins which I call *second order processes.* For we cannot demonstrate those first processes in the realm of actuality, but only their repetition by nature to the extent that it *reproduces their productive activity.* Visible nature presupposes those first-order processes and must have gone through them in order to exhibit them as a product. It is only nature which is productive in the second potency that goes through that series of stages before our eyes" (AA I,8:335; SW IV:43).

Why does the process repeat on a higher level? Let's suppose that a fixation of the alternation of the two forces, and hence a product, has come about. According to Schelling, such a product is actually just a seeming product, a *Scheinprodukt,* and fails to adequately express the absolute activity of nature: "Absolute activity cannot be represented by a finite product, but only by one that is *infinite*" (AA I,7:79; SW III:14). The finite product, as finite, fails to restore the original identity; it merely represents a local indifference in which nature's infinite productivity is now concentrated, but not extinguished. Since the product, as finite, only partially negates the original opposition, a new and distinct opposition arises which nature again strives to balance out. To put the same thing in other words, nature would not be absolutely active if it did not go on infinitely to resolve each of its products in turn: "Nature is absolutely active if the drive to an infinite development lies in each of its products" (AA I,7:83; SW III:19). "Everything that *is* in nature, must be viewed as something that has *come to be*" (AA I 7:93; SW III:33).

This is the reason why the original construction of matter must be repeated on a higher level. Since it is essential to *natura naturans* never to be a mere object, it must re-emerge from every objectivation as a higher power of activity: "This is therefore the reason why the first objectivation lays the ground for all the following potentiations [*Steigerung*] and hence for the movement itself. The explanation of this beginning, this initial being-something, is therefore the most important point" (SW X:100).

This first step, the explanation of how an original delimitation of forces and hence a 'being-something' (*Etwas-seyn*) can emerge—in short, the "construction of matter"—may well be called the Kantian element of Schellingian *Naturphilosophie,* for its starting point is Kant's explanation of the origination of matter in the interplay of repulsive and attractive forces. Since this is the very step, however, which will undergo the most extensive modification in the further development of the *Naturphilosophie,* I will return to it in more detail later on. For now, though, let us stick to the basic idea.

Once the original delimitation has been explained, then, the next step is to show how the specific differences in the products and their transformations are to be conceived: "It must be shown *how* the productivity is gradually materialized, transforming itself into increasingly fixated products which then constitute a *dynamic series of stages of nature*—the proper object of the whole system" (AA I,8:57; SW III:302).

This part of the system, which Schelling refers to as the "dynamic process," might be called the Fichtean element of *Naturphilosophie,* for to a large extent Schelling takes his bearings here from Fichte's pragmatic history of self-consciousness. "There will be exactly as many stages in the dynamic process as there are stages of transition from difference to indifference . . . Here it is not the *object,* but rather the *object's reproduction* which itself becomes objectivated" (AA I,8:67–68; SW III:315).

Since the reproduction of the object consists in a renewed transition from difference to indifference and thus necessarily *precedes* the product, these stages of the dynamic process do not occur in experience in their pure form, but only as an aspect of already finished products—that is, only through repetition in a higher power. Thus in general, the first moment of the construction (= "duplicity in identity") will have to be represented by products that still exhibit the opposed forces in their unity, as a positive and a negative pole, so to speak, and hence in magnetic phenomena in general. This means, however, that "magnetism is not the function of an individual matter, but a function of matter as such, and hence a genuine category of physics" (AA I,9,1:142; SW III:446).

In the second moment (= "alternation"), the two forces (positive and negative) appear not only as opposed, but as mutually external and separate forces, so that, for example, they can spread to cover surfaces. This

234

becomes manifest in visible nature in the form of electricity, which Schelling again characterizes not as the function of a single kind of matter, but as a general category of physics.

In the third moment (= "fixation of alternation," "indifference"), the forces unite once again and mutually penetrate each other so that a new product emerges. In this new product, the attractive and repulsive forces are equally present in every point. Schelling calls it the chemical process, whose paradigmatic empirical manifestation is the mixture of fluids and gases:

> The first step toward original production is the limitation of productivity by the original opposition which, *qua* opposition (and as the condition of all construction), is only distinguished in the case of *magnetism*. The second stage of production is the *alternation* of expansion and contraction which is visible *as such* only in the phenomenon of *electricity*. The third stage, finally, is the transition of that alternation to indifference, which as such is only discernible in *chemical* phenomena. **Magnetism, Electricity, and the chemical process** are the *categories* of the original construction of nature [of matter]—this construction itself eludes us and lies beyond our intuition, while those phenomena are its permanent, fixated remainder— and universal schemata of the construction of matter (AA I,8:71; SW III:321).[3]

As we have seen, it is impossible for nature's productivity to exhaust itself in the finite indifference of the chemical process. It re-emerges from production as incapable of complete and utter objectivation, as the higher power of a 'subject' that must become an object for itself, as a productivity which must realize itself in products, that is as the force of *organization*.

At this point the whole process of constitution unfolds anew. "Matter, which was reconstituted by the chemical process for a second time, is once again set back at the starting point of formation by organization" (AA I,8:72; SW III:322)—though of course it now unfolds on a higher level that involves products instead of the mere factors that characterize anorganic formation. "Anorganic nature is the product of the

---

[3] Since these are conceived as the three schemata of one and the same dynamic process, Schelling greeted Alessandro Volta's invention of the voltaic pile in 1800 and Michael Faraday's discovery of electromagnetic induction in 1831 as experimental vindications of his theory of the unity of electrical, chemical, and magnetic forces (cp. SW IX:439–52).

first potency, organic nature that of the *second*" (ibid.). Organic nature thus presupposes an anorganic, external nature on which it depends and in opposition to whose forces of disintegration it constitutes itself.

How do the stages of construction manifest themselves in this potentiation? Organic production, too, necessarily begins with delimitation, but in contrast to the non-living, living beings do not merely run up against the retarding, limiting factor—they *experience* it. For Schelling, the characteristic feature of life, the thing that distinguishes it from the non-living, is its fundamental openness toward an environment whose external influence it responds to as stimuli. Schelling also refers to this feature of organisms in the terminology of John Brown, calling it *excitability.* According to Schelling, however, this is only possible if at the same time we conceive an activity which reverts back into the subject of activity. This original organic receptivity, or excitability, is thus something "by means of which duplicity enters into an originally identical thing" (AA I,7:182; SW III:159).[4] In this way the activity becomes an *organon* (instrument) for itself; it divides itself, as it were, into an inside and an outside, such that its own outside serves as the medium through which external environmental influences can affect it and be answered by a corresponding reaction.

Consequently, the cause of excitability cannot lie within this medium, and hence neither in the organism itself, nor in the external environment whose very effects presuppose excitability. Its cause must therefore be sought in what precedes both: "Just as the organism is *duplicity in identity,* so too is *nature:* one, equal to itself, and yet also opposed to itself. Therefore, the origin of organic duplicity must be *one* with the origin of duplicity in *nature itself*" (AA I,7:183; SW III:160).

Excitability itself is not directly observable in experience. It can only be inferred from the phenomenon whose underlying condition it is: irritability or the *alternation* of contraction and renewed expansion with which the organism responds to external stimuli. Irritability thus marks organic activity's second stage of transition to a product. As such, it has up to now been nothing but mere alternation, nothing fixated: from excitability and irritability alone no product arises. In order for a product to emerge, irrita-

---

[4] "Though he was unable to give a derivation for it, Brown captured this concept very well with his concept of excitability, namely that organic activity that is outwardly directed is necessarily also receptivity for what is external, and vice versa, that this receptivity for what is external is necessarily also an outwardly directed activity" (AA I,7:179; SW III:153).

bility would have to become visible as an activity manifesting itself in an organic formation: "Irritability must therefore immediately be transformed into a *formative drive* or the *drive to production*" (AA I,7:190; SW III:171).

Even so, the productive force must again fail to exhaust itself in the product: "the continued existence of the organization has to be a constant being-reproduced, in a word, the force of production would have to be a *force of reproduction*" (AA I,7:191; SW III:172). Schelling finds an empirical instance of this in the fact that the force of production continually re-forms and reproduces its product (at least within the latitude possible for the type of organization): on the one hand as self-production via assimilation, metabolism, and secretion (the vital urge); on the other hand in the seeming artifacts of animals such as honeycombs, spider webs, beaver dams, and so on (the technical drive); and finally by way of self-opposition in the division of the sexes, whose renewed bonding (the reproductive drive) leads to the repetition of the organic product and the preservation of the species. Since the factors excitability, irritability, and reproduction can be related to each other in the individual products of organic nature in a great variety of different ways, the manifold forms of life can according to Schelling be understood on the basis of proportionality. Their differences ultimately reduce to the difference of the stages at which they divide themselves into opposite sexes (cf. AA I,7:107; SW III:53). "Just as a progressive series of functions occurs throughout the whole of nature, so it is with the individual as well, and the individual is itself nothing other than the *visible expression of a determinate proportion of organic forces*" (AA I,7:230–31; SW III:220).

Now, the organic forces, just like the anorganic ones, are supposed to be nothing but different expressions of the same world-producing force. Therefore they must be analogous to each other. According to Schelling, they do indeed represent the transformed moments of the original construction of matter, merely on different levels. Sensibility is accordingly the higher power of magnetism, irritability the higher power of electricity, and the formative drive the higher power of the chemical process, so that we arrive at the following general schema:

1st Stage	2nd Stage	3rd Stage
Duplicity in Identity	Magnetism	Excitability
Polarity	Electricity	Irritability
Indifference	Chem. Process	Formative Drive

Here I would like to pause for a moment. Schelling filled out this schema with a great variety of details and attempted to assign appropriate places to the rush of scientific discoveries and achievements of his day. The general schema of Schellingian *Naturphilosophie* should already have become clear without having to pursue those details here: The original productivity must be conceived as an "original duality" or as "duplicity in identity." A point of inhibition allows the duplicity to emerge into appearance, upon which it separates itself into opposing factors. In order for a product to arise, these polar factors must in turn be united and pass over into an "indifference." However, since this indifference does not exhaust the original productivity, it forces a renewed dissolution of the product and a repetition of the process at a higher stage, and so on.

Where could Schelling have gotten the schema that underlies his system of *Naturphilosophie* and what are we to make of it? His project as formulated in the *First Outline* was to "observe that which is [now] an *object* in its *first origin* . . . To philosophize about nature means to *create* nature" (AA I,7:78; SW III:13). Here, though, we find ourselves confronted by a fundamental difficulty, for of course nature already exists. In order to be sure that what I am *re-creating* is nature itself and not something else, I must therefore know its laws. As Schelling himself remarks, "Nature is its own law-giver (autonomy of nature)" (AA I,7:81; SW III:17). So I cannot very well recognize nature's laws on the basis of my own creative activity; I must learn them by observing nature. It is not on the basis of observation, however, that Schelling arrives at his schema, but rather through an act of Fichtean intellectual intuition, and only then does he transfer the schema to nature. Is this a legitimate move for him to make? He himself comments on this issue in the *Introduction* to the *Outline*. The gist is that the schema is based on the assumption that nature (like the I) is in its essence not merely a product, but is itself productive, and hence an absolute identity can never come about if rigor mortis is not to set in:

> Nature's oscillation between productivity and product must therefore appear as a universal duality of principles, by which nature is preserved in constant activity and prevented from exhausting itself in its product, and thus the principle of universal duality is as necessary to all natural explanation as is the concept of nature itself. —This absolute presupposition must carry its own necessity within itself, but it must also be subjected to empirical testing, *for if it*

should prove not to be the case that all natural phenomena can be derived from this presupposition, if in the universal nexus of nature there is a single phenomenon whose necessity is not grounded in that principle or which indeed contradicts it, then the presupposition is thereby shown to be false, and it henceforth ceases to be a valid principle" (AA I,8:34–35; SW III:277).

Here again we see the principle of the identity of nature and spirit at work which Schelling derives from section 76 of the *Critique of the Power of Judgment*. Like the I, nature too continually oscillates between productivity and product. Hence Schelling finds it unproblematic to apply to nature what he has learned through intellectual intuition of the I. Yet even if the identity is conceded, this is not sufficient in itself to legitimate the application to nature. For it glosses over the important difference that in the case of intellectual intuition—as Schelling himself writes in the *System of Transcendental Idealism*—"one always remains both the intuited (that which is doing the producing) and the one who is intuiting" (AA I,9,1:41; SW III:350–51). This is obviously not so in the case of nature: here that which is intuited (that which is doing the producing) and the one doing the intuiting (the philosopher) are not identical. Whether this difference necessarily has consequences for Schelling's approach is a question we will better be able to judge after we have dealt with that "most important point" that we have been putting off so far: How is it possible in the first place for there to be an original inhibition of productivity and hence how can the filling of space and an initial "being-something" come about?

IV.

Schelling's *Naturphilosophie* continued to develop even as he was formulating it. This development originates in his critique of Kant's theory of matter and ultimately leads to a modification of Schelling's own approach. Schelling arrived at this critique only gradually. In his first publication on *Naturphilosophie*, the *Ideas for a Philosophy of Nature* (1797), he was still an advocate of the Kantian theory of matter and, like Kant, he explained the filling of space as resulting from the interplay of repulsion and attraction. In this he had even gone a step further than Kant himself. Kant had started with the concept of matter as what is given in intuition and then asked how matter must be conceived if it is to fill space. The concept of matter itself he took to be "empirical" (4:470), while the analysis of the concept was metaphysical. In the *Ideas* (as in the later *System of Transcendental Idealism*), Schelling synthetically derives the concept of matter from that of intuition in order to show that the latter contains "in its origin the ground of [the former's] necessity." He does so by building on Fichte's derivation of intuition: the self-positing I, in order to become conscious of the original inhibition of its activity (sensation), reflects on sensation and posits a limiting factor in opposition to the sensed limitation. Since in reflection it is unconscious of *this* activity, it loses itself in the product of opposition and is as such intuitive. This product contains, however, nothing but what the productive activity has itself introduced into it: a force which strives to expand itself to infinity, and an opposed force which limits it. Schelling summarizes: "The essence of intuition, what makes intuition what it is, is that absolutely opposed, mutually limiting activities are united within it. Expressed differently, the product of intuition is necessarily a finite product, which arises from opposed, mutually limiting activities" (AA I,5:215; SW II:221).

Since the two activities balance out in the product, they necessarily appear as fixated, resting activities, i.e. as forces. Every product of intuition must therefore unite two opposed forces within itself, and the analysis of the concept of matter merely explicates *ex post* what was (unconsciously) introduced into external intuition as its condition of possibility: "This product does not therefore consist in the *composition of its parts,* but the other way around: its parts come into existence only after the whole (which only now becomes a possible object for the analytical understanding) has been made actual by a creative faculty (which can create only a *whole*)" (AA I,5:216–17; SW II:223).

Schelling sees this as a transcendental confirmation of Kant's model of the two forces proper to matter, and as a deduction of the ground of their necessity. Indeed, he asserts that in the *Metaphysical Foundations of Natural Science,* Kant analyzed the concept of matter with "such clarity and completeness" that nothing more is required than to paraphrase Kant's results (AA I,5:220; SW II:231). Only two years later, however, in his first publication after moving to Jena and then especially in the essays for the *Journal for Speculative Physics,* Schelling found himself compelled to reject Kant's account as circular. In the second edition of the *Ideas* (1803), Schelling retrospectively concedes that his own construction of matter in the first edition had repeated the flaws of Kant's theory (cp. SW II:241). How did Schelling arrive at this conviction?

240

Historical Excursus

In 1798 Franz von Baader had published a text which was to take on considerable importance for Schelling, *On the Pythagorean Square in Nature, or The Four Regions of the World* [*Über das pythagoräische Quadrat in der Natur oder die vier Weltgegenden*]. Although Baader himself states in the preface that his work was occasioned by Schelling's *On the World Soul* [*Über die Weltseele*], it is likely that the main features of Baader's text were already worked out prior to the publication of the latter work[5] and that Baader softened the tone in response to the fact that Schelling favorably comments on Baader's *Contributions to Elementary Physiology* [*Beiträge zur Elementar-Physiologie*] (1797) in several passages of the *On the World Soul* (AA I,6:188, 196, 235; SW II:499, 506, 546). In any case, what Baader particularly objects to is Schelling's uncritical adoption of the Kantian model of forces in the 1797 edition of the *Ideas*. Whereas Kant deserves praise as the first to have shown that the filling of space and hence matter would be inconceivable "without both repulsive and attractive force," giving a new and "beneficial breath of life" (Baader III: 185, remark) to the theory of material nature, Baader finds it "unforgiveable" that Schelling fails to see that Kant's theory is only a first step in the right direction, by no means exhausting the principles for the construction of matter. Thus he writes to Jacobi on February 2, 1798: "I know Schelling, but I am not very satisfied with him. When someone has progressed so far in the study of matter as to recognize its inner discord or the two conflicting elemental forces or natures, then it is really unforgiveable not to recognize the third force in which and by which the other two can alone achieve their efficacy and which by separating them preserves them. —Kant, Fichte, and Schelling etc. are thus still at the beginning $\wedge$ they still have to get to Δ and from there to Δ or to the relation of the active element to the three passive ones, before even the beginnings of a theory of body can be made" (Baader XV:181f.).

In his *Pythagorean Square,* Baader therefore attempts to prove (1) that in addition to the two fundamental forces of attraction and repulsion, a third principle, gravity, must be assumed in every point of matter-filled space. It unites the first two forces and both separates them and constrains them "as it were against their will . . . to act in unison towards a single point and to produce the phenomenon of matter" (Baader III:263).[6]

---

[5] See Baumgardt 1927, 213; cp. also the unpublished Munich dissertation by Hans Grassl 1952.

[6] This thought can be traced back at least as far as Plato, who has the Pythagorean Timaeus say, "It is not possible to combine two things well all by themselves, with-

(2) Gravity itself cannot be explained on the basis either of the attractive force or of its combination with the expansive force opposed to it. Rather, gravity is itself to be regarded as "the immediate expression of the individual inhering in and individualizing itself in all single or moveable bodies, and which for that very reason does not itself appear (as matter) since it is what lends all these their permanence, substance, and truth" (Baader III:257f.).

Over and above the three principles necessitated by the construction of matter, Baader therefore distinguishes a fourth, activating principle standing above them (symbolically: the point in the center of the triangle). Hence the title of the work: In harmony with the ancient Pythagoreans he "swears" by the "holy *Quaternarius*" as the "key to nature" (Baader XV:178, III:267).[7] He also adopts the Pythagorean principle that "The one is the primordial ground of everything,"[8] or, as he puts it in the *Pythagorean Square: "Totum (Unum) parte prius"* (Baader III:258).

In our context, three things are especially significant. (a) According to Baader it is impossible to construct matter from only two opposed forces since we must in any case already assume a third term holding them together in order for the conflict of the two forces to be realized in their mutual interplay.[9] (b) The concept of gravity Baader introduces as this third term has nothing to do with the attractive force. (c) Gravity itself is the expression of a whole, of a totality, which Baader calls "Substance" and which "vindicates" the apparent self-sufficiency of every single matter (Baader III:256).

After he became aware of Baader's text, Schelling repeatedly pointed out its importance. In his ensuing writings on *Naturphilosophie* he praises the *Pythagorean Square* as a work "of the greatest importance for the whole of dynamic physics" (AA I,7:268; SW III:265), in which the rights of gravity have been excellently reasserted (cp. SW II:241, VI:254). Yet this admission also compelled him to rethink his Kantian premises.

---

out a third; there must be some bond of union between them" (*Timaeus* 31c). Two elements, without a third term in common, are isolated individuals, each is *one* in and for itself and strictly speaking they cannot even add up to *two*.

[7] The Pythagoreans swore by "him [sc. Pythagoras] who discovered the *tetraktys* [fourfoldness, *quaternarius*] of our wisdom, the source which contains the springs of everlasting nature" (Iamblichos, *De vita Pythagorica*, 150).

[8] Capelle 1968, 477 and 475.

[9] For Kant the forces are the original elements from which matter then emerges. Thus they do not inhere in atoms existing prior to them. What, then, brings the two forces together so that they interact in conflict and fill up space?

V.

Schelling's critical engagement with Kant's theory of matter begins in his first publication of the Jena period, the *First Outline of a System of the Philosophy of Nature* (1799), in which Baader is called upon as the principle witness. The ensuing writings deepen the criticism. I would like to distinguish three levels of the Schellingian critique in order of increasing importance.

1) On the first level, at the beginning of the *First Outline*, the validity of the Kantian theory is merely qualified. It is still accepted as correct to the extent that one views matter as a 'product' and takes the filling of space to be the goal of explanation. On Schelling's interpretation, Kant derived his results on the basis of an analysis of *this* concept of matter, in the course of which he abstracted from all specific differences between matters of different kinds, considering only the degree to which it fills space (differences of density). For this reason, however, he cannot explain the formation "even of one single matter" (AA I,7:141; SW III:101) as specifically determined, and initially Schelling's criticism focuses only on this point. Of course he himself takes the opposite path of explaining the *production* of matter, affecting ignorance of the finished product. Here again, however, Schelling emphasizes that if one starts from matter as a product, as Kant does, "it cannot of course be constructed otherwise than from two [!] forces, whose varying relation results in differing degrees of density" (ibid.).

On this level, then, Schelling still believes that it is in principle possible to construct the degrees with which matter fills space on the basis of two forces.[10] But since Kant was not concerned with the problem of how specifically different kinds of matter originate, but only with the possibility of constructing the concept of matter as the object of outer sense in general, Schelling's critique really just amounts to the formulation of an alternative line of research. Moreover, the distinction between product and production (or construction) is by no means foreign to Kant himself; as we saw in Chapter 3 his systematic approach even requires that distinction. Hence Schelling is wrong when he claims that Kant treated the concept of matter purely analytically and that he did not intend to show

---

[10] By this time Kant himself no longer believed this possible. As early as 1792 he had realized that his explanation of the differing densities of matter in the *Metaphysical Foundations* is circular; compare Kant's letter to Beck, 11:376f.

how matter could be constructed from two forces and would indeed have thought such a task impossible. Schelling's appraisal of Kant's intentions only makes sense on the assumption that 'production' means the *construction of matter's specific differences*. But Kant's own approach clearly demands the fulfillment of both conditions, i.e. the analysis of the empirical datum of matter *and* proof that the concept 'matter' can be constructed from the elements found by that analysis; both conditions are necessary in order to prove the objective reality of the concept of matter. This requirement does not involve Kant in a contradiction. The real question is whether the two forces derived in the first, analytic step are sufficient to carry out the construction in the second step. And so we come to the second level of Schelling's critique.

2) Schelling's concentration on the productivity of nature leads him to a second objection which takes up Baader's second point from above, and which brings Schelling up to the level of reflection that Kant himself had reached in the meanwhile. If the genesis of nature is to be explained on the basis of pure productivity, an original, infinite activity or expansion which is itself not as yet a product, then one must also assume something equally original that retards and inhibits the infinite evolution of nature, giving it limits and determinacy or, as Schelling expresses it, a "finite velocity." This retarding factor is therefore to be understood as an intransitive force which is *used* for the 'construction' of a product, but also *used up* in the process. From this we must distinguish a *transitive* force such as gravitation which is supposed to exert an attractive influence on every matter and not just on the product. In regard to Kant's assumption "that the attractive force which is part of the construction of every finite matter, is the same as the one which also operates outside its sphere to infinity," Schelling now sees an "irresolvable difficulty in the [Kantian] system" (AA I,7:143–44; SW III:103f.): It is only from the standpoint of the product as the mere filling of space that "that retarding force is able to appear as attractive force" (AA I,7:143; SW III:102); from the standpoint of production, by contrast, the equation of attractive force with gravity must appear as a "failing" (SW II:241) and as unjustified.

3) In the "Universal Deduction of the Dynamic Process" [*Allgemeine Deduktion des dynamischen Prozesses*] (1800), the criticism is further specified. Indeed, it now casts a wholly different light on the Kantian approach, revealing a different kind of circularity than the one which Kant himself had noticed. Schelling concentrates on what I called (in Chapter 3)

the second step ("b") in the structure of the Kantian proof, and now claims that the circularity of Kant's account is made inevitable by the very nature of his approach. For Kant cannot characterize the forces from which the product matter is supposed to be constructed without having to presuppose matter as a product from the very outset—a "confusion," as Schelling now writes, of which more than a few traces are to be found in Kant's dynamics (AA I,8:319; SW IV:26): "When Kant characterizes the repulsive force as one that acts merely at the surface of contact, while the attractive force is characterized as penetrating through the whole body, it is obvious that he is considering these forces only in the third moment of the construction. For how is contact conceivable unless there is already impenetrability, i.e. matter? And how is penetration conceivable without something that is penetrated? All these predicates therefore apply to attractive and repulsive forces only when they are already represented by matter" (AA I,8:320; SW IV:27).

The two forces which are necessary for the construction of matter do not, *as such,* provide any reason for the degree of their limitation. In the first moment of the construction all we obtain is a continuous expansion and a negation of that expansion, but no limitation of determinate degree. In order to arrive at a determinate filling of space we are "obviously driven to assume a ground which is to be found neither in the attractive nor in the repulsive force of the body to be constructed, *and hence also not among the pure conditions of the construction*" (AA I,8:321; SW IV:28).

The question, then, is how Schelling's approach can avoid this "confusion." To answer it we will need to go back to the *First Outline* where, following Baader, Schelling first introduced gravity as the third force necessary for constructing matter. What exactly is this force? Obviously, its activity presupposes an original mutual externality, i.e. distinct masses between which it acts. This mutual externality cannot in turn be explained on the basis of the system of gravitation since it is itself the prerequisite of that system. Thus Schelling's first result is that gravity is simple while its condition is "duplicity" or "original difference," i.e. an original separation or division preceding gravity. More specific determination of gravity thus impels us to a consideration of the "history of the formation of the world in general . . . The phenomenon of gravity, which we cannot otherwise completely explain, leads us to an investigation of the system of the world" (AA I,7:149, 315; SW III:114).

Here, of course, Schelling again starts out from his fundamental assumption that there is an original productivity that has to be limited by an opposition or retardation lying within it. With this a difference arises—an "alternation of expansion and contraction" (AA I,8:62; SW III:308) which is the first condition of appearance as such. Now, within this to-and-fro of expansion and retardation something permanent is supposed to come about. How is that possible? Apparently, the alternation itself has to be fixated in a determinate way. It cannot be one of the two alternating terms that makes this happen; it must be some third term (gravity) that is therefore also included within the original alternation (for by hypothesis nothing is present outside the alternation—outside of nature).

How is the third force possible? All that is given to us is the condition under which it becomes active (i.e., the original diremption [*Entzweiung*]). If it is this diremption which first occasions its activity, as Schelling now argues, then it cannot be anything other than the absolute identity itself which only manifests itself (only *can* manifest itself) under this condition. If the absolute identity can only manifest itself under this condition, then precisely this set of conditions must also be assumed for every single one of its products. In another words, since every product in nature exists only by virtue of the third force, while this force itself exists only by virtue of "the continuous, uninterrupted existence of the opposition," the re-emergence of the opposition upon which every single product rests must somehow be guaranteed. It cannot be brought about by the product itself (since the product owes its own existence to the presence of the opposition), but only by some external influence– and since the condition is equally valid for all products, that external influence must be mutual. Consequently, Schelling now writes: "Hence neither can a single product, but only an absolute whole of products simultaneously come into existence, each of which contains the condition of opposition for every other" (AA I,8:328; SW IV:35).

With this step, however, the project of a genetic construction of nature in which "everything that *is* in nature, must be viewed as something that has *come to be*" (AA I,7:93; SW III:33), has been reduced to absurdity. If everything must come into existence at once, then we cannot really speak of an actual genesis at all.

VI.

Schelling confronted the consequences of this fact in the "Presentation of My System of Philosophy" which also appeared in the *Journal for Speculative Physics* in May 1801 and presents the first formulation of the *Iden-*

246

titätsphilosophie. What he here refers to as the "basic mistake of all philosophy" had until recently been his own point of departure, namely the assumption that "the absolute identity has actually come outside of itself, and the attempt to make intelligible how this coming-outside-itself could happen" (AA I,10:121; SW IV:119–20). This is impossible, as he now believes himself to have recognized, "because one can never specify a first point where the absolute identity has passed over into an individual thing, since the totality is what is original, and not individual things" (AA I,10:133; SW IV:132). With this Schelling has now arrived, as Baader had before him, at the principle "*Totum (Unum) parte prius,*" and the foundation of the *Identitätsphilosophie* has been laid.

By 1801, then, Schelling has re-affirmed his proximity to Spinoza to an astonishing degree: "The true philosophy [consists] in the demonstration that the absolute identity (the infinite) has not gone outside of itself, and everything that exists, insofar as it exists, is itself the infinite—a proposition which of all previous philosophers only Spinoza recognized" (AA I,10:121; SW IV:120). He borrowed Goethe's copy of Spinoza's *Ethics* and kept it in front of him on his writing desk throughout the composition of the "Presentation of My System": it served as his model for his own work: "As regards the mode of presentation, I have taken Spinoza as my example—not only because I had most reason to emulate the form chosen by that man to whom the content and substance of my system brings me closest, but also because this form also makes for the greatest brevity in the presentation and permits the reader to judge most accurately the cogency of the demonstrations" (AA I,10:115; SW IV:113).

VII.

Having now arrived at this result, I would like to return once more to the objection that I mentioned above while postponing any decision on it: namely that the intellectual intuition adapted from the *Wissenschaftslehre* is of no use in *Naturphilosophie* since it is not we who create nature, but nature itself which has already created itself, and in order to re-create nature we would have to learn its laws through experience, rendering a re-creation of nature superfluous for cognition.

Interestingly, A. K. A. Eschenmayer had already raised a similar objection in an article for Schelling's *Journal for Speculative Physics*: "I do not comprehend why anyone would want to take on the thankless labor of working out a method of constructing nature when nature constructs itself" (Eschenmayer 1801, 31). In his review of Schelling's *First Outline* he is even more explicit: "Now the *Naturphilosophie* takes upon itself the task of creating nature itself, or as Schelling has it, of eavesdropping on nature's self-construction. To do so I have to borrow the moments of this construction from the realm of experience, in order then to derive that very same sphere from those principles. I doubt whether this is a genuinely philosophical method and not rather a circle."[11]

Schelling responded in a short essay entitled "On the True Concept of Naturphilosophie and the Proper Method of Resolving its Problems" [*Ueber den wahren Begriff der Naturphilosophie und die richtige Art ihre Probleme aufzulösen*](1801). There he writes: "In the *Naturphilosophie* I do indeed consider that subject-object that I call nature, but I consider it in its self-construction. One must have raised oneself to the intellectual intuition of nature in order to comprehend this" (AA I,10:100; SW IV:96–97). Schelling explains what he means by an intellectual intuition of nature as follows: "It is only possible to behold the objective in its first becoming by depotentiating the *object* of all philosophizing, which in its highest potency is = I, and by beginning the construction with this object that has been reduced to the first potency" (AA I,10:89; SW IV:85).

On this view, Eschenmayer's mistake was to have remained at the standpoint of the I and *its* intellectual intuition. However, as Schelling now insists, it is necessary to start from an intellectual intuition "as it is required in the *Wissenschaftslehre*; however, I require in addition that we abstract from the intuiting subject in this intuition, an abstraction which leaves me with what is purely objective in this act, which in itself is a mere subject-object, but by no means = I" (AA I,10:92; SW IV:87–88). And in the "Presentation of My System" he states at the outset, in section 1: "thus in order to reach the standpoint which I require, it is necessary to abstract from the subject of thinking" (AA I,10:116; SW IV:114).

In other words, if intellectual intuition is to be retained as the method of our intuition of nature, that is only possible on the basis of a depotentiation (a suppression or neutralization) of the intuiting subject. The question however remains whether an intellectual intuition in which one abstracts from the intuiting subject can really amount to more than word-play. What exactly would such an intuition be, assuming it possible? In the case of intellectual intuition, being and thought are inseparable in the product

---

[11] In the *Erlanger Literaturzeitung* of April 4, 1801 (No. 67), 531, cited in Jantzen 1993, 78.

since in contrast to sensuous intuition it is a productive intuition. If we are now to abstract from the producing subject, then there would have to be a unity of being and thought which could exist without appearing as the product of a subject.

A mode of cognition of this kind, rightly understood, is however no longer intellectual intuition, but something quite different: *intuitive understanding*. For if we abstract from the subject, the subject cannot 'create' the object. If being and thought are nevertheless to remain inseparable in the object, then it must be the case "that my intuiting is itself a thinking, and my thinking an intuiting," as Goethe once put it ("Significant Help" [*Bedeutende Fördernis*], LA I,9:307; HA 13:37). An intuitive thinking of this kind, which does not 'create' its object, is the intuitive understanding. Whether it is available to humans or only to a divine being, as Kant claims, will be the subject of the next chapter.

I think Schelling is right when, following section 76 of the *Critique of the Power of Judgment* and Fichte's *Foundation,* he infers that, in principle, nature must in its essence be no less accessible to cognition than the I and that a philosophy of nature, understood thus, is a *desideratum.* He is also right, I think, when in opposition to Fichte he claims that the origin of nature is not in the I, but that the origin of both must lie in the realm of the supersensible. His lasting achievement is to have carried the modern philosophy of nature beyond its first beginnings in Kant's *Metaphysical Foundations of Natural Science* and to have demonstrated its importance as an independent discipline. His methodology, however, is wholly insufficient. And he is fundamentally mistaken when he infers that the method of cognition must be the same for both nature and the I, namely intellectual intuition, for he has clearly failed to learn the lesson of what I referred to above as Fichte's central insight: that "I am" and "it is" express two wholly distinct modes of being. Let us now consider how Goethe's philosophy of nature deals with this problem.

11

The Methodology of the Intuitive Understanding

I.

Before turning to Goethe, however, we must clarify why Kant denies intuitive understanding to humans. Since he introduced the notion of intuitive understanding as a contrasting concept that could shed greater light on the peculiar nature of our own discursive understanding, it will in turn illuminate the notion of the intuitive understanding if we start from the discursive understanding—the only kind of understanding Kant considers possible for humans. Kant elaborates this point in numerous passages: "From the side of the understanding, human cognition is *discursive*, i.e., it takes place through representations which take as the ground of cognition that which is common to many things, hence through *marks* as such ... All our *concepts* are marks, accordingly, and all *thought* is nothing other than a representing through marks" (9:58, cp. 16:300, 9:91).

A mark is that aspect of an object of which I become conscious, something that I can distinguish from other things: "External grounds of cognition are marks ... We cognize things only through marks" (16:297–98). In order for a mark to become a ground of cognition, however, I must compare representations with each other and reflect on marks which are common to several things[1] and can be combined in a concept: "To make concepts out of representations one must thus be able *to compare, to reflect,* and *to abstract,* for these three logical operations of the understanding are the essential and universal conditions for generation of

---

[1] The term 'discursive' derives from the Latin *discurrere*, to go to and fro: "*reflected* representation (*repraesentatio discursiva*)" (9:91). In general, the discursive understanding is for Kant the faculty of combining individual givens in a unity of consciousness.

every[2] concept whatsoever. I see, e.g., a spruce, a willow, and a linden. By first comparing these objects with one another I note that they are different from one another in regard to the trunk, the branches, the leaves, etc.; but next I reflect on that which they have in common among themselves, trunk, branches, and leaves themselves, and I abstract from the quantity, the figure, etc., of these; thus I acquire a concept of a tree" (9:94–95).

Discursive concepts are thus universal representations combining marks common to several objects: "[I] know that intuitions are given to the human senses, and brought under a concept and thereby under a rule by the understanding; that this concept contains only the common characteristic (leaving out what is particular), and is thus discursive" (5:484).

Discursive concepts, then, as Kant defines them, are precisely the kind of concepts of which Goethe's other source of philosophical inspiration, Spinoza, writes: "We see, therefore, that all the concepts [*notiones*] by which ordinary people are accustomed to explain nature are only modes of imagining [*modos imaginandi*], and do not indicate the nature of anything, only the constitution of the imagination . . . And because those who do not understand the nature of things, but only imagine them, affirm nothing concerning things, and take the imagination for the intellect, they firmly believe, in their ignorance of things and of their own nature, that there is an order in things" (E1app).

Now Kant would reject as uncritical dogmatism the basic assumption that one need not be satisfied with mere 'modes of imagination' but can, at least in principle, have knowledge of the nature of things; for as he writes in the *Prolegomena,* this is tantamount to wanting "to cognize determinately, like an object that is given, what is only an idea." According to Kant, however, that is misguided, "for the specific nature of our understanding consists in thinking *everything discursively,* i.e. through concepts, hence *through mere predicates,* among which the absolute subject must therefore always be absent. Consequently, all real properties by which we cognize bodies are mere accidents" (4:333, emphasis added).

Kant's language in the first *Critique* is even more pointed. There he writes in the amphiboly chapter that a so-called inner nature of things behind their properties is "nothing but a phantom," namely "a mere

---

[2] That is to say: of every *empirical* concept whatsoever. The pure concepts of the understanding (categories), the moral concepts, and the mathematical concepts are subject to other conditions (cp., e.g., Refl. 2850, 16:546).

something of which we should not understand what it is, even if someone were in a position to tell us," because we lack the necessary faculty of
cognition. "If by the complaints—*that we have no insight whatever into
the inner [nature] of things*—it be meant that we cannot conceive by pure
understanding what the things which appear to us may be in themselves,
they are entirely illegitimate and unreasonable. For what is demanded is
that we should be able to know things, and therefore to intuit them,
without the senses, and therefore that we should have a faculty of knowledge altogether different from the human, and this not only in degree but
as regards intuition likewise in kind—in other words, that we should be
not men but beings of whom we are unable to say whether they are even
possible, much less how they are constituted" (A277–78/B333–34).

II.

Thus we come to the crucial point—and to a seemingly irreconcilable
conflict. What Kant regards as a "phantom," Spinoza regards as a higher
"standard of truth"; what the former declares to be impossible for us humans, the latter holds to be the highest ideal of human knowledge. In one
point, however, Kant and Spinoza agree, and that is that intuitive thought,
in contrast to discursive thought, *cannot* derive its concepts by way of
reflection and abstraction from representations of the properties of things.
Thus we must consider why it is that Kant does not think it possible to
form concepts in this way, and why Spinoza does. What kind of concepts
would these be, and how are they acquired?

We have already seen that Spinoza takes mathematics as his point of
reference whereas Kant refers to a divine understanding. That mathematical concepts are not derived by abstracting from sensible experience
is, presumably, uncontroversial. The concept of a circle is not formed by
comparing various round things—e.g. the full moon, the horizon of the
open sea, the eyes of owls—in regard to their common marks and then
abstracting from their differences. A mathematical concept is not derived from intuition at all, but rather formed by pure thought (in Kantian terms, it is constructed in pure intuition). Spinoza, in turn, would
deny that I possess the concept 'circle' (in contrast to the mere representation 'circle') until I can identify its productive causes, for example until
I know that the circle is a plane surface described by a line, one point of
which is fixed and the other in motion. This definition expresses the es-

sence or the efficient cause and I can deduce the properties of the circle from it.[3]

What a concept[4] in this sense really expresses is what, according to Kant, Plato originally meant by "idea": "archetypes of the things themselves" (A313/B370). Kant only accepts that there can be such concepts in the realms of mathematics and morals since mathematics constructs its concepts in pure intuition while morality's concepts of what ought to be give us a paradigm by which to judge experience. Kant does not admit of such concepts in the realm of philosophical knowledge since only appearances are given to us whose archetypes we do not know. For this reason, they are not to be confused with Kant's transcendental ideas, which are merely what the categories become when they are expanded to include the unconditioned and thereby freed from their limitation to possible experience (A409/B435–36).

Since Kant himself approaches this issue from a conception of the divine understanding, for him non-mathematical knowledge can only be intuitive in case it proceeds from the whole to the parts and knows the parts through the whole. As we saw in the historical excursus in Chapter 6, for Kant such a faculty of understanding would not possess discursive concepts but rather *ideas,* since it would not cognize individual things through comparison and abstraction, but by way of a limitation of the whole. According to Kant, "the infinite being, for whom the condition of time is nothing" (5:123), beholds the whole of the world in a single intuition, whereas for our understanding, bound as it is to sensibility and hence to temporal conditions, such a world whole can only be given in the form of a task: the task of comprehending an endless succession of parts. In the *Critique of the Power of Judgment,* however, Kant was forced to introduce the idea of an intuitive understanding, in order to make comprehensible a

---

[3] Similarly we read in Letter 60, to Tschirnhaus: "In my view the crucial point is to discover an idea from which everything can be derived." And, "In order that I may know which out of many ideas of a thing will enable all the properties of the object to be deduced, I follow this one rule, that the idea or definition of the thing should express its efficient cause."

[4] Today it is common to ascribe possession of the concept of a circle to anyone who can discriminate circles from non-circles. Yet in this case, too, it is only properties ('marks') which are compared with one another, and so according to Spinoza we are dealing here not with concepts but with 'mere modes of representation'. On the contemporary theories of concepts see, for example, Margolis and Laurence 1999.

peculiarity of our discursive understanding. For this purpose, however, it was not necessary to proceed from the whole of the *world* to its parts, but only from the totality of a particular product of nature, such as an organism, to its parts. But in this case it is immediately apparent that one need not ascribe a *finite* intuitive understanding of this kind to a creator of worlds exclusively. Kant himself did not prove, but merely assumed, that such an understanding would be incompatible with a discursive understanding and hence must be impossible for us human beings.

Thus the claim that humans cannot be credited with a cognition that proceeds, for instance, from the whole of a plant to its parts, also struck Goethe as having little or no force since he believed himself already to have performed such cognition in his *Essay on the Metamorphosis of Plants,* even though he had done so more instinctively than consciously. Hence the crucial point for him was to give a conceptual account of his methodological procedure and to work out a methodology of the finite intuitive understanding. This project occupied him over the next several years. The philosophical attraction of Goethe's position consists not least in the fact that (and in the way that) he mediates between Spinoza and Kant and seeks to make discursive and intuitive thinking compatible.[5]

III.

Goethe had first conceived a methodological study while working on his *Contributions to Optics.* It is dated April 28, 1792, two years after the publication of the *Critique of the Power of Judgment,* and is entitled "The Experiment as Mediator between Object and Subject" [*Der Versuch als Vermittler zwischen Objekt und Subjekt*]. Although neither Spinoza nor Kant is mentioned by name, an attentive reader cannot fail to notice that what is being elaborated here is the project of a Spinozist *scientia intuitiva* on the basis of Kant's characterization of the intuitive understanding.

---

[5] In methodological terms, Goethe henceforth combines Spinoza's postulate that for every individual thing that we want to cognize, we must discover the 'idea' expressing its efficient cause and from which all the object's properties can be derived, with the Kantian postulate that knowledge of living beings requires a demonstration of how the whole and the parts of an organism mutually produce and condition each other.

254

What strikes one first is how close the content of the text is to the appendix of the first part of Spinoza's *Ethics* containing his methodological credo. Spinoza argues that since humans come into the world with no knowledge of the causes of things and are naturally inclined to seek out just what is useful to them, they come increasingly to represent things exclusively in relation to themselves and to regard the things of nature as existing for their own benefit. That this does not reveal the real nature of things would, says Spinoza, have remained eternally hidden to humans "if mathematics, which is concerned not with ends but only with the essences and the properties of figures, had not shown men another standard of truth" (E1app).

In "The Experiment as Mediator between Object and Subject," Goethe begins by aligning himself with Spinoza's reflections. He writes, "As soon as humans become aware of the things around them, they regard them in relation to themselves, and rightly so. For their whole fate depends on whether things are pleasurable or displeasurable to them, whether they attract or repel them, whether they are beneficial or harmful . . . and yet humans are thereby prone to a thousand errors" (LA I, 8:305; HA 13:10). If, however, they desire to know the objects of nature as they really are, they have to renounce the standard of pleasure and displeasure and develop their talent for observation in appropriate ways. They must train themselves to disregard all selfish interest and individual peculiarity—a "difficulty" which can be met by seeking cooperation with others, thereby multiplying one's perspectives and ways of representing the world.

Next the Kantian influence emerges into view. In the case of natural objects we do not at first know their 'essence' (idea), but must seek to discover it. Rather than deducing all the properties from the idea, the idea can only be known by way of the totality of the properties: in the case of natural things, the idea underlying the properties, *provided there is one,* can be recognized only at the end of the investigation. (And accordingly it is not until the end of the investigation that we can know *whether there is such an idea.*) This means that, first of all, all the properties of the relevant phenomenon must (discursively) be sought out and gathered together, in order then (intuitively) to bring the whole *as a whole* into view so that the idea can emerge.

Isolated experiments will inevitably be insufficient to this task. We saw in our discussion of Goethe's *Contributions to Optics* in Chapter 7 how central this thought is for him. Now he states that "everything depends on this point": "The *systematic variation of every single experiment* is therefore the proper duty of a natural scientist" (LA I,8:312; HA 13:18).

Goethe himself refers in this context to the experiments in the first two installments of his recently published *Contributions to Optics*. As Spinoza before him, Goethe too illustrates his point by appealing to mathematics; the influence of Kant's characterization of the intuitive understanding, to which the whole must be present *as a whole,* is also unmistakable:

> In the first two installments of my optical contributions I sought to conduct such a series of experiments which border on and immediately touch upon each other, and which indeed, once one has become thoroughly familiar with them and contemplates them as a whole, constitute but *one single* experiment, only *one* experience seen from the most various vantage points. —An experience of this kind, consisting as it does in a series of experiences, is manifestly of a *higher kind.* It represents the formula in which countless individual problems of arithmetic are expressed. To work towards such experiences is, I believe, the highest duty of the natural scientist (ibid.).

Goethe might thus appear to have taken the decisive step beyond Spinoza toward adapting the method of *scientia intuitiva* to natural objects as well. But as we saw in Chapter 7, his optimism was significantly dampened by Lichtenberg's objections against the explanation of colored shadows that Goethe had intended for the third volume of the *Contributions*. The example of the "so-called *couleurs accidentelles*" revealed that the continuous series of optical experiments did not allow him to derive both this phenomenon and that of colored shadows as differing manifestations of *one* underlying idea. It was not until several years later that he found a way to resolve this difficulty.

What is the problem? Let us consider once again Goethe's characterization of what he calls an experience of a *higher kind:* It comprises a number of different experiences and "represents the formula in which countless individual problems of arithmetic are expressed." Like a mathematical formula, the experience of a higher kind is meant to provide a means for deriving the individual phenomena from it. Is this the case? If for example I have the formula $y = 2x + 1$, I can express it in countless instances: 1, 3, 5, 7, 9, 11 . . . This does not present any problem. However, our task is still to *discover* the formula corresponding to the idea! Instead of generating the series on the basis of the formula, we have to derive the formula on the basis of the series. Thus to begin with all I have is (say) the series 1, 1, 2, 3, 5, 8, 13, 21 ... What is the formula on which the series is based? What would be the next number after 21?

And here we see: Just as little as the arithmetic series as such provides the formula that generates it, neither does the 'systematic variation of every single experiment' in a complete series reveal the underlying idea. Of course it is true (and this was presumably the decisive point for Goethe) that the mathematical method "reveals every gap in the reasoning on account of its fastidiousness and purity" (LA I,8:313; HA 13:18–19). When assembling the materials that comprise an experience of the higher kind, we must also take care not to leave out a single step if the underlying regularity is to be determined. However, the mere fact of having discovered all the parts (properties) is not in itself equivalent to having derived them from a single origin (idea).

At this point in time, then, Goethe is still under the sway of Spinoza's mathematical examples in which the idea is assumed as already given. Something crucial is still missing, but what is it?

IV.

Goethe's own path, the one that in the end actually led him to the solution of his problem, left hardly any traces in his writings. Even so, the mathematical example from above gives us a clue what to look for. What must I do in order to find the appropriate formula for the series 1, 1, 2, 3, 5, 8, 13, 21? Apparently I have to investigate the transitions between the numbers in order to see how one arises from the other and whether the intervals between them are based on some regularity. However I end up achieving this, there is no doubt that the path from the series to the formula lies in studying the *transitions*.[6]

A related clue is to be found in a passage from the later *Morphologischen Hefte* or notebooks on morphology. In the second *Heft*, under the heading "Doubt and Resignation" [*Bedenken und Ergebung*], Goethe

---

[6] An intellectual re-production of the transitions between 1, 1, 2, 3, 5, 8, 13, 21, is necessary in order to realize that, from the third element in the series onward, every number is the sum of the two preceding numbers; hence the next number must be 34, and we are dealing with the formula for the Fibonacci series, $f_n = f_{n-1} + f_{n-2}$, $n \geq 2$.

writes of the relation between idea and experience: "Here we encounter the real difficulty, which is not always clearly present to consciousness, that a certain gap seems to be entrenched between the idea and experience." Indeed, our own course of reflection has brought us to precisely this point, to this gap between idea and experience. Now Goethe continues: "The difficulty of *connecting* idea and experience with each other is a great hindrance to all scientific study of nature: the idea is independent of space and time, the study of nature is limited in space and time, and hence the simultaneous and the successive are intimately united in the idea, whereas from the standpoint of experience they are always separate, and a manifestation of nature which, according to the idea, we are to conceive as at once both simultaneous and successive, seems to drive us to a kind of madness" (LA I,9:97; HA 13:31–32, emphasis added).

Here, then, experience and idea are now joined by a third element, which 'is not always clearly present to consciousness', but whose importance for the whole conception is not to be underestimated: the *connection* between the two. This had, as it were, been *skipped over* when in "The Experiment as Mediator" Goethe stated that everything depends on putting together a series of experiments which "border on and immediately touch upon each other, and which indeed . . . constitute but *one single* experiment." For if the simultaneous and the successive are united in the idea, then, if an idea underlies the phenomena and is at work in them, both the simultaneous and the successive must also be united in the phenomena, *even though* "from the standpoint of experience they are always separate." The crucial point is thus to see *how* the simultaneous can be present in the successive. The suggestion is that if one wants to find the underlying idea, then what is separate in experience (the parts or properties) must be considered with a view to their *connection*, i.e. to the *transitions* between the parts.

In this initial formulation the thought is entirely abstract, so I would like to illustrate it (and examine it) a little further by taking a few examples from everyday experience.

V.

First example: Let's suppose we are watching a modern, 'experimental' film in which the scenes follow each other in a seemingly random, unconnected way: Times, places, and actors are constantly changing with no

indication of how they are connected. It seems as if every scene constituted an independent and self-contained episode. Then comes the final
scene, and suddenly everything that came before is illuminated in a flash.
This final scene provides the key to understanding the film and allows us
to recognize the idea that the director wanted to present. Now we might
perhaps wish to see the film for a second time, and then something decisive occurs: Although we see exactly the same scenes again, this time we
see every scene differently. When we watch the film again, the last scene
or rather our knowledge of the film's underlying idea is now present in
every single scene. And it now makes clear how the scenes which formerly appeared to be unconnected are in fact internally linked.

In this example we are at first, i.e. after seeing the film for the first
time, given all the parts (scenes) of a whole as well as the underlying idea,
but we are not yet given the internal link, the 'transitions' between the
scenes. With the aid of the idea, however, we can produce or reconstruct
these transitions for ourselves at a second viewing. This suggests that *if* a
whole consists of these three elements and two of them are given, then
I can infer the third element from them. We could put this to the test if
for example, differently than in the case of the film, we imagine a case in
which the idea and the transitions are given, but the parts still have to be
found.

Second example: A psychiatrist interested in philosophy delves ever
more deeply into the intellectual world of Nietzsche. Because of his profession, he takes a special interest in Nietzsche's insanity and its causes.
Time and again he wonders how it might have been if Nietzsche could
have undergone psychoanalysis. Since his illness took place in the period
in which psychoanalysis was first developed, the thought is not unrealis-
tic. It gradually grows into the idea for a novel: 'Nietzsche in Therapy'.
However: everything we know about Nietzsche indicates that he himself
would never have agreed to undergo therapy. How, then, is the idea to be
realized? Our author conceives the following plan: In the story, Nietzsche, who was very proud of his deep psychological insights, has to be
convinced that it is *he himself* who has to give therapy to someone since
only he, Nietzsche, can help that person, whereas in reality and without
Nietzsche's being aware of the fact, the 'patient' is the psychiatrist and
Nietzsche himself is the object of the therapy. To this end, one of Nietzsche's friends (Lou Salomé), who is deeply worried about his mental
health, persuades a doctor with whom she is acquainted (Josef Breuer,

259

Freud's mentor), to take part in the scheme and present himself as the 'patient'.[7] With this a narrative framework is in place which connects the beginning, middle, and end of the story and becomes a central thread, making transitions possible between the individual scenes. The only thing still missing are the scenes themselves—the different parts of the narrative in which the idea is to be realized. But now they can be 'found' in light of what is already given: they have to be realistic scenes in the sense that they are not only to reflect the locality and the Viennese milieu in the period when psychoanalysis was originally developed, but also to draw on Nietzsche's biography in such a way that a fictional narrative about *Nietzsche* comes about and not about someone who would bear no resemblance to the philosopher.

Whereas in the film example the parts and the idea were given and the transitions were to be discovered on their basis, in this second example the idea and the transitions (the 'central thread') are given and it is the parts which have to be found. Can we then also imagine a third case in which the parts and the transitions are given and the idea is to be discovered on their basis? Here I no longer need to construct an example, for this is exactly the case that Goethe seeks to solve with the help of his morphological method: all the parts ('the complete series') and the attentive observation of the transitions between them are to provide a basis for studying the idea underlying the whole. Here, too, I require two of the elements in order to find the third. The multiplication of the experiments on which Goethe insisted in "The Experiment as Mediator" thus represents only the *first* of two necessary steps: "Assiduously observe these transitions upon which, in the end, everything in nature depends," he would henceforth recommend.[8]

In contrast to the parts, of course, the transitions are not immediately given to sensibility—no more than they were in the mathematical series above. However, since the transitions have obviously taken place, it must be possible for me to re-produce them. Therefore it is particularly impor-

---

[7] This is the original idea of Irvin Yalom's bestseller *When Nietzsche Wept* (1992).
[8] Falk 1832, 27. In "The Experiment as Mediator" this moment is still missing, as we can tell by formulations such as this: "Once we have conducted such an experiment, once we have had such an experience, then, we cannot be meticulous enough in our examination of *what* immediately borders on it and *what* immediately follows upon it" (LA I,8:312; HA 13:18, emphasis added). Now Goethe would have to say: we cannot be meticulous enough in our examination of *how* that which immediately borders upon it, follows *from* it and *makes the transition* to the next form.

tant that in the course of my re-producing them, "my thinking not sepa-rate itself from the objects; the elements of the objects, the intuitions, must enter into my thinking and be intimately informed by it, so that my intuiting itself becomes a thinking and my thinking an intuiting" ("Sig-nificant Help," LA I,9:307; HA 13:37). As in the case of the mathemati-cal series, so too in the case of the succession of phenomena: I must simulate the transitions in thought; in imagination, I must re-produce the manner in which each part has emerged from the previous state and how it passes over into the succeeding state. And then I have to make all the transitions present to my mind *at once*—and with this the discursive understanding becomes intuitive and intuition becomes a single intuition—like the idea (or formula), I must be present at all points simultaneously in order to recognize its causality. As Goethe writes in a posthumously pub-lished remark:

> When I see an object before me which has come into existence, wonder about its genesis, and measure out the course of its becom-ing as far as I can follow it, I become aware of a series of stages [the individual parts] which I cannot perceive next to each other, but which I must make present to myself in memory as a certain ideal whole. At first I am inclined to imagine distinct steps, but since nature makes no leaps, I am finally compelled to intuit a *se-quence of uninterrupted activity as a whole by negating [aufhe-ben] the individual parts [qua individuals], but without destroying the impression* (LA I,10:131, emphasis added).

This requires both practice and of course a complete series on which to practice. Thus it was that Goethe, who had also taken over supervi-sion of the botanical garden in Jena, ordered that the specimens be planted "not where the soil is most suited to them, but where they *must* be placed on account of the systematic order";[9] he arranged for the cre-ation of botanical and physiological cabinets, started mineralogical col-lections, and spared no effort in directing attention to the transitions be-tween the phenomena (an issue which we will take up in more detail in the next chapter). With this, and with the elaboration of a Kantian meth-odology of the intuitive understanding, Spinoza's idea of a *scientia intu-itiva* had, in principle, been fruitfully adapted to natural objects.

---

[9] Cited in Irmtraut Schmid 1979, 50.

Before I go on to consider two concrete applications of this methodology of the intuitive understanding, I need to respond to an objection which at this point practically forces itself upon us: The two examples above, the objection goes, are not at all suited to illustrating the possibility of an intuitive understanding. For film and novel are products of art, created by certain individuals to represent their subjective ideas. Natural purposes, by contrast, as Kant had insisted, organize themselves; if we do not wish to relapse into pre-critical dogmatism, we cannot assume there to be some external 'artist' whose subjective ideas could explain them. Works of art thus shed no light on products of nature. The former originate in the subject, the latter in the object.

Before we go any further, a historical excursus may help us to gain some clarity on this issue.

VI.

Historical Excursus

According to legend, when the island of Delos was befallen by the plague in the fifth century B.C., the inhabitants appealed to the oracle in Delphi for advice. They were told to double the volume of the cubic altar in the temple of Apollo. In other words, they were ordered to geometrically construct the length of the side of a cube such that the whole cube would double in volume.

This problem went on to exercise the minds of a great many mathematicians, among them members of Plato's Academy. It was there that a solution was discovered by Menaechmus: since the construction is not possible using the classical means of compass and straightedge, he hit upon the expedient of basing it on the intersection of two second-order curves. In doing so, he 'discovered' the parabola and hyperbola, though he did not call them that. A century and a half later Apollonius of Perga integrated them into a general theory of the three conic sections ellipse, parabola, and hyperbola and gave them the names common today in his work *On Conic Sections.*

Apollonius was also an astronomer, but it would never even have occurred to him that conic sections might be the paths of planets and comets. The ancient view was that heavenly bodies necessarily moved along circular paths, because these were the most perfect. So Apollonius explained the orbits of the planets and their apparent retrograde motion as a combination of circular motions (epicycles), and this explanation became one of the pillars of Ptolemaic astronomy, which remained authoritative for many centuries. Even Copernicus, although he replaced Ptolemy's system with a heliocentric one, assumes in *De revolutionibus orbium caelestium* as a matter of course that the motions of the heavenly bodies are circular and of uniform velocity (Book 1, Ch. 4). The same is true for Galileo.

Kepler was the first to break with this assumption. His calculation of the orbit of Mars, based on Tycho Brahe's extensive observational data, showed that it could not be circular. He assumed that the planets move along ellipses and that one of their two foci is formed by the sun (Kepler's First Law). This turned out to be right. But how are we to understand the fact that a law discovered by Apollonius through sheer power of thought can turn out to underlie planetary motion? Or, to take a different example, why is it the case that a stone, tossed into the air at an angle, moves along a parabola, as Galileo claimed at about the same time? Newton ultimately integrated these discoveries into a unified theory, according to which the motion of a body around a central body always takes place along a conic section: depending on the initial velocity, its path will conform either to an ellipse, a parabola, or a hyperbola. The laws of the conic sections, which had been discovered by thought or rather by pure intuition, had proved to be regularities governing the physical world.

When for example Galileo writes in 1623 that the book of nature is written in mathematical language, or when in his widely read 1960 essay Eugene Wigner speaks of the "Unreasonable Effectiveness of Mathematics in the Natural Sciences," these are expressions of continually renewed astonishment over the fact that what is discovered in pure intuition can be *re-discovered* in the physical world. The laws, for example, of the conic sections were discovered without reference to nature, and yet they are realized (and demonstrable) in nature.

For now, I simply want to register this as a fact since it has an important implication for the objection raised above. As the example of mathematics shows, it cannot hold *in principle* that merely because something is found in the subject it cannot also be true in nature—even if we as yet have no insight into the ground of the agreement. The crucial point in our context, however, is that every mathematical construction, though carried out within the subject, is wholly free of any kind of subjectivity. It makes no reference whatsoever to the subject that carries it out. It stands beyond subject and object, we might say: *beyond the subject* because the construction is in no way affected by it; and *beyond the object* because the construction is valid not only for the individual object thus constituted, but for all objects of the same kind.

This is not the case, of course, with a film director or an author. They introduce their own personal representations into their work. Representations, however, in contrast to mathematical constructions, are not above and beyond subject and object. However, we also saw above that Spinoza and thus Goethe, too, desire to rise from representations to something corresponding to mathematical construction and which they call a concept (idea, essence). *Scientia intuitiva* is characterized by the fact that it does not seek to form representations, but rather concepts or ideas which are only to be found in the intuitive understanding and thus within the subject, yet which are realized in nature because they express the essence or inner nature of their object.

The hypothetical objection would thus only be valid if there were nothing outside of mathematics which, although it lies at the foundation of reality, can only be found within the subject; or in other words, it is valid only if all ideas are merely subjective. But that is precisely the unproven assumption that we are examining. To accept it without further scrutiny would be uncritical and dogmatic.

Now one might retort that it was Kant himself who showed that mathematics and philosophy follow completely different methods and that the imitation of mathematical procedures in philosophy is fundamentally misdirected. Kant first advocated this view in his 1764 essay *Inquiry Concerning the Distinctness of the Principles of Natural Theology and Morality,* and it is to be found in virtually identical form in the *Critique of Pure Reason*'s chapter on method. According to this view, philosophical cognition is the knowledge gained by reason from concepts, whereas mathematical cognition is based on the construction of concepts, where 'construction' is defined as exhibiting the a priori intuition corresponding to the concept. Mathematics contemplates the universal in the particular when, for example, it demonstrates in the case of a single (Euclidean) triangle that the sum of its angles is always equal to 180 degrees; the single case is valid for all cases in general. Philosophical cognition, by contrast, can only contemplate the particular in the universal, that is to say, by means of concepts (universal marks). To cognize something means in this case to subsume it under a concept under which it falls as a particular case. "The essential difference between these two kinds of knowledge through reason consists therefore in this formal difference, and does not depend on difference of their material or objects" (A714).

It has since become a dogma of Kantianism that this distinction captures the essences of mathematical and philosophical cognitions, and those who hold this dogma have forgotten that it rests on the assumption that *all* philosophical cognition is discursive. Yet that is precisely the assumption that Spinoza and Goethe are challenging, and its truth is what we need to examine here. In summary, then, we can say that *if* an idea lies at the basis of a set of phenomena and is operative in all its parts, then that fact can only be recognized by the method described here. *Whether or not* an idea in this sense lies at the foundation of a set of phenomena can also only be determined in this way. The bare assertion that the discursive understanding is the only humanly possible understanding has no philosophical bearing on this question.

VII.

To conclude my discussion of the procedures developed by Goethe I would like to illustrate them in two concrete cases. My reason for doing so is that I want to highlight the difference from Schelling's approach to *Naturphilosophie*. Whereas Schelling works with an *abstract* schema which he repeatedly 'potentiates' in order to explain the wealth of nature on its basis, Goethe's procedure—and the procedure of an intuitive understanding in general—is always *concrete* and follows the empirical phenomena. The two illustrations will exhibit all the methodological peculiarities of the intuitive understanding mentioned so far, namely (a) that the object's properties can be derived from its essence (Spinoza); (b) that the whole makes the parts possible and conditions them (Kant); and (c) that the methodical path lies in the observation of transitions (Goethe).

Illustration A: Theory of Colors

Comparison of Goethe's *Theory of Colors* (1810) with the fragmentary *Contributions to Optics* reveals that the most important difference is that the later work does not begin with light as such, but rather with the living eye in the act of seeing. More precisely, Goethe's first objects are the colors based on the action and reaction of the active eye. He calls them subjective or "physiological" colors. Only after he has dealt with these does Goethe turn to the "physical" colors arising outside the subject but requiring certain materials: colorless media such as prisms, lenses, water droplets, atmospheric vapors, and others. In the third place we find the so-called "chemical" colors which are permanent and adhere to the surfaces of objects, whereas physical colors are transient. Further chapters follow on the relation of the theory of colors to neighboring disciplines which we need not go into here. My illustration of Goethe's method will be drawn exclusively from the first two parts, touching only on the basic ideas.

Although light and darkness are naturally still required for the production of color, Goethe now sees "the foundation of the whole theory" in the colors which partially or wholly belong to "the subject," namely, to "the eye." These colors, which had been regarded hitherto as *couleurs accidentelles* or indeed as optical illusions, are fundamental to the *Theory of Colors* because they reveal the "chromatic harmony" (*Theory of*

Colors §1) which even Goethe himself had previously viewed as the subject of mere speculation and conjecture. For as Goethe's series of experiments demonstrates, these subjective colors are anything but accidental. They are governed by a strict regularity: a specific color, when viewed for a certain length of time, evokes a quite specific corresponding color when one afterwards gazes upon a white surface: yellow evokes violet, orange evokes blue, red green, and vice versa (cp. §50).

Now Goethe seems to have noticed that this regularity reflects a broader law. As he writes in §38: "We believe this again to be a proof of the great excitability of the retina, and of the silent resistance which every vital principle is forced to exhibit when any determinate state is presented to it . . . When darkness is presented to the eye it demands brightness, and vice versa: it shows its vital energy, *its fitness to apprehend the object, precisely by producing from within itself something that is opposed to the object.*"

The last clause of the sentence, which I have placed in italics, is so obviously an echo of Fichte's principle of reciprocal determination that it is worthwhile here to recall the details of that idea.

As we saw in Chapter 8, the third principle of Fichte's *Foundation* concerns a synthesis between the I and the non-I such that the divisibility of the originally posited totality allows for mediation between these elements which would otherwise contradict each other. Fichte does not fail to point out at once that all the following syntheses must be implicit in this fundamental synthesis if they are to be valid; i.e., that every further determination of the I and non-I have to be conceived as successive limitations (distributions of quantity) of the single totality of realities posited in consciousness. In section 4, which immediately follows, Fichte further elucidates this idea by means of the concept of reciprocal determination. Every determination fixates a certain quantity in such a way that the quantity of that which is excluded and posited as opposed is thereby also determined: "If the absolute totality of the real is to be conserved when the I is in a state of passivity," Fichte writes, "then, in virtue of the law of reciprocal determination, an identical degree of activity must necessarily be *carried over* into the non-I" (GA I,2:293f; W 1:135), and vice versa. However, since the activity of carrying over is independent of the elements of the alternation as such (which in themselves are individual and only become *alternating terms* by way of their connection), an independent activity must be posited, and this activity Fichte calls imagining. It is this faculty of connecting opposites which first makes consciousness possible.

By considering phenomena such as *couleurs accidentelles,* colored shadows, after-images, etc., in light of Fichte's reciprocal determination, Goethe discovered the eye's fundamental activity in constructing the visible world. For now his basic working assumption is that in every act of seeing the retina is simultaneously in diverse, indeed in opposed states (cp. §13), between which the eye *mediates* in order to produce connection and unity. He described the result as follows: "The eye of someone who is awake exhibits its vitality [*Lebendigkeit*] especially in its need to alternate its states . . . The eye cannot for a moment remain unchanged in a particular state determined by the object. On the contrary, it is forced to a sort of opposition, which, in opposing extreme to extreme, intermediate with intermediate, *at the same time combines that which is thus opposed,* and thus ever strives for a whole both in what is successive and in what is simultaneous and in the same place" (§33; emphasis added).

Just as Fichte had grounded the law of reciprocal determination in a "drive toward alternation in general," a drive which manifests itself in a "longing" for that part of the totality "which is opposed to that which is present" (GA I,2:444; W 1:320), so too Goethe identifies in the law of complementary colors a "need for totality" integral to our organ of sight and which manifests itself in the fact that the eye "brings forth the opposite of the single color forced upon it, thus producing a satisfying whole" (§812): "A single color excites the eye, by a specific sensation, to strive toward universality" (§805). Fichte's general principle of reciprocal determination is thus supplemented by a characteristic peculiar to the relevant set of phenomena, namely that the totality which the eye strives to fulfill is the totality of colors represented in the color circle (Figure 11.1).

Red

Orange   Violet

Yellow   Blue

Green

Figure 11.1

In other words, as soon as the eye is stimulated by a specific color it begins to strive to complete the color circle by producing its complementary color (i.e. the color opposite it in the circle) in and by itself. Indeed, in this way it has in fact realized the totality of the color circle, for "the violet color solicited by yellow contains red and blue; orange contains the yellow and red corresponding to blue; green unites blue and yellow and solicits red, and so forth through all the shades of the most various mixtures" (§60). "When the eye sees a color its activity is immediately triggered, and though it does so with a necessity unconscious to it, its nature is to produce another color which together with the given color contains the totality of the color circle" (§805).[10]

Today the law of complementary colors discovered by Goethe is an elementary part of every theory of vision. Yet why is the totality which the eye endeavors to complete the totality of *this* color circle? The idea that the dynamics of color alternation forms a natural sequence that can be represented as segments of a wheel is an idea that first emerged in the Middle Ages, and of course there are orderings of the colors that differ greatly from the one suggested by Goethe.[11] So why *this* color circle?

Here the 'physiological' part combines with the 'physical' part of the *Theory of Colors* in a way that exhibits interesting parallels with the case we considered in the last historical excursus.

As Goethe had already tried to show in the *Contributions*, the emergence of colors requires a coincidence of light and darkness or, as he now says, of "light and non-light" (Introduction and §744). Light itself is not visible as such, but only that which it illuminates.[12] In order to become visible it must enter into reciprocal action with "non-light," so that something new emerges: color. As I mentioned in Chapter 7 Goethe's very first experiment showed that colored edges did not appear until he directed the prism away from the white wall and toward the mullioned window.

---

[10] It is thus more than simply author's pride that occasions Fichte's remark to Schiller: "Goethe recently presented my system so clearly and coherently that I myself could not have done a better job" (cited in Schiller, *Der Briefwechsel zwischen Friedrich Schiller und Wilhelm von Humboldt,* 1:61.) It is presumably of equal significance that Goethe, during a stay at the spa in Teplitz shortly after completing the *Theory of Colors*, remarked upon seeing Fichte walking along the opposite side of the street: "There goes the man to whom we owe everything!" (H. I. Fichte, I:251).

[11] Cp. Gage 1993, 140, 9, 162, 171; see also Newton, *Opticks*, I, ii, prop. vi.

[12] "[W]e may call every light colored insofar as it is seen. Colorless light and colorless surfaces are to a certain extent abstractions" (§690).

A continuous series of related experiments finally led to the following general result: If we use the prism to move the light onto darkness thus illuminating it, blue is formed; if we move the darkness in front of light, thus darkening it, yellow is formed. These two colors are the first sensuous forms in which a fundamental polarity is manifested. They point to an *Urphänomen*—darkness through light produces blue; light through darkness produces yellow—from which all the other phenomena of color must be derivable.

As is well known, a pure mixture of the two colors yellow and blue produces green. Yellow and blue, however, can each be increased, augmented, or intensified in themselves; that is, they can be made darker or lighter without losing their specific properties. Such colors can be produced in numerous ways, e.g. when a semi-opaque medium is held in front of a light or dark surface in order to lighten or darken it, respectively. According to Goethe, we see the most impressive instance of this every day in the sky: the haze of the illuminated atmosphere causes the darkness of space to appear to us in the most various tones of blue and violet; the same medium intensifies the light of the setting sun and, depending on the degree of opacity, causes it to appear in the most manifold nuances of yellow-red and red. As a general rule, if the opacity of the medium through which the light is viewed increases or if it is thickened, yellow tones are intensified and shift toward yellow-red and red. If on the other hand the opacity of the illuminated medium is decreased, blue is intensified into blue-red or violet (cp. §§150–51).

Both extremes of the intensification (yellow-red and blue-red) thus converge; if they are brought together, say by producing them with a prism and then superimposing one upon the other, the result is a color which Goethe occasionally calls *Purpur:* a red tone of the greatest vivacity and intensity. Thus red is not truly a separate color of its own, but originates in a combination of the intensified primary colors. Opposed to it is the color which originates not in the combination of intensified yellow and blue, but in their simple mixture: green. Goethe summarizes the law governing the production of the colors in the Introduction to the *Theory of Colors:*

> We will here only anticipate our statements so far as to observe, that light and darkness, brightness and obscurity, or if a more general expression is preferred, light and non-light, are necessary to the production of color. Next to light, a color appears which we

call yellow; another appears next to darkness, which we name blue. When these, in their purest state, are so mixed that they balance out exactly, they produce a third color called green. Each of the two first-named colors can however of itself produce a new tint by being condensed or darkened. They thus acquire a reddish appearance which can be increased to so great a degree that the original blue or yellow is hardly to be recognized in it: but the most intense and purest red, especially in physical cases, is produced when the two extremes of the yellow-red and blue-red are united. This is the living view [*lebendige Ansicht*] of the appearance and generation of colors. But we can also assume an already existing red in addition to the specifically existing blue and yellow, and, working backwards, produce by way of mixing what we produced directly by augmentation or intensification. With these three or six colors, which may be conveniently arranged in a circle, the elementary theory of colors is alone concerned (LA I,4:20–21; HA 13:326).

Thus the colors combine in the physical sphere to form a circle, and it is the same circle we encountered with the physiological colors (Figure 11.2).

Figure 11.2

Moreover, given an identical degree of opacity in the medium of reciprocal action, light in front of darkness and darkness in front of light produce precisely the complementarily opposed pairs of colors in the physical sphere which the eye demands. What was initially discovered in the subject is now re-discovered in the external world. How is that possible? Goethe has obviously described something which is independent of whether it manifests itself within the subject or externally to the subject, something which is higher than both and which one may call the *essence* of color: a totality or whole which always manifests itself as a polarity, yet without compromising its inner unity: Every single color remains dependent on the totality and "solicits" the missing part of the whole to which it essentially belongs. Or, put differently, just as every angle in a triangle is determined by the two angles opposite it, so too every individual color is determined by the two opposed colors which, taken together, make up the solicited complementary color. It is only in the context of the specific 'whole' to which they belong that the individual angle and the individual color are what they are: the whole makes the individual part possible and determines it (Figure 11.3).

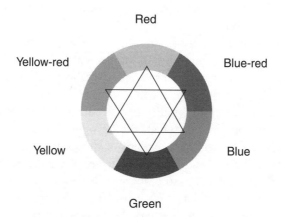

Red

Yellow-red   Blue-red

Yellow   Blue

Green

Figure 11.3

Illustration B: Metamorphosis of Plants

I would like to take my second illustration of Goethe's methodology from his *Metamorphosis of Plants*. It is instructive for showing how Goethe differs from Kant. Kant correlated plants and all other organisms with the reflective power of judgment, denying that the faculty of determinative judgment could produce genuine knowledge even *that* they are organisms. Goethe, on the other hand, begins by asking what makes certain products of nature *plants*—he asks what is common to all plants *as* plants such that they form a natural kingdom of their own. And he asks why this common element appears in such a plethora of forms.

If we consider the life-cycle of an annual plant (Figure 11.4), paying special attention with Goethe to the transitions between the individual

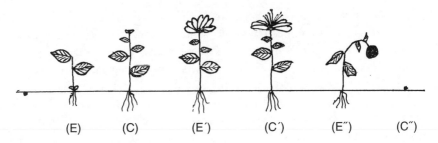

(E)   (C)   (E′)   (C′)   (E″)   (C″)

Figure 11.4

stages of development, we discover a progressive metamorphosis, "whose activity is always observable in stages from the first seminal leaves to the ultimate formation of the fruit and which by the transformation of one form into the next, as though by an intellectual ladder [*geistige Leiter*], ascends to that pinnacle of nature, reproduction by two sexes" (*Metamorphosis*, §6). What does this mean?

At first the plant's entire vitality is concentrated in the seed left over from the mother plant, with which the new process of formation now begins. This process starts with a point of division: something descends into the earth as a root and something strives upward toward the light: beginning with the cotyledons or embryonic leaves, we can observe a continuous movement upward and outward: the plant grows to height, the leaves become larger and differentiate themselves, expanding to a certain diameter (E). Then comes a sort of turning point: the rate of growth diminishes, the leaves may become smaller and their form less differentiated, the intervals between them decrease, and finally as sepals they form a circle around a common center (C). In the petals, the plant once again begins to expand (E′); at the same time, the delicate stamen and pistil take form (C′). In the fertilized plant, the pistil turns into a fruit (E″), in the interior of which a new seed forms. The series concludes with this new seed (C″).

If we retrace this movement in the imagination, paying attention to the transitions between stages of development, we notice a threefold alternation of expansion (E) and contraction (C): in the formation of the stem and leaves the alternation is *successive*, in the formation of the blossom it is *parallel*, and in the formation of the fruit and seed it is *nested* and interlocking (Figure 11.5).

272

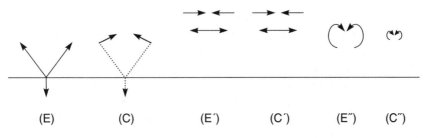

(E)　　　　(C)　　　　(E′)　　　　(C′)　　　　(E″)　　(C″)

Figure 11.5

Goethe writes: "From the seed to the highest development of the stem leaf we first observed an expansion, then we saw the calyx emerge by way of a contraction, the leaves by way of expansion, the reproductive parts once again by way of contraction; and we will soon witness the greatest expansion in the fruit and the greatest concentration in the seed. In these six steps, nature ceaselessly performs the eternal labor of reproducing the vegetable kingdom through two sexes" (§73).

But what exactly is it that is doing the expanding and contracting in these six stages?[13] It is obviously not any one of the visible parts of the plant. The sepal, for example, does not emerge from the stem leaf in any physical sense; it just follows upon it. So what expands and contracts and becomes concrete in such a variety of ways in the individual parts is, in the first instance, a form that can only be apprehended in thought. When Goethe first realized this he made the following note in his diary: "Hypothesis: Everything is leaf, and the greatest diversity becomes possible through this simplicity" (LA II,9A:55). What he means by 'leaf' is not the sensuously given stem leaf, but rather an ideal organ from which all the physical forms of the plant can be formed by way of transformation so that the petals, too, and the stamen and pistils must be considered as metamorphosed leaves.[14] The fact that they look different when viewed superficially is itself a merely superficial fact. According to the hypothesis,

---

[13] "In the progressive modification of the parts of the plant, *one single* force is at work which can only improperly be called expansion and contraction . . . *The force* contracts, expands, develops, transforms, connects, separates . . ." (LA I,10:58, emphasis added).

[14] "A leaf that only absorbs moisture under the earth is what we call a root; a leaf that is expanded by moisture is called a bulb. A leaf that expands uniformly is a stem, a stalk" (LA II,9A:55).

the plant's visible parts are merely particular formations of an underlying ideal form which presents itself anew at every nodal point, repeating its work. Thus, 'everything is leaf' must be understood as meaning that all the forms taken on by the plant are, *in respect to their idea,* identical:[15] "The same *organ* that expands on the stem as a leaf and has taken on such diverse forms, now contracts in the calyx, expands again in the petal, contracts in the organs of reproduction, in order to expand one final time as the fruit" (§115).

Once I have apprehended this ideal archetype in thought, I can mentally construct a plant by letting its essential forms emerge out of each other. I can produce plant forms which represent *real possibilities* since they conform to the archetype of the plant and hence *could* exist in nature given suitable conditions. This we could call a construction of the plant in inner intuition, whose governing law can be re-discovered in outer intuition. Goethe once put it like this: "Tell Herder that I am very close to unraveling the secret of the generation and organization of plants and that it is the simplest thing you can imagine . . . The *Urpflanze* will be the most remarkable creature in the world and even nature herself will envy me for it. With this model and the key to it, an infinite variety of plants can be invented, which are consistent, that is, they are such that, even if they do not exist, they *could* exist, and thus are more than just painterly or poetic shadows and apparitions, for they possess an inner truth and necessity" (HABr. 2:60).[16]

If the ideal "leaf" is the 'model' (the constructive element) for producing plants, then the key (the constructive rule) to its realization, i.e. to a construction in thought which qua real possibility would (in Kantian terms) possess objective reality, lies in the insight that this organ has to undergo a process of formation and transformation in "six steps" of ex-

---

[15] "No living thing is a single individual, but rather a plurality; even to the extent that it appears to us as an individual, it still remains a collection of living, self-sufficient beings which in their idea, their basic tendency, are identical, but which in their appearance can become identical or different, similar or dissimilar . . . The motile life of nature consists in the fact that that which is identical in the idea can appear to experience as either identical, or similar, or as wholly different and dissimilar" (LA I,9:8–9; HA 13:56–57).

[16] Goethe later replaced the term *Urpflanze* with the term *Typus,* but even the latter term is actually still too static: "In those days I was in search of the *Urpflanze,* unaware that I was looking for the idea, the concept according to which we could form it for ourselves" (letter to Nees von Esenbeck, August 1816, WA IV,27:144).

pansion and contraction in order to complete the life-cycle of an annual flowering plant.

However, that is only one side of the matter. Every idea also requires for its *physical* realization a material basis onto which it can imprint itself, but which in turn constrains and limits it. No single realization manifests the idea as such, but always only one of its countless possibilities to the exclusion of all others. The idea cannot therefore be discovered in the external world, but only in the intuitive understanding. Once it has been discovered, however, its effects can be re-discovered in experience.[17]

A plant that is present in material form can undergo a variety of transformations. The primordial form of plants not only actively determines the parts of the plant, but also possesses the ability to transform itself in the most various ways in reaction to external influences—it is a form, as Goethe writes in a letter to Charlotte von Stein, "with which nature always merely plays, as it were, and in playing brings forth the manifold of life" (HABr 1:514). The variations in form are a product of interaction with the environment. Goethe encounters the "innocent coltsfoot," familiar to him from Weimar, in the saline soil of Venice, but in a different form, "armed with sharp weapons" and with leaves of leather, and fatty mast-like stems (HA 11:90). In other climes the *Urform* appears in quite different plants. The whole wealth of the plant world is thus governed by two kinds of laws: on the one hand, the internal law proper to the plants as such that manifests itself in every individual plant; on the other hand, the laws of environmental effects, adaptation and selection, which manifest themselves in the varieties of plants:

> The metamorphosis of the plant . . . draws our attention to a twofold law:
>
> 1. The law of inner nature, by which plants are constituted.
>
> 2. The law of external circumstances, by which plants are modified ("Preliminary work for a physiology of plants" [*Vorarbeiten zu einer Physiologie der Pflanzen*], LA I,10:135).

---

[17] Goethe is convinced that what makes a plant a plant is the ideal whole that determines the parts and their succession and is simultaneously at work throughout that succession, so that the earlier states are just as determined by the later ones as the later ones are determined by the earlier ones: Not only does the formation of the petals, for example, presuppose the formation of the stem and the leaves; the possibility of the later formation of the fruit is already formatively at work in the development of the pistils and stamen in the blossom.

In order to study the second kind of laws, it is of course necessary to presuppose the first kind. Adaptation and selection can only take place in relation to something already equipped with the corresponding abilities. For inorganic products of nature are not subject to any process of selection, but only to chemical and mechanical processes. This is the reason why Goethe was so interested in the first kind of laws. In order to recognize it, a different kind of observation and thinking is necessary than in the study of inorganic nature. It is a kind of approach, as Goethe explained in a different context, "that forces me to consider all natural phenomena in a certain developmental sequence and attentively to follow the *transitions* forwards and backwards. For only in this way do I finally arrive at the living view of the whole [*lebendige Übersicht*] from which a concept is formed that soon will merge with the idea along an ascending line" ("*Wolkengestalt nach Howard*," LA I,8:74).

In other words, it is the method of an intuitive understanding.

12

Does Philosophy Have a History?

With the result of the preceding chapter I have once again skipped ahead in the order of events: Goethe was writing the *Theory of Colors*—the first work he *consciously* based on the methodology of the intuitive understanding—at the same time that Hegel was at work on the *Phenomenology of Spirit*. So we need to catch up on the steps leading up to this time. For when Hegel arrived in Jena in 1801, he was still very far from the *Phenomenology*. It is true that from 1802 onward he repeatedly announced a work that was to be entitled "Logic and Metaphysics,"[1] but this work never appeared. An account of the reasons why the book never materialized will constitute a final important step in understanding the 'twenty-five years of philosophy'.

After completing his studies in Tübingen together with Hölderlin and Schelling, Hegel was employed as a *Hofmeister* (a private tutor) in Bern and later in Frankfurt. When his father died, leaving him some money, Hegel decided to pursue an academic career, and so he went to Jena, where Schelling had already achieved notable success. "I have observed your public career with admiration and joy," Hegel wrote to Schelling on November 2, 1800, while still in Frankfurt. "In the course of my scholarly development, which began with men's subordinate needs, it was inevitable that I would be driven to science, and that the ideal of my adolescence would be transmuted into the form of reflection, into a system."[2]

---

[1] The Cotta publishing house announced the title "Dr. Hegel, Logic and Metaphysics 8°" as early as June 24, 1802 (see the document printed in *Briefe von und an Hegel*, 4,1:86).

[2] *Briefe von und an Hegel*, 1:59.

I.

What is the ideal of Hegel's adolescence that he obviously expects Schelling to know well enough that further explanation would be superfluous? When Hegel, Schelling, and Hölderlin parted ways in 1793, they sealed a bond of friendship, choosing as their watchword: *Reich Gottes,* the Kingdom of God, or the invisible church on earth.[3] This was a direct reference to Kant's *Religion within the Boundaries of Mere Reason,* which had come out at the Easter book-fair of 1793 and which the three Tübingen seminarians had studied intensively.[4] In Part Three of the work, Kant had introduced the idea of an invisible church as the idea of the unification of all the righteous under divine moral governance of the world, identifying it with the highest good as the ultimate purpose of practical reason. "The wish of all well-disposed human beings is, therefore, 'that the kingdom of God come, and that his will be done on earth'; but what preparations must they make in order that this wish come to pass among them?" (6:101).

The friends intended to dedicate themselves to this task. Thus Hegel wrote, presumably while still in Tübingen: "My intention is . . . to inquire . . . what means are required in order to integrate the doctrines and power of religion into the tissue of human sentiments, into the motives for action, and to ensure their vitality and effectiveness" (GW 1:90; TW 1:16). Political and historical studies were soon to follow, inquiring into the causes that had led to the positivity of religion, the alliance of a community originally based on faith with state authorities, and similar antagonisms characterizing the modern world.

Hegel initially remained true to his Kantian inspirations, but he too was soon to experience misgivings about their foundations. The seeds planted by Schelling in an early letter ("Kant has given results; the premises are still missing") received powerful nourishment when Hegel accepted a position as *Hofmeister* in Frankfurt at the beginning of

---

[3] Thus Hölderlin writes to Hegel in July 1794: "I am certain that you have on occasion thought of me since we took leave of each other with the watchword 'Reich Gottes'." And Hegel in turn writes to Schelling in January 1795: "May the kingdom of God come, and let not our hands be idle in our laps . . . Let reason and freedom be our watchword, the invisible church our point of unification" (*Briefe von und an Hegel,* 1:9, 18).

[4] F. Nicolin 1988 gives an excellent account of the traces left by this text in (among other places) Hegel's last sermon in Tübingen.

1797. His renewed proximity to Hölderlin brought him into contact with the developments following on Kant which I discussed in Chapters 7, 8, and 9.

Hölderlin, who had attended Fichte's lectures in Jena in 1794/95, had adopted from him the idea that all human consciousness is conditioned by two opposed tendencies or directions of striving which are locked in conflict with each other: one of them tends beyond everything finite into the infinite, while the other tends toward limitation and determinacy. Hölderlin argued that their common source or ground could not be located in an I, however, since an I without self-consciousness is inconceivable and self-consciousness in turn entails a "separation" of the thinker and what is thought (I=I). Their ground must therefore be a unity prior to all consciousness which Hölderlin, still under the influence of Jacobi's Spinoza reception, calls the 'being in all beings', '*das Sein in allem Dasein*'.[5]

These ideas provided Hegel with a new basis for his work. On the one hand, the original unity necessarily undergoes division in order to emerge into appearance. On the other hand, the resulting fundamental oppositions, including those which characterize the modern age, point beyond themselves: "even to be able to show that they are opposites, a unity is presupposed" (TW 1:251). Such a unity, such a being, however, cannot be theoretically demonstrated; it must be "believed." The understanding cannot comprehend this absolute unity; if it nevertheless attempts to conceive both the finite and the infinite at once, all it can do is either to oppose these to each other and formulate "antinomies,"[6] or to become a 'positive' faith which, in place of the true unification, ends up with a fixated and hence *finitized* unification. Hegel's basic concern thus appears in a new light: "If it is now shown that the opposed, limited terms cannot as such continue in existence, that they necessarily negate themselves [*sich aufheben*], and hence that, in order to be possible, they presuppose a unification . . . then it is proven that they have to be unified, that unification ought to take place" (ibid.).

I would like to take up the thread of Hegel's development at the end of his time in Frankfurt, shortly before his move to Jena. Two months

---

[5] See especially Henrich 1965/66 and 1991.

[6] "Belief [*Glaube*] is the way in which what has been unified, thereby unifying an antinomy, is present in our representation" (TW 1:250). In contrast to a mere contradiction, whose terms mutually annihilate each other, in the antinomy both terms are justified on independent grounds.

prior to the letter to Schelling mentioned above, Hegel completed the draft of a work, of which only a few pages have survived and which has therefore come to be known as the *Systemfragment 1800*. In this text Hegel gives more concrete expression to the 'being' that underlies all separation, calling it *infinite life*. What is significant about this is the indivisible unity of infinite life with its manifestations. On the one hand, there is only life where there are living beings; on the other hand, life is not identical with the sum of all living beings. Rather, it is what makes them into living beings at all. To be more precise, a living being is *individual* life in that it is distinct from the infinitude of life outside itself; it is individual *life* insofar as it is one with this infinitude.

The human being is himself a living being. In his reflections he distinguishes life in general from himself as a "single organized separated and unified whole," i.e. as nature. At the same time, however, this life in the form of conscious awareness of nature "feels" that external nature is something merely posited and not the true, infinite life. It feels that by having thus fixated life it has created for itself something "infinitely finite," something "unlimitedly limited," in short a "contradiction," an antinomy. Qua reason, whose nature is to desire knowledge of the true, it feels the "one-sidedness of this positing." Yet reflection is unable to escape from this one-sidedness:

> When I say it [sc. life] is the connection of opposition and relation, this connection can itself be taken in isolation and the objection raised that it is opposed to non-connection. A better expression would be to say that life is the connection of connection and non-connection, i.e. every expression is a product of reflection and it is therefore possible to prove of every expression, as something posited, that in positing something, something else is not posited, but excluded, and thus we are driven ceaselessly on with no place to rest. But we can put an end to this driving once and for all, if we do not forget that what we have called the connection of synthesis and antithesis, for instance, is not something posited, something belonging to the understanding and reflection, but that *its only character for reflection is that it is a being external to reflection* (TW 1:422; emphasis added).

Because, however, the finite thinking being is itself *life*, Hegel now argues, it can relate to the infinite in a way that differs from thought (or belief): it can seek to overcome what makes its life something *individual*.

The elevation of the finite to the infinite life would be tantamount to re-nunciation of everything that is merely self-serving; Hegel mentions the renunciation of property, willingness to make sacrifices, the merging of one's own subjectivity with that of the other believers in collective ritual acts, and so on. The suspension of finitude is thus not complete, but only partial—"religion is a certain elevation of the finite to the infinite" (TW 1:426); it starts with the particularities of determinate life and grows ever more complete as the life of the people (the *Volk*) grows less 'divided'.

The crucial point for Hegel is this. The elevation of the finite to the infinite is "necessary" for reflection "since the former is conditioned by the latter" (TW 1:426), and yet reflection cannot itself attain to the true infinite. Thus philosophy necessarily ends in religion:

> Philosophy must end as religion precisely because the former is a mode of thinking and therefore contains both an opposition to non-thinking and the opposition of a thinking subject and what is thought; it has to reveal the finitude in all things finite and to pos-tulate their complementation [*Vervollständigung*] through reason, especially the deceptions by its own infinite, in order to posit the true infinite beyond its own sphere. The elevation of the finite to the infinite is characterized as the elevation of finite life to infinite life, as religion, precisely by the fact that it does not posit the being of the infinite as a being through reflection, as something objective or subjective, which would be to complement what is limited by what limits it, to recognize the latter as something posited and hence limited in turn, and to seek anew that which limits it, and so on *ad infinitum*. This activity of reason is indeed also an elevation to the infinite, but this infinite is [merely something endless, not a true infinitude] . . . [gap in the text] (TW 1:422–23).

II.

Hegel arrived in Jena in January 1801—at the very moment that Schelling was embroiled in his controversy with Eschenmayer about the status of intellectual intuition presented at the end of Chapter 10. Schelling's reply to Eschenmayer, "On the True Concept of *Naturphilosophie*" [*Über den wahren Begriff der Naturphilosophie*], also came out in January 1801 in Schelling's *Journal for Speculative Physics*; the next number, which fol-lowed in May 1801, contained Schelling's "Presentation of My System"

[*Darstellung meines Systems*], the first account of his *Identitätsphiloso-phie*. The importance of this controversy for Hegel can be gleaned from his first publication in Jena, *The Difference between Fichte's and Schelling's Systems of Philosophy*, whose foreword is dated "July 1801."

As we saw in Chapter 10, Schelling now claims for philosophy not only the evidence of intellectual intuition, but over and above that an ability to abstract from the intuiting subject in this intuition: "The task is: to make the subject-object [as the object of intellectual intu-ition] objective and to bring it out of itself to the point where it wholly coincides with nature (as product); the point where it becomes nature is also the point where that which is illimitable within it elevates itself to the I, and where the opposition between the I and nature made by ordi-nary consciousness completely disappears, and nature=I, I=nature" (AA I,10:95–96; SW IV:91).

This idea took on great significance for Hegel, for whom intellectual intuition had hitherto played no role whatsoever, since it made it possible for him to take a decisive step beyond his Frankfurt *Systemfragment:* The infinite life, now called the absolute, no longer needs to be merely be-lieved or left wholly to religious experience; it is in principle accessible to philosophical cognition.[7]

A thumbnail sketch of the basic idea behind the new conception might go like this: Whereas philosophical reflection inevitably sets subject and object in opposition to one another, in intellectual intuition we have, "ex-pressed in terms of reflection: the identity of subject and object" (GW 4:77; TW 2:114). In order to produce such an intuition, Hegel now argues, the first requirement is a free act on the part of the subject, who must abstract from the manifold of empirical consciousness. To this extent, however, the intuition is still subjectively conditioned, and hence if phi-losophy makes *this* intellectual intuition its absolute principle—as Hegel believes Fichte does—then it has mistakenly elevated something that is in

---

[7] For a contrary view see for example Klaus Düsing: "It is astonishing that Hegel abandons this position of the superiority of religion to philosophy . . . at the very beginning of his time in Jena (1801) without any indication of his reasons for do-ing so, and henceforth insists on rational, speculative cognition of the absolute. Since external influences can hardly have played a role here, the reasons must be sought in Hegel's own later fragments from the Frankfurt period" (Düsing 1977, 40–41; Düsing 1988, 115 is even more explicit). Yet Düsing fails to question why intellectual intuition suddenly becomes so central for Hegel.

fact subjectively conditioned to an absolute principle: "the principle, the subject-object turns out to be a subjective subject-object" (GW 4:6–7; TW 2:11). And on Hegel's critical view of Fichte, all that can be derived from this is a series of finitudes from which the original identity can never be recovered but only set up as a postulate: "I=I is thus transformed into the principle: The I *ought* to be identical to itself" (GW 4:7; TW 2:12). Thus within the confines of transcendental philosophy the subject can never recognize its identity with the object, but neither can a true identity of subject and object be achieved in a *Naturphilosophie* which posits the object as absolute.

In order to get around this one-sidedness, Hegel suggests that both subject and object must each be posited as subject-object. This means that Fichte's subjective intellectual intuition and the objective intellectual intuition of the *Naturphilosophie* must both be "presented as unified in something higher than the subject," and this is achieved by abstracting from the intuiting subject in intellectual intuition. Intellectual intuition, understood thus, Hegel calls 'transcendental intuition': "To grasp transcendental intuition in its purity, one must also abstract from this subjective [element]; as the basis of philosophy, it is neither subjective nor objective, neither self-consciousness, opposed to matter, nor matter, opposed to self-consciousness, but absolute identity, neither subjective nor objective identity, pure transcendental intuition . . . [T]he opposition belonging to speculative reflection is no longer that of object and subject, but a subjective transcendental intuition and an objective transcendental intuition, the former the I, the latter nature, both the highest manifestations of absolute, self-intuiting reason" (GW 4:77; TW 2:115).

In Hegel's 'transcendental intuition', what formerly were opposites are now identical. This means on the one hand that, qua opposed terms, they have been negated (*aufgehoben*): "to this extent, nothing is present for reflection and knowledge" (GW 4:63; TW 2:95). At the same time, though—and this is the crucial idea—"because they are both in the absolute identity, *they also persist in being; and their persistence in being is* what makes knowledge possible, for in knowledge the partial separation of the two is posited" (GW 4:63; TW 2:95; emphasis added).

What exactly does this mean? The absolute is the identity of the ideal and the real, and only in both together is it complete. In order to be cognized, it has to be posited in both forms. In consciousness, this unity undergoes a diremption into subject and object, but in the object, too, the original unity must still be present, as must be the two sides of subject and object. If the subjective subject-object and the objective subject-object are both equally united in the absolute by transcendental intuition, then a cognition of the absolute becomes possible, *provided* that the opposed terms present in consciousness can be restored to their true unity in such a way that the original identity "gives birth to both, and is born of both" (GW 4:63; TW 2:94).

In the lectures Hegel was giving at this time he puts it this way: "the abstraction from everything else, this steady, clear intuition is the primary condition of all philosophizing"; it provides us with an "idea in its utmost simplicity" (GW 5:264). "Cognition must first exhibit the idea as such, and if we have previously only represented [*vorgestellt*] the intuition [of the absolute, the idea], we will now unfold this idea for cognition, undergoing a diremption into this cognition and hence into difference, yet remaining absolutely under the reign and the necessity of the idea itself, so that we do not lose the unity in this separation" (GW 5:262).[8]

In the *Differenzschrift*, however, Hegel at best only hints at the method for realizing the promised cognition: The task of philosophy must be to construct the absolute in consciousness (cp. GW 4:11; TW 2:19). To this end, the finitudes of consciousness have to be converted into antinomies. Once they are recognized as antinomies, they point toward the identity imperfectly expressed in them. However, in order for them to be recognized as antinomies and not merely as contradictions in which the opposed terms annihilate each other, reflection must always be "synthesized" (GW 4:16; TW 2:26) with the transcendental intuition which maintains the idea of the absolute in presence so that we 'do not lose the unity in this separation'. Therefore it is "of the deepest significance that it has been so seriously claimed that it is impossible to philosophize without transcendental intuition" (GW 4:28; TW 2:42).

---

[8] In the transcription by Troxler we accordingly read, "The separation [*Auseinandergehen*] of the ideal and the real now takes place in the transition from unconsciousness [*Bewußtlosigkeit*] to consciousness. The identical posits itself as different and relates the differences to each other, though this relation, taken in itself, is what is first, even though it appears as what is third. The foreign element which emerges is a product of itself, and the determinations which the ideal gives to the real are nothing but the affections which the latter transfers to the first by way of sensations" (74).

III.

Hegel adopts not only Schelling's conception of intellectual intuition, but also to a large extent the basic approach of his *Identitätsphilosophie*.[9] This approach is grounded in Schelling's conviction, laid out in Chapter 10, that the absolute or the infinite cannot have gone outside of itself, but that everything that exists, insofar as it exists, is the infinite itself. Outside of it is nothing, everything is within it.[10]

Schelling claimed that since it is the absolute identity of the ideal and the real, of being and cognition, the absolute identity only *is* in the form of its cognition of its self-identity: "Everything that exists is, in its *essence* (insofar as this essence is considered in itself and absolutely), the absolute identity itself, while in *the form of being* it is a cognition of the absolute identity" (AA I,10:123; SW IV:122).[11] This of course presupposes the emergence of a difference between the subjective and the objective. Since however, *in itself,* there is no opposition between subject and object, any difference between them can only be quantitative, a predominance of the one or the other—comparable to the two directions on the number line (cp. Hegel in the *Differenzschrift* GW 4:66; TW 2:100). Schelling expresses this in a scholium to section 30 of the *Presentation* as follows: "Our claim therefore, put in the most explicit terms, is that if we could behold everything that exists as it is in the totality, we would become aware of a perfect quantitative equilibrium of subjectivity and objectivity and thus nothing but a pure identity in which nothing is distinguishable, despite the fact that in regard to individual elements the preponderance

---

[9] Differences regarding the internal structure of the absolute, which do not affect the basic approach, can be disregarded here; on this see for instance Düsing 1988, 117, 186–87.

[10] In the preface to his *Presentation of My System of Philosophy,* Schelling now writes, "I have always presented what I call *Naturphilosophie* and transcendental philosophy as opposite poles of philosophizing; with this presentation I find myself at the point of indifference on which no one can stand safely and securely who has not constructed it beforehand from wholly opposite directions" (AA I,10:110; SW 4:108).

[11] In Troxler's notes on Schelling's lecture on his *Presentation of my System of Philosophy,* we find the following remark on the absolute identity: "Since being and cognition are one in it [sc. the absolute identity], it is unity, and since there is nothing outside of being and cognition, it is totality. Whoever has grasped this concept has reached the highest and the only standpoint of philosophy" (43).

may fall to the one or the other side, and thus that such quantitative differences, too, are by no means posited *in themselves,* but only in appearance" (AA I,10:128–29; SW IV:127).

And thus the quantitative difference between the ideal and the real is the ground of all finitude, whose measure is expressed by the specific potentiations. In Schelling's symbolism, if the absolute identity is A=A, then the form of any given potentiation is A=B, where B expresses the real principle and A the ideal principle. For this reason Schelling always expresses the absolute identity's form of being in the image of a line,[12] which he describes as "the fundamental formula of our whole system in which the same identical term is posited in both directions, but depending on which of the opposing directions it is posited in, either A or B is in preponderance, and at the point of equilibrium A=A" (AA I,10:139; SW IV:137).

$$\frac{\overset{+}{A}=B \qquad\qquad \overset{+}{A}=B}{A=A}$$

Before the year was out, Hegel and Schelling began publishing their *Critical Journal of Philosophy* [*Kritisches Journal der Philosophie*]. They were the journal's sole authors, but they did not sign any of the articles individually: the inevitable impression of a single common philosophical position was doubtlessly intended. In regard to the essence of philosophical cognition they were certainly in complete agreement: "That philosophy is One and can be only One, rests on the fact that reason is only One," we read in the jointly authored introduction to the first issue (GW 4:117; TW 2:172). Hegel had advocated the same position in the *Differenzschrift:* "If it is the case that the absolute, like its appearance, reason, is eternally one and the same (and it is the case), then every reason which has directed itself toward itself and come to know itself has produced a true philosophy and completed the task which, like its solution, is the same in all times. Since in philosophy reason, in knowing itself, has to do only with itself, the whole work and activity of philosophy lies in itself,

---

[12] On the meaning of this line and its background in the history of science, see Ziche 1996, 200–204.

and in regard to the inner essence of philosophy there are neither precursors nor successors" (GW 4:10; TW 2:17)

To the extent, namely, that every authentic philosophy is a systematic cognition of the absolute on the basis of the means available to its historical age and the idea of the absolute is always at the root of such systems, they are of equal worth and rank, like the great works of art. It is just as impossible for reason to view its own earlier incarnations as so many trial runs, Hegel writes, as it would have been for Shakespeare to consider the works of Sophocles or for Raphael to view those of Apelles as preliminary attempts along the path that ultimately led to themselves: "Every philosophy is complete in itself and, like an authentic work of art, contains the totality within itself" (GW 4:12; TW 2:19). This view rules out a historical *development* of philosophy in the sense of a steady course of progress just as it rules out the notion of historical progress in art. Thus he states in his lectures of 1801/02, "at all times there has always only been One and the same philosophy" (GW 5:274).

It is hard to imagine a more dramatic about-face than Hegel's announcement four years later in a lecture on the history of philosophy that "the further this development advances, the more perfect philosophy becomes" (TW 18:46). To understand how this change came about I would like to insert a further historical excursus.

IV.

Historical Excursus

In 1803, Schelling left Jena to accept a chair in Würzburg; in the same year, Franz Joseph Schelver, formerly in Halle, was called to the University of Jena. For Hegel, the newly arrived colleague, eight years his junior, was to prove a stimulating companion and it was not long before a close friendship formed between them. In order to appreciate its significance we need to know a little bit more about Schelver.

Franz Joseph Schelver, born in Osnabrück in 1778, had matriculated in Jena in April 1796 as a student of medicine, but he also studied botany with Batsch and philosophy with Fichte. In Autumn of 1797, Schelver switched to Göttingen where he earned his doctorate under J. F. Blumenbach one year later with a dissertation entitled *De irritabilitate*. From 1801 to 1803 he was employed as a lecturer

(*Privatdozent*) in Halle, and starting in 1802 he gave lectures on *Naturphilosophie* (among other things) that bear obvious marks of Schelling's influence.[13] In the same year, Schelver published a *Journal for Organic Physics* [*Zeitschrift für organische Physik*] whose sole author he was and of which only two issues were published. Through this undertaking he became more widely known.

Although Schelling was not uncritical of Schelver as a disciple, he nevertheless interceded with Goethe on his behalf when the University of Jena was looking for a professor of botany to replace Batsch, who had died in 1802.[14] This chair is of considerable importance in our present context. In 1794, Goethe and Batsch had founded the botanical garden still located at Fürstengraben in Jena, as well as the botanical institute connected to it. Despite resistance from the faculty of medicine, Goethe had also managed to have botany promoted from an ancillary discipline serving the study of medicine to an independent subject within the university; the professor in charge of it was henceforth to belong to the *philosophische Fakultät* or school of philosophy. In terms of university politics, this represented an important step towards establishing Goethe's methodology as a scientific discipline. The garden's design was to be determined neither by the needs and interests of the medical faculty nor by economic considerations; it was to serve purely morphological and systematic ends. In the founding documents Goethe took care to set down that the "purpose of a botanical garden is to maintain as many different plant varieties as possible of every genus, so that they are both well planted and suitable to be used for the study of botany. For this reason, a skillful botanical gardener will not plant where the conditions are most suited to them, *but where they ought to be planted to accord with the systematic order.*"[15] Even so, Goethe soon registered with disappointment that, in his own publications, Batsch took little heed of Goethean methodology.[16]

When Schelver succeeded Batsch in 1803, taking on the direction of the botanical garden as one of his duties, Goethe inserted a clause into Schelver's contract stating that he was not allowed to change anything in the "disposition of the garden, the order of the beds, etc.," but that everything was to be "carried on in the same way as heretofore."[17] Nor did Goethe miss the opportunity to instruct

---

[13] A transcript of these lectures can be found in the university library in Heidelberg, signature Hd-HS-1358.

[14] Cp. Schelling's letter to Goethe, January 24, 1803. In Schelling, *Briefe und Dokumente*, 2:485.

[15] Quoted in Schmid 1979, 49–50 (emphasis added).

[16] Cp., e.g., Goethe's letter to Batsch, February 26, 1794, WA IV, 10:144.

[17] The contract is included in Schmid 1979, 251–52.

Schelver personally in how to conduct the business of the garden and how to make use of it in his lectures on botany. In addition, however, Schelver was also given the task of building up various new collections and cabinets into "a small botanical museum."[18] Hegel, who by this time was already fast friends with Schelver and showing a lively interest in his activities, wrote to Schelling on November 11, 1803, that "Goethe is devoting all his energy to specimens and collections; not only is he having Schelver build up a botanical cabinet, he is erecting a physiological cabinet as well."[19]

The result was that Schelver, who had initially been inclined to dismiss Goethe's ideas on morphology, now increasingly identified with them. Whereas in the beginning he had dismissed the *Metamorphosis of Plants* as insufficiently speculative and criticized it to Schelling for resting content "with the worst kind of empirical necessity" and being "a very unimpressive abstraction,"[20] in short time the practical tasks entrusted to him under Goethe's own personal and intensive supervision would change Schelver's mind. After a visit by Schelver and Hegel at Goethe's house on November 27, 1803, Goethe wrote that very same evening to Schiller, "I passed a few very pleasant hours with Schelver, Hegel, and Fernow. Schelver is working in botany in a way that accords so beautifully with *what I think is right* that I can hardly believe my eyes and ears."[21]

Schelver's lecture announcements, too, reveal that he was busy assimilating what Goethe 'thought was right': whereas in the Summer semester of 1803, his first in Jena, he announced lectures on "botany" pure and simple, from 1804 onward he taught "botany in connection with botanical excursions" or "with the use of the Ducal botanical garden."[22] For Goethe had also begun to "take special care" of his lectures, as Schelver wrote to Schelling.[23]

When Schelver's original contract ended in 1805, Goethe recommended that it be renewed, arguing that it was "highly desirable that this young and very educated man who is continually cultivating himself for his profession should not be lost to the academy."[24] Yet lost to Jena he was soon to be. After Napoleon's devastating victory over the Prussian forces at the battle of Jena on October 14,

---

[18] Goethe had these requirements on Schelver put on record on April 23, 1803; cp. Schmid 1979, 34.

[19] *Briefe von und an Hegel,* 1:78.

[20] Schelver to Schelling, October 27, 1803; quoted in Müller 1992, 177–78.

[21] WA IV,16:356 (emphasis added). Cp. also the diary entry on this day, WA III,3:88.

[22] The lecture announcements are quoted in Bach 2001, 73.

[23] Quoted in Müller 1992, 175.

[24] Quoted in Schmid 1979, 35.

1806, Schelver's possessions were completely plundered and his natural history collection destroyed by French troops: "My lodgings have been ransacked," he wrote to Goethe four days after the battle. "The botanical museum is scattered all over the house and my herbarium is completely destroyed; it's lying all about the floor in water and dirt . . . My books have been used to light fires . . . I was forced to give up my clothes in my lodgings and the last of my money was robbed along with them."[25] Hereupon Schelver hastily departed Jena and eventually found a new position in Heidelberg.

In these three years, Schelver learned to practice botany as Goethe himself did. We can recognize the significance he himself accorded his apprenticeship with Goethe when we consider that a full sixteen years after leaving Jena he dedicates a book to Goethe with an inscription recalling "those unforgettable days during which the eyes of my mind were awakened in your collections so rich in meaning and under your guidance so full of affection" and expressing the hope that the dedicated work "will be some small return of that unclouded and free contemplation [*Schauen*, the stem of *Anschauung*, 'intuition'] into which I was first initiated by you."[26]

In our present context, however, the more important fact is that it was Schelver who brought Hegel closer to Goethe and his conception of science. Hegel took a lively interest in his friend's various activities and also involved himself in them in a practical way. His biographer, Rosenkranz, tells of the two friends' botanizing together, and also how Hegel carried out the experiments associated with Goethe's theory of colors for himself.[27] Together the two men paid regular visits to Goethe who was deeply impressed by Hegel's scientific abilities. In November of 1803 he writes to Schiller that Hegel is "a thoroughly excellent man,"[28] and his ministerial colleague Voigt reports to Frankenberg in a letter from July 2, 1804, that "Goethe cannot say enough good things about him [sc. Hegel]."[29] Paulus, the Jena professor of theology with whom Hegel had briefly cooperated on an edition of Spinoza, reports that "as concerns his knowledge of mathematics and physics, Goethe has a higher opinion of Hegel than of Schelling, as he said to me on several occasions."[30]

Even more revealing than Goethe's esteem for Hegel's abilities, however, is Hegel's own appraisal of his familiarity with Goethe's thought and his scientific

---

[25] Quoted in Keil and Keil 1882, 62.
[26] Schelver 1822, vi–vii. Cp. also Schelver's letter to Goethe from February 6, 1805, in Müller 1992, 167.
[27] Rosenkranz 1844, 220, 198.
[28] Letter to Schiller, November 27, 1803, WA IV,16:356.
[29] *Goethe. Begegnungen und Gespräche*, 5:510.
[30] *Hegel in Berichten seiner Zeitgenossen*, 79.

methodology. It is especially worth mentioning that after Schelver's departure from Jena Hegel made a move to become his academic successor. This was of course in part motivated by his hopes that a part of Schelver's salary, now unused, could serve to round out his own meager income. Yet Hegel also felt thoroughly qualified for the job. Thus he writes to Goethe in January of 1807, "Given the facilities present in the botanical garden, and if I might hope for Your Excellency's support, I think I would soon be in a position to offer lectures in botany as well as in philosophy."[31] After all that has been said, it is obvious that Hegel must have assumed that he would be able to lecture on botany as it was understood by Goethe. By this time, however, Goethe had already found another replacement for Schelver, and so he could not accept Hegel's offer; but this did not affect his high esteem for Hegel.

With this background in mind, let us return to the beginning of the period just described. In May of 1803, Schelling had left Jena and taken a position in Würzburg. Soon after this Hegel begins to distance himself unmistakably from Schelling.[32] At the same time, throughout this period of estrangement, a noticeable change takes place in Hegel's position, the reasons for which remain obscure to this day. Hegel scholars agree that beginning around 1803/04, Hegel's conception of his system undergoes a fundamental shift in orientation, but though I do not question the accuracy of the reasons that have been given for this shift, they are not really sufficient for a genuine understanding of what occurred. I will return to this point very soon.

Whatever the case, the fact is that in the summer of 1804 Hegel is busy revising his philosophical conception in hopes of being able to present it to Goethe, and with the hope that it might lead to a promotion. Thus he writes to Goethe on September 29, 1804, "My literary works till now have been too minor for me to dare bring them to Your Excellency's attention; the purpose of a work that I hope to finish in time for my lectures this Winter, a purely scientific treatment of philosophy, will permit me to present it to Your Excellency, if Your Excellency will most kindly allow it."[33] Today it is accepted as virtually certain that the 'purely scientific treatment of philosophy' that Hegel hoped would meet Goethe's scientific criteria, was the so-called Second Jena System from 1804/05, a

---

[31] *Briefe von und an Hegel,* 1:142.

[32] See for example Fuhrmanns 1962 and Krings 1977.

[33] *Briefe von und an Hegel,* 1:85.

fragment of which has been preserved from Hegel's own fair copy.[34] Hegel did not, however, present it to Goethe; instead, he suddenly broke off work before completing it. Why? And why was he at first certain that he would find Goethe's approval?

V.

The fragment of the manuscript begins with an assessment which in my opinion, although no names are named, constitutes a fundamental criticism of Schelling's *Identitätsphilosophie*: "Thus the so-called construction of the idea from two opposed activities, one ideal and the other real, as the unity of the two, has produced absolutely nothing but the boundary [*Grenze*]" (GW 7:3).[35] The editors of the Second System in the Critical Edition take this to be a critique of Fichte (cp. GW 7:369) and point to GW 4:395–400 to corroborate their interpretation. Now it is true that in Fichte the combination of opposed activities forms a boundary (the "limitation" of the third basic principle), but the point there is not at all to construct an "idea"; rather, Fichte wants to demonstrate that the limitation ("divisibility") of the two activities is a condition of consciousness.

Schelling, on the other hand—for example in the 1802 text *Further Presentation of the System of Philosophie* [*Fernere Darstellungen aus dem System der Philosophie*]—places the "idea of the absolute" as absolute identity at the beginning of philosophy and characterizes its goal as the "philosophical construction" of this idea or the "method of exhibiting all things as they are in the absolute": "By way of construction," the finite determinations "are re-immersed in the absolute unity": "In the construction, the particular (the determinate unity) is exhibited as absolute, that is, exhibited for itself as the absolute *unity of the ideal and the real*" (SW IV:372, 391, 398, 459).

Interpreted on the basis of these passages, Hegel's criticism would be that what is achieved in this 'so-called' construction is not the *absolute* unity of the ideal and the real, but only the combination of the two at a boundary. If this is right, then Schelling would be vulnerable to the same objection that Hegel had up to now directed only against Fichte—the objection, namely, that in the construction of his system he is unable to return to its starting point.

---

[34] Cp. the "editorial report" GW 7:360–62.
[35] It seems that Theodor Haering (1938, 2:160) was the first to see this as a criticism of Schelling.

Additional light is shed on this initially somewhat obscure objection by the elucidation that immediately follows it: Hegel goes on to explain that the problem here is the same as that previously described in the (so-called) construction of matter from the two forces attraction and repulsion.[36] Each of these forces is supposed to be something actual. But what are they really? To begin with they are distinguished exclusively on the basis of their direction. This, however, is an empty determination: each of the directions can arbitrarily be considered as an effect of attraction or of repulsion. "But that which in fact distinguishes the directions, a posited point, would already be the unity [Einssein] of the two in which all opposition and hence those directions themselves are extinguished. Outside of this state of their having been extinguished, they are nothing, i.e., they have no reality whatsoever. Matter is nothing but that unit [jenes Eins], or their absolute equilibrium in which they are neither opposed nor forces, and outside of which they do not exist either" (GW 7:4).

The difficulty surrounding the construction of matter Hegel alludes to here is the very one that led Schelling to follow Baader in introducing gravity as the third force required for the construction. This in turn had ultimately led to the conclusion that everything must exist simultaneously, and hence that there cannot have been any such thing as an original coming-into-existence—i.e., the basic premise of the Identitätsphilosophie in which the identity itself now figures as the required third term: "Together with these two unities which, sharing a single nature with the absolute and with each other, are comprehended within it, the absolute constitutes a trinitary being [drei-einiges Wesen] whose internal organism exhibits everything ad infinitum and strives to make cognizable—especially philosophy, which is contained within the absolute itself and must also be formed [gebildet] according to its form [Form]" (SW IV:423–24).

In order to make the original unity cognizable, philosophy must construct it from its two unities, real and ideal activity; however, these latter differ according to Schelling in their opposed directions: "Since in itself each of them is infinite, the former must be conceived as the positive, the latter as the negative infinite, in opposite directions" (AA I,10:138; SW IV:136).

Thus the problem of the construction of matter resurfaces in Schelling's Identitätsphilosophie. The two terms of the construction, real and ideal activity, differ only in their direction, which is to say they do not differ at

---

[36] Here we find ourselves on familiar terrain; cp. Ch. 10 above.

all except in their common product; yet in this very product they are extinguished. If they are not extinguished, then they must retain some individually specific determinateness or *quality* which persists after their combination; and in this case the constructed unity is in fact only a boundary
between two qualities, not an absolute unity. Thus Hegel now writes, "In
order to judge whether the unity is only a boundary, or whether it is absolute unity, one need only observe whether outside of or after their unification the two terms posited in it as one still exist for themselves . . . [If they
do, then it is clear] that the unity which *qua* beginning is wholly indeterminate and ambiguous as to whether it is true unity or [merely] unity as
quality, is indeed only the latter. For the absolute unification [*Einswerden*]
does not get any further than a mere *ought* [*ein Sollen*], that is, a *beyond*
over against the unity of the boundary, and the two sides fall apart" (GW
7:3–4). Hegel thus reproaches Schelling with the same shortcoming with
which he had charged Fichte in the *Differenzschrift*.

So what does Hegel have to offer instead? In contrast to the First Jena
System (1803/04) in which Hegel still grasped the differences in being as
Schellingian 'potentations', now, one year later, Hegel makes no mention
either of potentiations[37] or of intellectual ("transcendental") intuition.
Instead, in the Second System's treatment of logic Hegel focuses on the
transitions between the determinations of thought (the categories), in order to present them as *successively emerging from each other*. As we have
just seen, determinate quality is supposed both to negate itself and not to
negate itself. And this contradiction already implies a movement that leads
beyond the category of quality. Let us hear first how Hegel articulates this
idea before we try to work through its details: "In the boundary, quality
becomes what it is in its absolute essence, but what according to its concept (its posited essence) it is not supposed to be; and what it has become
is also that into which its concept must pass over [*übergehen*] when that
concept is posited as what it is supposed to be. Hence the boundary is the
totality or true reality [*wahrhafte Realität*]; and when this boundary is
compared with its concept, it turns out to contain [the concept's] dialectic,
for the concept negated itself [*hob sich auf*] in the boundary in such a way
that it has become the opposite of itself" (GW 7:6–7).

Let us try to understand Hegel's thought here. What does he mean
when he speaks of the concept of quality 'passing over'? Or first things

---

[37] The sole exception is GW 7:113.

first, what is a quality? According to its 'posited' concept or definition, quality is something that has its own separate existence for itself, an individual being.[38] It is a singular reality, an individual (*ein Einzelnes*) which, as Hegel puts it, "is identical only with itself, without regard to anything else" (GW 7:6). At the same time, however, it must also be something determinate, for an indeterminate quality would not be a quality at all. Now it is something determinate precisely to the extent that it is not something else: *omnis determinatio est negatio*. On the basis of its own determinateness, the quality necessarily excludes an indeterminate number of other determinatenesses (qualities) to which it is thereby negatively related. A quality thus only apparently exists "without regard to anything else." In truth, it only exists to the extent that other qualities exist at the same time, and *vice versa*. Hence the relation to others excluded from it is *essential* to every quality, and for Hegel this is what constitutes the concept of a *boundary*. For the essence of a boundary consists in being determined exclusively by the terms that are bounded or marked off from each other and with which the boundary is not identical since of course it excludes them. In the absence of bounded terms, the boundary does not exist, nor is it one of those terms. I.e., the boundary is something both determinate and non-determinate at the same time. According to Hegel, though, that is precisely the essence of *quantity*: it is a being from which the plurality of different determinatenesses (qualities) is excluded as indifferent to it.[39]

Let us now try to articulate the concept of quantity in more exact terms. Just as there cannot be a boundary in itself without something that is bounded by it, neither can there be quantity in itself without something whose quantity it is. Quantity is always a quantity *of something*. This 'something' to which it is essentially related is however at the same time excluded from it as indifferent: it could also be the quantity of something else (e.g. 'a dozen' can be the number of apples just as well as the number of apostles, etc.). Whereas a boundary excludes *two* determinate regions from itself, quantity excludes an indeterminate number of determinatenesses.

---

[38] It is therefore not a quality *of something*—for then it would already be the *property* of an other—but rather quality as such is a being that is for itself (cp. GW 9:39; TW 3:53).

[39] Here we have an excellent example of what Hegel means when he says that a concept (in this case, the concept of quality) 'has become the opposite of itself': Quality, as the simple *unity* of being and determinateness, passes over into the concept of quantity as a being in which the determinateness is *not one* with being, but instead is posited as external and indifferent to it.

More precisely, it is the negative (reflected) unity of what is excluded, of what it is not. "According to its concept, quantity in its immediacy is a negative [*negierende*] relation to itself" (GW 7:7). That which it excludes is therefore itself posited as an indifferent unity containing merely the "possibility of distinction."

However, it is *essential* to the excluded unity that it contain this possibility within itself, for it is the unity of determinate and hence distinguishable qualities, not something homogeneous and utterly lacking all distinctions. The unity excluded as indifferent is thus at the same time a plurality determinate in itself.

Now this being the case, quantity as that which is doing the excluding cannot in fact be a *simple* negative unity: "For the negation of the plurality by the unity is just as manifold as the plurality itself; and hence the unity itself is manifold in its negating—it is itself something manifold. And thus the negative unity is really a positive unity, and is posited as this plurality differentiated in itself, a multitude of numerical units [*numerische Eins*]" (GW 7:10). As a negative unity, quantity too is in truth the "possibility of plurality" and hence positive unity: it is like what is excluded from it, and what is excluded from it is like quantity—unity and plurality at one and the same time. In this way, however, the distinction between positive and negative unity has disappeared and passed over into their unity: "As the unit [*das Eins*] which has passed over into its opposite, the many units, and thus proven identical with it, it is totality [*Allheit*]" (GW 7:11). For to be unity and plurality at the same time is definitive of the concept of totality. The essence of quantity, the unity of unity and plurality, is totality.

Thus each of the concepts considered here passes over into another concept: unity passes over into plurality, plurality into totality (categories of *quantity*) as reality had passed over before into negation, and negation into limitation or boundary (categories of *quality*). Hegel claims that this is the case for *all* the categories of logic, and in this manuscript he attempts to substantiate his claim for the first time. I do not need to pursue the details any further here; right now it is more important to give precise articulation to the conceptual movement that Hegel has tried to demonstrate here for the first time. This *passing over into another* comes about when something that belongs to a concept, but which is missing from its initial definition, is set out or made explicit, thus deepening the concept or making it more precise. For example, in the concept of quality as an individual reality, the element of determinateness is made explicit. 'Determinateness' does not belong to the original definition since it is not something that distinguishes quality from non-quality, i.e., it is not a *differentia specifica* in the sense of the classical theory of definitions. Nonetheless, it is essential to quality. Because of this determinateness, quality is essentially related to an other, an excluded term, and hence it ceases to be something essentially singular. At this point the concept passes over into another concept for which the whole process begins anew.[40] What is important for Hegel in his presentation of logic is that it is only the trajectory of this conceptual movement *as a whole* that leads beyond the "boundary" (qua unification of enduringly self-sufficient opposites) to the "true infinity" in which the opposites have been negated or *aufgehoben*: "True infinity is the fulfilled demand that determinateness negate [*aufheben*] itself ... This alone is the true nature of the finite, namely that it is infinite, that it negates [*aufheben*] itself in its being" (GW 7:33). If however the very movement of the categories themselves reveals the essence of the finite to consist in the fact that it sublates itself, then an intellectual or transcendental intuition is superfluous as a guarantor of unity as envisioned in the *Differenzschrift*.

Compared with Hegel's earlier conceptions of logic, what is genuinely new in this fragment is its focus on the *transitions* between concepts. It is not hard to see either the influence of Goethe in this development or the reason why Hegel believed that this "purely scientific treatment of philosophy" would meet with Goethe's approval. And yet he never showed it to Goethe. In the section on philosophy of nature, the fair copy suddenly breaks off at the transition from the inorganic to the organic, never to be continued. What made Hegel finally reject the approach he had taken here?

VI.

In my opinion, this question can only be answered if we look at the project Hegel turned to instead: a series of lectures on the entire history of philosophy, delivered for the first time in the winter semester of 1805/06. One of the students present at them, Georg Andreas Gabler, gives this account: "The lectures that Hegel must have worked up on the basis of his own painstaking and prolonged study of the sources, were attended by

---

[40] This will be Hegel's method from now on; cp., e.g., *Encyclopedia* (1830), §88: "[Q]uite generally, the whole course of philosophizing, being methodical, i.e., *necessary*, is nothing else but the mere *positing* of what is already contained in a concept" (GW 20:125; TW 8:188).

everyone with the greatest interest, especially aroused by the dialectical transition from system to system, which at the time was an unheard-of innovation."[41] Such dialectical transitions were something wholly new for Hegel himself, as well, for until recently he had still subscribed to the view that there is no development in the history of philosophy, but that each philosophical system is of the same worth and rank as every other, like the great works of art, and that they have neither precursors nor successors. By 1805, however, things have come to look very different. Right in the introduction to the lectures he states: "We can condense the central claim of these lectures into the single concept 'development'. Once this idea has become clear to us, everything else will follow on its own" (TW 18:38).[42]

What we need to understand, then, is "the single concept 'development'." Interestingly, Hegel explains it by reference to the metamorphosis

---

[41] Quoted in Kimmerle 1967a, 69.

[42] Hegel lectured on the history of philosophy more frequently than on any other subject: after the lectures in Jena 1805/06, there followed two lecture courses in Heidelberg 1816/17 and 1817/18, and in Berlin he lectured on the subject no less than six times in alternating years. Since the manuscript of the Jena lecture course has not been preserved, but only the version that Karl Ludwig Michelet collated from all the available manuscripts, it may seem illegitimate to use it as the basis for any claims about Hegel's position in 1805. That may be right, but only with important qualifications: Michelet drew mainly from the later texts of the Berlin period because he found in them greater "clarity, solidity, and persuasiveness" (*Jubiläumsausgabe*, vol. 17:3) than in the text of 1805/06, which was also available to him. Thus there would seem to be no reason to assume any further difference *in content* between the various introductions. Rosenkranz, too, who was familiar with the Jena manuscript, states that "Hegel did not significantly modify this lecture on the history of philosophy in the later courses, as they have been printed, but merely provided them with a greater wealth of detail" (Rosenkranz 1844, 201). Two additional points can be made in support of my use of this sentence from the introduction: (1) In all the lectures, including that of 1805/06, it would have been necessary to discuss what makes the historical treatment of philosophy (in Hegel's sense) possible at all, and that is precisely "the single concept of 'development'." (2) Careful study of Michelet's text allows us to distinguish various temporal stages in the "Introduction": whereas at first it is stated that the central claim of the lectures can be condensed into "the *single* concept 'development'," two paragraphs further on it is said that it is above all important to understand *two* concepts: "These are the two concepts of *development* and of the *concrete*" (TW 18:39). This apparent contradiction, which seems to have escaped the notice of Michelet, can be taken to imply that the first statement is the original one and that Hegel did not realize the equal importance of the concrete until sometime after 1805, at which point he introduced it into the text. I will supply independent grounds for this claim in Chapter 14.

of plants. From the seed to the fruit, says Hegel, a plant goes through a cycle determined by its being-in-itself, its *Ansich* (in Goethean terms, the *idea*). At the end of the cycle we again find a seed—an individual which is numerically distinct from, but qualitatively identical to, the first seed and goes through the same process once again: "In the case of natural entities, of course, the subject there at the beginning and the existent that forms the end—the fruit, the seed—are two distinct individuals . . . but as regards the *content*, they are the same." Yet now Hegel goes on: "This is different in the case of spirit [*Geist*]. It is consciousness, and free because in it beginning and end coincide . . . The fruit, the seed does not exist for the first seed, but only for us; in the case of spirit, both are not only of the same nature in themselves, but there is a being-for-each-other and thus a being-for-itself. That *for which* the other is, is the same as the other. It is only in this way that spirit is at one with itself in its other [*bei sich selbst in seinem Anderen*]. The development of spirit is a going-out-of-itself, a differentiation of itself, and at the same time a coming-to-itself" (TW 18:41).

The idea is clear: When we apply the method of experience paradigmatically developed in the case of plant metamorphosis to the case of spirit, the result is something completely new. Instead of two distinct individuals with the same content, as in the case of the plant, we have *one* individual with two distinct contents. The cycles of a plant are repetitions, those of spirit are *developments*. That being so, however, philosophical systems can no longer be set side by side in equal worth and rank; they are expressions of a development.

If this is right, then what Hegel referred to as a "purely scientific treatment of philosophy" must also be modified: "Indeed, if the concept of philosophy is to be established not arbitrarily, but scientifically, a treatise of this kind must itself become the science of philosophy; for this science is characterized by the fact that it only seems to begin with its concept, whereas in truth the whole presentation of this science is the proof, indeed one might say the *discovery* of its concept, which is essentially a *result* of this science" (TW 18:17–18, emphasis added).

We can now understand why Hegel broke off work on the Second Jena System. For there the idea of the absolute formed the *beginning* of the science: "The logic began with the unity itself as what is self-identical" (GW 7:129). In this point Hegel had remained true to Schelling's original approach. If our interpretation regarding the "single concept 'development'" is right, though, then the absolute cannot stand at the beginning of the logic to guide the transitions among the concepts, be it in the form of (intellectual or transcendental) intuition (as in the *Differenzschrift*), be it in the form of the "self-identical" "base" of the logic (as in the Second Jena System, GW 7:129, 124): *It can only be a result.* "The essential nature of the idea is to develop, and to comprehend itself, to become what it is, only by way of development" (TW 18:39).

Hegel has taken a decisive step beyond Goethe: not only is it impossible to grasp the idea that philosophy strives to comprehend (the absolute) prior to the conclusion of the complete series of its realization; in fact, *it is not what it is* until the end of that series, i.e., it is itself essentially a dialectical process. This is the crucial point about the "single concept 'development'."

If the idea is nevertheless to be *cognizable,* philosophy itself as the (self-) knowledge of the idea must also have reached its conclusion. The history of philosophy would have to have come to completion *in this sense.* But who could reasonably claim such a thing?

Surely Hegel cannot have believed that he had proven such a claim in his lectures on the history of philosophy. For as he explicitly says, in order even to orient oneself in the overwhelming abundance of historical forms, one already has to have an idea of what one is looking for. Or as he writes in his introduction to the history of philosophy, written many years later in Berlin in 1820: "In order to recognize the development of the idea in the empirical form and appearance in which the progress of philosophy historically occurs, it is of course necessary that one be in possession of knowledge of the idea from the outset, just as one must already bring along the concepts of what is right and proper in order to judge human actions. Lacking the idea, the eye beholds nothing but a disorderly heap of opinions, as we see in so many histories of philosophy" (TW 20:479).

This clearly implies that in 1805/06 Hegel is in no position to claim scientific status for his interpretation of the history of philosophy. It can only have played an heuristic role.[43] Though of course the actual historical course of events must not contradict the assumed idea (this would

---

[43] The reference to concepts of what is "right and proper" is characteristic. For Kant, too, in the second chapter of the *Groundwork,* had of course made use of examples of duties which already assume a knowledge of the empirical nature of human beings in order to bring the moral law and hence "an idea of reason closer to intuition . . . and thereby to feeling" (4:436)—but not in order to demonstrate the law itself, which could only happen later, in the third chapter. Still, the idea of the moral law already needs to have been presented (4:402), in order to illustrate it by way of the examples.

constitute a refutation), neither can external history itself originally give rise to such an idea. This must be kept in mind when Hegel concludes his lecture in Spring of 1806 with the announcement that philosophy has come to an end: "This is the standpoint of the present time, and for now it is the last in the series of the forms of spirit [*geistigen Gestaltungen*]. — With this the history of philosophy is *concluded*" (ibid.).[44] Hegel must have been convinced at this point in time that the idea was demonstrable on independent grounds. I will return to this issue in the next chapter.

VII.

If we take a fresh look now at Hegel's former plans of publication, we see that his new insight that the idea develops of its own accord was bound to have two closely related consequences for the conception of his system. *First,* the division between logic and metaphysics, still unquestioned in the 1804/05 manuscript, has to be eliminated. In Hegel's earlier conception, logic had the task of revealing the dialectical nature of the finite and of thereby leading us to the standpoint of the idea. Accordingly, metaphysics was to be the "science of the idea" and its systematic presentation. In that conception, though, the idea was still conceived as "unity itself" (GW 7:129) which "is eternally one and the same" (GW 4:10). If however the idea develops of its own accord and if it is essentially dialectical in nature, then metaphysics as the science of the idea must also be dialectical and hence coincide with logic as Hegel understands it. The division into two separate disciplines has thus become obsolete—and so too has Hegel's previous plan for publication. From now on, logic must be the science of the idea and hence itself metaphysics, not just the

---

[44] Even though it cannot be proven beyond all doubt that Hegel employed this formulation in 1806, his claim that such a conclusion had been reached is attested to by Rosenkranz, who still had access to the Jena manuscripts: "At the end of the lecture course he spoke the words which have recently become so famous and been used so frequently as a motto: 'A *new epoch* has arisen in the world. It appears that the world spirit has now succeeded in casting off everything alien and objective and grasping itself as absolute spirit, and everything that comes to be objective for it, it itself produces and, unperturbed, retains power over it. The struggle of finite self-consciousness with the absolute self-consciousness which appeared external to it, ceases, etc.'" (Rosenkranz 1844, 202). It is exactly the same text as in TW 20:460, except that Rosenkranz breaks off at his "etc." shortly before the sentence quoted above.

introduction to metaphysics. As such, however, logic is constrained to presuppose the idea as demonstrated.

Secondly, then, logic must be preceded by an introduction that leads us up to the idea. Logic itself cannot perform this task, but nor can a history of philosophy, for it too must presuppose knowledge of the idea. Hegel's next step, therefore, prior even to the draft of a new logic, had to consist in providing a scientific introduction to the idea. But how?

Goethe had shown that we must be in possession of a *complete* set of phenomena before we can begin to discover its underlying idea. However, he gives no indication of the developmental stage required of the consciousness observing the phenomena; he merely stipulates that thought and intuition must remain conjoined if the transitions are to be grasped. Things are different, however, when it is philosophical consciousness itself that is being observed. Since it is observing itself, it must itself have arrived at the completion necessary in order to discover *its own* idea (assuming its development to be guided by an idea). The observing consciousness and the observed consciousness are not, albeit, numerically identical, but they are qualitatively the same; hence both must be "completed" to the same degree. Does such an assumption make any sense?

In any case, it raises a completely new difficulty, without precedent in the history of philosophy. Or perhaps there is a precedent after all. One single thinker had to a certain extent prepared the way for Hegel's innovation: Fichte. For he had written in the *Foundation of the Entire Wissenschaftslehre* that "anyone joining us in the present inquiry is himself an I, but one which has long since performed the actions which are here to be deduced . . . He has of necessity already completed the whole business of reason and now, of his own free will, determines as it were to go through the whole account once again and to observe the course once described by himself in another I that he arbitrarily posits and places at the point from which he himself once began and on which he conducts the experiment" (GA I,2:420; W 1:290f.).

I take it that this is the reason why Hegel now began a renewed and intensive study of Fichte, against whom he had previously raised such fundamental objections. This study left its trace in an entry from the notebook Hegel kept in Jena: "It is only since the history of consciousness [!] *that we know what we have in these abstractions,* by way of the concept: *Fichte's* achievement" (GW 5:502; TW 2:559).

This renewed study of Fichte in the latter half of the Jena period is well-known to scholars of Hegel, though previous studies have found its traces exclusively in Hegel's practical philosophy.[45] In his 1967 paper "Hegels Kritik des Naturrechts," for instance, Manfred Riedel takes note of the "striking terminological shift" that occurs "between the Jena lectures of 1803/04 and those of 1805/06," writing: "The gradual disappearance of Schellingian terminology and methods in these years, which seems to have run parallel to a renewed study of Fichtean philosophy, also entails the abandonment of a conception of natural law inspired by Aristotle and Spinoza."[46] Yet this fails to explain why Hegel saw the need for a *renewed study* of Fichte in the first place, especially since, as Riedel states, he returned in 1805/06 "to the position of Rousseau, Kant, and Fichte on natural law which he had subscribed to once before in the 1790s."[47]

Now I do not intend to deny that Hegel's conception of natural law in 1805/06 shows traces of this renewed interest in Fichte. Even so, the main reason for Hegel's return to Fichte seems to me to lie in the problem of a systematic introduction as implied by the notebook entry. In analogy to Fichte's methodological procedure in the *Foundation,* an introduction to logic would have to show that original or "natural" consciousness, constituted as it is by an opposition between subject and object that appears to it both natural and insurmountable, possesses an inner dynamic whose conclusion is already known to the author. As author and reader jointly recapitulate the stages of development of natural consciousness, the whole *qua whole* is brought into view and the underlying idea that logic begins from can now become available to cognition.

In the *Second Introduction to the Wissenschaftslehre* (1797) Fichte had emphasized that his procedure involves more than just two distinct levels of observation.[48] In contrast to the usual philosopher who spontaneously combines given concepts into judgments and whose philosophy thus consists in "thinking for himself," the *Wissenschaftslehre* is based

> not on an inert concept that is merely passively related to its investigation and has to wait for thought to make something out of it; rather, it is something living and active that produces cognitions out of itself and by itself, so that the philosopher merely watches it. His business in the matter exhausts itself in occasioning purposive

---

[45] An exception is Bowman 2006.

[46] Riedel 1967, 97.

[47] Riedel 1967, 105.

[48] The 'New Presentation of the *Wissenschaftslehre*' given here was also the subject of the lectures by Fichte that Schelver attended.

activity in that living thing, watching its activity, apprehending it and comprehending it in its unity . . . In the *Wissenschaftslehre* there are [consequently] two very different series of intellectual action [*geistiges Handeln*]: that of the I which the philosopher observes, and that of the philosopher's observations themselves. In the opposed philosophies to which I just referred, there is only *one* series of thinking: that of the philosopher's thoughts; for *the content itself is not conceived as thinking* (GA I,4:209–10; W 1:454, emphasis added).

We will rediscover these two series in Hegel's new introduction. Note, however, that since Hegel sets out to present the genesis of the philosophical consciousness not of an individual, but of humanity, it will not be the case that his business "exhausts itself" in occasioning purposive activity in living thought and "merely" watching it. It must have been clear to him from his own lectures on the history of philosophy that a given form of consciousness may be able to view itself as the successor of the previous forms, but not as the precursor of those which necessarily follow it. *These* transitions are in themselves no more visible than the transitions in the metamorphosis of plants, especially considering that they need not coincide with the chronological sequence of the forms. The reproduction of the transitions that allow us to see how a given form passes over into the next, revealing itself as part of a living whole, must therefore be the work of the observing consciousness; it is the observer who makes explicit what is implicit in the observed consciousness. In a *scientific* treatment of emerging consciousness, Hegel is soon to write,

> the new object is shown to have come into being through an *inversion of consciousness* itself. This way of viewing the matter is our contribution [*Zuthat*], by which the series of experiences of consciousness is raised to a scientific path and which is not present for the consciousness that we are observing . . . [T]he *emergence* of the new object, which presents itself to consciousness without the latter knowing what is happening to it, is what we see take place behind its back, as it were . . . but the *content* of that which we see emerge, is *for it,* and we merely comprehend its formal aspect or the pure fact of its emerging; for *consciousness* what has emerged exists only as an object, whereas *for us* it also exists as movement and becoming (#87 GW 9:61, TW 3:79–80).

Later Hegel was once again to touch upon "Fichte's achievement," and he explained it this way: "To *Fichtean* philosophy is owed the lasting achievement of having reminded us that the *determinations of thought* are to be demonstrated in their *necessity*, that it is essential to *derive* them" (GW 20:80; TW 8:117). Fichte himself had stated *expressis verbis* that the essence of philosophy consists in such a derivation (GA I,4:198; W 1:438). More precisely, it consists in showing that what is present in consciousness initially and *immediately* "is not possible without at the same time something else occurring, and that this other thing cannot happen without a third thing occurring, and so on until the conditions of what was initially shown to be present in consciousness are completely exhausted and the initial content of consciousness is thus made wholly intelligible as to its possibility." In this way, a "system of all the necessary representations, or the whole of *experience*" comes about. For, writes Fichte, in a scientific derivation of the kind proposed, "only the whole [occurs] in consciousness, and this whole is what we call *experience*" (GA I,4:205, 207; W 1:446, 448, emphasis added).

Hegel too has to derive such a whole of consciousness's necessary representations, in order to derive from it in turn the *idea* of the whole that must precede logic; this is the reason why he referred to his introduction to logic as a *Science of the Experience of Consciousness*. He began writing it in 1805, the very year in which he had broken off work on the Second Jena System, and by February of 1806 the unbound signatures were being printed in sequence—and hence concurrently with the lectures on the history of philosophy.[49]

---

[49] Hegel would later often refer to this work as his "voyages of discovery" (cp. Michelet 1837/38, 2:616). Why he did so will become clear in Chapter 14.

13

Hegel's "Voyages of Discovery": Incomplete

I.

Hegel's contractual negotiations with the Bamberg publisher Goebhardt make it evident that by this point in time he had a clear conception of the demonstrability of the idea. The volume they agreed on was to have the title *System of Science* and include two parts: the introduction entitled "First Part: Science of the Experience of Consciousness," and, as its second part, the "Logic." The printing of the first part commenced in February 1806 and the contract specified that it was to be completed by Easter, which fell on April 6, 1806. Only then was Hegel, whose financial situation was precarious, to receive the "honorarium stipulated *after half the work has been printed.*"[1]

The first sheets that were printed show that Hegel was already certain of the demonstrability of the idea.[2] There he describes the method he will follow in "The Science of the Experience of Consciousness." According to his description, any consciousness that claims to know something[3] is characterized by the fact that it has an object or that it is consciousness *of something.* Consciousness refers to this something and distinguishes it, as what is known, from its own act of knowing. But the known—i.e. the object—is here conceived as being as it is *in itself,* independently of whether it is known or not. Thus it is the standard against which knowledge is to be measured.

---

[1] Karl Hegel 1887, vol. 1, 62 (emphasis added).

[2] Only later (in the table of contents) did Hegel give this section the heading "Introduction."

[3] In the following, all mention of consciousness refers to such a philosophical consciousness in the broad sense.

Consciousness is *at once* both consciousness of the in-itself and con-sciousness of its knowledge of the in-itself, and thus it is the comparison of the two: "The very fact of its knowing any object at all gives rise to the difference that one thing is the *in-itself for it* [namely for consciousness], while knowledge, or the being of the object *for* consciousness, is a dis-tinct moment. The presence of this difference is the basis of the exami-nation" (#85 GW 9:59–60; TW 3:78). If the experience of consciousness reveals that its putative knowledge does not correspond to the in-itself, it has to change and revise its 'knowledge'. At the same time, however, this gives rise to a new in-itself that becomes the new standard against which to measure the new knowledge; for this knowledge is of course once again knowledge of something that is conceived as independent of its being known. According to Hegel, the task of a "science of the experi-ence of consciousness" is to record the path of successive examinations and corrections that consciousness is destined to travel as soon as it stakes a knowledge claim, and which it is bound to follow until it comes to a point where contradictions between knowledge and the in-itself cease to arise and knowledge is therefore completely adequate; that is the point at which the "logic" can begin.

So by the time Hegel signed the contract, he must in the first place already have been sure that this self-correcting movement of conscious-ness would not go on indefinitely. In the second place, he must have been sure that no contradiction would arise between knowledge and the in-itself that natural consciousness could not escape or overcome: In either case, no transition to the Logic would be possible. But as early as Febru-ary 1806, Hegel committed to print the statement that consciousness would in the course of its travails "reach a point at which it casts off the appearance of being caught up in something alien to it that exists only for it and as something other, a point where appearance and essence coincide . . . and finally, when it grasps this its own essence, it will denote the nature of absolute knowledge itself" (#89 GW 9:62; TW 3:81).

II.

Hegel enriched his presentation of the experience of consciousness with a prodigious amount of material and historical references, and I cannot hope to do justice to them here. Fortunately, however, I will not need to. Soon after the *work* was published, Hegel began to complain that re-viewers paid attention only to its content [!], failing to notice what was most important: "In any philosophy, and now more than ever, the greatest emphasis should be on the method of necessary connection, the *transition of one form into the other and origination from the other*."[4] So the focus should be on the transitions, for it is only by *reproducing them in thought* that we will be able to decide whether the series of shapes of consciousness as a whole is ultimately based on an idea that can serve as the starting point for Hegelian logic.[5]

That is what I intend to do in the following, but it requires that we abstract from all of our *own* thoughts and opinions and focus on nothing but the internal dynamics of the consciousness under consideration: "It is of the essence that we bear in mind throughout the entire investigation that these two moments, *concept* and *object, being-for-other* and *being-in-itself,* themselves fall within the knowledge under investigation, so that it is superfluous to bring in standards and to apply *our* thoughts and ideas to the investigation; it is by leaving them aside that we will be able to consider the matter as it is *in* and *for itself*" (#84 GW 9:59; TW 3:77). That, says Hegel, is how we have to approach the text.

III.

In order to survey the development of 'knowing' consciousness as a whole, we must begin with its simplest (its 'first') form. If it is truly the first, its content cannot be mediated by anything else; its object has to be an *immediate given,* and consciousness itself must be no more than a mere apprehending of the given. Hegel calls this first shape of consciousness "sense certainty": "Of what it knows, it says only this: it *is;* and the truth of this shape contains only the *being* of the matter at hand; in this certainty, consciousness for its part is only a pure *I;* or *I* am in it only as a pure *this,* and the object, too, is only a pure *this*" (#92 GW 9:63; TW 3:82). Let's take a closer look at this shape of consciousness.

---

[4] *Briefe von und an Hegel,* 1:330 (draft of a letter to van Ghert, end of Nov. 1810).
[5] The many contents that Hegel used to enrich his text are therefore always just *examples* of the particular stage that representational consciousness has reached; they could in principle be replaced by other examples. What is therefore crucial is not at all the particular content of consciousness, but the *way* it came to arrive at a content *of this kind*—i.e. the transitions. "We comprehend only the formal aspect of that content, or its pure origination" (#87 GW 9:61; TW 3:80).

First Object of Consciousness: Immediate Sensuous Being
("I. Sense Certainty")

(1) The object of knowledge is *this*—what is temporally *now* and spatially *here*. Thus it differs from everything else, but without the mediation of anything else. The question is whether sense certainty is in fact able, when its object is characterized in these terms, to lay hold of that object ('this here now') as it takes it to be in its essence, namely as being something independently of whether it is known. To grasp and hold on to its object, consciousness must be able to refer to it as identically the same, even as the perceptual context continues to change. But this it cannot do: 'now', 'here', and 'this' are indexical, i.e. context-dependent expressions, and what sense certainty claims to know as an existing being is actually something that ceases to exist as soon as the Now (e.g. "night") or the Here ("tree") has given way to another Now ("day") or Here ("house"): "The *Now* itself does endure, but as something that is not night; in the same way, it endures with respect to the day that it now is, as something that is also not day, or as something wholly negative [*ein negatives überhaupt*]. This enduring Now is thus not something immediate, but something mediated, for insofar as it is permanent and enduring, its determinateness *depends on the fact* that something else (namely day and night) is not" (#96 GW 9:65; TW 3:84).

The Now is an abiding, re-identifiable moment only to the extent that it excludes other Nows, and the case with Here and This is analogous. They are determinate, re-identifiable objects of knowledge only to the extent that they are mediated, i.e. to the extent that they exclude others.[6] But once the object turns out to be a universal, it no longer fits the description of what is true for sense certainty, namely an *immediate* given. The 'truth' of sense certainty must therefore be located in the other element of the relation, in knowledge. Hence we must now say that the object of sense certainty exists only because I am aware of it: "Its truth is in the object as *my* object . . . it exists because I am aware of it. Sense certainty has thus been driven out of the object, but it has not thereby been sublated but merely driven back into the I" (#100 GW 9:66; TW 3:86).

---

[6] The indexical expression must be replaced by corresponding expressions of the same kind if the subject is to be able to refer to the *same* thing from the point of view of a new perceptual situation: e.g. 'now' must be replaced by 'before', or 'yesterday', 'here' by 'there', and so on.

(2) The truth is now located in the I, in the immediacy of seeing, hearing, etc.: "The single Now and Here that we mean [*meinen*] is kept from disappearing by *my* holding fast to it" (#101 GW 9:66; TW 3:86).[7] But what is the I that holds fast to the This? On the level of immediacy it appears only as a pure I, "as a pure *this*," and hence the same problem recurs: a pure I can refer to itself only by using the same expression every other subject uses to refer to itself. 'I' is therefore just as context- or speaker-dependent as 'here' and 'now' were. It cannot be an identifying expression (one that 'holds fast' to its referent) except by excluding other subjects, except by being *mediated*.

(3) Now only one possibility remains if sense certainty is to maintain immediacy as its criterion of truth: the essence lies not in one or the other of the two terms, object or I, but in their immediate unity: "Its truth is preserved as an unchanging relation that makes no distinction between the I and the object in terms of essentiality, and in which therefore no difference at all can occur . . . rather, I am a pure act of intuiting" (#104 GW 9:67; TW 3:87–88). But this attempt is also destined to fail. Each moment, the 'Now' that I meant has already passed away and been replaced by a new Now; the 'Here' that I pointed out is not a point that is marked out by itself, but a continuum of many possible Heres (above, below, right, left) that form a determinate Here only by negating others. Once again, we see that what sense certainty means—the sensuous This—is a content that is mediated by exclusion (negation) and thus a *universal* content.

With this, sense certainty has exhausted the alternatives for identifying truth with the immediately given.[8] Experience forces it to concede that 'This' is a universal and hence the exact opposite of what it claimed to know. It contradicts itself and has no choice but either to assume the impossibility of any knowledge of the truth or to forget its experience and begin all over again.

We of course see more than this: "Every consciousness goes on to sublate truths such as *'the Here is a tree'*, or *'the Now is noon'*, and to assert

---

[7] [Tr.: Hegel is playing on the homonymy of *meinen*, 'to mean', and *mein(en)*, the possessive pronoun 'my' or 'mine'.]

[8] The fact that a particular shape of consciousness always has three options for locating the element of truth that is constitutive for it—in one of the two related terms or in both together—is valid for all the coming shapes and determines the course of the investigation. For clarity's sake, I will continue to identify them as (1), (2), and (3).

their opposite" (#109 GW 9:69; TW 3:90). If this is the case for *every* consciousness, then the result of sense certainty also has a positive significance: "what is actually true in sense certainty is the universal" (#96 GW 9:65; TW 3:85). The emergence of a new 'true' object is thus a necessary result[9]—an object for which sensuous individuality and universality are equally essential, or whose essence combines the moments of the one and the many independently of whether or not it is an object of knowledge: it must be *one* thing of *many* properties.

The consciousness of this new 'true' object is distinct from sense certainty; it is a consciousness for which the I and the object are universals. The object is once again conceived as being independent of whether or not it is known: "Its criterion of truth is therefore self-identity [*Sichselbstgleichheit*] and its approach is to apprehend things as self-identical" (#116 GW 9:74; TW 3:97). Hegel calls this new shape of consciousness "perception." For it, the object is not grasped as a result; perception finds it as something it merely encounters as *given*,[10] and our question is how it will be able to bring together individuality and universality in this new object.

New Object: The Sensuous Universal ("II. Perception")

(1) How does the perceiving consciousness bring together one and many? (a) Initially, the object appears to it as *one,* as a "pure unit" [*reines Eins*]. What it actually perceives, however, is a property and thus something that is universal, something that goes beyond the individual, something multiply instantiated.[11] Perception is forced to correct itself: what the

---

[9] "The [new] object is in its essence the same thing the [preceding] movement is; the movement is the development and articulation of the moments, the object is the same in condensed form" (#111 GW 9:71; TW 3:93).

[10] In a related context, Hegel writes: "What each generation has achieved in science and spiritual production is **inherited** by the following generation as constituting its soul, its spiritual substance as customs, and its principles, prejudices, and wealth—but at the same time it is a legacy to be treated as so much available *material*. Therefore, because each generation is itself spiritual vitality and activity, it invests its labor in what has merely been *handed down* to it, enriching the material it works on" (GW 18:37, emphasis added).

[11] This is the lesson learned from sense certainty: anything that is universal (e.g. red) can be the property of a book, of blood, of the setting sun, and so on, without

object is, independently of being known, must be a commonality with others (Hegel's word is *Gemeinschaft*) and hence a multiplicity. (b) On the other hand, the perceived property is a *determinate* property, and it can be determinate only by excluding others. And so once again perception corrects itself: Objectivity cannot be conceived as a commonality or continuity; it must be an "exclusive unit" [*auschließendes Eins*]. (c) Now this exclusive unit exhibits many properties that do no exclude each other but rather coexist indifferently one next to the other: Hegel's example is the white color of salt, its salty taste, and its cubic form. Thus consciousness must again correct itself: The object cannot be an exclusive *unit*; it cannot be more than a *common medium* in which diverse properties or matters exist indifferently, each for itself, even though each property, insofar as it is determinate, also excludes others. This, however, is tantamount to the loss of the thing's individuality, or rather, the thing loses its individuality to the individual property: "What is simple and true in my perception is therefore neither a universal medium, but the *individual property* taken in itself, which thus ceases to be either a property or a determinate being; for it now exists neither in a unit nor as related to others" (#117 GW 9:74; TW 3:98).

This step lands conscious back with the 'This' of sense certainty, and since sense certainty was already forced to pass over into perception, it threatens to fall into a perpetual oscillation back and forth between these first two shapes. The only thing that prevents it from doing so is the fact that when consciousness returns to its starting point, it has also been enriched by its intervening experience: through being repeatedly forced to correct itself it has learned that it is also liable to deceive itself and misapprehend what it takes to be the true. Unlike its predecessor (sense certainty), it no longer conceives of itself as a mere apprehending of the object; perception has become conscious of its own role in the object's dissolution. It can preserve the truth of the thing as self-identical only if it identifies itself as the cause of the (apparent) dissolution.

(2) Of its essence, the thing is a unit, and the multiplicity that seems to destroy its unity must therefore belong to consciousness. (a) More specifically, the apparent dissolution results from the fact that consciousness perceives the thing through distinct senses: the thing is white to *its* eye,

---

being identical with any one of these things; it is something simple that "exists by negation, neither this nor that, a *not-this,* and just as indifferently both this and that" (#96 GW 9:65; TW 3:85).

salty to *its* tongue (which is in turn *distinct* from its eye), cubic to *its* touch (which is *distinct* from both), and so on. Consciousness itself is therefore the element in which such moments appear as separate and being for themselves. The truth of the thing, namely its being a unit, is thereby preserved. Yet only apparently so. For the moments that consciousness takes upon itself are also determinate and as such they exclude others. But insofar as the thing is simply a unity, it is identical to all other things: each and every thing is a *unit*. The thing must therefore possess determinate properties in order to be distinguishable from others; i.e. the multiplicity of properties cannot belong merely to consciousness; they must belong to the thing itself.

(b) If consciousness has shown itself to be incapable of taking the *multiplicity* upon itself, it now has no option but to take upon itself the other side of the contradiction, the *unity* of the properties: it must itself be what unites the properties. For insofar as the thing is white, it is not cubic; insofar as it is cubic, it is not saline. The unification of these properties is the work of consciousness and thus need not be attributed to the thing. In this way, though, the 'properties' cease to be properties of *something,* strictly speaking, and become independent matters with nothing supporting them, and the thing is merely their aggregate: "In this way the thing has been elevated to a veritable *Also,* for now it is a collection of matters, and instead of being a unit, it has become merely the surface that contains them" (#121 GW 9:76, TW 3:101). (c) Hereby the individuality of the object is lost once more and perception is confronted with the same unacceptable alternative: 'propertyless unit distinguishable from nothing', or 'aggregate of independent matters without objective unity'.

(3) Consciousness has by turns made the object and also itself into a pure, distinctionless unit and then into the aggregate of independent matters—to no avail. The only remaining option is to take both sides together and conceive the entire movement as the object of consciousness. Each thing, then, is distinct not from itself but only from another thing. This last attempt is however once again destined to fail. For no thing can be posited as distinct from another unless it is determinate in itself. This determinateness must be essential to it, while its relation to others, though necessary, is not essential. In other words, the thing is a unit *distinct* from other things only insofar as it is essentially determined, i.e. related to others; it is essentially a *unit* only insofar as the relation to others is not part of its essence. The relation to others is supposed to be necessary and yet non-essential, and this contradiction destroys the object of perception

once and for all. Consciousness experiences that what it took to be the true *"is the opposite of itself in one and the same respect, for itself insofar as it is for others,* and *for others insofar as it is for itself"* (#128 GW 9:79; TW 3:104). For perception, this result is entirely negative.

New Object: The Unconditioned Universal ("III. Force and Understanding")

For us, however, a positive result has also emerged: "This content is at the same time universal; there can be no further content whose particular quality would prevent it from returning into universality" (#134 GW 9:83; TW 3:109). The object has been transformed once again: if the exclusion of others (individuality) and the relation to others (multiplicity) are equally essential to the object, while at the same time they mutually sublate each other, then they must be essential to the object only insofar as they are sublated. Individuality and multiplicity cannot therefore be independent elements; they belong to one and the same object as moments that mutually pass over into one another, and this mutual passing over is what is essential to the new object. For by its very definition, consciousness cannot help but represent this truth to itself in objective form: "But this movement is what is called *force;* one of its moments, namely the dispersal of the independent 'matters' in their immediate being, is the *expression* of the force; but force, taken as that in which they have vanished, is *force proper,* force which has been *driven out* of its expression and *back into itself"* (#136 GW 9:84; TW 3:110).

In truth, the object must be force since the nature of force consists precisely in what now constitutes the object of knowledge: it is essential to any force that it act, which is to say that it express itself in (seemingly independent) matters, even though it is not identical to that expression: *no force without expression, no expression without force.* Of course this new object must be capable in turn of being known to be independent of whether it is known: the distinctions exhibited by force must therefore be actual and exist in themselves, above and beyond their being represented. Can consciousness know its object as such?

(1) *No force without expression*—i.e., the force is realized (called forth or "solicited") by whatever allows for its expression. (a) This cannot be done by force itself, but only by something distinct from it, for a force that met with no resistance would be incapable of expressing itself; it would remain formless and dispersed. The very thing that resists the

force, enabling it to express itself, also drives it back into itself, making it (in contradistinction to its expression) force in itself. However, whatever solicits the force must itself be a force, for everything objective has proven in truth to be force. Hence the same thing goes for this force as well: it is actual only by virtue of being solicited and expressing itself. A force is actual only by virtue of another force, and vice versa. "Whence follows that the concept of force is *actualized* by being duplicated in two forces" (#141 GW 9:87; TW 3:114).

(b) The same thing that actualizes force—the play of forces—also robs it of its reality, and the difference we found to be necessary between two forces is sublated. For each force possesses its determinateness only by way of the other, i.e. in the common "middle term and contact" in which it receives expression. Only in contact, in the expression, is force something determinate, actual, and hence experienceable. Yet since force must be more than just its experienceable expression—*no expression without force*—there is nothing left for the "truth of force . . . except the *thought* of it" (#141 GW 9:87; TW 3:115). This means (c) that the essence of the object—force—is only intellectually apprehensible, in thought, and never by the senses: It is the concept of something *internal* to the thing, no longer sensibly given but accessible only to the understanding. It is an essence that merely *appears* in its sensible expression. And because it has its essence in something other than itself, the expression of force is *essentially* "appearance."

(2) (a) "This true essence of things now turns out to be determined in such a way that it is not immediate for consciousness; instead, consciousness has a mediated relation to what is internal, and as understanding it peers *through the play of forces as a terminus medius into the true background of things*" (#143 GW 9:88; TW 3:116). This move brings us back over to the subject's side of things. Consciousness has developed into a faculty of understanding that conceives itself as understanding what is given in intuition and penetrating the universal in thought. The true thus proves to be the interior of things, the "abiding beyond [*Jenseits*] behind the vanishing here [*Diesseits*]" (#144 GW 9:89; TW 3:117). It is free from all sensible appearances, but at the same time related to them by means of its concept. Hence it does not participate in the flux of appearances, being instead what *remains constant* in the flux: it is what regulates flux, the self-identical law of force.

(b) This *self-identical* law is supposed to be continuously present and efficacious in sensible appearances, but in fact it does not actually explain them since they are as various and variable as the continually fluctuating circumstances themselves. Appearance thus remains partly independent of the law, and this would be impossible if the appearance were that of the law *as such*. The self-identical law cannot therefore be something merely abstract and lacking internal differentiation; it must itself exhibit determinateness and hence distinctions in itself. In other words, the self-identical law must in truth be a realm of concrete laws, and therefore "indeterminately *many* laws must be present" behind the various appearances (#150 GW 9:92; TW 3:121).

However, an *unconnected* multiplicity of regularities cannot satisfy the understanding, "for which, as consciousness of the simple interior, the true is the unity that is universal in itself" (ibid.). It therefore seeks to derive the many regularities from a unified source or 'ground' (*Grund*), and to conceive the many laws as expressing a single unifying law. The result is a twofold law: in addition to the first law, which revealed itself to be a realm of *many* different laws (regularities), there is also a second law "in the form of a simple return-into-self that may still be called *force,* but which is not the same as the force that was driven back into itself, but rather force as such, the concept of force" (#152 GW 9:93; TW 3:122–23).

(c) Understanding cannot avoid making such a distinction, but the attempt to locate any real difference in content between the two sides must fail here as it did in the case of the play of forces. The understanding begins by trying to connect the two sides by deriving or "explaining" the one on the basis of the other. How does it go about this? First the fluctuating, contrary, but regularly occurring appearances are expressed in the form of a law. Then this law is supposed to express an underlying force that is the essence of the law.[12] In fact, however, the understanding has inferred this force from the regular appearances, which is to say that it has determined the cause on the basis of the effects, so the grounds of explanation are in point of fact just the same *content* as what they are

---

[12] For a scientist like Helmholtz, for example, this was self-evident: "Generally, as self-evident as the principle may seem and as important as it is, it is just as often forgotten—viz. the principle that natural science has to seek out the laws of facts. In recognizing the discovered *law* as a power that governs nature's processes, we objectify it as a *force,* and call the derivation of particular cases from a force that produces a specific effect under specific conditions a causal *explanation* of the phenomena" (Helmholtz 1877, 187).

supposed to be explaining (although the explanation may be formulated in such a way as to conceal this fact). The understanding therefore only *seems* to comprehend the appearances' behavior on the basis of the "nature" of the force they express. In truth, it is going round in a circle, explaining the differences *idem per idem*. "This necessity, which lies solely in the words, is just the recounting of the moments that form the circle of necessity; they are distinguished, but at the same time their difference expresses the fact that it is not a difference in the content itself [*die Sache selbst*] and so the distinction is sublated even as it is made; this movement is what we call *explanation*. A *law* is enunciated, and distinguished from its ground—the *force*—which is universal in itself; but this difference also turns out not to be a difference since the ground has exactly the same features as the law" (#154 GW 9:94–95; TW 3:125).

It might be objected that a movement of this kind just fails to be an explanation at all since the *explanandum* is not derived from any principle. In the next historical excursus I will discuss the reasons why Hegel nevertheless calls it an "explanation." Before that, though, I would like to follow the experience of consciousness qua understanding to the end.

Understanding cannot persist in this "tautological movement" forever. For its present experience with the *concept of the inner being of things* turns out to be the same experience of vanishing that it encountered before in the play of forces: Just as it proved necessary before to distinguish between the solicited and the soliciting term, only to see that distinction sublated at the very same moment, the distinction between *explanandum* (law) and *explanans* (force) now proves to be a necessary distinction which is not in fact a distinction at all. Yet since the understanding takes its *concept of inner being* to express the truth of the object, it is naturally led to experience the "tautological movement" of its concept as meaning that the flux of determinations is essential to the interior, as well, or "that the *law* of the *appearance itself* requires that distinctions emerge which are not distinctions, or that the selfsame is repelled from itself, while the resulting distinctions are in truth not distinctions at all and thus sublate themselves; or that what is not selfsame is *attracted* to itself" (#156 GW 9:96; TW 3:126–27).

(3) The understanding now has *two* laws of the interior or the supersensible. According to the first law, the interior is the stable, self-identical distinction; according to the second, which is the exact inverse of the first, the interior is the permanent instability of any distinction at all. If the understanding is to justify its claim to know its object as it is in itself,

it has to unify these two laws.[13] Initially it might seem as though the laws refer to separate spheres, e.g. the second law might apply to the world of appearances, while the first applies to what exists in itself. But the untenability of this notion of two separate worlds has just been shown by the experience of consciousness: "For if the distinction is an internal one, then the opposed term is not simply *one of two*;[14]—for otherwise it would be an indifferent being and not something defined by opposition;—rather, it is the opposite of an opposite, or the other is immediately present within it" (#160 GW 9:98; TW 3:130–31).

If consciousness is to persist in taking the essence of appearance as what is true, it must conceive that essence as a self-identical unity in which *all distinctions are immanent.* Since nothing outside this unity exists for itself, it has no limits, and is true "infinity"; moreover, since the dissolution of those distinctions is as essential to it as their positing, that unity is, in Hegel's words, "the simple essence of life . . . which . . . is itself both all distinction and the sublation of distinction, pulsating in itself without motion, trembling in itself without unrest" (#162 GW 9:99; TW 3:132).

Historical Excursus

Following Hegel's suggestion from above ("not just one of two"), I would like to try to clarify the final step of his argument with reference to the concept of number.[15] Since Aristotle, 'number' has ordinarily been understood to mean a multitude of independent units (cp. *Metaphysics* X.1, 1053a30). Euclid for example defines it this way: "A number is a multitude composed of units" (*The Elements,* Book VII, Def. 2). Similarly, Kant explains that the concept of a number arises "by successive addition of units in time" (4:283; cp. A103). Figure 13.1 is an illustration for the numbers 1 through 5.

There is, however, another (older) conception of number or unity, one we encountered above in the context of Kant's discussion of the intuitive understanding. According to this conception, multiplicity does not come about through "successive addition" of units, but is rooted instead in the unit itself, arising *'limitando'*

---

[13] Since each of these two positions, when seen from the perspective of the other, appears to be "the inversion of the truth" (#26 GW 9:23; TW 3:30), Hegel calls the experience that recognizes the equal validity of both sides the experience of the "inverted world."

[14] On this see the historical excursus immediately following.

[15] See also TW 18:235–240.

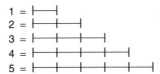

Figure 13.1

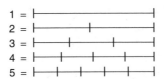

Figure 13.2

through internal differentiation or division, rather like organic cell division (See Figure 13.2).

The additive concept of unity is more familiar to us today since it suits discursive thought. As Kant insisted in the *Critique of the Power of Judgment,* however, that concept is no longer sufficient when it comes to understanding living things. The only problem is that the two concepts of unity appear to be mutually incompatible, and this was Kant's belief as well.

Now as Hegel describes it, what the understanding learns from its experience with "explanation" is that the distinction between two concepts of unity has to be made *and* sublated at the same time. Up to this point, consciousness has tried to conceive the one-many relation as additive. In light of its experience with explanation, however, it is forced not only to invert this relation, but to view the contradiction between the two as itself an inversion of the actual state of affairs, i.e. as in truth not a contradiction at all. Two significant consequences follow from this.

First. When numbers are formed by division, there is never any need to go outside the original unity; two, three, four, and so on, are all contained within the unit. So unity is present in the multiplicity. If we understand reality according to this model, then its "infinity" (since it is not limited by anything external to it) must be clearly distiguished from a "bad infinity" (which would be an endless addition of external units).

Second. In the case of organic differentiation, the potential to pass over from the unit to the dyad, from one to two, must be contained in the original unity itself, whereas in the case of addition this potential is external to the units. This is

319

the reason why Hegel insists that if the absolute unity is to be conceived as organic ("vital"), then it must be characterized by a "negativity" that drives it to continual self-determination (self-differentiation).

These observations indicate that we should understand 'explanation' as essentially belonging to the first, additive conception of unity. Fichte, for example, had written in the *Foundation*: "[E]xplanation is never an instantaneous grasp, but rather a gradual ascent from one to the other . . ." (GA I,2:413; W 1:281). At the same time, we begin to see why Hegel finds the concept of explanation to be particularly suitable for expressing what is specific to the understanding: it enables him (via Schelling) to draw a quite specific connection to Spinoza (and hence also to Goethe). For it was precisely the inference from the effect to its cause that Spinoza identified as characteristic of the second kind of knowledge, whereas the third kind of knowledge derives the properties (effects) from a thing's essence or first cause. Spinoza writes: "There is the Perception that we have when the essence of a thing is inferred from another thing, but not adequately [second kind of knowledge]. This happens, either when we infer the cause from some effect* [Asterisked footnote in the original: *When this happens, we understand nothing of the cause except what we observe in the effect*] or when something is inferred from some universal, which some property always accompanies. Finally, there is the Perception we have when a thing is perceived through its essence alone, or through knowledge of its proximate cause [third kind of knowledge]" (TIE, sect. 19).

Schelling had adopted this distinction, but characterized it in other terms: he referred to the inference from effect to cause as 'explanation' (presumably following Jacobi's interpretation of Spinoza),[16] but he called the knowledge of a thing on the basis of its essence or true cause its "construction."[17] On this account, explanations are given when we are unable to derive an object from its

---

[16] As we saw in Chapter 4, in his *Letters on the Doctrine of Spinoza* Jacobi had sought to identify philosophical thought as such with the project of explaining the conditioned on the basis of its conditions, and had insisted that this inevitably leads to Spinozism and fatalism. We also saw that Jacobi failed to recognize the role of Spinoza's third kind of knowledge; in the present context, we are only interested in his identification of "explanation" with the "inference from the effect to the cause."

[17] Schelling frequently commented on this, for example in the *Further Exposition* (SW IV:342–45), in the *Critical Journal of Philosophy* he produced with Hegel (SW 5:125–51), and most clearly in the "*Miscellen vom Herausgeber*" in the second issue of the first volume of the *Journal for Speculative Physics* (AA I,8:441–46; SW IV:527–33).

origin (or to cognize it in the third kind of knowledge): "Explanations occur only when we work back from the appearance to its cause, i.e. when the cause is determined on the basis of the effect—in a word, in the field of empiricism—but not when the effect is derived from the self-sufficient and independently known cause. In this latter case only *constructions* are possible. The notion of *explaining* nature's appearances must therefore be banned from all true natural science" (AA I,8:413; SW IV:530).

Hegel speaks of explanation in this sense. More specifically, he is concerned to show that understanding must pass over into a new form of consciousness as soon as it comes to see that it has only seemingly explained sensible determinate being from its cause, whereas in reality it has inferred the latter from the former.

In passing, note Hegel's extraordinary acumen in criticizing the concept of force in this way. "For example, the attractive force of the earth and sun is given as the reason why the planets revolve about the sun. This adds nothing to the content than what is already contained in the phenomenon (viz. the relation between the motions of these two bodies), only now it is put in the form of a determination that is reflected into itself, i.e. force. If we ask what kind of force attractice force is, the answer is that it is the force that makes the earth revolve about the sun; which is to say that it has exactly the same content as the determinate being whose ground it is supposed to be. The relation of the earth and sun in respect to their motion is the identical basis of both the *explanans* and the *explanandum* . . . Leibniz charged *Newton's* attractive force with being the same kind of occult quality that the scholastics appealed to in their explanations. In fact, it would be more accurate to criticize it for being an all too *familiar* quality, for it has no other content than the appearance itself" (GW 11:304–5; TW 6:98–99).

Toward the end of the nineteenth century, similar reflections led physicists like Heinrich Hertz, Robert Kirchhoff, and Ernst Mach to formulate a theory of mechanics that could do without the concept of force.[18] Indeed, physicists went even further, discovering that in the interior of things distinctions arise that are not distinctions. "We shift back and forth between images, describing it [sc. the elementary

---

[18] In *Concepts of Force,* Max Jammer puts it this way: "For it became increasingly clear that the concept of force, if divested of all its extrascientific connotations, reveals itself as an empty scheme, a pure relation. In fact, like 'the king for a day' in the fairy tale, it came back to where it started . . . 'Force,' so to say, was the common denominator of all physical phenomena and seemed thereby to be a promising instrument to reduce all physical events *to one fundamental law*" (Jammer 1957, 242, emphasis added). Cp. Hertz 1894, 1–49.

particle] alternately as both a particle and a wave or wave packet. We know, however, that neither of these descriptions is exact . . . If an exact description of the elementary particle is desired . . . the only thing we can offer in way of a description is the probability function. What this shows, however, is that *not even the property of 'being,'* if we can call that a property, can be ascribed to the elementary particle without qualification."[19] And hence neither can we speak here of an 'explanation' of the appearances, at least not in the proper sense of the term.

But now let us resume our consideration of consciousness which, after its experiences in the shape of understanding, has now reemerged in a new shape.

IV.
New Shape of Consciousness: Immediate Infinity
("IV. The Truth of Self-Certainty")

We now meet with a consciousness characterized by the 'knowledge' that all distinctions are in truth internal distinctions. Unlike the preceding objects, then, the new object cannot be distinct from nor, to that extent, alien to consciousness. But since it is nonetheless still representational consciousness, it represents this internal distinction (the distinction that is not a distinction) to itself as objective in character. That is, as consciousness it makes distinctions, but what is distinguished from it is nothing other than itself: it is thus self-consciousness, consciousness whose object is the *I*. "The *necessary progression* from the previous shapes of consciousness, which took the true to be a thing or a term distinct from consciousness, expresses not only that consciousness of a thing is only possible for self-consciousness, but that this alone is the truth of those shapes" (#164 GW 9:102; TW 3:135).[20]

In its initial shape, self-consciousness is the immediately present, individual, sensible I. We have returned to our starting point—to the certainty of sensuous immediacy—but on a higher level. We must now see whether consciousness, in being certain of itself in this way, has also come to know the truth of what it takes itself to know.

(1) As self-consciousness, consciousness is immediately certain of its identity with what it distinguishes from itself. In formal terms, this refers

---

[19] Heisenberg 1970, 50–51 (emphasis added).
[20] Of concern here is therefore not the genealogical origin of self-consciousness, but rather its certainty of being the truth of the preceding shapes of consciousness.

to the unity of the thinker with what is thought: the undifferentiated I = I. In terms of content, however, the I that is thought is empirical consciousness, consciousness that is rooted in the world. Thus "the whole expanse of the sensible world is retained, though at the same time it is retained only as existing in relation . . . to the unity of self-conscousness with itself" (#167 GW 9:104; TW 3:138). The sensible world, then, insofar as it exists only in relation to the unity of self-consciousness, is a manifold composed of the contingent and non-essential; that is, self-consciousness is what possesses true being and the sensible world has its truth in self-consciousness. Hegel says of this self-consciousness that "it is desire as such" (ibid.). The term of art "desire as such" combines three moments: (α) the certainty that what is distinct from the I is at the same time compatible with the I, an object capable of fulfilling its needs; (β) the certainty that what is distinct from the I (what is *mine*) possesses no being of its own (its lack of self-independence); and (γ) the striving to elevate this certainty to truth by sublating or assimilating what is distinct from the I (the desired object). "Certain of the nullity of this other, it posits that nullity as its truth, annihilates the independent object and thereby attains its self-certainty as *true* certainty, as certainty that has taken on *objective form* for it" (#174 GW 9:107; TW 3:143).

(2) This means that in order for self-consciousness to *know* that what is distinct from it truly possesses no being of its own, it has to sublate what is other. We know from the case of the understanding, however, that both consciousness and its other are determinations of *life*—of that eternally self-renewing being that eternally posits and negates distinctions and which is "the universal, inexhaustible substance" (#177 GW 9:108; TW 3:145). What for us is a *result,* is encountered by consciousness as something *given.* It therefore experiences the renewal of desire after every sublation of what is distinct from it, and so it must continually renew its demonstration of the nullity of the inexhaustible sensible world. By the same token, its experience shows that, *qua* desire, it owes all its satisfaction to the continually renewed *being* of the other. In this way, the object of desire also shows itself to be an independent life whose essence is in fact *external* to the desiring consciousness. "It is therefore something other than self-consciousness and the essence of desire after all; and self-consciousness has learned this truth through its experience" (#175 GW 9:107–8; TW 3:143).

(3) The certainty of being at one with itself in the other therefore receives its truth for self-consciousness only by being confirmed by the other existence. That other existence must negate itself, thereby proving that

sensuous life is of no account to it. This is something that only another self-consciousness can do: *"Self-consciousness attains satisfaction only in another self-consciousness"* (#175 GW 9:108; TW 3:144). Of course the same thing goes for this other self-consciousness as well: it cannot elevate its certainty to truth until another self-consciousness carries out its own negation. Self-consciousness has hereby duplicated itself along with the actions necessary for elevating its certainty to truth. For us, this signals the emergence of a new shape of consciousness faced with the task of uniting the individuality of self-consciousness with its otherness.[21]

New Shape of Consciousness: Unity in Duplication ("IV.A. Independence and Dependence of Self-Consciousness")

(1) To establish itself as *self-consciousess,* consciousness must negate the other, thereby demonstrating its nullity. And to establish itself as *pure* self-consciousness, it must demonstrate its ability to relinquish all ties whatsoever to its sensuous life (its immediately determinate being), representing instead the negation of all such elements. In other words, in negating what is other than itself, it must also prove its readiness to risk its own life in doing so. And this is the case for both opposing beings, each of whom is driven to elevate its certainty to truth. The second self-consciousness must risk its life in striving for the annihilation of the first self-consciousness, and the latter must do the same at the risk of its own life. "They have to enter into the struggle because each needs the other in order to elevate its certainty of *being for itself* to truth, just as it must elevate this certainty to truth in regard to its own life. And it is only by risking its life that self-consciousness demonstrates its freedom and shows that it does not take its essence to be *being,* the *immediate* form in which it comes into existence, submersion in the expanse of life, but that there is nothing present in it that could not be regarded as a vanishing moment, and that it is pure *being-for-self"* (#187 GW 9:111; TW 3:149).

---

[21] Self-consciousness has thereby repeated the experience of sense certainty at a higher level: "a) the pure, undifferentiated I is its first, *immediate* object. b) This immediacy is, however, absolute *mediation;* it exists only as the sublating of the independent object, i.e. it is desire. The satisfaction of desire is the reflection of self-consciousness into itself, or the certainty that has become truth. c) Even so, its truth is really the double reflection, the *duplication* of self-consciousness" (#176 GW 9:108; TW 3:144; emphasis added). Now, like perception before it, it must strive to reconcile exclusive individuality with the necessary relation to others.

(2) At this point, however, self-consciousness comes to appreciate that "life is as essential [to it] as pure self-consciousness is" (#189 GW 9:112; TW 3:150). For should the opponents lose their lives, neither will experience the truth for the sake of which they entered the struggle. Indeed, if the struggle ends with the death of either of the two opponents, the victor still achieves no more than the satisfaction of mere desire and must therefore repeat the whole process. If, on the other hand, both opponents resign, then neither will have established itself as pure self-consciousness and the struggle for recognition will not have produced a result. Hence there remains only one option if self-consciousness is to prove itself: faced with its imminent death, *one* of the two opponents must choose life over being-for-self while the other remains committed to pure being-for-self as its essence. When this occurs, what began as a symmetry between two identical self-consciousnesses devolves into a relation between two unequal and opposed shapes: "the one is the independent consciousness for whom being-for-self is essential, and the other is that for whom life or being-for-other is essential; the former is the lord, the latter the bondsman" (ibid.).

(3) The lord's conduct in the struggle has demonstrated his power over the life that he accounts as nothing; and since life has power over the other opponent, he is subjugated to the lord. By making his vanquished opponent work on the objects of his, the lord's, desire, preparing them for his consumption, the lord leaves his bondsman to toil with the independent side of things while he himself has only to enjoy their nullity.

(a) This state of affairs appears to secure the lord's recognition by another self-consciousness: this other self-consciousness posits itself as having no essential being (α) by allowing its devotion to life to sublate its being-for-self and (β) by working on what the lord desires and preparing it for his consumption instead of enjoying it himself. In this way it does to itself what was done to it by the lord, and the dependent consciousness presents the lord with the truth of his self-certainty. Once again, however, the object fails to correspond to its concept since the consciousness that is doing the recognizing is not a consciousness that the lord himself could recognize as independent: "The *truth* of the independent consciousness is therefore the *servile consciousness* ... lordship proved that its essential being is the reverse of what it wants to be" (#193 GW 9:114; TW 3:152).

(b) On the other side, neither is servitude what it first appears to be. At the moment of imminent death, the bondsman experienced the dissolution of his entire being and the threat of nothingness: "but the absolute liqui-fication of all that is solid is the simple essence of self-consciousness, the absolute negativity, *pure being-for-self* which hereby *belongs to* this con-sciousness" (#194 GW 9:114; TW 3:153). In the fear of death, then, it has (α) *experienced* this pure being-for-self, and being-for-self is objec-tively present to it in the form of the lord. And since (β) it invests its labor in preparing the objects of the lord's desire, it imprints its own form upon those objects, thereby making it permanent. Whereas desire per-petually renews itself in response to the continual disappearance of its object, work is "*inhibited* desire, *checked* vanishing, or *formative activ-ity*" (#195 GW 9:115; TW 3:153). Work forms both the worker and his object. Step by step, the bondsman works off his devotion to natural ex-istence while at the same time coming to see his own independence re-flected in the object whose independent form he has replaced with his own by working on it. Servitude is thus crucial to advancing conscious-ness: "Without the discipline of service and obedience, fear retains a merely formal character and fails to permeate the conscious actuality of determinate being. Without formative activity, fear is something inward and mute, and consciousness does not come to be for itself. If on the other hand consciousness' formative activity lacks that first, absolute fear, it is merely vain self-will; for in that case its form or negativity is not negativity *in itself* and so its formative activity cannot lead it to con-sciousness of itself as essential being . . . As long as the whole content of its natural consciousness has not trembled and quaked, it still partici-pates, *in itself,* in determinate being" (#196 GW 9:115; TW 3:154–55).

(c) The bondsman's consciousness now has an *external* intuition of its own essential being (its unity with what is distinct from it): it sees itself reflected in the object, in the forms of being modifed by its labor, and it beholds its pure being-for-self in the sight of the lord. Up to this point, it still exists as the mediation between these two, or their middle term. *For it,* these two sides of its own essential being are still separate; *in itself,* however, this middle term between self and being already constitutes a "new shape of self-consciousness; a consciousness . . . that *thinks,* or that is free self-consciousness" (#197 GW 9:116; TW 3:156). Consciousness has thereby assumed a *form* corresponding to that which we first en-countered in Chapter 11, where we distinguished it from mere represen-tation. This form of thinking is characterized by the fact that it no longer identifies itself with the subject side of the relation, representing the ob-ject as fundamentally opposed to itself. This consciousness is as yet still

326

unaware of having overcome the subject-object opposition. Even so, as the 'middle term' between the two, it is no longer *merely* representational consciousness of an object which is essentially alien to it; it has become certain that *in thought* it possesses the essence of what is superficially distinct from itself. As constituted by *thought* in this sense, consciousness is no longer dependent on heteronomous grounds of determination; it is determinate in and of itself—it is free. "For *in thinking,* the object does not present itself in representations, or shapes, but in *concepts,* i.e. in a distinct being-in-itself which consciousness knows at the same time not to be distinct from itself. Anything *representational, figurative,* or which exists as an *indifferent being* has by definition the form of being something other than consciousness; a concept, however, is at the same time an *indifferent being* . . . In thinking, I *am free* because I am not in another, but absolutely at one with myself" (#197 GW 9:116–17; TW 3:156).

New Shape of Consciousness: Thinking Self-Consciousness ("IV.B. Freedom of Self-Consciousness")

Consciousness is now certain of its freedom in thought, and its next series of experiences again result from the fact that its certainty still has no truth, i.e. the fact that knowledge and the known do not agree.

(1) Self-consciousness now takes its own thought as the essential being from which distinctions arise, and as indifferent to natural being. At this point, its freedom of thought is abstract; it has returned into itself from the other and therefore has no content of its own, but only an externally given content by which it is continually solicited and from which it continually abstracts. But *that* the form of thought is also the form of being—of this self-consciousness is certain. The criterion of truth and value is therefore conformity with the form of thought, i.e. rationality. This shape of self-consciousness, which Hegel calls "stoicism" in reference to its most familiar historical instantiation (though without identifying the two), succumbs to empty formalism. In this formalism, thought seeks its own truth in vain—a fact that manifests itself in experience when, sooner or later, thought grows "bored" with its formalism (cp. #200 GW 9:118; TW 3:159).

(2) The reason for this is that thought is by its very nature universal and hence the negative of particularities and distinctions. Accordingly, thought is driven to realize the negation which in stoic consciousness is merely abstraction from content. The content that is merely indifferent in

stoicism, must be actively negated. Self-consciousness, qua thought, can do this by thinking through the dialectical experiences it has undergone up to this point and appropriating them as moments of its own activity of negation. The contradictions that so far have merely befallen consciousness in the course of its dialectical movement, now come to be associated with its own feeling of independence and freedom, and it finds itself able "to make whatever purports to be real vanish in the certainty of its freedom": "It exhibits the *dialectical movement* that is sense certainty, perception, and understanding, as well as the inessential being of what in the relation of lord and bondsman and in abstract thinking itself was taken to be something *determinate* . . . [T]hrough this self-conscious negation it attains *for itself* the *certainty of its own freedom,* produces the experience of that freedom, and thereby elevates it to *truth.* What vanishes is what is determinate, or difference . . . For there is nothing permanent about it, and it *must* vanish to thought because what is different consists precisely in being nothing in itself, but having its essential being in another" (#203–4 GW 9:119–20; TW 3:160–61).

The skeptical consciousness that now emerges is not aware of itself as resulting from the preceding movement, but only as the "absolute dialectical unrest" that transforms and dissolves everything solid, and whose negative activity affords certainty of its freedom and immutability. It is important to notice, however, that the object of skeptical negation is the same as that of stoic abstraction: the negation of whatever happens it chances to find as empirical, contingent consciousness. But this means that consciousness immediately depends for the certainty of its freedom and essential *immutability* on what is contingent and *mutable* in its own *empirical* existence. It requires action and experience in order to assert the nullity of what is done and experienced, and thereby to experience its freedom and immutability. As a consequence, skeptical consciousness is divided: "Its actions and words continually contradict one another, and its consciousness of immutability and identity, and of utter contingency and non-self-identity, is equally divided and contradictory" (#205 GW 9:121; TW 3:162).

(3) Self-consciousness now experiences itself as divided *in itself;* its two extremes are utterly disparate both from each other and from self-consciousness. The simple, immutable element counts as essential being, while the empirically mutable counts as inessential. As the consciousness of this contradiction, skepticism strives to resolve it and thus to free itself

of its inessential being: "it is itself immediately both, and the *relation of the two* is for it a relation of the essential to something inessential and worthless [*Unwesen*], so that the latter has to be sublated" (#208 GW 9:122; TW 3:164). Once again therefore, consciousness is involved in a struggle, but this time it is a struggle against itself and to win is also to lose. In Hegel's words, it is "unhappy consciousness."

(a) Unhappy consciousness suffers under the nullity of its mutable, sensuous existence, and strives to rise to the immutable as to its own essential being. Yet since as consciousness it is itself their very unity, the immutable and sensuous individuality are inseparably linked in its experience, for the immutable is present exactly to the extent that it rises above sensuous individuality and in no other way. Its own sensuous individuality is in turn present only in and through the emergence of the immutable, and so consciousness immediately experiences the necessary relation of the two sides in its own self: "Consciousness becomes aware of individuality *as such* in the immutable, and at the same time it experiences *its own* individuality in the immutable. For the truth of this movement is precisely the *oneness* of this dual consciousness. This unity becomes for it one in which, *at first, the difference* of both is still the dominant feature" (#210 GW 9:123; TW 3:165).

What consciousness experiences is that there is *no immutability without individuality, no individuality without immutability.* This implies that the same distinction must also surface in the immutable, so whereas before the immutable was just an empty abstraction, it now comes into view as having a concrete shape, indeed as having the shape of individuality; it is "pure *thinking* that *thinks* itself *as individuality*" (#217 GW 9:125; TW 3:169). Since the unhappy consciousness has not yet come to understand itself in these terms, it does not perceive this as its own doing, but as something that befalls it: it *finds* that its individuality depends on the immutable. And with this it becomes religious consciousness.[22]

Even so, the immutable itself remains alien, otherworldly, and wholly absent from the empirical world. The unhappy consciousness is therefore caught in the middle between an immutable but alien being and sensuous individuality; both sides exist *for it,* but what is not present *for it* is that

---

[22] In the original sense of the word "*religio,*" which means both man's passive ties to a power distinct from him (*religare*), and his active celebration of and devotion to that binding power (*religere*).

it is itself the immutable being. Its attitude is that of prayer (*Andenken*), not thought (*Denken*), and its object is not an object of conception, but of feeling and painful longing. For while consciousness is certain of depending on the immutable and of being recognized as an individual "since [the immutable] thinks itself as individuality," it is still unable to elevate its certainty to truth because its object is necessarily absent: "for it is supposed to be a beyond, something nowhere to be found" (#217 GW 9:126; TW 3:169).

(b) Consciousness itself mutates in the course of this experience. Its feeling of self, attained through work and satisfaction of desire, has deepened. To the extent that it now experiences its individuality as depending on the immutable, it also recognizes something that is not of its own doing, but which it simply *comes upon* as a kind of gift or endowment. Its activity depends on abilities and powers that are not of its own making, but which constitute "a gift from an alien source that the immutable makes over to consciousness to be used by it" (#220 GW 9:127; TW 3:171). The fulfillment of its desires and the success of its labors depend upon these abilities and powers—no less than on the continual renewal of the external reality as a source of satisfaction and an object of labor. Its own activity is thus commensurate with external reality: reality is not simply a nullity in relation to desire and work, rather, it is *like consciousness itself*: "a reality *broken in two,* on the one hand intrinsically null, but also a sanctified world; this reality is the shape of an immutable that has preserved its individuality" (#219 GW 9:127; TW 3:170–71).

In light of this experience, consciousness must conceive the immutable as enabling its activity and as the source of its feeling of self. "Instead therefore of returning into itself after its activity and being satisfied with having proven itself, it reflects this movement of its activity back into the other extreme, which is thereby represented as a pure universal, as the absolute power in which all movement originates and which is the essential being both of the disintegrating extremes as they first appeared and of the flux itself" (#221 GW 9:128; TW 3:172). In refusing to allow itself to take pride in its success, consciousness becomes consciousness of *gratitude* for its continuing existence. And in the grateful reliquishing of its independence, it seems finally to have attained unity with the immutable to which it surrenders its individuality: "That the immutable consciousness *renounces* and *surrenders* its shape, whereas the individual consciousness gives *thanks,* i.e. *denies* itself the satisfaction of being conscious of its *inde-*

pendence and ascribes the essence of its activity not to itself but to the beyond—through the *mutual self-surrender* of these two sides, consciousness attains its *unity* with the immutable. Only ... the opposition of the universal and individual again emerges from it [sc. the unity]" (#222 GW 9:128; TW 3:172).

The impression of unity proves illusory. While gratitude is indeed the response to a gift that consciousness has no right to demand, the feeling of gratitude itself does not originate with the giver. It is essential to gratitude that it have its origin in the inner freedom of the one who is grateful; it cannot be brought about externally. That consciousness expresses true gratitude for its continued existence is thus its own inalienable deed, further confirming it in its individuality. If gratitude appears to stifle consciousness's sense of its own individuality, it does so only superficially; in truth, the grateful consciousness experiences itself "as actual and active consciousness, or consciousness for which what is *true* is that it exists *in and for itself*" (#223 GW 9:129; TW 3:173).

(c) In order to become one with the immutable external to it, consciousness must therefore surrender its individual will. Only by having its action be the expression of obedience to an *external* command does it cease to be the expression of its *own will*. But since the immutable is external and beyond comprehension, a mediator is called for, a priest who "presents the two extremes to each other and ministers to each in its service for the other" (#227 GW 9:130; TW 3:175). The unhappy consciousness repudiates the *essence* of its will and transfers it to the mediator who stands in immediate relation to the immutable and whose counsel links them like the middle term in a syllogism. Consciousness equally repudiates the *product* of its will, relinquishing all property and means of enjoyment—the fruits of its labor and desire—through sacrificial offerings, fasting, and mortification of the flesh.

The result is twofold. In relating *negatively* to itself, consciousness surrenders the actuality of its being-for-self: "it is certain of having truly divested itself of its *I* and of having made its immediate self-consciousness into a *thing*, an objective being" (#229 GW 9:130; TW 3:175–76). But this surrender of its will is at the same time a *positive* expression of the will of the immutable, which is thereby determined not as individual, but as universal will. The activity of consciousness is thus an expression of the universal. At first, it is the mediator who affirms the positive significance of consciousness's activity, expressing the individual's abnegation to the immutable consciousness and assuring the individual that the immutable is reconciled with him and hence no longer alien: "In this movement it has also become aware of its *unity* with the universal" (#231 GW 9:132; TW 3:178). This however implies that the individual is, *in itself*, an absolute being; the extremes of the unhappy consciousness cease to be extremes and now exist only as sublated. This in turn renders the mediator unnecessary, or rather the mediator turns out to be merely the external appearance of the new truth of this consciousness: "This middle term is the unity that knows both [sc. extremes] immediately and relates them to one another, and is consciousness of their unity, which it proclaims to consciousness, thereby proclaiming *to itself* its certainty of being all truth" (ibid.).

With this we have come full circle for a second time. *Taken in itself,* being-other initially vanished to consciousness in its experience of the inverted world, in which all distinctions turned out to be immanent distinctions. This experience transformed consciousness into self-consciousness. As self-consciousness, the experience of the unhappy consciousness has now also sublated the being-other that was only *for it*. In other words, "There appeared two aspects, one after the other . . . But the two reduced themselves to the single truth that what *is* or the *in-itself*, only *is* insofar as it is *for* consciousness, and what is *for* consciousness is *in itself*" (#233 GW 9:133; TW 3:180). Consciousness now 'knows' itself to be absolutely essential being, the unity of self and other, individuality and universality.

V.

New Shape of Consciousness: Abstract Reason
("V. The Certainty and Truth of Reason")

For us a new shape of consciousness has emerged. The 'unhappiness' of the previous shape has vanished and its negative relation to the world has turned positive. It neither seeks to negate worldly things nor does it cling to the particularity of the self over against the world. What has thereby emerged for consciousness is the notion of "reason" as the unity of "self and being," subject and object. In place of the free but empty thought that emerged from servitude and sought only to withdraw from the world, consciousness has now to embrace the certainty that, in thought, it possesses all that is real and the unity of what exists. On the other hand, it is the case that, "in its *immediate* emergence as reason, the consciousness

332

that is this truth has this path behind it and has forgotten it, or reason in its immediacy is at first only the *certainty* of that truth" (#233 GW 9:133; TW 3:180).

(1) Reason is initially abstract and present in a merely formal way. It is characterized as the certainty that self-consciousness and being are essentially one or (in philosophical terms) the pure "category." It must also contain distinctions, however, since it is part of reason's essence to be immediately identical to itself in its *being-other*. The distinction is therefore at once both necessary and sublated in the unity of reason, and so the pure category must also contain a multiplicity of categories.

(2) This multiplicity is opposed to unity and yet also related to it. The unity of reason is thus a *negative* unity of distinctions, i.e. *individuality* ("a new category which is consciousness as exclusive, i.e. consciousness for which there is an *other*" [#236 GW 9:135; TW3:183]). What this consciousness excludes are the other categories, and therefore consciousness remains purely at one with itself even though *the other* is equally essential. "Each of these different moments refers to another; and yet at the same time no being-other can arise within them" (ibid.).

(3) The consciousness that is certain of being all reality is therefore necessarily both, simple unity and exclusive consciousness, abiding unity and a restless movement that runs through all of its moments in search of what is other than itself. In this way it experiences that its certainty is an empty and abstract unity still lacking content. "This idealism is involved in this contradiction because it asserts the *abstract concept* of reason to be true; and so a reality emerges for it that is in fact not the reality of reason, even though reason is supposed to be all reality . . . Being at first only the *certainty* that it is all reality, in this *concept* [reason] is aware that as *certainty,* as the *I,* it is not yet in truth all reality, and it is driven to elevate its certainty to truth and to give filling to the *empty* 'mine' " (#239 GW 9:137; TW 3:185).

New Shape of Consciousness: Observing Reason ("V.A. Observing Reason")

Consciousness thus seeks to fill its empty certainty with content and to elevate it to truth. It seeks its truth in the *object* because even though it is certain of the unity of self and being, thereby possessing a *representation* of reason, it has yet to grasp *itself* as reason, as elevated above *both* subject and object. This consciousness "*has* reason" or is the "rational instinct," as Hegel puts it, but it has not yet taken up the *standpoint* of reason that encompasses both subject and object, being the exclusive standpoint of neither. Instead, it clings to the standpoint of the subject, seeking in objects that unity of individuality and universality it knows itself to be: "If it knew *reason* to be the identical essence both of things and of itself and knew that, in its proper shape, reason can only be present in consciousness, it would descend into its own depths and seek it there instead of in things. And finding reason in those depths, it would be directed back out toward reality in order to behold therein reason's sensuous expression, but now taking it essentially as the *concept*" (#242 GW 9:138; TW 3:186–87). Discovering the *concept* in oneself would lead to its *rediscovery* as the essence of external things as well, as we learned from the various examples we considered in Chapter 11. In other words, by rightly understanding itself, consciousness would become intuitive reason, *scientia intuitiva,* and it would know itself to have the "same essence" as external things. This it is not yet able to do. Because it is just emerging from the sensuous sphere, it is still *representational* consciousness and so it does not seek the concept in itself but in objects. In this way, it becomes discursive empirical science, *scientia discursiva,* or 'observing reason'.[23] It seeks to find in sensuous being that unity of individuality and universality it knows itself to be. Certain that actual reality must be conformable to reason and hence fundamentally intelligible, consciousness sets out "to find in the form of the concept what had been a thing for sense certainty [*Meinen*] and perception, i.e. it seeks to possess in thinghood the consciousness only of itself" (#240 GW 9:137; TW 3:186).

Here again, there are basically three ways that consciousness might find itself in the objective sphere: as nature, as spirit in its determinate being, or in both together. Accordingly, observing reason is (1) the science of nature; (2) the science of self-consciousness; (3) the science of self-consciousness as a natural entity.

---

[23] "For rational intelligence does not belong to the particular subject the way desire does, but as something that is at the same time universal in itself. In relating to things in accord with this universality, it is man's universal reason that strives to discover itself in nature and thereby to re-establish the inner essence of things that cannot be revealed by sensuous existence, even though it is the ground of sensuous existence. This theoretical interest whose satisfaction is the work of *science* . . ." (TW 13:59).

(1) *The Observation of Nature*

(a) *Inorganic Nature.* (α) Since what reason is seeking in the objective sphere is *itself*—i.e. the conceptual, the universal—it soon loses interest in merely describing things. It begins to search for the identifying criteria of things, distinguishing between essential and inessential properties. It classifies things according to their essential characteristics and groups them in genera, species, and so on. At the same time, however, these characteristics are supposed to be more than just a means of identification—they are supposed to mark the essential determinations of the things themselves: the artificial system is meant to represent the system of nature itself.

The actual experience and practice of observing reason, however, reveals that the notion of essential properties and the seemingly sharp boundaries they allow us to draw between species and genera, are "taunted by instances" (#247 GW 9:141; TW 3:191) that blur and confuse those boundaries, continually forcing them to be redrawn. What was essential proves inessential, and the inessential turns out to be essential. This leads reason to give up the idea of seemingly identical, 'essential' characteristics and to view them instead as vanishing moments, continuously passing over into their opposites: it begins to seek the *laws* that governs these appearances and of which the visible characteristics are mere outward indications.

(β) The law as such is not identical to the characteristics that manifest it. It is initially "something alien" (#250 GW 9:142; TW 3:193) to reason whose presence is only suggested by the appearances. All that is immediately observable are its sensuous manifestations, so it never appears in pure form, unadulterated by contingency. Reason therefore seeks to purify the law from everything contingent; it performs *experiments* with the law under the most various conditions in order to discover its pure form and to free its moments from any dependence on determinate being.[24] In short, it becomes experimental reason.

(γ) In this way, the law becomes a universal purified of everything sensuous; although it manifests itself in the particularities of being, it is not

---

[24] "Negative electricity, for example, which originally manifested as resinous electricity, while positive electricity manifested as vitreous electricity, gradually lost this meaning over the course of the many experiments and became purely *negative* electricity, no longer belonging to one specific kind of things; it ceased to be possible to say that there are some bodies that are positively electric while other kinds are negatively electric" (#251 GW 9:143–144; TW 3:194).

essential to them. The law of gravitation is indifferent and external to the apples, for instance, that fall from the tree to the earth. And vice versa. The one can exist without the other. Universal law and individual thing do not form an essential unity, and reason therefore begins to look for things in which the law is really immanent and essential: "What is in truth the *result* and *essence* is now present to this consciousness itself, but as an *object;* precisely because it is not a *result* for consciousness and bears no relation to the preceding movement, it emerges as a *special kind* of object, and consciousness's relation to it constitutes a different kind of observation" (#253 GW 9:144–45; TW 3:196).

(b) *Organic Nature.* The result of the previous movement, represented as an object, is organic life. For in the case of organisms, the law is *internally* present as the vital whole without which none of its parts would have existence or determinateness.

(α) In contrast to the outward 'characteristics' of the inorganic sphere, in the organic world it is never an isolated property that appears essential and then passes over into its opposite. Rather, it is precisely through its relation to others that the organism is maintained *as itself.* Because this is the case, to locate the law exclusively in the individual organism is to isolate it from its *true expression* as a universal.

(β) Observing reason must therefore seek the universal in the organism's relation to the environment in which it is necessarily situated, but against whose forces of dissolution the organism must also constantly assert its individuality to stay alive. Hence an "essential relation" appears to obtain between the two such that "the law is present as the relation of the natural environment to the structure of the organism" (#255 GW 9:145; TW 3:197).

(γ) In reason's experience, however, the organism's observable dependence upon and adaptation to its inorganic element (e.g. the structure of the fish in relation to water, the coat of fur in relation to cold climates, etc.) fail to reveal anything essential or necessary since every seemingly likely principle is simultaneously confronted with a host of bewildering exceptions.[25] Though reason observes a multitude of regularities, all they

---

[25] "[A]s frequently as a thick coat of fur is found together with the northern climate, the structure of the fish together with water, or that of birds with the air, the concept of a northern climate does not contain that of a thick coat of fur, that of the sea does not contain that of the structure of the fish nor that of the air that of the structure of birds. As though to underscore this freedom of the two sides in relation to each other, there are land animals with the essential characteristics of birds, of fish, etc." (#255 GW 9:146; TW 3:197–98).

show is that the environment exerts a *"great influence,"* and so "the relations of the organic to the natural elements cannot therefore be called *laws"* (#255 GW 9:146; TW 3:197). Since they are indifferent beings, the relata remain mutually external, and it is impossible to derive the properties of the one from the concept or essence of the other.

(c) *Both together.* (α) The sought-for unity of individual and universal, failing to be observed in the organism's immediate relation to its environment, is now projected outside the environment and conceived as a *teleological* relation. On this conception, natural things are only means to ends that are external to them, but which constitute their proper 'essence'. Individuality and universality are thus united in a supersensible concept of purpose and by the same token in an understanding external to the organisms.

(β) However, as we saw in our earlier discussion of Kant, organisms cannot be understood on the basis of purposes external to them. They are *self-organizing* and therefore manifest an *internal* purposiveness that forces us to conceive them not as governed by the purposes of some external understanding, but as natural purposes: "Since [the organism] preserves *itself* in its relation to the other, it is just that kind of natural existence in which nature reflects itself into the concept, combining into a single unity those moments of cause and effect, active and passive, which are sundered in the relation of necessity. Consequently, here nothing appears merely as a *result* of necessity; rather, because it [sc. the organism] has returned into itself, what comes last, the result, also comes *first* and is the starting point of the movement and the *purpose* that it realizes. The organism does not produce something but only *preserves itself,* or the product is already there as it is being produced" (#256 GW 9:146; TW 3:198).

This means that the organism's relations to the environmental elements in their immediacy are contingent and fail to reveal any necessity. Such necessity emerges only at the end of the organic life-cycle: the entire movement of the life-cycle is its own purpose and through interaction with the environment it produces what the organism was from the beginning. It is an end in itself, and in the end it attains itself. "We have here, it is true, the distinction between what it *is* and what it *seeks,* but this is *the mere appearance of distinction,* and consequently it is in its own self a concept" (#257 GW 9:147; TW 3:199).

In this distinction that is no distinction, observing reason finally discovers something identical to itself; but it discovers it in the form of an objective life distinct from itself. In distinguishing this life from itself, it also draws a distinction between organic activity and its own activity: "However, this unity of universality and the activity is not present for this *observing* consciousness because that unity is essentially the inner movement of the organism and can only be grasped as concept"—to which we might add: by an intuitive understanding that actively simulates and reproduces the organic movement and transitions—"but observation seeks the moments in the form of *being* and *permanence;* and because the nature of what is organically a whole is such that the moments are not contained in it nor can be found in it in that form, consciousness transforms the opposition [between universality and activity] into one that conforms to its point of view" (#261 GW 9:149; TW 3:202).

To comprehend the experience of organic life, observing reason would have to become intuitive understanding. However, since what it means to be *observing* reason is to view things only "as sensuous things opposed to the I" (#242 GW 9:138; TW 3:187), it does not perceive the necessity of an intuitive understanding and instead transforms the opposition into one that 'conforms to its point of view'. The consequence is that "thought sinks to the level of representation" (#262 GA 9:149; TW 3:202). The terms that before were opposed, individual (organism) and universal (external world, purpose), are now viewed as united in the organism itself as its internal purpose. Reason conceives the organic entity as the essential relation of two different but inseparable moments, the inside and the outside that belongs to it, and these are assumed to be related to each other by a law.

(γ) Reason's formulation of that law is *"the outer is an expression of the inner"*(#262 ibid.). The details of the various possibilities for understanding this law are not important here; suffice it to say that this strategy, too, is destined to fail. Laws establish a necessary connection between determinations that are distinct from and independent of one another: e.g. the connection between motion and heat (principle of the conservation of energy) or between crime and punishment (penal law). But since organic life is "essentially a *pure transition*" and has its determinate being not in static determinations but in coming to be and passsing away, there are "no such indifferent beings as are required for a law" (#279 GW 9:156; TW 3:212).

In neither the organic nor the inorganic world, then, does observing reason find what it seeks: the necessary unity of individuality and universality. It must therefore continue its search in the other element of observation—in the subject whose individuality is at the same time associated with having a *consciousness* of the universal. Objectively represented, this is self-consciousness in its determinate being.

(2) *Observation of Self-Consciousness*

(a) The laws that determine this object are laws of thought, and reason accordingly begins by identifying them as the sought-for universal. To the extent that such 'laws' formulate relations among static, unchanging elements, they fail to express precisely what is essential to their contents, viz. their being vanishing moments of active thinking, of the synthetic unity of self-consciousness: "This absolute truth of fixed determinatenesses, or of a number of different laws, contradicts, however, the unity of self-consciousness or of thought and form in general" (#300 GW 9:168; TW 3:228).

(b) Consciousness therefore turns to the observation of the *activity of thought*—and it does so once again by representing it as something objective and distinct from itself. This prevents reason from thematizing the concept's self-movement, their transitions into each other, just as before it prevented reason from thematizing *intuitive* reason in its observation of the organic. As merely representational consciousness it once more fails to grasp the internal unity of the universal and individual: "Because this connection is not present to observing consciousness, it imagines that thought, in its laws, remains over on one side, and that, on the other side, it finds a new being in what is now its object, viz. the active consciousness, which is *for itself* in such a way that it sublates being-other and, in this intuition of itself as the negative, has its actuality" (#301 GW 9:168; TW 3:229). And so reason plunges itself into psychology, observing the various ways in which individual consciousness responds to the various actualities it encounters.

(c) It must therefore seek to discover a law relating active individuality to the universality opposed to it, and so to understand the individual on the basis of its environment. It posits the law that *the inner is an expression of the outer.* Here again, however, observation fails to discover what it is looking for. On the one hand, the universal (the environment) is supposed to shape and determine the individual, while on the other hand the kind and extent of environmental influence depends on the determinate individual—on the degree to which it resists, yields, or remains indifferent to the pressures of the enviroment: "[T]hat by such and such an influence this individuality has become *this specific individuality* means

339

nothing else than that it has been this all along" (#306 GW 9:170; TW 3:231). The observed influence could therefore just as easily not have oc-curred, and talk of psychological laws is just that—empty talk of laws: "Psychological observation discovers no law for the relation of self-consciousness to actuality, or the world over against it; and, through the mutual indifference of both, it is forced to fall back on the *peculiar deter-minateness* of real individuality which exists *in* and *for itself,* i.e. it con-tains within it the opposition between *being for itself* and *being in itself* effaced within its own absolute mediation. This real individuality has now become the object for observation or the object to which it now turns" (#309 GW 9:171; TW 3:233).

(3) *Observation of the Relation of Self-Consciousness to Its Immediate Actuality*

Finally to abandon the search for psychological laws is to abandon the conception of individuality and universality as two separate but neces-sarily related terms. Reason, having set out in search of necessity, has in the end been thrown back upon the peculiar *determinateness* of real in-dividuality. The latter is in fact itself an inseparable unity of inner and outer, individuality and universality. For on the one hand, a perfectly universal human shape is proper to each individual, while on the other each individual is also individually formed, with an expression distinct from all other human shapes. It is an immediate unity of being as given (the universal) and being as made (the individual), being in itself and be-ing for itself. This unity becomes the next object of observation.

(a) Reason begins by observing this unity in the individual's essential activity or being for itself. The individual's *interior* is conceived as a com-bination of its original character with what influence and cultivation have made of it; its corporeal *exterior,* by contrast, is an organ for rendering the interior visible—the speaking mouth, for example, or the working hands. What these organs manifest in speech and works are on the one hand ex-ternalizations of the inner; on the other hand, though, they are also some-thing that action has transferred into the sphere of mere being—and so they externalize the inner both too much and too little. They externalize it too much in that the works cease to contain anything internal (i.e. ac-tive); and too little in that the interior remains distinct from what is manifested in the works. "The action, then, as a completed work, has the double and opposite meaning of being either the *inner* individuality and

340

not its *expression,* or, qua external, a reality *free* from the inner, a reality quite different from the inner" (#312 GW 9:173; TW 3:235).

(b) The unity of inner and outer must thus be conceived in such a way that the outer is not separate from the inner. Reason therefore now goes on to consider the external shape that is part of the individual as a permanent expression of its actions and which functions as a sign of its interior. Reason refers characteristic gestures and facial features (physiognomy), peculiarities of handwriting (graphology) etc. to an interior whose outward sign and actuality consist in this reflected being.

At the same time, though, the inner and the outer are supposed to stand in a recognizably necessary, law-like relation to one another. Yet they fail to do so. For a sign is always also something indifferent in relation to the signified and the signifier. Since it remains inner in its externalization, the inner could express itself just as well in a different appearance, just as the same appearance could express some different inner state.[26] This inner freedom of the individual in relation to the sign frustrates observing reason anew. There is nothing left but to assume that the corporeal exterior is relevant neither as an organ nor as a sign of the inner, but only as its static shape: "an actuality that is completely at rest, not a sign that could speak for itself, but a mere thing that presents itself as separate from the movement of self-consciousness" (#323 GW 9:179–80; TW 3:244).

(c) The outer is now conceived as a static, corporeal being that is nonetheless supposed to stand in a necessary relation to the inner. Lacking the concept, a relation of this kind seems as though it could only be a causal relation. As such, the cause (the inner) would have to be just as corporeal as its effect, so that the two would be related as, say, the brain (as the *being* of self-conscious individuality) is related to the cranium (as its external actuality).[27] Their relationship would be roughly comparable to that between a walnut and its shell.

---

[26] "Lichtenberg is therefore right to say, 'Supposing the physiognomist actually succeeded once in capturing a man, a single honest decision would be enough to render him incomprehensible for another several millennia" (#318 GW 9:176; TW 3:239).

[27] Here again, of course, we should note that phrenology as popularized in Hegel's time by F. J. Gall, is only an illustration, an *example* for the shape of consciousness under description. Cp. note 29.

(α) But how exactly are we to conceive such a causal relation? Every particular spiritual sensation would have to have its particular location in the brain, and any increase or decrease in that region's activity would show some effect on the corresponding part of the cranium—just as a high forehead is traditionally associated with thoughtfulness, a receding chin with weakness of the will, and so forth. With this, however, the comparison has already reached its limits. For even if we could ascertain a correspondence between specific kinds of intellectual activity and some localized cerebral activity (which would be associated in turn with a certain cranial form), the cerebral activity would still be just as detectable when the individual performs the relevant action, as when it performs a modified action because it seems to him appropriate for certain *reasons*. There is therefore a certain tension between the latitude for variation that is characteristic of intellectual activity, and the strict localization of neural activity, which is necessarily underdetermined. The form of the cranium may indeed correspond to the brain as the shell does to the nut, but the concrete, reflected versatility of intellectual activity, which is never just "thoughtfulness" or "weakness of will," finds no counterpart in the non-reflected being of the cranium. On the contrary: "the versatility [*Vielseitigkeit*] of the spirit gives rise to an equal degree of ambiguity [*Vieldeutigkeit*] in its determinate being" (#332 GW 9:184; TW 3:250).

(β) If reason is going to hold onto the idea of a law-like correspondence between the two sides, it must assume an *indirect* causal relation in lieu of the direct relation it has failed to discover. "If, all the same, the relation is still to exist, what remains and is necessary to form it is a *concept-less* [*begrifflos*], free, pre-established harmony of the corresponding determination of the two aspects . . . On the one side there is a multitude of fixed locations on the cranium, and on the other a multitude of spiritual properties, the number and nature of which will depend on the state of psychology" (#335 GW 9:185; TW 3:252). Since both sides have their common origin in the vital process, we can also imagine that a specific spiritual property is correlated with a specific protuberance or indentation in the skull, even without there being any direct causal relation between them. Whatever the case, since reason lacks all insight into the possible source of such a pre-established harmony, it gets no further than imagining various hypotheses. Above all, this shape of observing reason is thwarted by the fact that none of the hypothesized relations are genuinely law-like. Unlike the other bones in the human body, each skull is as individual as a fingerprint; assumptions about *necessary* connections between a certain spiritual property and a specific cranial form will therefore always be liable to falsification.

If a direct causal relation is ruled out (α) by the underdetermination of the 'original being', while pre-established harmony is ruled out (β) by the specificity of the skull's static external being, observation has only one alternative: (γ) to assume that underdetermination and specificity are realized together so that one side of the relation is variable, the other invariable.

(γ) Accordingly, reason now tries to understand the 'spiritual properties' constituting the side of being-for-self, as *original dispositions* whose presence is expressed in various cranial forms (the in-itself). Within the parameters of these original dispositions, the individual has a certain latitude in the actions it can take, and these in turn are actualized only under specific circumstances; it is therefore also possible for them to remain latent or underdeveloped. The sought-for law thus states that, if the behavior corresponding to the disposition does not occur, it ought nevertheless to have occurred as dictated by the cranial form. Or as Hegel says, "that this individual *really ought* to be as the cranium predicts, and that he has an original disposition, which however has failed to develop" (#337 GW 9:187; TW 3:255). To the extent that the spirit's original being is a disposition, it is in fact a non-being whose only *actuality* lies wholly with the shape of the skull. "When therefore a man is told: 'You (your inner being) are this kind of person *because* your *skull-bone* is shaped as it is', this means nothing else than 'I regard a bone as *your reality*'" (#339 GW 9:188; TW 3:256).

Observing reason has now exhausted its constitutive array of options. As long as it seeks by observation and representation to discover itself in individual being, its own essence will always appear to it in materialist terms. "When *being* as such, or thinghood, is predicated of spirit, the true expression of this is that spirit is the same kind of thing that a *bone is*. It must therefore be regarded as extremely important that the true expression has been found for the bare statement about spirit—that '*it is*'" (#343 GW 9:190; TW 3:259–60). This is where we have ended up. Self-consciousness recognizes its self in the shape of an individual thing, finds its being-for-self in the form of a being-in-itself, and succeeds thereby in expressing only something from which spirit is profoundly absent.[28] That is the one thing.

---

[28] "What is so lacking in spirit in this thought . . . is not to be the *thought* of what it says, or not to know what it is saying; in other words, that *being* is still used with

The other is that this result signifies the death of this shape of consciousness. For if reason is *all reality,* it is impossible that its being-for-itself has its actuality in being-in-itself. Difference is just as essential to reason as unity and oneness is. Reason could not be the 'category' and all reality if the category's actuality was reducible to one or the other of its two moments. "Reason, essentially the concept, is immediately divided into itself and its opposite, an opposition which for that very reason is just as immediately sublated" (#346 GW 9:192; TW 3:262). The result of observing reason therefore sublates itself; the two moments that are immediately opposed in the category exist only insofar as they are sublated and mediated: "Through this result, then, the category is further determined as being this self-sublating opposition" (#344 GW 9:191; TW 3:260).

Reason is thereby forced to comprehend its essential being. If it has been concerned up to now exclusively with the things in which it sought to *find* itself, it now comes to be the purpose of its own activity and sets out to realize itself *as* reason and to *actualize itself.*[29]

New Shape of Consciousness: Active Reason ("V.B. The Self-Actualization of Rational Self-Consciousness")

For us a new shape of consciousness has emerged. Since the truth of observing reason consists in the self-sublating opposition of self and being, consciousness (after having had its self tranformed into a thing) can no longer regard the *objectivity* of the actual as anything more than a mere surface whose essence is reason itself. Its new object is therefore a self-consciousness that it encounters as objective and independent of itself, but which is nevertheless not alien for consciousness: for it knows

---

a meaning that it only has for the initial sense certainty, and similarly that the I is taken as something entirely particular that cannot even be said as it is meant, as we have seen in earlier remarks" (GW 9:440).

[29] Like each one of the shapes of consciousness considered heretofore, observing reason is also capable of forgetting its experience and beginning again from the top. For instance, it could follow brain research in taking being-for-self as an effect (an epiphenomenon) of matter, and replace Gall's cranial measurements with Libet's experiments. Instead of: "You (your inner being) are this kind of person *because* your *skull-bone* is shaped as it is" (#339 GW 9:188; TW 3:256), one would say: "You find yourself willing as you do *because* your *neurons* are firing in this region."

of this other self-consciousness that "*in itself* it is recognized by it," and so it is certain "of having its unity with itself in the duplication of its self-consciousness and the independence of each" (#347 GW 9:193; TW 3: 263). This certainty must now be elevated to truth, and to this end the stations of self-consciousness must once more be traversed:

> Just as observing reason repeated, in the element of the category, the movement of *consciousness,* viz. sense certainty, perception, and understanding, so will reason again run through the double-movement of self-consciousness, passing over from independence into freedom. This active reason is initially conscious of itself only as an individual, and as such it must demand and produce its actuality in the other—whereupon, by elevating its consciousness to universality, it becomes *universal* reason, and is conscious of itself as reason, as a consciousness already recognized in and for itself, and which in itself unites all self-consciousness. It is the simple spiritual being which, in attaining consciousness, is at the same time *real substance,* into which the earlier forms return as into their ground, so that in relation to it they are merely particular moments of its becoming, moments which may break loose and appear as independent shapes, but which in fact are supported only by it [sc. the ground, the real substance] and have determinate being and actuality only through it, and which have their truth only to the extent that they are and remain within it (#348 GW 9:193; TW 3:263–64).

Even here, then, in the chapter's introductory passage, Hegel already hints that the experience of consciousness will reach its goal in this movement and that the opposition between certainty and truth will vanish. But first let's have a closer look at this final stage.

(1) "*Pleasure and Necessity.*" Active self-consciousness once more begins as being aware of itself as an individual. It is certain of being all reality and thus has its true object in itself. However, at first this object is only *for it,* not yet there for others. It finds itself confronted with an actuality different from its own, which however it knows cannot be more than a mere surface. Accordingly, it must strive to recognize its own being-for-self, as an independent being, in this other. "The *initial purpose* is to recognize itself qua individual being in the other self-consciousness, or to make this other into itself; it has the certainty that, in itself, it is itself already that other . . . It plunges therefore into life and brings its

role as pure individuality to the stage" (#360–61 GW 9:198–99; TW 3:270–71).

(a) Now, in possession of reason, the self-conscious indidividual no longer sets out as mere desire to annihilate the other. Instead, since it knows itself to be in the other (i.e. that it is of the same essence as the other), it is concerned to sublate the other's independent surface and to find and enjoy itself in the other self-consciousness. In this way, desire has been sublimated to pleasure. "It attains therefore to the enjoyment of *pleasure,* to the consciousness of its actualization in an apparently independent consciousness, or to the intuition of the unity of two independent self-consciousnesses" (#362 GW 9:199; TW 3:272). It finds that in the enjoyment of pleasure it loses itself as *this individual,* experiencing itself instead as the unity with another self-consciousness and hence as sublated individuality. The truth of its pleasure thereby proves to be something universal and the opposite of individuality.

(b) At the same time, however, this experience also shows the universal to be something independent. For the extent to which pleasure can be satisfied depends on things beyond the individual's control, things which it therefore encounters as alien to itself: e.g. public mores with their many rules and regulations, but also factors like chance and fate. And thus the pleasure of being united with the other self-consciousness does not lead to a sublation of the surface beneath which the individual hoped to discover itself. Instead, it experiences the universal as something it cannot comprehend as its own essence: it is confronted with the universal as an alien necessity.

(c) "Through the experience that was supposed to reveal its truth, consciousness has instead become a riddle to itself; the consequences of its deeds are for it not the deeds themselves; it is befallen by an experience which, *for it,* is not the experience of what it is *in itself . . . Abstract necessity,* therefore, has the character of the merely negative, uncomprehended *power of universality,* on which individuality is smashed to pieces" (#365 GW 9:201; TW 3:274).

(2) *"The Law of the Heart."* A consciousness that is certain of being all reality can only regard this alien necessity as an illusion whose seeming force and actuality it must sublate. Its purpose now is, therefore, to make this seeming necessity into an expression of its own essence, and hence to make its pleasure universal, giving it the form of law. Since such a law immediately unites individuality and universality, everyone else must also be able to recognize themselves in the particular law it establishes. Up to

now, however, the established order has been set over against the individuals, so that humanity obeys a law that is foreign to its essence, a law to which it is subjected and in relation to which it is therefore passive. The explicit goal of this shape of active reason is to sublate this passivity so that everyone can take pleasure in identifying with the law. "And so it is no longer characterized by the levity of the previous shape of self-consciousness, which sought only the particular pleasure of the individual, but with the seriousness of high purpose it seeks its pleasure in displaying the *excellence* of its own nature, and in promoting the welfare of mankind" (#370 GW 9:202–3; TW 3:276).

(a) The individual acts according to its law and makes 'the excellence of its own nature' into a universally binding actuality. The content of this law still characterizes it as that of the single individual, but insofar as it is universally binding, it has become indifferent to the individual The *immediate* unity of self and law has been lost in its actualization. Although it is the individual's own doing, it fails to recognize itself in the very deed by which it intended to assert itself *as this single individual*. In the actualization of its law, it experiences itself as alienated, and hence its own actuality is at the same time felt by it to be something unreal, and so it is divided within itself.

(b) The others, by contrast, do not experience the law as a realization of their pleasure, but as the carrying out of another's law, and they turn against the reality that has been forced upon them just as the first individual had turned against the reality he saw himself confronting. Through the others' resistance, this first individual now experiences that the reality he previously encountered as an abstract necessity is in fact animated by the consciousness and actions of everyone. The power of the universal order turns out to be the actions of the other individualities who have their own reality therein and who are therefore prepared to fight for it as their very essence.

(c) "The *universal* that we have here is, then, only a universal resistance and struggle of all against one another ... What seems to be the public *order* is thus a universal state of war in which each wrests what he can for himself, executes justice on the individuality of the others while asserting his own, which is equally nullified throught the action of others. This is the *way of the world,* the illusion of an unchanging course that is only *meant* to be a *universality* and whose content is in reality an insubstantial play of asserting and nullifying individual particularities" (#379 GW 9:207; TW 3:282).

The way of the world turns out, then, to be an actuality whose law is particularity, individuality—a law that is no law. It is the "illusion" of an insubstantial actuality where untruth is actual, not truth and universality—an inverted actuality, turned upside down by the private interests of individuals. On the opposing side we have the true universal which has yet to be actualized and which can become actual only by means of "sublating the individuality that has arrogated actuality to itself" (#380 GW 9:207; TW 3:283). The next goal of active consciousness must therefore be informed by the insight that what is essential is the truly universal, the law, and that all individual assertiveness whatsoever is to be sublated, both in the way of the world and in one's own consciousness.

(3) *"Virtue and the Way of the World."* Consciousness is now committed to the truth only of such laws as are necessary in themselves and not merely relative to some individual purpose. On the one hand, this law of virtue, purified of all particular interests, has yet to be realized; for the moment, it remains a mere object of "faith." At the same time, however, it is supposed to constitute the "true," inner essence of the way of the world, and it must therefore be enforced against all individuals who are committed to the truth of their own particular private interests. This can only happen if the virtuous consciousness dedicates all its talents, abilities, and powers to this purpose—abilities that the virtuous consciousness is certain of wielding for the good, whereas all the other individuals misuse them for their own ends.

(a) What is the experience of virtuous consciousness? Since the good can only be realized by the powers and abilities the individual finds itself to have been born with, the good accomplishes itself through the individual. The good is therefore already realized, at least in the actions and abilities of the individuals. To this extent, then, the good emerges equally in both the virtuous consciousness and the way of the world. "Therefore, wherever virtue comes to grips with the way of the world, it always hits upon places which are the actual existence of the good itself which, as the in-itself of the way of the world, is inextricably interwoven in every manifestation of the way of the world. And in the actuality of that in itself, virtue has its own existence, too; therefore, the way of the world is invulnerable" (#386 GW 9:211; TW 3:287). In other words, virtue is engaged in purely illusory battle with an invulnerable opponent and thus mired in internal contradiction.

(b) How do things look on the opposing side? Since the opponent is concerned exclusively with his own *being-for-self,* nothing is sacred to him; there is nothing he is not prepared to sacrifice or whose loss he is not prepared to endure. Where the virtuous consciousness feels bound by what it takes to be the in-itself, the opponent sees only a moment to be negated or preserved as he chooses. He holds in his power what the virtuous consciousness holds to be the in-itself—and thereby wields power over the consciousness who is devoted to the law of virtue as the bondsman was devoted to life. The way of the world triumphs over virtue for the same reason that the lord conquered the bondsman. "However, it does not triumph over something real, but over the creation of distinctions that are no distinctions; it triumphs over pompous talk of what is best for humanity, about the oppression of humanity; over talk of self-sacrifice for the sake of the good and the misuse of talents;—all such ideal entities and purposes melt into empty words that uplift the heart but leave reason unsatisfied—that edify but raise no edifice" (#390 GW 9:212; TW 3:289).

(c) In this way, the final distinction that is no distinction vanishes. The active consciousness experiences the untenability of the notion of something good in itself that is yet to be actualized and must be brought about by a self-sacrificing individuality: the way of the world *is* the actuality of the universal, its reality consists in the activity of all individuals—the individual, particular, and universal are in truth inseparably one. With this, however, the opposition that has governed the path of consciousness to this point has also finally vanished—the opposition between what is *in itself* and what is *for itself*. "However, with this result, that which as the *way of the world* stood opposed to the consciousness of what exists in-itself has likewise been conquered and has vanished. Before, individuality's *being-for-itself* was opposed to the essence or the universal, and appeared as an actuality separate from *being-in-itself*. But since actuality has proved to be in undivided unity with the universal, then, just as the in-itself of virtue is merely an aspect, so does the being-for-itself of the way of the world also prove to be no more than that" (#392 GW 9:213; TW 3:291).

VI.

When we recall the course taken by the experience of natural consciousness up to this point, we see that its dialectical movement began by traversing the object sphere ("consciousness"), then the subject sphere ("self-consciousness"), and finally the subject-object sphere ("reason"). It passed through the stations of the in-itself, the for-itself, and the in-and-for-itself. It appears as though nothing further could follow after this. The original goal has therefore now been reached. At the outset, Hegel had predicted that consciousness would "reach a point at which it casts off the appearance of being caught up in something alien to it that exists only for it and as something other, or where appearance and essence coincide." The last experience of active reason has finally brought consciousness to this point: "*It encountered* an *actuality* that was supposedly the negative of itself, and only by sublating it was it able to realize its *purpose*. Since, however, *purpose* and *being-in-itself* have turned out to be the same thing as *being-for-others* and *actuality as it is given*, truth and certainty no longer come apart . . . Its account with its previous shapes is thereby closed" (##394, 395 GW 9:214–15; TW 3:292–93).

VII.

But now something exceedingly strange occurs. The publisher who had printed Hegel's text up to this point suddenly refuses to go on printing. Hegel writes to Niethammer: "I have now started a written discussion with him . . . he usually has the bad manners of not answering, of ignoring what I have written, and of acting just as he pleases."[30] Moreover, the publisher refused to pay the honorarium he had promised upon completion of the first part and that Hegel so desperately needed, explaining "that he would first have to have the entire ms. in hand before he could decide how much the half of it was."[31]

How could it have come to this?

---

[30] Hegel to Niethammer, August 6, 1806, *Briefe von und an* Hegel, 1:113.
[31] Karl Hegel 1887, 62.

14

Hegel's "Voyages of Discovery": Complete

I.

Why the dispute with the publisher? An answer begins to emerge when we look back at the actual course that consciousness has taken up to this point, which comprises three circles or three turns along a spiral ascent (Figure 14.1).

The last circle is not yet complete; only the dialectic of natural consciousness has come to an end. One step beyond section V.B still remains to be taken before the final circle is completed. Natural consciousness, at the conclusion of its dialectic, has arrived at 'our' standpoint, that of the philosophical observer. It now knows, as we do, that the opposition of subject and object with which it started has been sublated, and that both subject and object are moments of a spirit higher than either, and that this spirit therefore cannot be identical to just one or the other. This standpoint of *spirit,* a standpoint beyond subject and object, the standpoint of "absolute" knowledge is the appropriate starting point for logic, but that does not mean that it is identical with "our" standpoint. The logic, as the pure self-movement of the concept, must be able to unfold as though "we" had no part in it. As Hegel makes clear, this last step from our knowledge to the standpoint of absolute knowing remains to be taken: "Of the moments noted as constituting the concept of knowledge, one seems still to belong only to us and not yet to self-conscious spirit itself, as it must if this is to be its perfectly self-transparent return to self, unadulterated by anything alien . . . This moment, that spirit has returned into itself and is for itself within the object as such, in *being,* which is *opposed* to being-for-itself, this moment seems to be only for us who know that I = I, or pure being-for-itself, is self-identity, or *being. . . .* However, if the present shape of spirit [is to be] its [sc. spirit's]

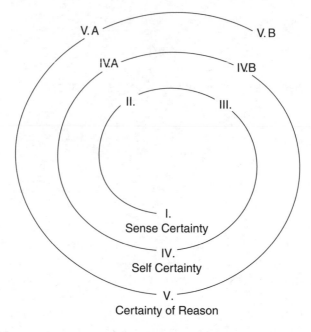

V. A   V. B

IV.A   IV.B

II.   III.

I.
Sense Certainty

IV.
Self Certainty

V.
Certainty of Reason

Figure 14.1

perfect self-knowledge, this moment must not remain merely our reflection."

Since the progress of reason up to this point has been divided into chapters designated as "A" (Observing Reason) and "B" (Active Reason), this last chapter would have to be designated by the letter "C". And since the remaining movement is supposed to be not just our reflection, but the "final and absolute [reflection] of spirit" through which spirit expresses its "perfect self-knowledge", it would be fitting if this last chapter were entitled 'Science', or both together: "C. Science". As a matter of fact, Hegel did write exactly such a chapter, and the quotation above is taken from it (GW 9:438–39).

II.

Astonishingly, Hegel scholars have (so far as I am aware) completely failed to notice the significance of this text. Following its first editor, Johannes Hoffmeister, they have persistently mis-identified the text with this heading as a draft of the *Phenomenology's* closing chapter, despite the impossibility of reconciling this conjecture with the structure of the *Phenomenology* as a whole.[1] But we should let the text speak for itself. In what sense does "C. Science" contain the solution to the remaining problem just decribed? Why can Hegel say that the final reflection no longer belongs merely to us? Or in other words, why is it not merely our reflection that spirit's being-for-itself is also being?

In order for spirit's being-for-itself to be being, it must have both the *I* and the *world* in *one and the same* consciousness, i.e. it must both have rediscovered itself in the world and have found in consciousness that which truly *is*. In the strongest terms, spirit must have the consciousness that the world is the I and I the world. As soon as the individual conceives itself *as a moment* of the universal, it transcends itself as an individual and *thinks* itself as sublated in spiritual substance. This however is tantamount to spirit's return into itself: consciousness "passes over into spirit through this reflection" (GW 9:438). This marks the *form* of the final reflection. However, we cannot speak of spirit's self-consciousness ($I = I$) until the *content* is also present, such that thinking and the object of thought, being-for-itself and being-in-itself, are the same. Consciousness, in its transition into spirit, also brings about this content in a final retrospective act: "In fact, however, this moment has already come about for us at an earlier point" (GW 9:439). Recall that the last section of Observing Reason (craniology) ended by identifying being-for-itself with a thing; and the last chapter of Active Reason ("Virtue and the Way of the World") resulted in the insight that "the side of *actuality* is itself nothing other than the side of *individuality*" (#389 GW 9:212; TW 3:289). So in

---

[1] Hoffmeister, who originally published "C. Science" in 1932 in *Hegels Jenenser Realphilosophie I* (259ff), characterized the text this way: "It is an immediate preliminary draft for the final part of the *Phenomenology*, 'Absolute Knowledge', into which it was incorporated verbatim" (259). He apparently failed to notice that the basic problem addressed in "C. Science", namely that the final reflection must not be merely our own, would no longer be able to arise in the chapter "Absolute Knowledge". Despite this fact, Otto Pöggeler not only adopted Hoffmeister's appraisal of "C. Science", he even added to it, reflecting that "since here B must certainly [*sic*] have denoted religion, a question remains as to what was dealt with under A" (Pöggeler 1973a, 221). And thus not only was a lapse of judgment rendered authoritative for future research; at the same time, the senseless task was set of identifying chapter 'A', which of course now could no longer be "A. Observing Reason". The absurd fruit that efforts in this direction were to bear can be gleaned from the survey in Bonsiepen 1977.

both moments, being and self, spirit's being-in-itself (the unity of being and being-for-itself) has already emerged *prior to* the final reflection, so that Hegel can now go on to write: "This moment thus completes spirit's simple reflection into itself; it completes it insofar as we only needed to show that it has already occurred, since it is already contained in the concept of that reflection. Hence we also see that this reflection is the final and absolute reflection of spirit. For in it, self-certainty and its truth have become entirely equal to one another" (GW 9:440).

And so the "science of the experience of consciousness" has arrived at its intended destination. What Hegel announced at the outset has now been realized in every point: Consciousness has not only arrived at the point "at which it casts off the appearance of being caught up in something alien to it that exists only for it and as something other." Hegel had predicted that in grasping "its own essence, it will denote the nature of absolute knowledge itself" (#89 GW 9:62; TW3:81). That point has now been reached.

III.

And yet Hegel never published the chapter "C. Science". According to Hegel's son Karl, twenty-one sheets had already been printed by the time the dispute with the publisher began.[2] A sheet comprises sixteen pages; hence the editors' commentary in volume 9 of the *Gesammelte Werke*: "21 sheets, 336 pages, and thus up to C. *Individuality that takes itself to be real in and for itself* had been printed" (GW 9:462)—which would therefore have included "Virtue and the Way of the World". But this statement is not exact. As a matter of fact, "Virtue and the Way of the World" ends on page 329. This means that another 7 pages had been printed in the 21st sheet at the time the dispute began! And that corresponds pretty exactly to the length of the text "C. Science".[3] So had this chapter, too, already been printed?

Here is one obvious objection: If "C. Science" had really already been printed, it would no longer have been found among Hegel's posthumous

---

[2] Cp. Karl Hegel 1887, 62.

[3] Seven pages of the original edition correspond to just about 130 lines in the *Gesammelte Werke,* where "C. Science" comprises 135 lines. (I am not counting the last four lines; these are written on a new page and they break off mid-sentence, and I see in them a first attempt at formulating the new conception.)

papers; it would have been in the possession of Goebhardt, the publisher. And so it must have been. As the editors tell us (GW 9:466–67), the manuscript that has been preserved is full of deletions and additions and hence could not have been Hegel's fair copy. Rather, it must represent the final draft prior to the fair copy, or the manuscript submitted to the typesetter, as indicated by the complete absence of the abbreviations and shorthand symbols typical of Hegel's drafts and lecture notes. In other words, what remained in Hegel's possession was the *penultimate* version; the final version or fair copy has not been preserved.

Assuming that "C. Science" had in fact already been printed along with the 21st sheet, the publisher's indignation suddenly becomes understandable: he would have had to pulp the whole sheet, which with an edition of 750 copies at the exorbitant price of paper at the time would have been a considerable loss. For Hegel's plans had changed utterly unexpectedly and indeed fundamentally. Not only was the chapter after "Virtue and the Way of the World" no longer to be the concluding chapter of the 'first part' of the book, upon which the logic was supposed to follow. According to Hegel's new plan, this first part, that had been conceived as an *introduction* to the logic, would expand to twice its originally intended length, no longer leaving any room in the volume for the logic that was to have been its 'second part'. On top of that, the book was to have a completely different title. Instead of "First Part: Science of the Experience of Consciousness," it was going to be called "I. Science of the Phenomenology of Spirit." As a result, the original title had to be cut out of the first page of the first sheet (designated sheet 'A'), which had already been printed in February.[4]

---

[4] In the first edition of 1807 the regular designation of the sheets therefore begins with 'A2' (the first page of what at this point was not yet called the "Introduction"), since the old title page ('A') has been excised. The new title page, on the other hand, exhibits no designation whatsoever since it is now the *last* page of the last sheet of the "Preface" which was written and printed only after the whole work had been completed. I have access to such a copy. There are, however, also copies whose owners purchased the sheets individually and had them bound themselves, so that page 'A' with the original title was preserved. That is the case, for example, in one copy whose owner had his own name (A. Loga) printed together with Hegel's on the spine of the book; this copy is now in possession of the Butler Library of Columbia University (New York) under the signature B2925/1807g. (On the question of the title, see also Nicolin 1967.)

Hereupon, Goebhardt refused to go on printing the book and also withheld the honorarium promised when the first half of the book had been printed. When Hegel's effort to change his mind failed, he finally asked his friend Niethammer to negotiate directly with the publisher in Bamberg. His efforts were similarly unsuccessful until finally, "after fruitless negotiations with the obstinate publisher, [he] attained his goal only by the heroic means of signing a contract with him on September 29, 1806, obliging him (Niethammer) to pay for the entire edition of the work, as far as it had been printed (21 sheets), at a price of 12 florins a sheet,—in case the author failed to deliver the entire rest of the manuscript by October 18; whereas Goebhardt, in case of timely delivery, promised to pay the honorarium in two installments for the twenty-four printed sheets that would have comprised half of the work."[5] So the new half is now made up of twenty-four sheets, rather than twenty-one as previously.

If my conjectures are right, then the new 21st sheet would have allowed Hegel to re-write the conclusion of "Virtue and the Way of the World", adapting it to the changed situation, for the 21st sheet begins with the third section of that chapter, "The universal is true for the virtuous consciousness . . ." (#384 GW 9:209; TW 3:285). All the evidence points to Hegel's having done exactly that. And this is the reason why it is no longer as obvious as it must originally have been that "C. Science" was intended to follow immediately upon the conclusion of "Virtue and the Way of the World".

Especially the beginning of "C. Science" with its talk of "spirit as represented in absolute religion" may seem not to fit what Hegel has said up to this point. But that is only apparently the case. For at that period, Hegel used the term "absolute religion" for the representation that the immediate shape of the divine being is self-consciousness. Take the "Third Jena System Draft" (1805/06) for example: "Absolute religion is this knowledge—*that God is the depth of spirit that is conscious of itself,*—in this way he is the Self of all—It is the essence of pure thought,—*but when divested of this abstraction he is an actual Self; a human being,* who has *the ordinary spatial and temporal form of existence—and all individuals are this individual—the divine nature is not different from human nature*" (GW 8:280, cp. #759 GW 9:405; TW 3:552).

---

[5] Karl Hegel 1887, 62.

"Absolute religion" thus denotes precisely the representation of the divine that we encountered in the unhappy consciousness and from which reason emerged as universal self-consciousness. In light of this, we can see more clearly that at the beginning of "C. Science", Hegel is summarizing spirit's movement from unhappy consciousness through the three stations of reason to the present standpoint:

> The nature of spirit's final reflection into itself, which constitutes *knowledge,* has already become apparent. Spirit as represented in the absolute religion [of unhappy consciousness] [has] passed over into the Self of consciousness[6] [= Reason]; the latter has for its part also recognized itself as the essence[7] [= Category], in contradistinction to this essence that is sealed off, in its being-for-itself, from the essence it excludes, the essence that is in-itself [= observing reason];[8] but the Self's I = I is the simplicity and self-identity of its being-for-itself, and hence being-in-itself;[9] in this reflection, it passes over into spirit[10] [= active reason]. The first movement was the content of absolute religion itself; since the second [sc. movement] belonged to self-consciousness, we recalled that it was a mode of self-consciousness that had previously occurred; it is therefore to be viewed as a moment belonging to the actuality of spirit and constituting one of the conditions for its final reflection into itself (GW 9:438).

---

[6] "In grasping the thought that the *single* individual consciousness is *in itself* Absolute Essence, consciousness has returned into itself" (#231 GW 9:132; TW 3:178).

[7] "I is therefore only the *pure essentiality* of indifferent being [*des Seienden*], or it is the simple *category* . . . in other words, the category means this, that self-consciousness and being are the *same* essence" (#235 GW 9:134; TW 3:181).

[8] "It is true that we now see this consciousness, for which *being* means what is *its own* [*das Seine*], revert to the standpoint of meaning [*Meinen*] and perceiving, but not in the sense that it is certain of what is merely an *other,* but rather as the certainty that it is itself this other" (#240 GW 9:137; TW 3:185).

[9] "Self-consciousness found the thing to be like itself, and itself to be like a thing; i.e. it is aware [*es ist für es*] that it is *in itself* objective reality . . ." (#347 GW 9:193; TW 3:263).

[10] "It is spirit which, in the duplication of its self-consciousness and in the independence of both, has the certainty of its unity with itself" (ibid.).

This perspective therefore further confirms that "C. Science" was originally intended as the final chapter of "the science of the experience of consciousness".

Hegel learned of Niethammer's contract on October 6. In order to get the rest of the manuscript to Bamberg by October 18, Hegel had to send it off by October 13, giving him exactly *one week*. As we know, he wrote the last pages within earshot of Napoleon's approaching cannons. Things could not have been much quieter in his mind, either.[11] Why did Hegel take all this upon himself instead of sticking with the original plan and receiving the honorarium he so desperately needed?

IV.

Historical Excursus

At the very latest, by the time the semester began in May it must have been clear to Hegel that the publisher could not be prevailed upon either to continue printing or to pay out the honorarium.[12] He was therefore facing extreme financial straits. Unexpected help came barely a month later when Goethe was able to secure for Hegel a yearly salary of 100 *Reichstaler*.[13] He writes to Hegel on June 24, "Please regard this, my dear *Herr Doktor,* at least as proof that I have not ceased to work in your favor behind the scenes" (WA IV,19:151). Can we infer from this

---

[11] In this connection, Hegel's son writes that "the greater the gratitude Hegel owed to Niethammer for such a proof of his friendship, the more distressing his situation became when at the last moment, after war had broken out, it seemed very doubtful whether the manuscript, which had already been dispatched, would reach the publisher in time" (Karl Hegel 1887, 62).

[12] Hegel to Niethammer, August 6, 1806: "Printing began in February, and according to the original contract this part was to be finished by Easter; I had this extended till the beginning of the semester—but this again was not fulfilled . . ." (*Briefe von und an Hegel* 1:113).

[13] Through the mediation of Christian Gottlob von Voigt, Goethe had secured a salary for Hegel from the Duke as *recompense for the services Goethe himself had rendered* in connection with the university's collections! Thus Voigt writes to Goethe on June 26, 1806: "My son has described to me in part your Excellency's many efforts regarding our scientific collections, and yesterday the librarian presented the case to me in even greater detail . . . So as to contribute something for my own part as well, I have tried to do something to help Hegel *in light of your Excellency's recommendation* and *in recognition of the man's merits*" (GVB 3:116, emphasis added).

that Goethe was not only aware of Hegel's decision, but also approved and supported it?

At the same time that Hegel was working on his "science of the experience
of consciousness", Goethe was busy with the first part of his *Theory of Colors,*
which he too had originally intended to finish by Easter 1806[14] and which had
been being printed in successive sheets since October 1805. Concurrently with
this work on the *Theory of Colors,* Goethe also gave a series of lectures on natural philosophy for a select audience from October 2, 1805, until May 14, 1806,
always on Wednesday from 10 in the morning until 1 in the afternoon: "I have set
aside one morning a week", he wrote to Zelter on November 18, 1805, "when
I present my results and convictions regarding natural objects to a small society.
In this way I myself become aware of *what I do and do not possess*" (WA IV,19:75;
emphasis added).

That was exactly the purpose of these private lectures: Goethe wanted to find
out whether he merely *had* his 'results and convictions' or whether he *possessed*
them such that he could demonstrate their validity to an audience. At this time
Goethe was also just finishing his work on the first part of *Faust,* and his scientific
concerns also left a trace in that text, to which he now added a sentence found
neither in the *Urfaust* nor in the *Faust Fragment* of 1790: "What you have inherited from your fathers / earn it to possess it" [*Was du ererbt von Deinen Vätern
hast, / Erwirb es um es zu besitzen*] (line 682).

An *inheritance* is something that already exists, something that has been completed and left behind by others; a *possession,* by contrast, is something one has
worked for and earned for oneself. Something similar is true of intellectual property: opinions and representations are also handed down, adopted from others,
and to this extent they are familiar, *bekannt,* without being properly understood,
erkannt—i.e. one is unable to derive what is familiar (the properties)[15] from the
essence of the thing. It is true that Goethe's "convictions" (*Urphänomene,* ideas)
are not inherited in this sense; he *earned* them through rigorous investigation of
the transitions between phenomena. In his lectures, however, he wanted all the
same to ascertain whether he also *possessed* them in the sense of being able to
reproduce them—i.e. to derive the phenomena from ideas and thereby to reproduce

---

[14] Cp. Goethe's letter to Zelter of October 12, 1805: "I ... will try to have my
work on colors out by Spring" (WA IV: 19:68). On December 6, 1805, Goethe's
brother-in-law Vulpius writes to N. Meyer: "Goethe is working on his theory of
colors which is supposed to come out this Spring, and has no time for anything
else" (LA II,3:155).

[15] See also Chapter 13, n. 10.

them in one's own mind as required by *scientia intuitiva*.[16] The controversy with Lichtenberg that had forced him to abandon his *Contributions to Optics* had left a deep impression on Goethe! Before presenting his *Theory of Colors* to a wider audience, he needed to be sure that it was immune to similar objections. Thus he sets out the real task of the lectures at the very beginning: "*We meet with two requirements* in the study of natural phenomena: [1.] to become familiar with the phenomena in their entirety and to *appropriate* them to ourselves through reflection . . . When we are able to survey an object in all of its parts, to grasp it properly and [2.] to reproduce it mentally, then we can say that we intuit it in the strict and higher sense, that it *belongs* to us, that we have obtained a certain mastery over it.[17] *And so the particular continually leads us to the universal, and the universal to the particular*" (LA I,11:55; emphasis added).[18]

Hegel was not among the audience at Goethe's actual lectures, but he met with Goethe in Jena several times during this period and it is also documented that Goethe showed him the proofs of his *Theory of Colors*.[19] Striking in any case is the fact that at this exact moment, Hegel modified his plans in a way that corresponds directly to Goethe's second "requirement", namely that the ascent from the particular to the universal be followed by a descent from the universal to the particular. It is hardly less striking when Hegel appeals to Goethe's distinction between property and possession in order to explain the necessity of expanding his original plan. In the Preface to the *Phenomenology,* composed after its completion, he writes:

> The task of leading the individual from his uneducated standpoint to knowl-
> edge had to be seen in its universal sense, **and** the universal individual,

---

[16] In this way Goethe "was able to forget everything external and to awaken in [himself] a vivid awareness of what was soon to be communicated to a wider audience" (LA I,6:429; HA 14:268–69).

[17] In December, one member of Goethe's audience, Schiller's wife, Charlotte, writes of the lectures, "I derive much enjoyment from these hours, and I have felt as though I were looking on as the world takes form" (quoted in Steiger 1982–96, IV:635).

[18] The decisive point, Goethe wrote in another context, is that "we arrive at the *Urphänomene* which we contemplate face to face in their unfathomable glory, *and then return back to the world of appearances* where that which is incomprehensible in its simplicity reveals itself in the thousands upon thousands of manifold appearances, immutable in all the mutability" (LA I,8:164; emphasis added).

[19] Hegel mentions this in a letter to Schelling from February 23, 1807 (*Briefe von und an Hegel,* 1:151).

world spirit, had to be studied in its formative education[20] . . . This past existence is the already acquired **property** of universal spirit which constitutes the substance of the individual, and hence appears externally to him as his inorganic nature. —In this respect, formative education, regarded from the side of the individual, consists in his **earning** [*erwerben*] what thus lies at hand, devouring his inorganic nature, and taking **possession** of it for himself. But, regarded from the side of universal spirit as substance, this is nothing but the process by which it gives self-consciousness to itself, that is, the bringing about of its own becoming and reflection into itself . . . The existence that has been taken back into the substance has only been *immediately* transposed into the element of the self through that first negation, and it therefore still has the same character of uncomprehended immediacy or unmoved indifference that existence itself had; existence has thus merely passed over into *representation* . . . The fact that what is represented becomes the **property** of pure self-consciousness, this elevation to universality as such, is only the *one* side, not yet its completed education (##28–33 GW 9:24–28; TW 3:31–36; emphasis added).

Completed education—*vollendete Bildung*—and therefore knowledge too require that we also traverse the opposite direction, descending through a series of transitions from the 'elevation to universality' back into concrete existence. Here is a further characteristic passage: "The proposition cited above, namely that truth is essentially *one,* is still abstract and formal. In a deeper sense, the starting point and the final goal of philosophy is to know this *one* truth, but at the same time to recognize it as the source from which all else, all laws of nature, all the phenomena of life and consciousness merely flow, of which they are merely reflections; in other words, all these laws and phenomena must be derived from that source **by a seemingly reversed path**, but only in order to comprehend them on its basis, i.e. **to recognize their derivation from it**. The essential point is thus to recognize that the *one* truth is not a one-dimensional [*einfach*] and empty thought, but a thought that is determinate in itself" (TW 18:38–39; emphasis added).

The passage is taken from the Introduction to Hegel's *Lectures on the History of Philosophy* in which now suddenly (as mentioned above in Chapter 12, n. 42) "the two [!] concepts of *development* and of the *concrete*," are said to be essential, whereas in 1805 Hegel had still insisted that everything depends on "the *single* concept of 'development' " (ibid.).

---

[20] Originally, all that had been planned was to consider "the history of the *education* of consciousness itself to the standpoint of science" (#78 GW 9:56; TW 3:73).

It therefore looks as though Hegel's decision to revise his original plan of publication was informed by Goethe's parallel endeavor of the same period. To be exact, he seems to have become *quite generally* convinced that the mere ascent to the idea—be it the idea of color, the idea of the plant, or the idea of the absolute—is only half the truth, and that it is always necessary to demonstrate the possibility of descending from the idea back to the phenomena if we are to provide scientific proof that the idea is the source of the phenomena and that it is therefore objectively real.[21] Goethe insisted that this must be shown for *every particular* idea; Hegel now seeks to demonstrate it in the case of the highest idea, the absolute idea. However, this also saddles Hegel with a problem that Goethe does not have— and to which I will return at the end of this chapter.

In a letter to Goethe written many years later, Hegel was to write: "When I survey the path of my spiritual development, I see you interwoven in it everywhere and I think of myself as *one of your sons; you have nourished in me a tenacious resistance to abstraction,* and your creations [*Gebilde*] have marked out my path like torches."[22]

I can now return to "C. Science".

V.

At the end of "C. Science" the standpoint of absolute knowledge, or the self-consciousness of spirit, has been reached: "What is true, and what is present here, is just this movement of positing *being* as the negative of the Self, and also abstracting [from it] or the Self; and its immediacy is therefore itself only this movement" (GW 9:443). Thus we come full circle one last time, and yet the resulting immediacy is just as abstract as it was each time before:

"I. Sense Certainty": *abstract being*

"IV. The Truth of Self-Certainty": *abstract self-consciousness*

"V. Certainty and Truth of Reason": *abstract reason*

"C. Science": *the abstract absolute*

---

[21] "In its immediacy, spirit is not yet true, it has not yet made its concept into an object for itself, that which is present within it in an immediate way has not yet been transformed into something posited by it . . . only through the cognition of spirit's nature does the science of spirit itself become true" (*Encyclopedia* [1830] §378Z, TW 10:15).

[22] *Briefe von und an Hegel*, 3:83, emphasis added.

If the system of philosophy that Hegel had been promising since the beginning of his time in Jena is to unfold on the basis of the idea of the absolute, then that idea must be more than an abstract standpoint; it must potentially contain within itself everything that is to develop out of it, just as the seed potentially contains the whole plant with all its parts. The introduction to the system cannot therefore end with "C. Science". As Hegel was later to explain:

> In my *Phenomenology of Spirit* . . . I began with the first, simplest manifestation of spirit, *immediate consciousness,* and unfolded its dialectic up to the standpoint of philosophical science, thus demonstrating the necessity of this standpoint. It was not possible to do this, however, by halting at the formal element of mere consciousness; for the standpoint of philosophical knowledge is at the same time the most concrete standpoint and the one richest in content, and in order to emerge as a result it presupposes the concrete shapes of consciousness, for example morality, ethical life, art, and religion. Therefore, the elaboration of the content, the objects of specific branches of philosophical science, also forms a part of what might initially appear as an exclusively formal development of the consciousness behind whose back, as it were, that development takes place, insofar as the content constitutes consciousness's being-*in-itself.* The exposition is complicated by this requirement, and what is really part of the concrete branches [sc. of philosophical science itself] also partly constitutes the matter of its introduction (*Enz.* [1830] §25; GW 20:68–69; TW 8:91–92).

This does indeed render the exposition more complicated, and it does so in two different respects. For one, a further part must be added corresponding to the preceding movement of consciousness, a part in which it is now spirit that *gives itself* the contents that natural consciousness had taken as the given ("the concrete shapes of consciousness"). The stages described up to this point ("consciousness", "self-consciousness", "reason") therefore have to be traversed once more, this time from the standpoint of spirit ("Spirit", "Religion", "Absolute Knowledge").[23] Spirit

---

[23] After completing the work, Hegel taught in Nürnberg, where he characterized the relation between the two parts as follows: "The theory of spirit considers spirit according to its various types of consciousness and its various types of activity . . . Consciousness as such is knowledge of an object, be it external or internal, and

"must progress to consciousness of what it immediately is . . . and by passing through a series of shapes attain to knowledge of itself. These shapes, however, are distinguished from the previous ones by the fact that they are real spirits, actualities in the strict meaning of the word, and instead of being shapes merely of consciousness, are shapes of a world" (#441 GW 9:240; TW 3:326). For this very reason, however, the book can no longer properly be called a "Science of the Experience of Consciousness"; this characterization now fits only the first part of the work and must therefore give way to the more comprehensive title, *Phenomenology of Spirit*.

Chapter V.C., rather than being the *terminus* of the introduction, now becomes its midway point, or to be exact: the *turning point* at which, now that the ascent to the standpoint of spirit has been completed, the descent into the particular must begin. This chapter, of which Hegel will say later in the book that it marks the sphere "with which *spiritual reality* first made its appearance" (#641 GW 9:345; TW3:471), now receives in place of the old title, "C. Science", the new heading "C. Individuality that takes itself [but is not taken by us!] to be real in and for itself". This individuality, which is the immediate expression of active spirit, begins as the "*result*" of the preceding movement and hence as "the *abstractly universal*" reality. By the same token, however, this individuality is also concrete, an "originally determinate nature" which has "not yet exhibited its movement and reality", and which therefore still contains it only implicitly within itself. "We have to see how this concept of intrinsically real individuality characterizes itself in its moments, and how its concept of itself enters into its consciousness" (##398, 397 GW 9:216; TW 3:294).[24]

---

regardless of whether it presents itself with or without an activity on the part of spirit or whether it is produced by spirit. Spirit is considered according to its activities insofar as the determinations of its consciousness are ascribed to spirit itself." And: "I distinguish the two parts by the fact that spirit *qua consciousness* is active in relation to its determinations as though they were *objects,* so that its activity of determining appears to it as the relation to an object; whereas *qua spirit*, spirit is active only in relation to its own *determinations,* and the changes it undergoes are characterized as its own activities and are considered as such (GW 10,1:8–9, 10,2:825, emphasis added).

[24] The first step has to show how the distinctions to be worked off by spirit arise within spiritual substance in the first place. In a posthumous remark Hegel notes: "Absolute Knowledge [!] makes its first appearance in the guise of reason as lawgiver; in the concept of ethical substance itself there is not distinction between consciousness and being-in-itself; for the pure thinking of pure thought is both in-itself, i.e. self-identical substance, and consciousness at the same time. This means,

That is the first reason why the exposition gets more complicated. The second reason is this. The twenty-one sheets that had already been printed were not originally intended to be followed by a second pass, and now they were supposed to form a harmonious unity with the new part of the book. But the truth is that they clash with the new conception. Since chapter V.C. represents the conclusion of a cycle, the following chapter, "VI. Spirit", ends up—utterly inappropriately—next to V.A (Figure 14.2).

The problems Hegel now came to face show up in the table of contents, where he tries to account for the altered plan by introducing chapter divisions that do not correspond to the text as it had already been printed. At this point, a genuinely satisfying solution was no longer possible. This explains why, according to the table of contents, the book is divided into six main sections, whereas in the text itself we find eight such sections and Hegel himself mentions seven "main sections" in the advertisement he wrote after completing the *Phenomenology*.[25]

When the book was finally printed, Hegel sent a copy to Schelling, writing, "I am curious to hear what you say about the idea of this 1st part which is actually the introduction—for I got no further than the business of introducing, *in mediam rem*.—I feel that working my way into the details was damaging to the general view of the whole, which is by its

---

however, that a determinateness arises within this substance; and the first such determinateness turns out to be that *laws* are promulgated, and in this way a difference arises between consciousness and being-in-itself; this being-in-itself is however ethical substance itself, or absolute consciousness" (GW 9:437).

[25] Whereas the text itself is divided into chapters I through VIII, the table of contents introduces the following division which does not occur as such in the text: (A) consciousness; (B) self-consciousness; (C) (AA) reason; (BB) spirit; (CC) religion; (DD) absolute knowledge. —In Hegel's advertisement, in turn, he writes of his book that it "considers the various *shapes of spirit* as stations along the path into itself by which it becomes [7] pure knowledge or absolute spirit. Accordingly, in the main divisions of this science, which are subdivided in turn, we considered [1] consciousness, [2] self-consciousness, [3] observing reason and reason in action, [4] spirit itself, [5] as ethical, cultured, and moral spirit, and finally [6] as religious spirit in its various forms" (GW 9:446; TW 3:593). It is striking that the fourth "main division", "spirit itself", is to be found neither in the book nor in the table of contents. Since it is situated between "reason in action" and "ethical spirit", it must be identical with the new chapter V.C. ("Individuality that takes itself to be real in and for itself"). There spirit is indeed considered for the first time as *active* spirit that "comes to actuality through its own activity", i.e. as what it is in truth: "spirit itself".

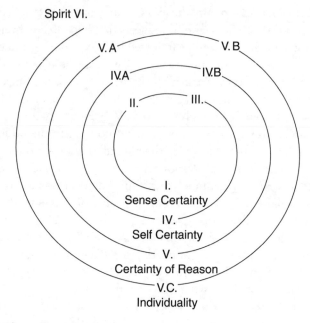

Spirit VI.

Figure 14.2

very nature such an entangled process of passing back and forth that even if it had been made to stand out more distinctly, it would still have cost me a great deal of time before it was really clear and complete."[26]

VI.

I would like to pause here and step back a pace so as to situate Hegel's altered plan in the perspective we have taken up to this point.

The "Science of the Experience of Consciousness" was intended to be an introduction to the logic, leading the reader to the "standpoint of science" from which the logic begins. For this Hegel would not have needed "the concrete shapes of consciousness" that he now decided to include, for the logic itself is a pure movement of the concept, and the "moments of its movement no longer appear there as determinate *shapes* of *consciousness*"

---

[26] Hegel to Schelling, May 1, 1807, *Briefe von und an Hegel,* 1:161.

(#805 GW 9:432; TW 3:589). Because that is so, the original introduction, conceived as an introduction to the logic, was able to limit itself to showing that natural consciousness inevitably develops into the standpoint of science. A reversal of direction from the standpoint of science back to the concrete shapes of consciousness only becomes relevant once we move from logic to *Realphilosophie*.

On the other hand, once the original introduction had been expanded to twice its intended length, there was no longer any room to include the logic in the same volume. Consequently, it would have to be published *together* with the *Realphilosophie* in a second volume. And this is in fact how Hegel announces his plans in his advertisement for the *Phenomenology*: "A *second volume* will contain the system of *logic* as speculative philosophy as well as the two remaining branches of philosophy, the *science of nature* and of *spirit*" (GW 9:447; TW 3:593. Cp. GW 11:8; TW 5:18). It was for this reason that he finally decided to write a "Preface" to the *Phenomenology*, now characterizing the book as an introduction to the *entire* system and not only to the logic.[27]

This, however, goes one step beyond the purpose for which the "science of the experience of consciousness" had originally been conceived, which had been to demonstrate the *actuality* of the (absolute) idea and thereby to justify the claim with which Hegel had concluded his lectures on the history of philosophy in the Summer of 1806:

> This is the standpoint of the present time, and the series of shapes of spirit has for now reached its end.—*Herewith,* this history of philosophy comes to an end. *Hereafter* our standpoint will be the cognition of the idea (TW 20:461, emphasis added).

We must therefore distinguish between two claims:

(1) "This" history of philosophy reaches its end once it has led to the standpoint of knowledge. At that point, philosophy is no longer "love of knowledge", as its name implies, but can finally become "actual knowledge" (#5 GW 9:11; TW 3:13). This is the case as soon as philosophical consciousness, for which the opposition of subject and object initially appeared insurmountable, has been driven by its own nature to

---

[27] However, since the logic was also steadily expanding, Hegel published the *Science of Logic* first (two vols., 1812/16), and the *Realphilosophie* followed in 1817 as part of the *Encyclopaedia of the Philosophical Sciences*.

a standpoint beyond that opposition, a standpoint "at which it gets rid of its semblance of being burdened with something alien, with what is only for it, and some sort of other, and where appearance becomes identical with essence" (#89 GW 9:62; TW 3:81).

(2) "Hereafter", i.e. after completion of this history, Hegel will be concerned to fill this standpoint with content, to move on to cognition of the idea, and to erect a system of "actual knowledge".

VII.

By integrating the concrete parts of his system into the introduction he had now come to refer to as the *Phenomenology of Spirit,* Hegel had not merely conflated these two points of view; he also tried to cover up the resulting cracks (for example in the table of contents and the preface). As a consequence, the notion of philosophy's coming to an end was placed in a false light; for now the impression arose that Hegel's *own system* meant the end of philosophy, an idea that later generations would find unworthy of serious discussion.

And that for good reason. For by definition Hegel's system of science can only be a system of what is present and past. This system is necessarily a closed circle whose end returns (on a higher level) to its beginning, namely spirit's knowledge of itself, the absolute idea. Taken this way, the 'end of philosophy' can only signify a definitive closure after which nothing else can come.

And this is in fact how Hegel understood it: "Talk of the absolute idea might lead one to expect that it is only here that one finally gets around to what is right . . . However, the true content is none other than the entire system whose development we have observed . . . The absolute idea is in this respect comparable to an old man who utters the same religious tenets as the child, but for whom they are invested with the meaning of his whole life" (*Encyclopaedia* [1830] §237Z, TW 8:389). It is a direct consequence of this that, for Hegel, a philosophical science can only shed proper light on what already exists—like the lived life the old man looks back upon.

It may be hard to accept this systematic exclusion of all that is genuinely new from philosophical science. But neither are we forced to accept it since, on my view, there is no need to limit scientific activity to what already exists. Hegel's system is not the only possible science after the end of philosophy in sense (1) above. In fact, *two* alternatives emerge "hereafter" for filling out the standpoint of science with content:

(a) Hegel's own top-down path from the absolute idea to the system of actuality in the *Realphilosophie;* and

(b) the bottom-up path, the path from concrete phenomena to the ideas that correspond to them. This latter path is that of *scientia intuitive* as we became familiar with it in Chapters 4 and, especially, 11.

If we now look back at Chapter 6, at Kant's discussion of a non-discursive understanding in section 77 of the *Critique of Teleological Judgment,* we can see that, in a certain way—*mutatis mutandis*—the two alternatives (a) and (b) correspond to the distinction Kant makes there between two different conceptions of intuitive understanding: (α) an intuitive understanding that has as its object nature as a *whole,* "indeed the whole of nature as a system" (5:409), which we must conceive as "the cause of the world" (5:410); and (β) an intuitive understanding that focuses on *individual* products of nature in order to "represent the possibility of the parts (in their individual character and in their combination) as dependent on the whole" and so to determine the particular on the basis of the "synthetic universal" (5:407), i.e. the idea.

Kant thought that both paths were equally incapable of being realized since he believed that human understanding is exclusively discursive. That belief proved untenable, and both Goethe and Hegel agree that we must move beyond it. Even so, the distinction between the two is notable: Hegel's concern is to provide determinate content for the standpoint of the infinite understanding (which is also the cause of the world) in such a way as to derive the system of philosophical knowledge from it; in *scientia intuitiva* as conceived for example by Goethe, on the other hand, the goal is to see how, in the case of concrete natural phenomena, the particular emerges from a synthetic universal. Although it was Goethe who inspired Hegel's procedure in the *Phenomenology of Spirit* of following the ascent to the universal with a descent into the particular, Hegel's overarching goal is nonetheless quite different from Goethe's.

In contrast to (a), (b) represents a path that is, though seldom taken, fundamentally open to the new. Like (a), (b) also presupposes a scientific standpoint beyond the subject-object dichotomy. The notion that the essence of things can be discovered within the intuitive understanding is comprehensible from this standpoint alone: the idea manifests itself in things, on the one side, as their essence, and in the subject, on the other side, as their concept (in contradistinction to *representation*).[28] *Scientia intuitiva* therefore begins with the assumption that there are no fewer ideas than there are *Urphänomene* in which those ideas manifest themselves. For as we saw in Chapter 11, the phenomena of color are based on a wholly different idea than, say, the life-cycle of an annual flowering plant.

Nor, of course, does a multiplicity of ideas contradict the fact of a single, unified reality. Just as a concept (the manifestation of the idea in the subject) is impossible in isolation from the broader conceptual network, and just as an isolated *Urphänomen* is an impossibility, neither is it conceivable that there could be ideas existing apart from any connection with other ideas. They too must be moments of an internally differentiated whole: they must stand to each other in relations of greater or lesser affinity, mutually conditioning, facilitating, impeding, or excluding one another, and hence they must be hierarchically ordered and subordinated to a highest (absolute) idea constituting the internal nexus of the whole. Goethe remarks in this connection: "What is highest is the intuition of the different as identical" (HA 12:366). "Man must be able to elevate himself to the highest reason if he is to touch the deity that is revealed in *Urphänomenen,* physical and moral, behind which it lies and from which they arise."[29]

Differently from Hegelian science, *scientia intuitiva* is methodologically characterized by the fact that it does not take the highest idea as its point of departure, but strives on the contrary to ascend ever closer to it in cognition. "The more we know individual things, the more we know God," Spinoza had said of the third kind of knowledge in the *Ethics* (E5p24); in this he inspired Goethe's unqualified agreement (cp. HABr 1:475–76). And so we read in the *Theory of Colors:*

> We believe ourselves to have earned the philosopher's gratitude for having sought to pursue the phenomena all the way to their original sources [= the *Urphänomene*], to the point at which they merely appear and are and where there is nothing left in them to explain (Introduction, LA I,4:21; HA 13:327).

---

[28] 'Concept' is here to be understood strictly in the sense worked out in Chapter 11. In a so-called concept that has been formed from representations by a subject, the idea and hence also the essence of things *cannot* manifest themselves—as became evident in the presentation of "observing reason".

[29] Eckermann, *Gespräche mit Goethe,* February 13, 1829.

If . . . the physicist can attain to knowledge of what we have called an *Urphänomen,* he may rest secure and the philosopher with him; *he* is secure because he can convince himself that he has reached the limit of his science, that he is standing at the empirical summit from where he can gaze back and survey all the stages of his experiments, and gaze forward into the realm of theory into which, though he may not enter, he still may peer. And the philosopher is secure since from the hand of the physicist he takes a final result that in his own becomes a starting point (§720 LA I,4:211; HA 13:482–83).

That in his own becomes a starting point. With this phrase Goethe states why philosophy need not come to an end even after the completion of its history. It would fall within philosophy's domain as a science to investigate the internal connections among the ideas that are manifest in the *Urphänomene,* and to generate a systematic presentation of them. And insofar as metaphysics is the scientific cognition of the supersensible, the systematic ordering of all the ideas derived from *Urphänomene* would constitute a metaphysics of the future.

It seems that Goethe himself would liked to have taken some steps in this direction: "Perhaps we will find an opportunity in the future . . . to establish connections among the elementary phenomena of nature by our method" (§757 LA I,4:223; HA 13:493). At the same time, however, he was aware that the requisite knowledge of all the *Urphänomene* lay in the distant future, as did a metaphysics of the ideas they manifest, and also that *scientia intuitiva* was bound at first, like all things genuinely new, to meet with disapproval and incomprehension.

So let us summarize: When speaking of the "end of philosophy", two senses of "end" must be distinguished: completion and cessation. One cycle comes to completion in order to give way to a new one; for something to cease is for it to have exhausted its inner drive.[30]

In this sense, we can say that "this" history of philosophy is *complete* when it has sublated the subject-object dichotomy that previously constituted it, thereby giving birth to a new kind of thought distinct from the

---

[30] This corresponds, on a temporal level, to the distinction Kant makes in §57 of the *Prolegomena* between 'boundary' [*Grenze*] and 'limit' [*Schranke*]: "[I]n all boundaries there is also something positive . . . whereas limits contain mere negations". A boundary is something positive "which belongs both to that which lies inside it and to the space external to a given content" (4:354, 361).

discursive thought which had been appropriate within the dichotomy that previously laid claim to (almost) exclusive validity. This would mean that all previous philosophy had reached its boundary: a new cycle and a new 'history' could begin.

Alternatively, the history of philosophy may be said to have *come to an end* in the sense that, in the end, only a closed system is possible, and once such a system is erected philosophy would have exhausted its potential.

If we are careful to distinguish between these two senses of 'end', it becomes clear that even if Hegel's system were successful on its own assumptions (a question I would answer in the negative, but which I can leave aside here), this still would not entail the end of *philosophy* since, after the "science of the experience of consciousness" has led to the standpoint of science, another kind of philosophical science is still possible, a kind that is not identical with Hegel's system and which is in contrast to it fundamentally open to the future: *scientia intuitiva*. With his "science of the experience of consciousness", provided it was successful, Hegel would in fact have provided philosophical justification for *scientia intuitiva*, i.e. for the form of cognition that Spinoza had demanded without being able to formulate it in methodologically adequate terms, and whose methodology Goethe was the first to work out, yet without being able to provide philosophical justification. In the first half of the *Phenomenology*, Hegel would have given philosophical proof that the postulated standpoint beyond the subject-object dichotomy is in fact an objective reality.

Therefore: on the assumption (to which I will return once more in the epilogue) that Hegel's description of the path of philosophical consciousness to the standpoint of science is in principle correct, I believe that our conclusion from the twenty-five years of philosophy must nevertheless diverge from Hegel's: The path of *scientia intuitiva* alone is still open.

Epilogue: An End of Philosophy

The twenty-five years of philosophy are the years in which philosophy became a science, thereby also arriving at knowledge of itself. Let us look back over the path that we have traveled.

Philosophy (metaphysics) claims to be cognition of the world purely on the basis of thought. It thus presupposes non-empirical, but nonetheless veridical reference to objects. In order to investigate whether and in what way such a thing could be possible at all, Kant inaugurates transcendental philosophy, which accordingly abstracts from all given objects in order to consider the human cognitive faculty by itself. Before it had arrived at the results of its investigation, philosophy as a science was not possible (Ch. 1).

This first characterization of transcendental philosophy proves upon reflection to be insufficient. On the one hand, it is not possible for it to abstract from *everything* that is given, since the objective reality of the categories cannot be demonstrated without an a priori determination of the *empirical* concept of matter. On the other hand, it turns out that the conditions under which a metaphysics of morals is possible are no less in need of explanation than are the conditions that make a metaphysics of nature possible, since the highest principle of morality still requires proof (Ch. 2).

In this way, it becomes necessary to expand transcendental philosophy in two directions. It requires (a) proof of the constructibility of the object of outer sense; (b) the discovery and justification of the highest principle of morality. Since in the case of morality objective reference as such is unproblematic, transcendental philosophy must now be defined more broadly as an investigation into the possibility of synthetic propositions a priori (Ch. 3).

With Lessing's assertion that Spinoza's philosophy is the only possible philosophy, a competing alternative to transcendental philosophy arises. For according to Spinoza, the criterion of scientific knowledge is the ability to derive the properties of an object from its essence or its proximate cause (*scientia intuitiva*) (Ch. 4).

In the meantime, the integration of morality into transcendental philosophy entails a twofold problem: Since the moral law is to be realized in the sensible world, and since the sensible world is subject to a causal determinism that rules out the existence of purposes, a conflict arises between the legislation of practical reason and that of theoretical reason, which thus appear as disjoint and indeed as incompatible (Ch. 5).

Only in the supersensible substrate of appearances is it possible to unify these two legislations with each other and with a nature that agrees with them, which in turn is necessary if reason is to accord with itself. Contrary to its original conception, transcendental philosophy thus comes to have its foundation in the object of outer sense and the condition of its internal unity in a supersensible substrate (Ch. 6). Moreover, precise consideration of the reflective power of judgment also shows that we are compelled to conceive of the supersensible as something unconditional in which thought and being, what is and what ought to be, mechanism and purpose are inseparably one.

Although it is a conceptual necessity, Kant continues to insist that the link between the sensible and the supersensible is fundamentally beyond human cognition. In order to prove this, he contrasts the human cognitive faculty with something which, according to him, it is not and cannot be: intellectual intuition and intuitive understanding. In this way, though, he also gives the first precise characterization of these two faculties (Ch. 6). Yet by doing so, Kant also casts doubt on his own assertion that they are inaccessible to the human mind and that the supersensible is therefore necessarily beyond human cognition: According to Fichte, we realize an intellectual intuition in every single self-intuition of the I; and Goethe sees that he has already realized Kant's intuitive understanding by basing his study of the metamorphosis of plants on it (Ch. 7). From this point on, the question of the knowability of the supersensible takes center stage.

According to Fichte, the essence of the I is that it (a) is what it is only *through itself* (self-positing); and that it (b) must be what it is *for itself* (self-consciousness). This, however, entails further that (a') the I knows its being as its deed, and this consciousness of the unity of thought and being is not a receptive intuition, but a productive, an intellectual intuition. And (b') the determinate actions that the supersensible I must perform in order to posit itself can be brought to consciousness step by step and made into objects of cognition. In this way, what was for Kant an unfathomable root in which the sensible and supersensible worlds are united becomes, in the case of the human I, a legitimate object of investigation (Chs. 8, 9).

374

However, if we must conceive of the supersensible as something unconditional, in which thought and being, spirit and nature are inseparably one, then Fichte's philosophy of freedom is only a first step toward its cognition. Schelling therefore insists on an exposition of nature's origination from the common root (Ch. 9).

Schelling's attempt to base the method of his *Naturphilosophie* on Fichte's intellectual intuition inevitably leads to the dissolution of intellectual intuition. For in order to employ it for cognition of *nature,* it would have to be possible to abstract from the subject of intuition in the act of intuition itself. With this step, intuition ceases to be productive, however, and becomes intuitive understanding (Ch. 10).

It was Goethe who elaborated a methodology of intuitive understanding based on Spinoza and Kant. It consists in bringing together related phenomena and grasping them in such a way as to form a whole. In a further step, the transitions between the phenomena must be re-created in thought in order to tell whether the whole was already at work in them or whether the parts are only externally connected. If the former is the case, then an idea becomes accessible to experience as the ideal whole to which the sensible parts owe their existence and their specific character (Ch.11).

Hegel applied this method to philosophy itself in order to achieve philosophical knowledge of the supersensible. Since philosophical consciousness is a consciousness that makes a truth claim, he began by setting up a complete series of such shapes of consciousness in order to make the transitions between them reproducible in thought. (Whether or not the series is in fact complete can be determined only by actually going through and trying to re-produce the transitions one by one.) When the philosophical consciousness of the present now looks back over its past shapes and reproduces the transitions between them in thought, it grasps what it thereby experiences as the knowledge of something that consciousness itself has not produced but merely aided in making visible. This is a self-moving, spiritual content which, although discoverable only in the thinking subject, exists independently of it and is objectively real. In this experience, consciousness apprehends the effects of a supersensible spiritual reality. In this way, it has attained the standpoint of *scientia intuitiva* (Chs. 12–14).

And thus these twenty-five years of philosophy come to an end. What remains open, however, is the question of the legitimacy of the assumption with which the last chapter ended: the question whether Hegel's presentation of the transitions in his 'science of the experience of consciousness'—and hence also the introduction to the standpoint of science—is correct. The majority of readers have denied that it is. The classical and continually recurring objection is that the steps in Hegel's argumentation are lacking in necessity; that the historical shapes that he discerns do not exhaust the alternatives; that, on the contrary, many new alternatives have emerged since Hegel's time in science, art, and so on.

I cannot subscribe to this objection for the following reasons:

(1) As we saw at the beginning of Chapter 13, Hegel is not concerned in the *Phenomenology* with 'historical shapes'—these are ultimately no more than examples and could be replaced by equally serviceable 'alternatives'. Rather, Hegel is interested in the 'method of the passing over of one form into another and the emergence of one form out of the other'. But then the question is not whether there are alternatives to Hegel's examples, to the historical shapes chosen by him, but whether there are alternatives *to the transitions between them.*

(2) And here again, the question is not whether we today, with the conceptual means placed at our disposal by the current level of development, might be able to imagine different transitions, but whether a different transition would be possible for the observed consciousness *on its level.* What *we* can imagine is therefore irrelevant to answering this question.

(3) If this is conceded, then the objection ought rather to be formulated this way: it is not convincing that a specific transition is supposed to be necessary for consciousness at its given level. And such an objection may, in any given case, in fact be justified. Then the question becomes: Is the transition itself not necessary, or has its necessity simply not been convincingly presented? As long as we find that some of the *other* transitions are necessary, we can always be sure that the problem is one of *presentation.* That is the crucial point! If a whole makes its parts possible and gives them their shape, then it must be active in all the parts and in all their transitions, not only in some. If that activity (necessity) has been recognized in some of the transitions but not in others, all this implies is that the latter have not yet been adequately grasped and presented.

(4) Hegel's project could therefore only be said to have 'failed' if no necessity whatsoever was to be found in the 'science of the experience of consciousness', and if instead the transitions between shapes were contingent and thus might have happened differently. But that assumption is unwarranted, as I hope to have shown in Chapter 13 despite the undeniable imperfections in my presentation.

When I say that this is the result of the twenty-five years of philosophy, I do not mean to imply that there had not been philosophical approaches prior to that which exhibited some similarities with what I have described as intuitive thought. Compared with what we have explored here, however, those approaches seem rather more like side paths branching off from the main course of philosophical development. Nor were they demanded by what preceded them, in contrast to the epoch described in this book.

Nor do I wish to assert that the line of argument presented here robs discursive thought of its legitimacy. On the contrary: it must be mastered before one can move beyond it. It does, however, seem to me that today discursive thought has lost its position of exclusive dominance. In this respect it could perhaps be compared with Euclidean geometry which, too, was long held to be the only possible geometry and hence by default the one that describes reality; today we know that spaces with zero-curvature are merely one possibility, and that the validity of Euclidean geometry is limited to these.

I think something similar is also true of discursive thought. Consider Kant's starting point one last time. The existence of an antinomy proved to him that discursive thought, shaped as it is by sensibility and dependent as it is on sensibility, leads to contradictions as soon as it is applied to anything other than sensibility. This led Kant to conclude that the supersensible cannot be known. That, however, is an incomplete disjunction. One can as easily conclude that if supersensible reality is to be known, non-discursive thought is required. What I have tried to show in this book is that between 1781 and 1806 a *philosophical* justification was worked out, demonstrating that this is not idle speculation but a real possibility—a possibility whose potential has still to be realized. The future of a philosophy 'that will be able to come forward as a science' has only just begun.

This book is an English translation of *Die 25 Jahre der Philosophie: Eine systematische Rekonstruktion* (Frankfurt am Main: Vittorio Klostermann 2011). Förster's work represents a sustained engagement with the texts of classical German philosophy and associated primary literature in the original language. The question thus arises as to how best to deal with this variety of primary texts, some of them available in English translation and some of them not. It fortunately happens that for several of the philosophers who figure most prominently in the book, widely available, authoritative, and relatively complete translations are there to be drawn upon. This is especially so in the case of Immanuel Kant: the translations comprising the *Cambridge Edition of the Works of Immanuel Kant* (1995–) have been consulted throughout and most frequently adopted. For the *Critique of Pure Reason,* Norman Kemp Smith's translation (London: Macmillan 1929) has also been consulted. With the exception of the *Critique of Pure Reason,* Kant's works are cited by volume and page number of the Akademie-Ausgabe (Berlin: de Gruyter 1900–); the Cambridge edition includes the pagination of this edition. References to the *Critique of Pure Reason* are given in the customary form, indicating the first (A) or second (B) edition and the page numbers. Here and in the case of the English editions mentioned below, all translations have been tacitly modified where necessary for accuracy and to maintain consistency with the main text and each other.

Wherever possible, Fichte's works have been cited according to Daniel Breazeale's translations, specifically his English version of the "Review of *Aenesidemus,*" "Concerning the Concept of the *Wissenschaftslehre,*" and the "Outline of the Distinctive Character of the *Wissenschaftslehre* with Respect to the Theoretical Faculty." All of these are to be found in the volume edited by Breazeale, *Fichte: Early Philosophical Writings* (Ithaca,

NY: Cornell University Press 1988). In the case of the *Grundlage der gesammten Wissenschaftslehre,* I have consulted the only available complete English translation, that of Peter Heath and John Lachs, *Science of Knowledge (Wissenschaftslehre), with First and Second Introductions* (New York: Appleton Century Crofts 1970). Here again, Fichte's texts are cited on the basis of the standard German editions: *Gesamtausgabe der Bayerischen Akademie der Wissenschaften* [GA] (1964ff.) and *Sämtliche Werke,* edited by I. H. Fichte [W] (1854ff.). The translations by Breazeale and Heath/Lachs include the pagination of one or both of these editions.

Despite increasing attention in recent years, there is no authoritative and complete edition of Schelling's works in English. The following translations were consulted and adopted where appropriate: *Philosophical Letters on Dogmatism and Criticism,* in *The Unconditional in Human Knowledge: Four early essays 1794–6,* trans. F. Marti (Lewisburg, PA: Bucknell University Press 1980); *On the History of Modern Philosophy,* trans. and ed. Andrew Bowie (Cambridge: Cambridge University Press 1994); *First Outline of a System of the Philosophy of Nature,* trans. Keith R. Peterson (Albany: State University of New York Press 2004); *System of Transcendental Idealism,* trans. Peter Heath (Charlottesville: University Press of Virginia 1978). Schelling's works are cited on the basis of the standard German editions: *Sämmtliche Werke,* edited by Karl Friedrich August Schelling [SW] (Stuttgart and Augsburg 1856–), and where available, to the ongoing critical edition of the Schelling Kommission of the Bayerische Akademie der Wissenschaften [AA] (Stuttgart-Bad Cannstatt: frommann-holzboog 1976–). The Heath and Peterson translations include the pagination of one or both of these editions.

Similarly, for many of the texts by Hegel cited in this book, there is no widely recognized standard English edition, and in some cases there is no previous translation at all. Hence all translations of Hegel's works are my own, with the exception of the *Phenomenology of Spirit.* In this latter case, I have consulted the widely used English translation by A. V. Miller (Oxford: Oxford University Press 1977) throughout, again modifying it where necessary for accuracy and consistency with the main text. This edition has the added benefit that Miller has numbered Hegel's paragraphs consecutively, greatly facilitating reference; his numbering is included here in addition to the page numbers of the standard German editions: *Werke in zwanzig Bänden,* edited by Eva Moldenhauer and Karl Markus Michel [TW] (Frankfurt am Main: Suhrkamp 1971); and

Gesammelte Werke, edited by the Rheinisch-Westfälische Akademie der Wissenschaften [GW] (Hamburg: Meiner 1968–). In the case of Hegel's correspondence, I have consulted the English translation *Hegel: The Letters,* by Clark Butler and Christiane Seller (Bloomington, IN: Indiana University Press 1984), modifying it tacitly and supplying my own translations when necessary. Hegel's letters are cited according to the edition *Briefe von und an Hegel,* edited by Johannes Hoffmeister (Hamburg: Meiner 1952), and are identified by date and sender or recipient.

Goethe's letters and other texts have with few exceptions been translated directly on the basis of the German editions, and all references are to these. In the case of his scientific writings, however, I have consulted Douglas Miller's translation: J. W. von Goethe, *Scientific Studies* (Princeton, NJ: Princeton University Press 1988).

Friedrich Heinrich Jacobi's main works are available in the widely used English translation by George di Giovanni: *The Main Philosophical Writings and the Novel "Allwill"* (Montreal: McGill-Queen's University Press, 1994). This translation has been adopted wherever possible, and references to it are given together with those to the German editions (eds. Roth and Köppen 1812–25 [JW]; eds. Hammacher and Jaeschke (1998—) [JWA]), separated by a slash (e.g., JWA 1,1:13/183). Di Giovanni's translation contains only selections from Jacobi's writings. In the case of texts or passages not included in the English edition, the translations are my own.

Except where noted, the translations of all other primary and secondary texts in German are my own. In the case of primary texts that are not in German, wherever possible I have adopted the translations of standard English editions; these are listed in the main bibliography of this book.

6:12	*Kant's Gesammelte Schriften* (Akademie Ausgabe), volume and page number
A/B	First/Second Edition, *Kant's Critique of Pure Reason*
AA	Schelling, *Historisch-Kritische Ausgabe*
E	Spinoza, *Ethics, Demonstrated in Geometric Order* (app = appendix, p = proposition, c = corollary, s = scholium, d = definition, dem = demonstration, lem = lemma)
GVB	*Goethes Briefwechsel mit Christian Gottlob Voigt*
GA	Fichte, Gesamtausgabe der Bayrischen Akademie der Wissenschaft
GW	Hegel, *Gesammelte Werke* (Akademie Ausgabe)
HA	*Goethes Werke* (Hamburger Ausgabe)
HABr.	*Goethes Briefe* (Hamburger Ausgabe)
JW	Jacobi, *Werke*. Eds. F. Roth and F. Köppen
JWA	Jacobi, *Werke*. Eds. K. Hammacher and W. Jaeschke
LA	Goethe, *Die Schriften zur Naturwissenschaft* (Leopoldina Edition)
MGS	Mendelssohn, *Gesammelte Schriften*
SW	Schelling, *Sämmtliche Werke*. Ed. K. F. A. Schelling
TIE	Spinoza, *Treatise on the Emendation of the Intellect*
TW	Hegel, *Werke in zwanzig Bänden*. Eds. E. Moldenhauer and K. M. Michel
W	*Fichte Werke*. Ed. I. H. Fichte
WA	*Goethes Werke* (Weimarer Ausgabe)
#	Number of paragraph in Hegel, *Phenomenology of Spirit*

1. Primary Texts

Alhacen. *De aspectibus.* Ed. A. Mark Smith. Philadelphia: American Philosophical Society 2001.

Aristotle. *The Complete Works.* Ed. Jonathan Barnes. 2 vols. Princeton, NJ: Princeton University Press 1984.

Baader, Franz von. *Sämtliche Werke.* Ed. Franz Hoffmann et al. Reprint Aalen: Scientia Verlag 1987.

Bayle, Pierre. *Historisches und kritisches Wörterbuch.* Nach der neuesten Auflage von 1740 ins Deutsche übersetzt etc. von J. Chr. Gottsched. Leipzig 1744. Reprint Hildesheim: Olms 1978.

Berkeley, George. *A Treatise Concerning the Principles of Human Knowledge* (1710). Ed. G. Warnock. London: Collins/Fontana 1975.

———. *Three Dialogues between Hylas and Philonous* (1713). Ed. G. Warnock. London: Collins/Fontana 1975.

Böttinger, Karl August. *Literarische Zustände und Zeitgenossen. Begegnungen und Gespräche im klassischen Weimar* (1838). Berlin: Aufbau-Verlag 1998.

Briefe von und an Hegel. Ed. Johannes Hoffmeister. 3rd ed. Hamburg: Meiner 1952.

Capelle, Wilhelm, ed. *Die Vorsokratiker.* Stuttgart: Kröner 1968.

Descartes, Rene. *Oeuvres.* Ed. Charles Adam and Paul Tannery. Paris: Cerf 1897–1913.

Diels, Hermann, ed. *Die Fragmente der Vorsokratiker.* 7th ed. Berlin: Weidmann 1954.

Diogenes Laertius. *Lives of Eminent Philosophers.* Trans. R. D. Hicks. Cambridge, MA: Harvard University Press 1925.

Eckermann, J. P. *Gespräche mit Goethe in den letzten Jahren seines Lebens.* Frankfurt am Main: Insel 1981.

Eschenmayer, K. A. "Spontaneität=Weltseele oder das höchste Prinzip der Naturphilosophie", *Zeitschrift für speculative Physik.* Bd. 2, Heft 1 (1801), 3–68.

Euclid. *The Thirteen Books of the Elements.* Trans. Sir Thomas Heath. 2nd ed. New York: Dover 1956.

———. *The Optics of Euclid.* Trans. Harry Edwin Burton. In *Journal of the Optical Society of America* 35:5 (1945).

Euler, Leonhard. *Briefe an eine deutsche Prinzessin* (1769). Leipzig: Johann Friedrich Junius. Reprint Braunschweig: Vieweg 1986.

Fichte, I. H., ed. *Joh. Gottl. Fichtes Leben und literarischer Briefwechsel.* 2nd ed. vol. 1. Leipzig 1862. (1st ed. 1830)

Fichte, J. G. *Fichtes Werke.* Ed. Immanuel Hermann Fichte. Berlin: de Gruyter 1971.

———. *Gesamtausgabe der Bayrischen Akademie der Wissenschaft.* Ed. H. Gliwitzky, H. Jacob, and R. Lauth. Stuttgart-Bad Cannstatt: frommann-holzboog 1961ff.

———. *Züricher Vorlesungen über den Begriff der Wissenschaftslehre: Februar 1794.* Nachschrift Lavater. Ed. Erich Fuchs. Neuried: Ars Una 1996.

J. G. Fichte im Gespräch. Ed. Erich Fuchs. 6 vols. Stuttgart-Bad Cannstatt: frommann-holzboog 1978–92.

J. G. Fichte in zeitgenössischen Rezensionen. Ed. Erich Fuchs, Wilhelm G. Jacobs, and Walter Schieche. 4 vols. Stuttgart-Bad Cannstatt: frommann-holzboog 1995.

Garve, Christian. *Gesammelte Werke.* Reprint Hildesheim: Olms 1986.

Goethe, Johann Wolfgang. *Die Schriften zur Naturwissenschaft.* Ed. im Auftrage der Deutschen Akademie der Naturforscher Leopoldina. Weimar: Böhlaus Nachfolger 1947ff.

———. *Goethes Werke.* Ed. im Auftrage der Großherzogin Sophie von Sachsen (Weimarer Ausgabe). Weimar: Hermann Böhlau 1887–1919.

———. *Goethes Werke.* Hamburger Ausgabe, 14 vols. Ed. Erich Trunz. 14th ed. München: C. H. Beck 1989.

———. *Goethes Briefe.* Hamburger Ausgabe, 4 vols. Ed. Karl Robert Mankelow. 3rd ed. München: C. H. Beck 1986.

———. *Tagebücher. Historisch-kritische Ausgabe.* Ed. A. Döhler. vol. 3. Stuttgart: J. B. Metzler 2004.

———. *Corpus der Goethe Zeichnungen.* Ed. der Nationalen Forschungs- und Gedenkstätten der klassischen deutschen Literatur in Weimar. Leipzig: E. A. Seemann Buch- und Kunstverlag 1958–73.

Goethe. *Begegnungen and Gespräche.* Ed. Renate Grumach. Berlin: 1965ff.

Goethes Gespräche. Biedermannsche Ausgabe, ed. Wolfgang Herwig. München: Deutscher Taschenbuch Verlag 1998.

Goethes Briefwechsel mit Christian Gottlob Voigt. Schriften der Goethe-Gesellschaft. vols. 53–56. Weimar: H. Bohlaus Nachfolger 1949ff.

Hamann, Johann Georg. *Briefwechsel.* Ed. Arthur Henkel. Frankfurt am Main: Insel 1965.

Hegel, Georg Wilhelm Friedrich. *Werke in zwanzig Bänden.* Ed. Eva Moldenhauer and Karl Markus Michel. Frankfurt am Main: Suhrkamp 1971.

———. *Gesammelte Werke.* Ed. Rheinisch-Westfälische Akademie der Wissenschaften. Hamburg: Meiner 1968ff.

———. *Dissertatio Philosophica de Orbitis Planetarum.* Ed. and trans. Wolfgang Neuser. Weinheim: Acta humaniora d. VCH 1986.

Hegel in Berichten seiner Zeitgenossen. Ed. Günther Nicolin. Hamburg: Meiner 1970.

Hegel, Karl, ed. *Briefe von und an Hegel.* Leipzig: Dunker & Humblot 1887.

Herder, Johann Gottfried. *Gott. Einige Gespräche* (1787). In *Johann Gottfried Herder Werke*. vol. 4. Frankfurt am Main: Deutscher Klassiker Verlag 1994.

———. *Werke*. Ed. Wolfgang Pross. München: Hanser 1984.

———. *Briefe*. Ed. Wilhelm Dobbek and Günter Arnold. Weimar: Hermann Böhlaus Nachfolger 1977ff.

———. *Ideen zur Philosophie der Geschichte der Menschheit* (1784–1791). Darmstadt: Joseph Merzer 1966.

Hölderlin, Friedrich. *Sämtliche Werke*. Ed. Friedrich Beisner. Stuttgart: Kohlhammer 1943ff.

———. *Sämtliche Werke*. Ed. D. E. Sattler. Frankfurt am Main: Stroemfeld/Roter Stern 1975ff.

Hume, David. *A Treatise of Human Nature* (1739). Oxford: Oxford University Press 1978.

———. *Enquiries concerning Human Understanding and concerning the Principles of Morals* (1777). Oxford: Oxford University Press 1975.

Iamblichus. *On the Pythagorean Life*. Trans. Gillian Clarke, Liverpool: Liverpool University Press 1989.

Ibn Esra, Abraham ben Meïr. *Buch der Einheit* [*Sefer ha-Echad*]. Trans. Ernst Müller. Berlin: Welt-Verlag 1921.

Jacobi, Friedrich Heinrich. *Werke*. Ed. F. Roth and F. Köppen. Leipzig: Gerhard Fleischer d. Jüng. 1812–25.

———. *Werke*. Ed. Klaus Hammacher and Walter Jaeschke. Hamburg: Meiner 1998ff.

Kants Gesammelte Schriften. Akademie Ausgabe. Berlin: Reimer, later de Gruyter 1900ff.

Kant, Immanuel. *Prolegomena zu einer jeden künftigen Metaphysik, die als Wissenschaft wird auftreten können*. Ed. Rudolf Malter. Stuttgart: Reclam 1989.

Kepler, Johannes. *Weltharmonik*. Ed. and trans. Max Casper. München: Oldenbourg 1997.

Leibniz, Gottfried Wilhelm. *Essays de Théodicée* (1710). Ed. and trans. Herbert Herring. Darmstadt: Wissenschaftliche Buchgesellschaft 1985.

———. *Die philosophischen Schriften*. Ed. C. I. Gerhardt. 7 vols. Berlin: Weidmann 1875–90. Reprint Hildesheim: Olms 1978.

The Leibniz-Clarke Correspondence (1715/1716). Ed. H. G. Alexander. Manchester: Manchester University Press 1956.

Lessing, Gottfried Ephraim. *Werke*. Ed. Kurt Wölfel. Frankfurt: Insel 1967.

Lichtenberg, Georg Christoph. *Aphorismen, Schriften, Briefe*. Ed. Wolfgang Promies. München: Hanser 1974.

Lucretius. *On the Nature of Things*. Trans. W. H. D. Rouse. Ed. M. F. Smith. Cambridge, MA: Harvard University Press 1992.

Maimon, Salomon. *Versuch über die Transzendentalphilosophie* (1790). Ed. Florian Ehrensperger. Hamburg: Meiner 2004.

Meister Eckhart. *Deutsche Predigten und Traktate*. Ed. Josef Quint. München: Hanser 1963.

Mendelssohn, Moses. *Gesammelte Schriften*. Ed. F. Bamberger u. a. Stuttgart-Bad Cannstatt: Friedrich Frommann 1971ff.

Newton, Isaac. *Philosophiae Naturalis Principia Mathematica, the Third Edition with Variant Readings*. Ed. A. Koyré and I. B. Cohen. 2 vols. Cambridge, MA: Harvard University Press, 1972.

———. *Opticks, or a Treatise of the Reflections, Refractions, Inflections & Colours of Light*. New York: Dover 1952.

Novalis. *Schriften*. Ed. Richard Samuel. vol. 2. Stuttgart: Kohlhammer 1981.

Plato. *Complete Works*. Ed. John M. Cooper. Indianapolis: Hacket 1997.

Reinhold, Karl Leonhard. *Die Hebräischen Mysterien oder die älteste religiöse Freymaurerey*. Leipzig: Georg Joachim Göschen 1788. Ed. Jan Assman. 2nd ed. Neckargmünd: Edition Mnemosyne 2006.

———. "Briefe über die Kantische Philosophie". In *Teutscher Merkur* 1786/7.

———. *Versuch einer neuen Theorie des menschlichen Vorstellungsvermögens*. Prag: C. Widtmann and J. M. Mauke 1789.

———. *Beyträge zur Berichtigung bisheriger Mißverstände der Philosophen*. Jena: J. M. Mauke 1790.

———. *Über das Fundament des philosophischen Wissens*. Jena: J. M. Mauke 1791.

Schelling, Friedrich Wilhelm Joseph. *Briefe und Dokumente*. Ed. Horst Fuhrmans. Bonn: Bouvier 1962.

———. *Sämmtliche Werke*. Ed. Karl Friedrich August Schelling. Stuttgart and Augsburg 1856ff.

———. *Historisch-kritische Ausgabe*. Ed. Hans Michael Baumgartner, et al. Stuttgart-Bad Cannstatt: frommann-holzboog 1976ff.

———. "Timaeus" (1794). Ed. Hartmut Buchner. Stuttgart-Bad Cannstatt: frommann-holzboog 1994.

Schelver, Franz Joseph, ed. *Zeitschrift für organische Physik*. Bd. 1, Heft 1. Halle: Rengerschen Buchhandlung 1802.

———. *Die Aufgabe der höheren Botanik*. Verhandlungen der Kaiserlich Leopoldinisch-Carolinischen Academie der Naturforscher. vol 2. Bonn: Adolph Marcus Buchhandlung 1821.

———. *Lebens- und Formgeschichte der Pflanzenwelt*. Heidelberg: Joseph Engelmann 1822.

Schiller, Friedrich. *Werke*. Nationalausgabe. Weimar: Hermann Böhlaus Nachfolger 1943ff.

———. *Der Briefwechsel zwischen Friedrich Schiller und Wilhelm von Humboldt*. Ed. Siegfried Seidel. Berlin: Aufbau 1962.

Schlegel, Friedrich. *Kritische Ausgabe*. Ed. Ernst Behler. München: Schöningh 1958ff.

Schopenhauer, Arthur. *Die Welt als Wille und Vorstellung*. Ed. Ludger Lütkehaus. 2 vols. Zürich: Haffmans Verlag 1988.

Schulze, Gottlob Ernst. *Aenesidemus oder über die Fundamente der von dem Herrn Reinhold in Jena gelieferten Elementar-Philosophie. Nebst einer Vertheidigung des Skepticismus gegen die Anmaassungen der Vernunftkritik* (1792). Reprint Berlin: Reuther & Reichard 1911.

Spinoza. *Collected Works*. Trans. E. M. Curley, vol.1. Princeton, NJ: Princeton University Press 1985.

———. *The Letters*. Trans. S. Shirley. Indianapolis: Hackett 1995.

Steffens, Henrich. *Was ich erlebte. Aus der Erinnerung niedergeschrieben.* 10 vols. Breslau: Max und Komp 1840–44.

Steiner, Rudolf. *Gesamtausgabe.* Dornach: Rudolf Steiner Verlag 1955ff.

Troxler, Ignaz P. V. *Vorlesungsnachschrift von Schellings und Hegels erster absoluter Metaphysik (1801–1802).* Ed. Klaus Düsing. Köln: Jürgen Dinter 1988.

Wolff, Christian. *B. v. S. Sittenlehre, widerlegt von dem berühmten Weltweisen unserer Zeit Herrn Christian Wolff.* Trans. Johann Lorenz Schmidt. Frankfurt and Leipzig 1744.

2. Secondary Texts

Abeken, Bernhard Rudolf. 1904. *Goethe in meinem Leben. Erinnerungen und Betrachtungen.* Ed. Adolf Heuermann. Weimar: Böhlaus Nachfolger.

Al-Azm, Sadik J. 1972. *The Origins of Kant's Arguments in the Antinomies.* Oxford: Oxford University Press.

Allison, Henry E. 1983. *Kant's Transcendental Idealism.* New Haven: Yale University Press.

———. 1989. "The Hidden Circle in Groundwork III". In G. Funke and T. M. Seebohm, eds., *Proceedings of the Sixth International Kant Congress,* 149–60.

———. 1990. *Kant's Theory of Freedom.* Cambridge: Cambridge University Press.

———. 2001. "The *Critique of Judgment* as a 'True Apology' for Leibniz". In Gerhardt et al. 2001, 286–99.

———. 2001. *Kant's Theory of Taste.* Cambridge: Cambridge University Press.

Ameriks, Karl. 2000. *Kant and the Fate of Autonomy.* Cambridge: Cambridge University Press.

———, ed. 2000. *The Cambridge Companion to German Idealism.* Cambridge: Cambridge University Press.

Arber, Agnes. 1954. *The Mind and the Eye. A Study of the Biologist's Standpoint.* 3rd ed. Cambridge: Cambridge University Press 2009.

Arnheim, Rudolf. 1969. *Anschauliches Denken,* 7th ed. Köln: DuMont 1996.

Asmuth, Christoph, Alfred Denker, and Michael Vater, eds. 2000. *Schelling zwischen Fichte und Hegel.* Amsterdam: Grüner.

Assmann, Jan. 1996. "Denkformen des Endes in der altägyptischen Welt". In Stierle and Warning 1996, 1–31.

———. 2006. Afterword to Carl Leonhard Reinhold, *Die Hebräischen Mysterien.*

Bach, Thomas. 2001. "'Für wen das hier gesagte nicht gesagt ist, der wird es nicht für überflüssig halten.' Franz Joseph Schelvers Beitrag zur Naturphilosophie um 1800". In Breidbach and Ziche 2001, 65–82.

———. 2005. "Mineralogische Suiten—ein Weg von der Anschauung zur Erkenntnis". In Marcus Bertsch and Johannes Grave, eds., *Räume der Kunst. Blicke auf Goethes Sammlungen.* Göttingen: Vandenhoeck & Ruprecht, 289–312.

Baum, Manfred. 1986. *Die Entstehung der Hegelschen Dialektik.* Bonn: Bouvier.

———. 2000. "The Beginnings of Schelling's Philosophy of Nature". In Sedgwick 2000, 199–215. Also in Asmuth et al. 2000.

Baumgardt, David. 1927. *Franz von Baader und die philosophische Romantik.* Halle/Saale.

Baynes, Kenneth et al., eds. 1987. *After Philosophy. End or Transformation?* Cambridge, MA: MIT Press.

Beck, Lewis White. 1960. *A Commentary on Kant's Critique of Practical Reason.* Chicago: University of Chicago Press.

Becker, Oskar. 1931. "Die diairetische Erzeugung der platonischen Idealzahlen". *Quellen und Studien zur Geschichte der Mathematik, Astronomie und Physik 1*, 464–501.

Beierwaltes, Werner. 1985. *Denken des Einen.* Frankfurt am Main: Klostermann.

Bell, David. 1984. *Spinoza in Germany from 1670 to the Age of Goethe.* Bithell Series of Dissertations. vol. 7. University of London, Institute of Germanic Studies.

Benacerraf, Paul. 1973. "Mathematical Truth". *Journal of Philosophy 70,* 661–79.

Benn, Gottfried. 1932. "Goethe und die Naturwissenschaften". In Bruno Hillebrand, ed., *Essays und Reden in der Fassung der Erstdrucke.* Frankfurt am Main: Fischer Taschenbuch Verlag 1989, 175–205.

Bernecker, Sven. 1995. *Wandlungen der Elementarphilosophie. Die Folgen der Systemkrise K. L. Reinholds (1792–1823).* Unpublished manuscript.

———. 1997. "Reinhold". Lecture, University of Munich, Dec. 16, 1997.

Beyer, Wilhelm Raimund. 1975. "Kunst und Natur. Goethes Interesse am Jenenser Schelling". *Goethe Jahrbuch 22,* 9–28.

Boenke, Michaela. 1990. *Transformation des Realitätsbegriffs. Untersuchungen zur frühen Philosophie Schellings im Ausgang von Kant.* Stuttgart-Bad Cannstatt: frommann-holzboog.

Bonsiepen, Wolfgang. 1977. "Zur Datierung und Interpretation des Fragments 'C. Die Wissenschaft' ". *Hegel-Studien 12,* 179–90.

Bortoft, Henri. 1986. *Goethe's Scientific Consciousness.* The Institute for Cultural Research.

Boucher, Wayne I., ed. 1999. *Spinoza: Eighteenth and Nineteenth Century Discussions.* vol. 1 (1700–1800). Bristol: Thoemmes Press.

Bowman, Brady. 2003. *Sinnliche Gewissheit: zur systematischen Vorgeschichte eines Problems des deutschen Idealismus.* Berlin: Akademie Verlag.

———. 2006. "Ist Hegels frühe Logik eine 'Geschichte des Selbstbewußtseins'?". In Ralf Beuthan, ed. *Die Geschichtlichkeit der Vernunft.* Heidelberg: C. Winter, 81–92.

———. ed. 2007. *Darstellung und Erkenntnis. Beiträge zur Rolle nichtpropositionaler Erkenntnisformen in der deutschen Philosophie und Literatur nach Kant.* Paderborn: mentis.

Brandt, Reinhard. 1988. "Der Zirkel im dritten Abschnitt von Kants Grundlegung der Metaphysik der Sitten". In H. Oberer and G. Seel, eds., *Kant. Analysen-Probleme-Kritik.* Würzburg: Königshausen & Neumann, 169–91.

———. 1989. "Analytic/Dialectic". In Eva Schaper and Wilhelm Vossenkuhl, eds., *Reading Kant: New Perspectives on Transcendental Arguments and Critical Philosophy.* Oxford: Basil Blackwell, 179–95.

Breazeale, Daniel. 1995. "Check or Checkmate? On the Finitude of the Fichtean Self". In Karl Ameriks and Dieter Sturma, eds., *The Modern Subject: Conceptions of the Self in Classical German Philosophy.* Albany: State University of New York Press, 87–114.

————. 2000. "The Spirit of the *Wissenschaftslehre*". In Sedgwick 2000, 171–98.

Breazeale, Daniel, and Tom Rockmore, eds. 2001. *New Essays in Fichte's Foundation of the Entire Doctrine of Scientific Knowledge*. Amherst, NY: Humanities Books.

Breidbach, Olaf, and Paul Ziche, eds. 2001. *Naturwissenschaft um 1800. Wissenschaftskultur in Jena-Weimar*. Weimar: Böhlauf Nachfolger.

Bubner, Rüdiger. 1991. "Hegel and the End of History". *Bulletin of the Hegel Society of Great Britain* 23/24, 15–23.

Burnyeat, M. F. 1982. "Idealism and Greek Philosophy: What Descartes Saw and Berkeley Missed". *Philosophical Review 90*, 3–40.

Carl, Wolfgang. 1989a. "Kant's First Draft of the Deduction of the Categories". In Eckart Förster, ed. *Kant's Transcendental Deductions. The Three 'Critiques' and the 'Opus postumum'*. Stanford, CA: Stanford University Press, 3–20.

————. 1989b. *Der schweigende Kant. Die Entwürfe zu einer Deduktion der Kategorien vor 1781*. Göttingen: Vandenhoeck & Ruprecht.

————. 1992. *Die Transzendentale Deduktion der Kategorien in der ersten Auflage der Kritik der reinen Vernunft*. Frankfurt am Main: Klostermann.

Carrier, Martin. 1981. "Goethes Farbenlehre—ihre Physik und Philosophie". *Zeitschrift für allgemeine Wissenschaftstheorie 12*, 209–25.

————. 1994. *The Completeness of Scientific Theories*. Dordrecht: Kluwer.

Cartwright, Nancy. 1983. *How the Laws of Physics Lie*. New York: Oxford University Press.

Cassirer, Ernst. 1921. "Goethe und die mathematische Physik". In Cassirer, *Idee und Gestalt*. Reprint Darmstadt: Wissenschaftliche Buchgesellschaft 1989, 33–80.

————. 1932. *Goethe und die geschichtliche Welt*. Ed. Rainer A. Bast. Hamburg: Meiner 1995.

————. 2006. "Über Linné und die gewöhnliche Art, die Botanik zu behandeln". In Cassirer, *Nachgelassene Manuskripte und Texte,* vol. 10: *Kleinere Schriften zu Goethe und zur Geistesgeschichte 1925–1944*. Hamburg: Meiner, 146–54.

Cesa, Claudio. 1996. ". . . ein Doppelsinn in der Bedeutung des Wortes Setzen". In Fuchs and Radrizzani 1996, 134–44.

Christ, Kurt. 1988. *Jacobi und Mendelssohn. Eine Analyse des Spinozastreits*. Würzburg: Könighausen & Neumann.

Claesges, Ulrich. 1974. *Geschichte des Selbstbewusstseins*. Den Haag: Nijhoff.

Cooper, W. A. 1909. "Goethe's Quotation from Hutten in *Dichtung und Wahrheit II*". *Modern Language Notes* 24(4), 101–5.

Cramer, Konrad. 1978. "Bemerkungen zu Hegels Begriff vom Bewußtsein in der Einleitung zur Phenomenologie des Geistes". In Horstmann 1978, 360–93.

————. 2003. "Kants 'Ich denke' und Fichtes 'Ich bin'". *Internationales Jahrbuch des Deutschen Idealismus*, 57–92.

Danto, Arthur C. 2004. "Hegel's End-of-Art Thesis". In David E. Wellbery et al., eds., *A New History of German Literature*. Cambridge, MA: Belknap Press of Harvard University Press.

Danz, Christian, Claus Dierksmeier, and Christian Seysen, eds. 2001. *System als Wirklichkeit. 200 Jahre Schellings "System des transzendentalen Idealismus"*. *Kritisches Jahrbuch der Philosophie*, vol. 6.

Della Rocca, Michael. 2008. *Spinoza*. London and New York: Routledge.

Dilthey, Wilhelm. 1905. *Das Erlebnis und die Dichtung*. Leipzig and Berlin: Teubner.

Duhem, Pierre. 1969. *To Save the Phenomena*. Trans. E. Dolan and Ch. Maschler. Chicago: University of Chicago Press.

Duquette, David A., ed. 2003. *Hegel's History of Philosophy. New Interpretations*. Albany: State University of New York Press.

Durner, Manfred. 1990. "Schellings Begegnung mit den Naturwissenschaften in Leipzig." *Archiv für Geschichte der Philosophie* 72(2), 220–36.

———. 1991. "Die Naturphilosophie im 18. Jahrhandert und der naturwissenschaftliche Unterricht in Tübingen. Zu den Quellen von Schellings Naturphilosophie". *Archiv für Geschichte der Philosophie* 73(1), 71–103.

Düsing, Klaus. 1971. "Das Problem des höchsten Gutes in Kants praktischer Philosophie". *Kant-Studien* 62, 5–42.

———. 1976. *Das Problem der Subjektivität in Hegels Logik*. Bonn: Bouvier.

———. 1977. "Jugendschriften". In Pöggeler 1977, 28–42.

———. 1980. See Henrich, Dieter.

———. 1980. "Idealistische Substanzmetaphysik. Probleme der Systementwicklung bei Schelling und Hegel in Jena". In Henrich and Düsing 1980, 25–44.

———. 1988. "Absolute Identität und Formen der Endlichkeit. Interpretationen zu Schellings und Hegels erster absoluter Metaphysik". In Troxler, 99–193.

———. 1993. "Hegels 'Phänomenologie' und die idealistische Geschichte des Selbstbewußtseins". *Hegel-Studien* 28, 103–26.

Düttmann, Alexander García. 2000. *Kunstende*. Frankfurt: Suhrkamp.

Emundts, Dina. 2012. *Erfahren und Erkennen. Eine Studie zu Hegels* Phänomenologie des Geistes. Frankfurt am Main: Klostermann.

Engelhardt, Wolf von, ed. 2004. *Goethes Fichtestudien*. Weimar: Hermann Böhlaus Nachfolger.

Evans, Gareth. 1980. "Things Without the Mind—A Commentary upon Chapter Two of Strawson's *Individuals*." In Zag van Straaten, ed., *Philosophical Subjects. Essays Presented to P. F. Strawson*. Oxford: Clarendon Press, 76–116.

Falk, Johann. 1832. *Goethe aus näherm persönlichen Umgange dargestellt*. Reprint Hildesheim: Gerstenberg 1977.

Feuerstein-Herz, Petra. 2007. *Die grosse Kette der Wesen. Ordnungen in der Naturgeschichte der Frühen Neuzeit.*Wiesbaden: Harrassowitz.

Fischer, Kuno. 1852. *Logik und Metaphysik oder Wissenschaftslehre*. Ed. Hans-Georg Gadamer. Heidelberg: Manutius Verlag 1998.

———. 1865–69. *Geschichte der neuern Philosophie*. 5 vols. Mannheim: Friedrich Wassermann.

Forster, Michael N. 1998. *Hegel's Idea of a Phenomenology of Spirit*. Chicago: University of Chicago Press.

Fowler, D. H. 1987. *The Mathematics of Plato's Academy: A New Reconstruction*. Oxford: Clarendon Press.

Fragstein, Artur von. 1967. *Die Diairesis bei Aristoteles*. Amsterdam: Verlag Adolf M. Hakkert.

Frank, Manfred. 1996. "Wechselgrundsatz". *Zeitschrift für philosophische Forschung 50*, 26–50.

Frank, Manfred, and Gerhard Kurz, eds. 1975. *Materialien zu Schellings philosophischen Anfängen*. Frankfurt am Main: Suhrkamp.

Franks, Paul. 1997. "Freedom, *Tatsache* and *Tathandlung* in the Development of Fichte's Jena *Wissenschaftslehre*". *Archiv für Geschichte der Philosophie 7*, 331–44.

———. 2005. *All or Nothing*. Cambridge, MA: Harvard University Press.

Friedman, Michael. 1992. *Kant and the Exact Sciences*. Cambridge, MA: Harvard University Press.

Friedman, Michael, and Alfred Nordmann, eds. 2006. *The Kantian Legacy in Nineteenth-Century Science*. Cambridge, MA: MIT Press.

Fuchs, Erich, and Ives Radrizzani, eds. 1996. *Der Grundansatz der ersten Wissenschaftslehre Johann Gottlieb Fichtes*. Neuried: Ars Una.

Fuhrmans, Horst. 1962. "Schelling und Hegel. Ihre Entfremdung". In Fuhrmans 1962–75, vol. 1, 451–553.

———, ed. 1962–75. *F. W. Schelling. Briefe und Dokumente*. 3 vols. Bonn: Bouvier.

Fulda, Friedrich, and Dieter Henrich, eds. 1973. *Materialien zu Hegels "Phänomenologie der Geistes"*. Frankfurt am Main: Suhrkamp.

Fulda, Hans Friedrich. 1973. "Zur Logik der Phänomenologie". In Fulda and Henrich 1973, 391–425.

———. 1975. *Das Problem einer Einleitung in Hegels Wissenschaft der Logik*. 2nd ed. Frankfurt am Main: Vittorio Klostermann.

———. 1978. "Hegels Dialektik als Begriffsbewegung und Darstellungsweise". In Horstmann 1978, 124–74.

Gadamer, Hans-Georg. 1989. "Anfang und Ende der Philosophie". In Marcel F. Fresco, Rob J. A.van Dijk, and H. W. Peter Vijgeboom, eds., *Heideggers These vom Ende der Philosophie*. Bonn: Bouvier, 7–19.

Gage, John. 1993. *Kulturgeschichte der Farbe: von der Antike bis zur Gegenwart*. Ravensburg: Otto Maier.

Gaier, Ulrich, Valérie Lawitschka, Wolfgang Rapp, and Violetta Waibel. 1995. *Hölderlin Texturen 2. Das "Jenaische Project". Das Wintersemester 1794/95*. Tübingen: Hölderlin Gesellschaft.

Gerhardt, Volker, Rolf-Peter Horstmann, Ralph Schumacher, eds. *Kant und die Berliner Aufklärung. Akten des IX. Internationalen Kant-Kongresses*. Berlin: de Gruyter 2001.

Geulen, Eva. 2002. *Das Ende der Kunst. Lesarten eines Gerüchts nach Hegel*. Frankfurt am Main: Suhrkamp.

Gögelein, Christoph. 1972. *Zu Goethes Begriff von Wissenschaft*. München: Hanser.

Grassl, Hans. 1952. *Franz von Baaders Lehre vom Quaternar*. PhD. Diss., University of Munich.

Grumach, Ernst. 1949. *Goethe und die Antike*. Berlin: de Gruyter.

Guyer, Paul. 1979. *Kant and the Claims of Taste*. Cambridge, MA: Harvard University Press.

Haag, Johannes. 2006. "Descartes über Willen und Willensfreiheit". *Zeitschrift für philosophische Forschung 60*, 483–503.

———. 2010. *See* Perler, Dominik.

Haering, Theodor. 1934. "Die Entstehungsgeschichte der Phänomenologie des Geistes". In *Verhandlungen des dritten Hegelkongresses vom 19. bis 23. April 1933 in Rom*. Tübingen: J. C. B. Mohr (Paul Siebeck), 118–38.

———. 1938. *Hegel. Sein Wollen und sein Werk*. 2 vols. Reprint Aalen: Scientia Verlag 1963.

Hampshire, Stuart. 1951. *Spinoza*. Harmondsworth, U.K.: Penguin Books.

Harnack, Adolf von. 1901. *Geschichte der Königlich Preußischen Akademie der Wissenschaften zu Berlin*. Berlin: Verlag von Georg Stilke.

Hasler, Ludwig, ed. 1981. *Schelling. Seine Bedeutung für eine Philosophie der Natur und der Geschichte*. Stuttgart-Bad Cannstatt: frommann-holzboog.

Heidegger, Martin. 1976. "Das Ende der Philosophie und die Aufgabe des Denkens". In Heidegger, *Zur Sache des Denkens*. Tübingen: Max Niemeyer Verlag, 61–80.

Heidemann, Ingeborg. 1958. "Spontaneität und Zeitlichkeit". *Kantstudien Ergänzungshefte 75*.

Heilinger, Jan-Christoph, ed. 2007. *Naturgeschichte der Freiheit*. Berlin: de Gruyter.

Heimsoeth, Heinz. 1956. "Studien zur Philosophie Immanuel Kants". *Kantstudien Ergänzungshefte 71*.

———. 1970. *Studien zur Philosophie Immanuel Kants II*. Bonn: Bouvier, 133–280.

Heisenberg, Werner. 1970. *Physik und Philosophie*. Frankfurt, Berlin: Ullstein.

Helmholtz, Hermann von. 1877. "Das Denken in der Medizin". In Helmholtz, *Vorträge und Reden,* 5th ed., vol. 2. Braunschweig: Friedrich Vieweg und Sohn 1903.

Henrich, Dieter. 1965/66. "Hölderlin über Urteil und Sein". *Hölderlin-Jahrbuch 14,* 73–96.

———. 1966. "Zu Kants Begriff der Philosophie". In Kaulbach and Ritter 1966, 40–59.

———. 1967. *Fichtes ursprüngliche Einsicht*. Frankfurt am Main: Klostermann.

———. 1971. *Hegel im Kontext*. Frankfurt am Main: Suhrkamp.

———. 1975. "Die Deduktion des Sittengesetzes". In A. Schwan, ed., *Denken im Schatten des Nihilismus*. Darmstadt: Wissenschaftliche Buchgesellschaft, 55–112.

———. 1976. *Identität und Objektivität. Eine Untersuchung über Kants transzendentale Deduktion*. Heidelberg: C. Winter.

———. 1978. "Formen der Negation in Hegels Logik". In Horstmann 1978, 213–29.

———. 1982. "Andersheit und Absolutheit des Geistes. Sieben Schritte auf dem Wege von Schelling zu Hegel". In Henrich, *Selbstverhältnisse*. Frankfurt am Main: Suhrkamp, 142–72.

———. 1988. "Die Identität des Subjekts in der transzendentalen Deduktion". In H. Oberer and G. Seel, eds., *Kant. Analyse-Probleme-Kritik*. Würzburg: Königshausen & Neumann, 39–70.

———. 1989. "Kant's Notion of a Deduction and the Methodological Background of the First *Critique*". In Eckart Förster, ed., *Kant's Transcendental Deduc-*

tions. The Three 'Critiques' and the 'Opus postumum'. Stanford, CA: Stanford University Press, 29–46.

———. 1991. *Konstellationen. Probleme und Debatten am Ursprung der idealistischen Philosophie (1789–1795)*. Stuttgart: Klett-Cotta.

———. 2003. *Between Kant and Hegel*. Ed. David S. Pacini. Cambridge, MA: Harvard University Press.

Henrich, Dieter, and Klaus Düsing, eds. 1980. *Hegel in Jena*. Bonn: Bouvier.

Hertz, Heinrich. 1894. *Die Prinzipien der Mechanik in neuem Zusammenhange dargestellt*. Leipzig: Johann Ambrosius Barth.

Hildebrandt, Stefan. 1995. *Wahrheit und Wert mathematischer Erkenntnis*. München: Carl Friedrich von Siemens Stiftung.

Hinske, Norbert. 1971. "Antinomie". In Joachim Ritter, ed., *Historisches Wörterbuch der Philosophie*. Basel: Schwabe, 393–96.

Hoeltzel, Steven. 2001. "Fichte's Deduction of Representation in the 1794–95 *Grundlage*". In Breazeale and Rockmore 2001, 39–59.

Horstmann, Rolf-Peter. 1972. "Probleme der Wandlung in Hegels Jenaer Systemkonzeption". *Philosophische Rundschau* 19 (1972), 87–118.

———. 1977. "Jenaer Systemkonzeptionen". In Pöggeler 1977, 43–58.

———, ed. 1978. *Seminar: Dialektik in der Philosophie Hegels*. Frankfurt am Main: Suhrkamp.

———. 1990. "'Kant hat die Resultate gegeben . . .' Zur Aneignung der Kritik der Urteilskraft durch Fichte und Schelling". In *Hegel und die "Kritik der Urteilskraft"*. Stuttgart: Klett-Cotta, 45–65.

———. 1991. *Die Grenzen der Vernunft*. Frankfurt am Main: Anton Hain.

———. 2000. "The early philosophy of Fichte and Schelling". In Ameriks 2000, 117–40.

———. 2003. "Den Verstand zur Vernunft bringen? Hegels Auseinandersetzung mit Kant in der *Differenzschrift*". In Welsch and Vieweg 2003, 89–108.

Hübener, Wolfgang. 1975. "Zu Spinozas Satz 'Omnis determinatio est negatio'". In Harald Weinrich, ed., *Positionen der Negativität*. München: Fink, 499–503.

Jacobs, Wilhelm G. 1967. *Trieb als sittliches Phänomen*. Bonn: Bouvier.

———. 2004. *Schelling lesen*. Stuttgart-Bad Cannstatt: frommann-holzboog.

Jähning, Dieter. 1966–69. *Schelling. Die Kunst in der Philosophie*. 2 vols. Pfullingen: Neske.

James, William. 1890. *The Principles of Psychology*. 2 vols. New York: Henry Holt.

Jamme, Christoph. 1983. *"Ein ungelehrtes Buch". Die philosophische Gemeinschaft zwischen Hölderlin und Hegel*. Bonn: Bouvier.

Jamme, Christoph, and Helmut Schneider, eds. 1984. *Mythologie der Vernunft*. Frankfurt am Main: Suhrkamp.

———. 1990. *Der Weg zum System. Materialien zum jungen Hegel*. Frankfurt am Main: Suhrkamp.

Jammer, Max. 1957. *Concepts of Force*. Cambridge, MA: Harvard University Press.

Jantzen, Jörg. 1994. "Eschenmayer und Schelling. Die Philosophie in ihrem Übergang zur Nichtphilosophie". In Walter Jaeschke, ed., *Religionsphilosophie und spekulative Theologie*. Hamburg: Meiner, 74–97.

————. 1998. "Die Philosophie der Natur". In Hans Jörg Sandkühler, ed., *F. W. J. Schelling*. Stuttgart: Verlag J. B. Metzler.

————. 2005. "Adolph Karl August von Eschenmayer". In Thomas Bach and Olaf Breidbach, eds., *Naturphilosophie nach Schelling*. Stuttgart-Bad Cannstatt: frommann-holzboog.

Jürgensen, Sven. 1994. "Die Unterscheidung der Realitäten in Fichtes *Wissenschaftslehre* von 1794". In *Fichte-Studien 6*, 45–70.

Kaehler, Klaus Erich, and Werner Marx. 1992. *Die Vernunft in Hegels Phänomenologie des Geistes*. Frankfurt am Main: Klostermann.

Kaulbach, Friedrich, and Joachim Ritter, eds. 1966. *Kritik und Metaphysik*. Berlin: de Gruyter.

Keil, Geert. 2007. *Willensfreiheit*. Berlin: de Gruyter.

Keil, Richard, and Robert Keil, eds. 1882. *Goethe, Weimar und Jena im Jahre 1806. Nach Goethes Privatacten*. Leipzig: Edwin Schloemp.

Kimmerle, Heinz. 1967a. "Dokumente zu Hegels Jenaer Dozentenzeit (1801–1807)". In *Hegel-Studien 4*, 21–99.

————. 1967b. "Zur Chronologie von Hegels Jenaer Schriften". In *Hegel-Studien 4*, 125–76.

————. 1970. *Das Problem der Abgeschlossenheit des Denkens. Hegel-Studien, Beihefte 8*. Bonn: Bouvier.

Kleinschnieder, Manfred. 1971. *Goethes Naturstudien*. Bonn: Bouvier.

Klimmek, Nikolai F. 2005. *Kants System der transzendenten Ideen*. Berlin: de Gruyter 2005.

Klotz, Christian. 2002. *Selbstbewußtsein und praktische Identität*. Frankfurt am Main: Klostermann.

Köhl, Harald. 1990. *Kants Gesinnungsethik*. Berlin: de Gruyter.

Köhler, Dietmar. 1998. *See* Weisser-Lohmann, Elizabeth.

————. 2000. "Hegels Vorlesungen über die Geschichte der Philosophie. Anmerkungen zur Editionsproblematik". *Hegel-Studien 33*, 53–83.

Köhler, Dietmar, and Otto Pöggeler, eds. 1998. *G. W. F. Hegel. Phenomenologie des Geistes*. Berlin: Akademie Verlag.

Kordales, Lambros. 1998. *Hegels kritische Analyse der Schädellehre Galls in der "Phänomenologie des Geistes"*. Würzburg: Königshausen & Neumann.

Krings, Hermann. 1977. "Die Entfremdung zwischen Schelling und Hegel (1801–1807)". *Sitzungsberichte der Bayrischen Akademie der Wissenschaften, Philosophisch-Historische Klasse,* Jahrgang 1796, Heft 6, 3–24.

————. 1994. "Genesis und Materie—Zur Bedeutung der 'Timaeus'—Handschrift für Schellings Naturphilosophie". In Schelling, *"Timaeus"*, Ed. Hartmut Buchner, Schellingiana vol. 4. Stuttgart-Bad Cannstatt: frommann-holzboog.

Krohs, Ulrich, and Georg Toepfer, eds. 2005. *Philosophie der Biologie*. Frankfurt am Main: Suhrkamp.

Kroner, Richard. 1977. *Von Kant bis Hegel*, 3rd ed. Tübingen: Mohr.

Krüger, Gerhard. 1933. "Die Herkunft des philosophischen Selbstbewusstseins". *Logos 22*, 225–72.

Kwade, Anne-Kristina. 2000. *Grenze. Hegels 'Grenz'-Begriff 1804/5 als Keimzelle der Dialektik*. Würzburg: Königshausen & Neumann.

Landgrebe, Ludwig. 1966. "Das philosophische Problem des Endes der Geschichte". In Kaulbach and Ritter 1966, 224–43.

Lang, Heinwig. 1983. "Goethe, Lichtenberg und die Farbenlehre". *Photorin. Mitteilungen der Lichtenberg-Gesellschaft 6*, 12–31.

Laurence, Stephen. 1999. *See* Margolis, Eric.

Lauth, Reinhard. 1975. *Die Entstehung von Schellings Identitätsphilosophie in der Auseinandersetzung mit Fichtes Wissenschaftslehre.* Freiburg: Karl Alber.

———. 1984. *Die transzendentale Naturlehre Fichtes nach den Prinzipien der Wissenschaftslehre.* Hamburg: Meiner.

———. 1989. *Transzendentale Entwicklungslinien von Descartes bis zu Marx und Dostojewski.* Hamburg: Meiner.

———. 1994. *Vernünftige Durchdringung der Wirklichkeit: Fichte und sein Umkreis.* Neuried: Ars Una.

———. 1996. "Die konstituierenden Momente des Setzens in Fichtes erster Wissenschaftslehre". In Fuchs and Radrizzani 1996, 121–33.

———. 1998. *Descartes' Konzeption des Systems der Philosophie.* Stuttgart-Bad Cannstatt: frommann-holzboog.

Libet, Benjamin. 1985. "Unconscious Cerebral Initiative and the Role of Unconscious Will in Voluntary Action". *Behavioral and Brain Sciences 8*, 529–66.

———. 2004. *Mind Time: The Temporal Factor in Consciousness.* Cambridge, MA: Harvard University Press.

Lindberg, David C. 1976. *Theories of Vision from Al-Kindi to Kepler.* Chicago: University of Chicago Press.

Longuenesse, Béatrice. 1998. *Kant and the Capacity to Judge.* Princeton, NJ: Princeton University Press.

———. "Kant über den Satz vom Grund". In Gerhardt et al. 2001, 66–85.

Loock, Reinhard. 1997. "Gefühl und Realität". *Fichte-Studien 10*, 219–37.

Löw, Reinhard. 1980. *Philosophie des Lebendigen.* Frankfurt am Main: Suhrkamp.

MacIntyre, Alaisdair, ed. 1972. *Hegel. A Collection of Critical Essays.* Reprint: Notre Dame, IN: University of Notre Dame Press 1976.

———. 1972. "Hegel on Faces and Skulls". In MacIntyre 1972, 219–36.

Margolis, Eric, and Stephen Laurence, eds. 1999. *Concepts: Core Readings.* Cambridge, MA: MIT Press.

Martin, Gottfried. 1950. *Immanuel Kant.* 4th ed. Berlin: de Gruyter 1969.

———. 1961. "Zu den Voraussetzungen und Konsequenzen der Kantischen Antinomienlehre". *Kant-Studien Ergänzungshefte 81*, 51–54.

———. 1966. "Kants Auseinandersetzung mit der Bestimmung der Phänomene durch Leibniz und Wolff als verworrene Vorstellungen". In Kaulbach and Ritter 1966, 99–105.

Marx, Werner. 1986. *Das Selbstbewußtsein in Hegels Phänomenologie des Geistes.* Frankfurt am Main: Klostermann.

———. 1992. *See* Kaehler, Klaus Erich.

Matthaei, Rupprecht. 1958. *Zur Morphologie des Goetheschen Farbenkreises.* Köln: Böhlau.

Melamed, Yitzhak. 2004. "Salomon Maimon and the Rise of Spinozism in German Idealism". *Journal of the History of Philosophy 42*, 67–96.

————. 2012. *Spinoza's Metaphysics of Substance and Thought*. Oxford: Oxford University Press.

Menasse, Robert. 1995. *Phänomenologie der Entgeisterung*. Frankfurt am Main: Suhrkamp.

Michelet, Carl Ludwig. 1837/38. *Geschichte der letzten Systeme der Philosophie in Deutschland von Kant bis Hegel*. Zwei Theile. Berlin: Duncker and Humblot.

————. 1839. *Schelling und Hegel*. Berlin: Ferdinand Dümmler.

Miller, David Marshall. 2008. "*O male factum*: Rectilinearity and Kepler's Discovery of the Ellipse". *Journal of the History of Astronomy 39*, 1–21.

Molnar, Géza von. 1994. *Goethes Kantstudien*. Weimar: Hermann Böhlaus Nachfolger.

Mommsen, Momme. 1999. *Lebendige Überlieferung*. Bern: Lang.

Moyar, Dean. 2011. *Hegel's Conscience*. Oxford: Oxford University Press.

Müller, Klaus-Dieter. 1992. *F. J. Schelver 1778–1832. Romantischer Naturphilosoph, Botaniker und Magnetiseur im Zeitalter Goethes*. Stuttgart: Wissenschaftliche Verlagsgesellschaft.

Müller-Wille, Steffan. 1999. *Botanik und weltweiter Handel. Zur Begründung eines Natürlichen Systems durch Carl von Linné (1707–78)*. Berlin: Verlag für Wissenschaft und Bildung.

Nicolin, Friedhelm. 1967. "Zum Titelproblem der Phänomenologie des Geistes". In *Hegel-Studien 4*, 113–23.

————. 1988. "Verschlüsselte Losung. Hegels letzte Tübinger Predigt". In Annemarie Gethmann-Siefert, ed., *Philosophie und Poesie. Otto Pöggeler zum 60. Geburtstag*. Stuttgart-Bad Cannstadt: Frommann, vol. 1, 367–99.

Nordmann, Alfred. 2006. *See* Friedman, Michael.

Ott, Gerhard, and Heinrich O. Proskauer. 1979. *Das Rätsel der farbigen Schatten*. Basel: Zbinden Verlag.

Perler, Dominik, and Johannes Haag, eds. 2010. *Ideen. Repräsentalismus in der frühen Neuzeit*. Berlin: de Gruyter.

Pester, Thomas. 1994. "Goethe und Jena. Eine Chronik seines Schaffens in der Universitätsstadt". In Strack 1994, 663–88.

Pinder, Tillmann. 1969. *Kants Gedanke vom Grund aller Möglichkeit*. PhD diss., Freie Universität Berlin.

————. 1986. "Kants Begriff der transzendentalen Erkenntnis". *Kant-Studien 77*, 1–40.

Pinkard, Terry. 1994. *Hegel's Phenomeology. The Sociality of Reason*. Cambridge: Cambridge University Press.

————. 2008. "What Is a Shape of Spirit?" In D. Moyar und M. Quante, eds., *The Phenomenology of Spirit: A Critical Guide*. Cambridge: Cambridge University Press, 112–29.

Pippin, Robert. 1989. *Hegel's Idealism. The Satisfaction of Self-Consciousness*. Cambridge: Cambridge University Press.

————. 1993. "You Can't Get There from Here: Transition Problems in Hegel's *Phenomenology of Spirit*". In Frederick C. Beiser, ed., *The Cambridge Companion to Hegel*. Cambridge: Cambridge University Press, 52–85.

————. 2008. "Eine Logik der Erfahrung? Über Hegels *Phänomenologie der Erfahrung*". In Vieweg and Welsch 2008, 13–36.

Pitt, Gustav Leopold. 1869/70. *Aus Schellings Leben in Briefen*. 3 vols. Leipzig: S. Hirzel.

Pöggeler, Otto. 1973a. *Hegels Idee einer Phänomenologie des Geistes*. Freiburg: Alber.

———. 1973b. "Die Komposition der Phänomenologie des Geistes". In Fulda and Henrich 1973, 329–90.

———. 1984. "Hegels philosophische Anfänge". In Jamme and Schneider 1984, 126–43.

———. 1998. *See* Köhler, Dietmar.

———, ed. 1977. *Hegel*. Freiburg and München: Karl Alber.

Proskauer, Heinrich O. 1979. *See* Ott, Gerhard.

Recki, Birgit. 2001. *Ästhetik der Sitten*. Frankfurt am Main: Klostermann.

Reich, Klaus. 1932. *Die Vollständigkeit der kantischen Urteilstafel*. Berlin: Richard Schoetz.

———. 1935. *Kant und die Ethik der Griechen*. Tübingen: J. C. B. Mohr (Paul Siebeck).

———. 1958. Introduction to Immanuel Kant, *De mundi sensibilis atque intelligibilis forma et principiis*. Hamburg: Meiner, vii–xvi.

Reimann, Angelika. 1982–96. *See* Steiger, Robert.

Ribe, Neil, and Steinle, Friedrich. 2002. "Explanatory Experimentation: Goethe, Land, and Color Theory". *Physics Today 55*, 43–49.

Richards, Robert J. 2002. *The Romantic Conception of Life. Science and Philosophy in the Age of Goethe*. Chicago: University of Chicago Press.

Riedel, Manfred. 1967. "Hegels Kritik des Naturrechts". *Hegel-Studien 4*, 177–204.

Ritter, Joachim. 1966. *See* Kaulbach, Friedrich.

Rosenkranz, Karl. 1844. *Georg Wilhelm Friedrich Hegels Leben*. Reprint Darmstadt: Wissenschaftliche Buchgesellschaft 1977.

Sandkaulen, Birgit. 2000. *Grund und Ursache. Die Vernunftkritik Jacobis*. München: Fink.

Schabel, Lisa A. 2003. *Mathematics in Kant's Critical Philosophy*. New York: Routledge.

Schadewaldt, Wolfgang. 1978. *Die Anfänge der Philosophie bei den Griechen*. Frankfurt am Main: Suhrkamp.

Schmid, Irmtraut. 1979. *Die naturwissenschaftlichen Institute bei der Universität Jena unter Goethes Oberaufsicht*. PhD diss. Humboldt-Universität zu Berlin.

———. 1994. "Goethes Verantwortung für die Alma Mater Jenensis. Amtliche Pflichten—Oberaufsicht—Wissenschaft". In Strack 1994, 80–93.

Schmitz, Hermann. 1957. *Hegel als Denker der Individualität*. Meisenheim: Anton Hain.

———. 1959. *Goethes Altersdenken im problemgeschichtlichen Zusammenhang*. Bonn: Bouvier.

Schneewind, Jerome B. 1998. *The Invention of Autonomy*. Cambridge: Cambridge University Press.

———. 2010. *Essays on the History of Moral Philosophy*. Oxford: Oxford University Press.

Schneider, Michael S. 1994. *A Beginner's Guide to Constructing the Universe*. New York: HarperCollins.

Schöne, Albrecht. 1987. *Goethes Farbentheologie*. München: C. H. Beck.

Schrader, Wolfgang H. 1979. "Philosophie als System—Reinhold und Fichte". In Klaus Hammacher and Albrecht Mues, eds., *Erneuerung der Transzendentalphilosophie im Anschluß an Kant und Fichte*. Stuttgart-Bad Cannstatt: frommann-holzboog, 331–44.

Schulz, Günter. 1955. "Die erste Fassung von Fichtes Abhandlung 'Über Geist und Buchstab in der Philosophie. In einer Reihe von Briefen' 1795". In *Goethe. Neue Folge des Jahrbuchs der Goethe-Gesellschaft 7*, 114–21.

Schwaetzer, Harald. 1997. *"Si nulla esset in Terra Anima". Johannes Keplers Seelenlehre als Grundlage seines Wissenschaftsverständnisses*. Hildesheim: Olms.

Sedgwick, Sally, ed. 2000. *The Reception of Kant's Critical Philosophy*. Cambridge: Cambridge University Press.

Siep, Ludwig. 1992. *Praktische Philosophie im Deutschen Idealismus*. Frankfurt am Main: Suhrkamp.

———. 2000. *Der Weg der Phänomenologie des Geistes*. Frankfurt am Main: Suhrkamp.

Spahn, Christian. 2006. *Lebendiger Begriff—Begriffenes Leben. Zur Grundlegung der Philosophie des Organischen bei G. W. F. Hegel*. Würzburg: Königshausen & Neumann.

Speiser, Andreas. 1932. *Die mathematische Denkweise*. Zürich: Rascher.

———. 1934. *Leonhard Euler und die deutsche Philosophie*. Zürich: Orell Füssli.

Steiger, Robert, and Angelika Reimann. 1982–96. *Goethes Leben von Tag zu Tag*. 8 vols. Zürich and München: Artemis.

Steiner, Mark. 1998. *The Applicability of Mathematics as a Philosophical Problem*. Cambridge, MA: Harvard University Press.

Steinle, Friedrich. 2002. "'Das Nächste ans Nächste reihen': Goethe, Newton und das Experiment". *Philosophia Naturalis 39*, 141–72.

———. 2002. *See* Ribe, Neil.

Stern, Robert. 2002. *Hegel and the Phenomenology of Spirit*. London: Routledge.

Stewart, Jon. 1995. "The Architectonic of Hegel's *Phenomenology of Spirit*". *Philosophy and Phenomenological Research 55*, 747–76.

———. 2000. *The Unity of Hegel's Phenomenology of Spirit*. Evanston, IL: Northwestern University Press.

———, ed. 1996. *The Hegel Myths and Legends*. Evanston, IL: Northwestern University Press.

Stierle, Karlheinz, and Rainer Warning, eds. 1996. *Das Ende. Figuren einer Denkform*. München: Wilhelm Fink.

Stolzenberg, Jürgen. 1986. *Fichtes Begriff der intellektuellen Anschauung. Die Entwicklung in den Wissenschaftslehren von 1793/94 bis 1801/02*. Stuttgart: Klett-Cotta.

———. 1994. "Fichtes Satz 'Ich bin.' Argumentanalytische Überlegungen zu Paragraph 1 der 'Grundlage der gesamten Wissenschaftslehre' von 1794/95". In *Fichte-Studien 6*, 1–34.

———. 2003. "'Geschichte des Selbstbewußtseins'. Reinhold—Fichte—Schelling". *Internationales Jahrbuch des Deutschen Idealismus*, 93–113.

Strack, Friedrich, ed. 1994. *Evolution des Geistes: Jena um 1800*. Stuttgart: Klett-Cotta.

Strawson, Peter F. 1959. *Individuals*. London: Methuen.

———. 1966. *The Bounds of Sense*. London: Methuen.

———. 1974. "Imagination and Perception". In *Freedom and Resentment and other Essays*. London: Methuen, 45–65.

Surber, Jere Paul. 2003. "The 'End of History' Revisited: Kantian Reasons, Hegelian Spirit, and the History of Philosophy." In Duquette 2003, 205–23.

Szlezák, Thomas A. 1993. *Platon lesen*. Stuttgart-Bad Cannstatt: frommann-holzboog.

Taylor, Charles. 1972. "The Opening Arguments of the Phenomenology." In MacIntyre 1972, 151–87.

———. 1975. *Hegel*. Cambridge: Cambridge University Press.

Theunissen, Michael. 1975. "Begriff und Realität. Hegels Aufhebung des metaphysischen Wahrheitsbegriffs." In Horstmann 1978, 324–59.

Tilliette, Xavier. 2004. *Schelling. Biographie*. Stuttgart: Klett-Cotta.

Tonelli, Giorgio. 1966. "Die Voraussetzungen zur Kantischen Urteilstafel in der Logik des 18. Jahrhanderts". In Kaulbach and Ritter 1966, 134–58.

———. 1994. *Kant's* Critique of Pure Reason *Within the Tradition of Modern Logic*. Ed. David H. Chandler. Hildesheim: Olms.

Tugendhat, Ernst. 1979. *Selbstbewußtsein und Selbstbestimmung. Sprachanalytische Interpretationen*. Frankfurt am Main: Suhrkamp.

Vater, Michael. 2000. "Intellectual Intuition in Schelling's Philosophy of Identity 1801–1804". In Asmuth et al. 2000, 213–34.

Vieweg, Klaus, and Wolfgang Welsch, eds. 2008. *Hegels Phänomenologie des Geistes. Ein kooperativer Kommentar zu einem Schlüsselwerk der Moderne*. Frankfurt am Main: Suhrkamp.

Wackwitz, Stephan. 1985. *Friedrich Hölderlin*. Stuttgart: Metzler.

Wagner, Hans. 1966. "Platos Phaedo und der Beginn der Metaphysik als Wissenschaft (Phaedo 99D–107B)". In Kaulbach and Ritter 1966, 363–82.

Waibel, Violetta L. 2002. *Hölderlin* und *Fichte 1794–1800*. Paderborn: Ferdinand Schöningh.

Walther, Manfred, ed. 1992. *Spinoza und der deutsche Idealismus*. Würzburg: Königshausen & Neumann.

Warning, Rainer 1996. *See* Stierle, Karlheinz.

Waschkies, Hans-Joachim. 1986. *Physik und Physikotheologie des jungen Kant*. Amsterdam: Verlag B. R. Grüner.

Wegenast, Margarethe. 1990. *Hölderlins Spinoza-Rezeption und ihre Bedeutung für die Konzeption des "Hyperion"*. Tübingen: Max Niemeyer.

Weisser-Lohmann, Elizabeth. 1998. "Gestalten nicht des Bewußtseins, sondern einer Welt—Überlegungen zum Geist-Kapitel der Phänomenologie des Geistes". In Köhler and Pöggeler 1998, 183–207.

Weisser-Lohmann, Elizabeth, and Dietmar Köhler, eds. 1998. *Hegels Vorlesungen über die Philosophie der Weltgeschichte*. Hegel-Studien, Beiheft 38. Bonn: Bouvier.

Weizsäcker, Carl Friedrich von. 1962. "Kopernikus, Kepler, Galilei". In Klaus Oehler and Richard Schaeffler, eds., *Einsichten*. Frankfurt am Main: Vittorio Klostermann, 376–94.

————. 1981. "Einige Begriffe aus Goethes Naturwissenschaft". In *Goethes Werke. Hamburger Ausgabe*. München: C. H. Beck, vol. 13, 539–55.

————. 1991. "Goethes Farbentheologie—heute gesehen". *Nachrichten der Göttinger Akademie der Wissenschaften*, No. 9.

Wellbery, David E. 1996. *The Specular Moment*. Stanford, CA: Stanford University Press.

Welsch, Wolfgang. 2008. *See* Vieweg, Klaus.

Welsch, Wolfgang, and Klaus Vieweg, eds. 2003. *Das Interesse des Denkens. Hegel aus heutiger Sicht*. München: Wilhelm Fink Verlag.

Wieland, Wolfgang. 1966. "Hegels Dialektik der sinnlichen Gewißheit". In Fulda and Henrich 1973, 67–82.

————. 1967. "Die Anfänge der Philosophie Schellings und die Frage nach der Natur". In Frank and Kurz 1975, 237–78.

————. 1982. *Platon und die Formen des Wissens*. Göttingen: Vandenhoeck & Ruprecht.

Wigner, Eugene. 1960. "The Unreasonable Effectiveness of Mathematics in the Natural Sciences". *Communications in Pure and Applied Mathematics 13*, 1–14.

Williams, Bernard. 1998. *Plato: The Invention of Philosophy*. London: Phoenix. Reprinted in *The Sense of the Past. Essays in the History of Philosophy*. Ed. Myles Burnyeat. Princeton, NJ: Princeton University Press 2006.

Wundt, Max. 1929. *Fichte-Forschungen*. Stuttgart-Bad Cannstatt: Friedrich Frommann.

————. 1932. *Die Philosophie an der Universität Jena in ihrem geschichtlichen Verlaufe dargestellt*. Jena: Verlag von Gustav Fischer.

Ziche, Paul. 1996. *Mathematische und naturwissenschaftliche Modelle in der Philosophie Schellings und Hegels*. Stuttgart-Bad Cannstatt: frommann-holzboog.

Zimmermann, Rolf Christian. 1969–79. *Das Weltbild des jungen Goethe*. 2 vols. München: Wilhelm Fink Verlag.

Ziolkowski, Theodore. 1988. *Das Wanderjahr in Jena*. Stuttgart: Klett-Cotta.

Zocher, Rudolf. 1966. "Der Doppelsinn der Kantischen Ideenlehre". *Zeitschrift für philosophische Forschung 20*, 222–26.

Zöller, Günter. 2001. "Positing and Determining in Fichte's *Foundation of the Entire Wissenschaftslehre*. In Breazeale and Rockmore 2001, 138–52.

Tschirnhaus, E. W. von, 253
Tugendhat, E., 163

unconditioned, the, 32, 33, 37, 38, 82, 112, 227, 253
Urpflanze, 274
Urphänomen, 269, 359, 360, 370, 371

Vinci, L. da, 172
Voigt, C. G., 174, 221, 222, 223, 290, 358
Volta, A., 235
Vries, S. de, 80
Vulpius, C. A., 359

Weißhuhn, F.A., 180
Wieland, Ch. M., 77, 173
Wigner, E., 263
Wolff, Ch., 3, 33, 75, 76, 77, 79, 84, 85, 86, 154

Yalom, I., 260

Zedler, J. H., 121
Zelter, K. F., 359
Zeno of Elea, 116
Ziche, P., 286
Zocher, R., 34